Epic Lives and Monasticism in the Middle Ages, 800–1050

This is the first book to focus on Latin epic verse saints' lives in their medieval historical contexts. Anna Lisa Taylor examines how these works promoted bonds of friendship and expressed rivalries among writers, monasteries, saints, earthly patrons, teachers, and students in Western Europe in the Central Middle Ages. Using philological, codicological, and microhistorical approaches, Professor Taylor reveals new insights that will reshape our understanding of monasticism, patronage, and education. These texts give historians an unprecedented glimpse inside the early medieval classroom, provide a nuanced view of the complicated synthesis of the Christian and Classical heritages, and show the cultural importance and varied functions of poetic composition in the ninth, tenth, and eleventh centuries.

Anna Lisa Taylor is an assistant professor in the Department of History at the University of Massachusetts, Amherst.

Epic Lives and Monasticism in the Middle Ages, 800–1050

ANNA LISA TAYLOR

University of Massachusetts, Amherst

CAMBRIDGE
UNIVERSITY PRESS

CAMBRIDGE
UNIVERSITY PRESS

32 Avenue of the Americas, New York, NY 10013–2473, USA

Cambridge University Press is part of the University of Cambridge.

It furthers the University's mission by disseminating knowledge in the pursuit of
education, learning, and research at the highest international levels of excellence.

www.cambridge.org
Information on this title: www.cambridge.org/9781107030503

© Anna Lisa Taylor 2013

First published 2013

Printed in the United States of America

A catalog record for this publication is available from the British Library.

Library of Congress Cataloging in Publication Data
Taylor, Anna Lisa.
Epic lives and monasticism in the Middle Ages, 800–1050 / Anna Lisa Taylor,
University of Massachusetts, Amherst.
pages cm
ISBN 978-1-107-03050-3
1. Christian poetry, Latin (Medieval and modern) – History and criticism.
2. Epic poetry, Latin (Medieval and modern) – History and criticism.
3. Monasticism and religious orders – Biography.   4. Authors and patrons –
Europe – History.   5. Poetics – History – To 1500.   6. Monks' writings – History
and criticism.   7. Christian saints – Biography – Early works to 1800.   I. Title.
PA8056.T39   2013
871'.03093823–dc23   2013004472

ISBN 978-1-107-03050-3 Hardback

For my parents, Elizabeth and Bruce.

Contents

Figures and Illustrations

Acknowledgments

The research for this book began as a dissertation at the University of Texas at Austin, and was supported by the Mellon Foundation, the Bibliography Society, the Medieval Academy, the Hill Monastic Manuscript Library, a Dora Bonham Award, and a Harrington Fellowship. The University of Massachusetts, Amherst, provided a publication subvention.

My research would have been impossible without access to the manuscripts. I therefore thank the librarians and archivists at the Bibliothèque nationale de France at Richelieu, the Bibliothèque municipale de Valenciennes, the Bibliothèque municipale de Rouen, the Bibliothèque municipale de Saint-Omer, the Bibliothèque municipale de Boulogne-Sur-Mer, the Archives départementales du Nord, the Institut de recherche et d'histoire des textes, the Bibliothèque royale de Belgique, the Biblioteca Apostolica Vaticana, and the Bodleian library. Particular thanks go to Jean Vilban, of the Bibliothèque Marceline Desbordes-Valmore, who was exceptionally generous with his time and expertise. Jim Kelly of the University of Massachusetts was very helpful in acquiring research materials.

Many scholars lent assistance to this project. Jean Oblin showed great kindness in guiding me through Marchiennes and Hamage and in sharing his immense local knowledge, which transformed my understanding of the relations between those houses.

I owe much gratitude to all those who provided feedback on written drafts and on presentations of the material (all errors are entirely my own). Foremost are my two incomparable dissertation advisors and *patronae*, Alison Frazier and Martha Newman. They shaped the project and dissected it in the best possible ways, challenging me to think differently about the

ix

material and my arguments, while also giving me the necessary confidence to proceed. I cannot possibly repay their care and concern, nor can I hope to ever be such a great mentor to my own students. The book would have been impossible without them, and their influence is present on every page.

The project benefited at its formative stages from the best dissertation committee ever, Jennifer Ebbeler, Brian Levack, and Marjorie Woods. I owe special thanks to Jennifer Heuer, who read multiple versions of every chapter and provided extensive feedback at every stage. Brian Ogilvie read chapters and helped me navigate all aspects of publication. I profited from conversations on hagiography and monasticism with Felice Lifshitz, who also allowed me to read her dissertation, and Thomas Head. Scott Bruce was extremely generous with his time, providing detailed comments on the manuscript and saving me from numerous errors. Elizabeth Brown kindly shared her unpublished work on Saint-Denis. Thomas Noble made constructive suggestions in response to my work on Hilduin. Anna Grotans and the anonymous reader for the Cambridge University Press provided numerous helpful criticisms and suggestions.

In addition, I wish to thank the other scholars and long-suffering civilians who have supported my academic life more generally. I have had a series of wonderful mentors: Suzanne Dixon, Lisa Kallet, Paula Perlman, and Sabine MacCormack, who is much missed. I have been fortunate in my colleagues including Keith Bradley, Katy Schlegel, Audrey Altstadt, Joye Bowman, Anne Broadbridge, Jenny Adams, Robert Sullivan, Jon Olsen, Jennifer Fronc, and Carlin Barton. My students at UMass were a constant source of sanity and good humor (thank you especially to the Monsters – Amy, Brittany, Chris, Elyse, Jim, Lauren, Meghan, and Nick). Amanda provided indispensable moral support and sandwiches, and forced me to write the first draft. Meli and her clan were my second family all these years. Al was the best.

Most of all I wish to thank my parents, Elizabeth and Bruce. In appreciation of their unremitting enthusiasm for and encouragement of my intellectual life, this book is dedicated to them, with much love.

Abbreviations

AASS	Acta Sanctorum, edito novissima. Paris, 1863–1875
AB	*Analecta Bollandiana*
Abou-El-Haj, *Medieval Cult*	Barbara Abou-El-Haj, *The Medieval Cult of Saints: Formations and Transformations* (Cambridge, 1997).
Alcuin, York Poem	Alcuin, *Versus de patribus, regibus et sanctis Euboricensis ecclesiae* [Alcuin: The Bishops, Kings, and Saints of York], ed. Peter Godman (Oxford, 1982).
ASE	*Anglo-Saxon England*
Astronomer	The Astronomer, *Vita Hludovici*, ed. Ernst Tremp in MGH SRG 64 (Hannover, 1995), pp. 279–555.
BEC	*Bibliothèque de l'école des chartes*
BHL	Bibliotheca Hagiographica Latina, 2 vols. and suppl. (Brussels, 1898–1901, 1986).
Bischoff, "Bücher"	Bernhard Bischoff, "Bücher am Hofe Ludwigs des Deutschen und die Privatbibliothek des Kanzlers Grimalt," *Mittelalterliche Studien*, vol. 3 (Stuttgart, 1981), pp. 187–212.
Bischoff, *MAS*	Bernhard Bischoff, *Mittelalterliche Studien: Ausgewählte Aufsätze zur Schriftkunde und Literaturgeschichte*, vols. 1–3 (Stuttgart, 1966–1981).

Björkvall and Haug, "Performing Latin Verse"	Gunilla Björkvall and Andreas Haug, "Performing Latin Verse: Text and Music in Early Medieval Versified Offices," in *The Divine Office in the Latin Middle Ages: Methodology and Source Studies*, Regional Developments, Hagiography, ed. M.E. Fassler and R.A. Baltzer (New York, 2000), pp. 278–299.
Carolingian Learning	John J. Contreni, *Carolingian Learning: Masters and Manuscripts*, Variorum Collected Studies Series 363 (Hampshire, 1992).
CCCM	Corpus Christianorum, Continuatio Mediaevalis
CCSL	Corpus Christianorum, Series Latina
CH	Pseudo-Dionysius, *The Celestial Hierarchy*, ed. G. Heil, *Corpus Dionysiacum* II (Berlin, 1991), and Hilduin's Latin translation, ed. Théry, *Études Dionysiennes*.
Charlemagne's Heir	*Charlemagne's Heir: New Perspectives on the Reign of Louis the Pious, 814–840*, ed. Peter Godman and Roger Collins (Oxford, 1990).
CSEL	Corpus Scriptorum Ecclesiasticorum Latinorum
Curtius, *European Literature*	Ernst Robert Curtius, *European Literature and the Latin Middle Ages* (Princeton, 1953).
de Gaiffier, "Hagiographe"	Baudouin de Gaiffier, "L'hagiographe et son public au xie siècle," in *Miscellanea Historica in honorem Leonis van der Essen* (Brussels, 1947), pp. 135–166.
Dehaisnes, *Catalogue*	Chrétien Dehaisnes, *Catalogue général de manuscrits des bibliothèques publiques des departments*, vol. 6 (Paris, 1878).
Depreux, *Prosopographie*	Philippe Depreux, *Prosopographie de l'entourage de Louis le Pieux (781–840)* (Sigmaringen, 1997).
DHGE	Dictionnaire d'histoire et de géographie ecclésiastiques (Paris, 1912–).
DN	Pseudo-Dionysius, *The Divine Names*, ed. B. Suchla, *Corpus Dionysiacum* II (Berlin, 1991), and Hilduin's Latin translation, ed. Théry, *Études Dionysiennes*.
Dolbeau, "Domaine négligé,"	François Dolbeau, "Un domaine négligé de la littérature médiolatine: les textes hagiographiques en vers," *Cahiers de civilisation médiévale* 45 (2002): 129–131.

EH	Pseudo-Dionysius, *The Ecclesiastical Hierarchy*, ed. G. Heil, *Corpus Dionysiacum* II (Berlin, 1991). In Hilduin's Latin translation, ed. Théry, *Études Dionysiennes.*
EHR	*English Historical Review*
EME	*Early Medieval Europe*
Ermenric	*Ermenrich d'Ellwangen, Lettre à Grimald*, ed. Monique Goullet. Sources d'histoire médiévale 37 (Paris, 2008).
Fleckenstein, *Hofkapelle*	Josef Fleckenstein, *Die Hofkapelle der deutschen Könige*, vol. 1. *Grundlegung. Die karolingische Hofkapelle*. MGH Schriften 16/1 (Stuttgart, 1959).
Flodoard	Flodoard, *Historia Remensis Ecclesiae*, ed. Martina Stratmann, MGH SS 36 (Hannover, 1998).
Gesta Ep. Cam.	*Gesta episcoporum Cameracensium*, ed. Ludwig Bethmann, MGH SS 7 (Hannover, 1846), pp. 393–489.
Godman, *Poetry*	Peter Godman, *Poetry of the Carolingian Renaissance* (Norman, 1985).
Godman, *Poets*	Peter Godman, *Poets and Emperors: Frankish Politics and Carolingian Poetry* (Oxford, 1987).
Goullet	Monique Goullet, ed. and trans., *Ermenrich d'Ellwangen, Lettre à Grimald*, Sources d'histoire médiévale 37 (Paris, 2008).
Grotans, *Reading*	Anna A. Grotans, *Reading in Medieval St. Gall* (Cambridge, 2006).
Hucbald, *VR*	Hucbald, *Vita Rictrudis* (prose) (BHL 7247), PL 132, 827C–48C.
Irvine, *Textual Culture*	Martin Irvine, *The Making of Textual Culture: "Grammatica" and Literary Theory, 350–1100* (Cambridge, 1994).
Jaeger, *Envy*	C. Stephen Jaeger, *The Envy of Angels: Cathedral Schools and Social Ideals in Medieval Europe, 950–1200* (Philadelphia, 1994).
JMH	*Journal of Medieval History*
JML	*Journal of Medieval Latin*
Johannes, *VR*	Johannes, *Vita Rictrudis* (metric) (BHL 7248), MGH Poetae 5/3, pp. 565–596.

Jonsson, *Historia*	Ritva Jonsson (Jacobssen), *Historia: Études sur la genèse des offices versifiés*, Studia Latina Stockholmiensia 15 (Stockholm, 1968).
Kirsch, *Laudes Sanctorum*	Wolfgang Kirsch, *Laudes Sanctorum: Geschichte der hagiographischen Versepik vom IV. bis X. Jahrhundert*, v. 1 (IV.–VIII. Jahrhundert), Quellen und Untersuchungen zur lateinischen Philologie des Mittelalters, 14/1 (Stuttgart, 2004).
Lapidge, "Lost Passio"	Michael Lapidge, "The Lost 'Passio Metrica S. Dionysii' by Hilduin," *MJ* 22 (1987): 56–79.
Leclercq, *Love of Learning*	Jean Leclercq, *The Love of Learning and the Desire for God: A Study of Monastic Culture*, trans. Catharine Misrahi. 2nd ed. (New York, 1974).
Lifshitz, "Beyond Positivism"	Felice Lifshitz, "Beyond Positivism and Genre: 'Hagiographic' Texts as Historical Narrative," *Viator* 25 (1994): 95–113.
Manitius, *Geschichte*	Max Manitius, *Geschichte der lateinischen Literatur des Mittelalters*, 3 vols. (Munich, 1911–1959).
McKitterick, *Frankish Kingdoms*	Rosamond McKitterick, *The Frankish Kingdoms under the Carolingians 751–987* (Essex, 1983).
McKitterick, *History and Memory*	Rosamond McKitterick, *History and Memory in the Carolingian World* (Cambridge, 2004).
MGH AA	Monumenta Germaniae Historica Auctores Antiquissimi
MGH Ep.	Monumenta Germaniae Historica Epistolae (in quart.)
MGH Ep. 3	Merowingici et Karolini Aevi 1. Ed. Societas Aperiendis Fontibus Rerum Germanicarum Medii Aevi (Berlin, 1892).
MGH Ep. 4	Karolini Aevi 2. Ed. Ernst Dümmler (Berlin, 1895).
MGH Ep. 5	Karolini Aevi 3. Ed. Ernst Dümmler (Berlin, 1899).
MGH Ep. 6	Karolini Aevi 4. Ed. Societas Aperiendis Fontibus Rerum Germanicarum Medii Aevi (Berlin, 1925).
MGH Ep. 7	Karolini Aevi 5. Ed. Societas Aperiendis Fontibus Rerum Germanicarum Medii Aevi (Berlin, 1928).

MGH Poetae	Monumenta Germaniae Historica Poetarum Latinorum Medii Aevii
MGH Poetae 1	Poetae Latini Aevi Carolini, vol. 1, ed. Ernst Dümmler (Berlin, 1881).
MGH Poetae 2	Poetae Latini Aevi Carolini, vol. 2, ed. Ernst Dümmler (Berlin, 1884).
MGH Poetae 3	Poetae Latini Aevi Carolini, vol. 3, ed. Ludwig Traube (Berlin, 1896).
MGH Poetae 4/1	Poetae Latini Aevi Carolini, vol. 4/1, ed. Paul von Winterfeld (Berlin, 1899).
MGH Poetae 4/3	Poetae Latini Aevi Carolini, vol. 4/3, ed. Karl Strecker (Berlin, 1923).
MGH Poetae 5/3	Poetae Latini medii aevi Die Ottonenzeit, ed. Gabriel Silagi with Bernhard Bischoff (Munich, 1979).
MGH Poetae 6/1	Nachträge zu den Poetae aevi Carolini, ed. Karl Strecker (Weimar, 1951).
MGH SRM	Monumenta Germaniae Historica Scriptores Rerum Merovingicarum
MGH SRM 3	Passiones vitaeque sanctorum aevi merovingici 1, ed. Bruno Krusch (Hannover, 1896).
MGH SRM 4	Passiones vitaeque aevi merovingici 2, ed. Bruno Krusch (Hannover, 1902).
MGH SRM 5	Passiones vitaeque sanctorum aevi merovingici 3, ed. Bruno Krusch and Wilhelm Levison (Hannover, 1910).
MGH SRM 6	Passiones vitaeque sanctorum aevi merovingici 4, ed. Bruno Krusch and Wilhelm Levison (Hannover, 1913).
MGH SRM 7	Passiones vitaeque sanctorum aevi merovingici 5, ed. Bruno Krusch and Wilhelm Levison (Hannover, 1920).
MGH SS	Monumenta Germaniae Historica Scriptores (in folio)
MJ	*Mittellateinisches Jahrbuch*
Molinier, Catalogue	Auguste Molinier, *Catalogue général des manuscrits des bibliothèques publiques de France. Départements*, vol. 25 (Paris, 1894).
MT	Pseudo-Dionysius, *The Mystical Theology*, ed. A.M. Ritter, *Corpus Dionysiacum* II (Berlin,

	1991), and Hilduin's Latin translation, ed. Théry, *Études Dionysiennes.*
Novem vitae	*Novem vitae sanctorum metricae ex codicibus monacensibus, parisiensibus, bruxellensi, hagensi, saec. IX–XII,* ed. William Harster (Leipzig, 1887).
PD (metric)	Hilduin of Saint-Denis, *Passio Dionysii* (metric) (no BHL). Unpublished.
PD (prose)	Hilduin of Saint-Denis, *Passio Dionysii* (prose), PL 106, cols. 25D–50C.
PG	Patrologiae cursus completus, series Graeca, ed. J.P. Migne.
PL	Patrologiae cursus completus, series Latina, ed. J.P. Migne.
Platelle, *Temporel*	Henri Platelle, *Le temporel de l'abbaye de Saint-Amand des origines à 1340* (Paris, 1962).
Poleticum	*L'histoire-polyptyque de l'abbaye de Marchiennes (1116/1121), étude critique et édition,* ed. Bernard Delmaire (Louvain-la-Neuve, 1985).
Poncelet, "Catalogus"	A. Poncelet, "Catalogus codicum hagiographicorum latinorum bibliothecae publicae Duacensis," *AB* 20 (1901): 361–470.
RBPH	*Revue belge de philologie et d'histoire*
Springer, "Sedulius"	Carl P.E. Springer, "The Manuscripts of Sedulius: A Provisional Handlist," *Transactions of the American Philosophical Society* N.S. 85 (1995): i–xxii and 1–244.
Stock, *Implications*	Brian Stock, *The Implications of Literacy: Written Language and Models of Interpretation in the Eleventh and Twelfth Centuries* (Princeton, 1983).
TAPA	*Transactions and Proceedings of the American Philological Association*
Texts and Transmission	L.D. Reynolds, ed., *Texts and Transmission: A Survey of the Latin Classics* (Oxford, 1983).
Thegan	Thegan, *Vita Hludovici,* ed. Ernst Tremp in MGH SRG 64 (Hannover, 1995), pp. 167–277.
Théry, *Études Dionysiennes*	Ed. Gabriel Théry, *Études Dionysiennes,* vol. 2 (Paris, 1937).

Tilliette, "Modèles"	Jean-Yves Tilliette, "Les modèles de sainteté du ixe au xie siècle, d'après le témoignage des récits hagiographiques en vers métriques," in *Santi e demoni nell'alto Medioevo occidentale (secoli V–XI)*, Settimane di studio del Centro italiano di studi sull'alto medioevo, 36 (Spoleto, 1989), pp. 381–406.
Tilliette, "Poésie metrique"	Jean-Yves Tilliette, "La poésie metrique latine: ateliers et genres," in *Religion et culture autour de l'an mil: Royaume capétien et Lotharingie*, ed. Dominique Iogna-Prat and Jean-Charles Picard (Paris, 1990).
Ugé, *Monastic Past*	Karine Ugé, *Creating the Monastic Past in Medieval Flanders* (Woodbridge, 2005).
VA	Milo, *Vita Amandi* (metric) (BHL 333), MGH Poetae 3, pp. 561–612.
VE (prose)	Anon., *Vita Eusebiae* (prose) (BHL 2736), AASS March, vol. 2, pp. 447–450; and Act. SS. Belgii, 4, pp. 557–564.
VE (metric)	Anon., *Vita Eusebiae* (metric) (BHL 2737). Excerpts of book 1 in AASS February, vol. 1, p. 304; and excerpts of book 2 in AASS March, vol. 2, pp. 450–452.
VG	Heiric of Auxerre, *Vita Germani* (metric) (BHL 3458), MGH Poetae 3, pp. 428–517.

Introduction: Saints, Princes, Teachers, and Students

Milo, the ninth-century poet and monk of Saint-Amand-les-Eaux, shuffles sideways into the frame of a miniature to present an unbound booklet to a larger (and therefore more powerful) seated figure, his teacher Haimin, a monk of Saint-Vaast (Figure 1).[1] Haimin reaches for the work with his left hand and raises his right in benediction. The front of the booklet bears the first words of Milo's *Vita Amandi*, composed around 845–855.[2] Written in almost 2,000 lines of epic dactylic hexameter, the poem recasts the seventh-century prose life of the monastery's founding saint into a much longer, more elaborate work.[3] This full-page miniature, from the codex Valenciennes, Bibliothèque municipale, MS 502 (produced at Saint-Amand between 1066 and 1107) is the visual counterpart to the letter in which Milo dedicates the *Vita Amandi* to Haimin.[4] Milo, in a stereotypical profession of humility, asks Haimin to correct his epic poem.

---

[1] Valenciennes, Bibliothèque municipale, MS 502, fol. 77r. See Molinier, *Catalogue*, pp. 403–405; and Abou-El-Haj, *Medieval Cult*, pp. 156–159 and 378–443. I follow the French convention of referring to monastic foundations (e.g., Saint-Gall, Saint-Amand) to distinguish them from their saints (Saint Gall, Saint Amand). In cases in which the house is usually referred to by its place name, rather than that of its church, such as Fulda, Reichenau, Marchiennes, and Hamage, I have followed common practice.

[2] The *incipit* of the *prohemium* is "festa propinquabant nostri." Milo, who was born after 809, was a student at the abbey of Saint-Vaast and then a monk and teacher at Saint-Amand. See Traube's introduction to Milo, *Vita Amandi*, pp. 557–558; Platelle, *Temporel*, p. 66.

[3] Milo's *VA*, comprising 1,818 lines of dactylic hexameter and a fifty-line preface, was based on the *Vita* by Amand's disciple Baudemund (BHL 332), ed. Bruno Krusch in MGH SRM 5, pp. 428–449.

[4] Fols. 74v–75v.

FIGURE I. Valenciennes, Bibliothèque Municipale, MS 502, fol. 77r. Milo
presents his epic *Vita Amandi* to his teacher Haimin.

The full-page miniature on the folio's verso shows Milo receiving his
work back (Figure 2). In contrast to his obsequious demeanor in the
previous image, Milo breezes into the room. Haimin looks up from the
parchment on which he is writing (presumably his reply to Milo) to hand
back the *Vita Amandi*. Each monk has a hand on the pamphlet, which is

FIGURE 2. Valenciennes, Bibliothèque Municipale, MS 502, fol. 77v. Milo receives his epic *Vita Amandi* back from Haimin.

open toward the viewer, inviting him or her to read the *Vita Amandi* that follows.[5] Rubricated capitals that begin beneath the miniature read "the Life of Saint Amand transformed from prose speech into heroic song," that is, epic meter.[6] This miniature corresponds to Haimin's response to Milo, in which he says that after he had judged the *vita* to be doctrinally sound, metrically correct, and eloquent:

> I showed the brothers who are with me how this whole stream should be navigated. . . . I urge our brothers who do not shrink from such studies to freely take up this work and I beseech them so that they might be goaded to a similar pursuit rather than inflamed by the torches of jealousy.[7]

This exchange reflects the pedagogical context of epic saints' *vitae*. Milo cast his epic as one of the *praeexercitamina*, the composition exercises undertaken by a student advanced in language arts. Haimin responded that he read the *vita* with others and encouraged them to emulate it.[8] Epic *vitae* were read in the monastic classroom and composed as a result of this education. The earliest manuscript of Milo's *Vita Amandi*, very different from this luxury codex, is a ninth-century schoolbook.[9]

---

[5] Fols. 78r–117r.

[6] "Vita Sancti Amandi de prosa oratione in aeroicum carmen transfusa." All translations are my own unless otherwise noted.

[7] Haimin, *Rescriptum* in MGH Poetae 3, pp. 566–567 (on fols. 75v–76v of this MS): "totum id flumen fratribus, qui mecum sunt, quomodo sit navigandum ostendi. . . . hortor fratres nostros, qui in talibus studiis non abhorrent, munus hoc libenter suscipere et obsecro, ut satius velint ad simile studium provocari quam invidiae facibus concremari."

[8] The term comes from Priscian's *Praeexercitamina*, exercises for rhetorical training adapted from Hermogenes widely used in the Middle Ages for teaching composition and textual interpretation. Priscian, *Opuscula*, ed. Marina Passalacqua, vol. 1, *De figuris numerorum; De metris Terentii; Praeexercitamina* (Rome, 1987), pp. xxix–xxx. Haimin wrote a *Miracula* (BHL 8510) and a *Sermo* (BHL 8511) on his abbey's patron, Vedast. On Saint-Vaast, see Denis Escudier, "Le scriptorium de Saint-Vaast d'Arras des origines au XIIe siècle," *Positions de thèses de l'École nationale des chartes* (1970): 75–82.

[9] Valenciennes, BM, MS 414, copied at Saint-Amand (late ix). This unornamented and utilitarian book (106 folios, 245 mm × 155 mm) includes Bede's treatise on verse composition and other classroom texts: Bede's *De arte metrica*; a brief passage (in an untrained hand) on the death of Nero; Milo's letter to Haimin and Haimin's response; Milo's *VA*; the *Versiculi Vulfai*; Milo's verse *De sobrietate*, with verse dedication to Charles the Bald; the poem *Conflictum veris et hiemus*, and an *abecdarium*. For this manuscript, see Lièvre, *Catalogue général des manuscrits*, p. 452. The *conflictum* is printed under Alcuin's name in MGH Poetae 1, p. 270. *De sobrietate* is printed in MGH Poetae 3, pp. 611–675. Brussels KBR MS 8721–8728 (3214) (ix), a collection on Amand, contains Hucbald's poems of dedication, the letters by Milo and Haimin, Milo's *VA*, and Vulfaius's *Versiculi*. The composite codex Copenhagen, KB, MS Thott. 520, includes ninth-century fragments of the *VA*. See J. Van den Gheyn, *Catalogue des manuscrits de la Bibliothèque Royale de Belgique*, vol. 5 (Brussels, 1905), p. 188.

The other images framing Milo's *Vita Amandi* in Valenciennes, BM, MS 502 indicate other contexts and functions of epic *vitae*. Another full-page miniature shows a monk presenting a bound codex to a large, crowned, and seated individual (Figure 3). This man is the work's second dedicatee, Charles the Bald, and the monk is Milo's student Hucbald, who, after his teacher's death in 872, sent the *Vita Amandi* to the emperor.[10] Charles inclines his head toward Hucbald and reaches out his left hand for the *Vita Amandi*. His right hand is raised, holding a small scepter. The artist connects the dedications to Haimin and Charles by using almost identical composition for both scenes. The image corresponds to the acrostic poems with which Hucbald addresses the *Vita Amandi* to Charles, redeploying it to impress the abbey's most important patron.[11] The twin dedications, to a teacher and to the emperor, point to two contexts of the epic lives, pedagogy and patronage, which were closely related in this case, because Milo had taught two of Charles's sons at Saint-Amand.[12] Similarly, Heiric of Saint-Germain in Auxerre had written his epic *Vita Germani* at the request of his student, Charles's son Lothar, before sending it to the emperor.[13]

A half-page miniature of the monk Vulfaius follows the text of Milo's *Vita Amandi* (Figure 4). The nimbed figure sits at a writing desk in an elaborate architectural setting reminiscent of Carolingian evangelist portraits.[14] Like the depiction of Charles the Bald, the image invokes Saint-Amand's ninth-century golden age. In his right hand, Vulfaius holds a quill; in his left, a scraper. He writes on parchment, composing his *versiculi* (little verses) in response to Milo's *vita*. His eyes rest on an open codex representing Milo's work. His *versiculi* are copied in the miniature (Figure 4).

The portrait of Vulfaius, the only figure represented alone with a copy of Milo's *Vita Amandi*, points to another function of epic lives, as the objects of solitary devotional reading. By showing this reader's poetic response, the artist emphasizes the dynamic aspect of the *vita*; as Haimin says, an epic life

---

[10] On Charles as a patron, see Rosamond McKitterick, "Charles the Bald (823–877) and his Library: The Patronage of Learning," *EHR* 95 (1980): 29–47, and "Manuscripts and Scriptoria in the Reign of Charles the Bald, 840 – 877," in *Giovanni Scoto nel suo Tempo: L'organizzazione del sapere in età carolingia*, ed. Claudio Leonardi and Enrico Menestò (Spoleto, 1989), pp. 201–234.

[11] Fols. 73v–74r, ed. in MGH Poetae 3, pp. 462–465.

[12] On Charles's policy of cloistering extra heirs, see Janet Nelson, *Charles the Bald* (London, 1992), p. 226.

[13] Heiric, *VG*.

[14] Fol. 117v, Abou-El-Haj, *Medieval Cult*, p. 89.

FIGURE 3. Valenciennes, Bibliothèque Municipale, MS 502, fol. 73r. Hucbald presents Milo's epic *Vita Amandi* to Charles the Bald.

could spur readers to compose their own works.[15] Read intensively in the classroom, guided reading, or private meditation, they could inspire new compositions, such as Vulfaius's verses or other epic *vitae*.

The four miniatures that frame Milo's epic *vita* depict the work's exchange and reception. The artist represents a book containing the epic

[15] Haimin, *Rescriptum*, ed. in MGH Poetae 3, pp. 566–567.

FIGURE 4. Valenciennes, Bibliothèque Municipale, MS 502, fol. 117v. Vulfaius composes his *Versiculi* in response to Milo's *Vita Amandi*.

vita four times (twice open and twice closed), its author twice, and its readers (Haimin, Charles, and Vulfaius) a total of four times. By contrast, all but one of the thirty-two miniatures accompanying the prose *Vita Amandi* in the same codex show the saint's deeds. The single depiction of a book of the prose *Vita Amandi* is static; in Baudemund's author portrait, the *vita* is nearly closed and he holds his pen aloft (Figure 5).[16] In each of the images accompanying the epic *vita*, the work is central to the action: in three instances, it is being exchanged between men of unequal status (a student and a teacher or a monk and an emperor), and in the fourth, it is being read and inspiring new verse. Like the written materials transmitted with this copy of Milo's *Vita Amandi* (Hucbald's acrostics, the correspondence of Milo and Haimin, Vulfaius's *versiculi*), the epic's pictorial program emphasizes the poem not the saint.[17] As Rosamond McKitterick has shown, "representations of books in Carolingian book illuminations ... stress the power of the written word and by implication those who controlled and produced books."[18] By choosing to represent the epic *vita*, the artist signaled its importance. McKitterick has argued that elites defined themselves by their use of the written word. In this case, the epic poem – learned and difficult, requiring considerable education to read or write – was a particularly apposite way for the hypereducated elite to constitute their identity and relations.

The pictorial emphasis on the uses of Milo's text demonstrates the importance of epic *vitae* for monasteries in western Francia during the ninth, tenth, and eleventh centuries. By writing, reading, emulating, excerpting, teaching, memorizing, and exchanging these works, monks (and sometimes nuns and canons) created and perpetuated "textual communities" characterized by the use of erudite saints' lives written in epic

---

[16] Valenciennes, BM, MS 502, fol. 1v. The half-page author portrait on fol. 125v is almost certainly of Gislebert, author of the *Miracula Amandi* (BHL 345) on fols. 126r–136v. A twelfth-century addition depicts Amand dictating his will (fol. 123r). Reproduced in Abou-El-Haj, *Medieval Cult*, pp. 443, 435.

[17] An eleventh-century manuscript from the abbey of Marchiennes (Douai, BM, MS 849), Saint-Amand's neighbor, several kilometers away on the River Scarpe, shows a similar contrast between illustrations of prose and epic *vitae*, with the epic *VE* prefaced by a half-page inhabited initial with an author portrait of a monk, kneeling in prayer, offering up a leaflet, while a hand reaches down from heaven (fol. 43r). The prose works are accompanied by scriptural scenes and saints. See Appendix B.

[18] McKitterick, *History and Memory*, p. 243; Rosamond McKitterick, "Essai sur les représentations de l'écrit dans les manuscrits carolingiens," in *La Symbolique du livre dans l'art occidental du haut moyen âge à Rembrandt*, ed. F. Dupuigrenet Desroussilles (Bordeaux, 1995), pp. 37–64.

FIGURE 5. Valenciennes, Bibliothèque Municipale, MS 502, fol. 1v. Baudemund, author of the prose *Vita Amandi*.

Latin verse.[19] By depicting three generations of teachers and students (Haimin, Milo, and Hucbald), the illustrations indicate the importance of epic *vitae* in educating monks and creating a community of scholars. Showing Milo's *Vita Amandi* as a physical object that changes hands, the pictures also point to how the exchange of these works created and cemented bonds of *amicitia* – friendship and patronage – with important figures outside the monastery. The manuscript itself – a lavish collection of works on Saint Amand made for the abbey and probably kept on the altar – points to another function of the epic life; it glorified the saint.[20] In return for homage, poets could hope to attain the heavenly patron's intercession in their own salvation.[21]

None of these individual functions was unique to epic *vitae* – various works glorified saints, inveigled patrons, and challenged students – but the precise combination of features and purposes was distinct and significant. Of particular importance was the combination of saintly subject with epic form. During the Central Middle Ages (ca. 800–1100), a church's patron saints, manifest in their relics, were its main source of influence and revenue.[22] Texts, rituals, art, and architecture could all convey the saint's power and narrative to patrons, adversaries, and pilgrims. The epic *vita* was a particular way of promoting the saint. Poetry was central to medieval grammar education, and epic was its most prestigious form. Virgil's *Aeneid* – the ultimate model for the *vitae* – was the central school text, making epic saints' lives the quintessential expression of the synthesis of pagan and Christian culture that underlay the Carolingian Renaissance.

By combining the *virtus* of their patron saints with the cachet of epic, poets imbued their works with celestial and worldly authority and combined two potent forms of spiritual and cultural capital. Accordingly, epic *vitae* possessed a set of meanings and social functions distinct from their prose counterparts and from other kinds of poetry. In order to show the significance of the epic *vitae*, I will return to the functions indicated by the images in Valenciennes, BM, MS 502, before suggesting reasons for the

---

[19] The term is from Stock, *Implications*, p. 88.

[20] An illustrated *libellus* on the patron saint, such as Saint-Omer's *codex argenteus* (now lost), could be kept on the altar. See Rosemary Argent Svobada, "*The Illustrations of the Life of St. Omer (Saint-Omer, Bibliothèque Municipale, MS 698)*" (PhD diss., University of Minnesota, 1983), p. 16.

[21] For example, Milo, *Prohemium*, lines 1–16; *VA*, 3.201.

[22] Patrick Geary, *Furta Sacra: Thefts of Relics in the Central Middle Ages* (Princeton, 1999), p. 15. Geary uses the term "Central Middle Ages" for 800–1100.

scholarly neglect of these sources. Finally, I discuss the sources and features of epic *vitae*.

THE USES OF EPIC *VITAE*

Epic *vitae* were integral to the culture of Carolingian monasteries and, from the tenth century, Ottonian and Capetian cathedral schools. These institutions educated most of the age's leading churchmen, courtiers, and writers. Children of the lay elite as well as oblates and future clerics attended these schools. Emperors used them to house superfluous heirs. Monasteries and cathedral schools produced courtiers, reformers, diplomats, and bishops. Accordingly, the readers and writers of epic lives belonged to networks of friendship and patronage that included kings, princes, and bishops.

Epic *vitae* were read in the classroom. Poems, both Classical and Christian, provided the fundamental curriculum texts, and verse composition represented the apex of learning in monastic and cathedral classrooms of the Central Middle Ages.[23] From antiquity, epic was considered to be the most authoritative form of poetry.[24] The epic *vita*, read in the classroom, could combine the abbey's institutional history and an edifying exemplum with many of the features that made Classical epic so useful for teaching. Further, the pleasures of poetry meant that readers would return to and remember it. Laid down in the memory at a formative age, poetry provided ideas and language for the reader to draw on later. In his letter to Macedonius, Sedulius, author of the *Paschale carmen* (ca. first half of the fifth century), explains his rationale for composing epic Christian verse:[25]

I will not refuse, however, to briefly explain why I wished to write according to metrical rules. Rarely, best of fathers, just as your experience of reading also knows from diligent practice, has anyone shaped the gifts of divine power into song, and there are many who delight instead in the study of worldly pursuits due to its poetic

---

[23] Irvine, *Textual Culture*, p. 7; *Grammatica* (education in the language arts) was the basis of education, and poetry was fundamental to *grammatica*. Quintilian defines *grammatica* as "recte loquendi scientia et poetarum enarratio"; Hraban Maur, as "scientia interpretandi poetas atque historicos et recte scribendi loquendique ratio." Quintilian, 1.4, 2, ed. Harold Edgeworth Butler (Cambridge, MA, 1922); Hraban, *De clericorum institutione*, iii, 18 (PL CVII, 395). On poetry's centrality to the curriculum, M.B. Ogle, "Some Aspects of Medieval Latin Style," *Speculum* 1 (1926): 170–189.

[24] Irvine, *Implications*, p. 236; Isidore, *Etymologiae*, 1.39; 1.38.1–2.

[25] Carl P.E. Springer, *The Gospel as Epic in Late Antiquity: The Paschale Carmen of Sedulius*, Supplements to Vigiliae Christianae 2 (Leiden, 1988), c. 2; Michael Roberts, *Biblical Epic and Rhetorical Paraphrase in Late Antiquity* (Liverpool, 1985), p. 83.

decorations and the pleasures of songs. They read over whatever has rhetorical charm, but they pursue it [Scripture] more neglectfully since they do not love it at all. Any verses they have seen, however, sweetened with charm, they take up with such heartfelt enthusiasm, that by going over these things more often, they store them deep in their memory and repeat them.[26]

This passage abounds in terms for pleasure (*deliciae, voluptates, facundia*), emphasizing the allure of verse. Sacred literature, sweetened with poetic charm (*blandimento mellitum*), could lure those who normally rejected Scripture into reading Christian texts avidly and often.[27]

Epic *vitae* were written in a classroom milieu. Advanced students learned and practiced verse composition and could embark on writing an epic life as a kind of "qualifying examination."[28] The ability to compose poetry was a mark of education and, accordingly, moral worth.[29] Because epic verse was the most revered form, its composition spoke most highly of the poet's intellect, culture, and training.[30]

The reading and writing of epic lives as part of the curriculum helped define not only individual houses but also wider "textual communities," which shared a literary inheritance and modes of interpretation.[31] We will see that these communities were constituted by an education that allowed writers and readers to engage in recondite games of allusion and intertext.

---

[26] Sedulius, *Ep. ad Macedonium* (prefacing *Paschale carmen*), in *Sedulii Opera Omnia*, CSEL 10, ed. Johann Huemer (Vienna, 1885), pp. 4–5. "Cur autem metrica voluerim haec ratione conponere, non differam breviter expedire. Raro, pater optime, sicut vestra quoque peritia lectionis adsiduitate cognoscit, divinae munera potestatis stilo quisquam huius modulationis aptavit, et multi sunt quos studiorum saecularium disciplina per poeticas magis delicias et carminum voluptates oblectat. Hi quicquid rhetoricae facundiae perlegunt, neglegentius adsequuntur, quoniam illud haud diligunt: quod autem versuum viderint blandimento mellitum, tanta cordis aviditate suscipiunt, ut in alta memoria saepius haec iterando constituant et reponant."

[27] On the mnemonic function of late antique didactic verse, see Julius Ziehen, "Zur Geschichte der Lehrdichtung in der spätrömischen Literatur," *Neue Jahrbücher für das klassische Altertum* 1 (1898): 404–417, esp. 404–405.

[28] Michael Lapidge, "Tenth-Century Anglo-Latin Verse Hagiography," *MJ* 24–25 (1989/1990): 260.

[29] The equation of education and moral formation was pronounced in the cathedral schools discussed by Jaeger, *Envy*, p. 42. Horace implies that composition expresses character in *Ars Poetica*, line 309. "Wisdom is the beginning and the source of writing correctly" (Scribendi recte sapere est et principium et fons).

[30] On epic's prestige, see Llewelyn Morgan, "Getting the Measure of Heroes: The Dactylic Hexameter and its Detractors," in *Latin Epic and Didactic Poetry. Genre, Tradition and Originality*, ed. M. Gale (Swansea, 2004), pp. 4–5.

[31] Stock, *Implications*, p. 90.

As the pinnacle of studies, poetry was the elite language of *amicitia*.[32] The exchange of poetry for patronage dated to antiquity. There are numerous examples of poets courting favor through their song.[33] Poetry, writes Hibernicus Exul at Charlemagne's court, is a gift for kings, superior to the gold, gems, horses, and finery given by the world's most important men.[34] It will last "as long as the stars turn in the sky."[35] In return for the gift of literature (and other services as a courtier), the writer could acquire the power and status that came from close contact with the ruler, and perhaps offices and benefices. Dudo of Saint-Quentin lays bare this exchange of literature and reward within the framework of *amicitia*. In the preface to his prosimetric history of the Normans (which draws on epic saints' lives),[36] he describes a conversation with his benefactor, the Norman Duke Richard I:

> Two years before his death, I was with that outstanding duke, Richard, son of Count William [Longsword], as was my custom, and I wanted to return the duty of my service (*meae servitutis officium*) to him, because of the countless acts of generosity (*beneficia*), he had bestowed on me, from no merit on my part.... On a certain day, when we were walking, he began to embrace me with the arms of most pious love and to persuade me with the sweetest words and to soften me with pleasant imprecations ... to [record] the customs and deeds of the Norman land, particularly of his own forbear Rollo, who established the laws in the kingdom.[37]

Dudo describes his work as an act of *caritas* toward his benevolent employer. He does not present the exchange of *beneficia* for literature as a cynical transaction, but couches it in the language of affection.[38]

---

[32] On *amicitia*, see Gerd Althoff, *Family, Friends and Followers: Political and Social Bonds in Medieval Europe*, trans. Christopher Carroll (New York, 2004), pp. 67–90.

[33] See Peter Godman, *Poets*, passim.

[34] Hibernicus Exul II, lines 1–11, 39 (an Irish poet, either Dungal or Dicuil), ed. in MGH Poetae 1, pp. 396–397; Alfred Ebenbauer, *Carmen historicum. Untersuchungen zur historischen Dichtung im karolingischen Europa* I (Vienna, 1978), pp. 18–19.

[35] Hibernicus Exul II, line 24.

[36] Leah Shopkow, "The Carolingian World of Dudo of Saint-Quentin," *JMH* 15 (1989): 19–37.

[37] Dudo, *Praefatio* to *De moribus et actis primorum Normanniae ducum*, ed. Jules Lair (Caen, 1865), p. 119: "ante biennium mortis eius ut more frequentativo fui apud eximium ducem Ricardum Willelmi Marchionis filium volens ei reddere meae servitutis officium; propter innumera beneficia quae absque meo merito mihi ... erat impertiri. Qui quadam die adgrediens, coepit brachiis piissimi amoris me amplecti; suisque dulcissimis sermonibus trahere atque precibus iocundis mulcere ... scilicet ut mores actusque telluris Normannicae quin etiam proavi sui Rollonis quae posuit in regno iura describerem."

[38] Dudo apparently received more benefits in return for the *De moribus*, completed under the duke's son, Richard II, around 1015: he became the Norman court's chaplain and

Epic lives, as an ideal currency in this economy of patronage, were often dedicated to kings and bishops.[39] Heiric quotes a letter in which the bishop Aunarius asks the presbyter Stephen to compose an epic *vita* of Germanus on account of their *amicitia*.[40] Heiric transmits their correspondence in his letter dedicating his own epic *Vita Germani* to Charles the Bald.[41] Heiric explains that because Prince Lothar, who had requested the work, had died before its completion, he had sent the epic to Lothar's father Charles. Heiric creates a flattering fiction in which the patron is part of the intellectual community. He depicts Charles as the pinnacle (*culmen ac fastigium*) of the arts, a philosopher king who single-handedly keeps learning alive and flourishing throughout his realm. The *Vita Germani* was a gratifying gift, implying that the recipient could appreciate its abstract and metrically diverse prefatory poems, its theology drawn from Eriugena, and its use of Greek. In the case of Charles, educated at court by Walafrid Strabo (who was author of two epic saints' lives), this was not implausible.[42]

Nonetheless, the dedication reflected Charles's cultural patronage, rather than the violent realities of his reign. Heiric locates the gift of the *vita* in an imaginary realm, a republic (*respublica*) of letters ruled over by a merciful ruler: "many are the monuments of your clemency, many the symbols of your piety."[43] In Heiric's formulation, the palace could "deservedly be called a school" (*merito vocitetur scola palatium*).[44] Because Charles, emulating his grandfather Charlemagne's zeal, has brought about this republic, all its literary ornaments redound to his glory.[45]

The epic *vita* was a gift not only for the earthly benefactor, but for the heavenly patron, the saint, who is asked to intercede for the poet's salvation. Milo presents his epic *vita* as a festal offering to "noster patronus" Amand and himself as the saint's suppliant (*supplex*).[46] Similarly, a

---

chancellor and was allowed to keep his benefices when he left Normandy. See Shopkow, "Carolingian World," p. 21.

[39] The earliest examples are the *Vitae Martini* of Paulinus of Périgueux and Fortunatus, discussed in the following.

[40] *Commendatio* to *VG*, p. 430.

[41] Ibid., pp. 429–430.

[42] McKitterick, "Charles the Bald (823–877)," p. 30. On Walafrid, see Chapters 2 and 3.

[43] Heiric, *Commendatio*, p. 429: "multa sunt vestrae monumenta clementiae, multa simbola pietatis."

[44] For a discussion of this passage, which does not present evidence of a royal court or court school, see Godman, *Poetry*, pp. 57–58.

[45] Heiric, *Commendatio*, p. 429.

[46] *VA, Prohemium*, lines 1–16; 3.201.

century and a half later, Johannes addresses Amand as *"alme patrone"* (nurturing patron).[47]

Poetry was also the preeminent language of rivalry, and competitive verse took many forms.[48] A struggle between rival epic poets informs the context of the monk Ermenric's mid-ninth-century letter and, I argue, competition among local abbeys prompted the production of the epic *Vita Eusebiae*, just as it motivated the writing of prose and epic *vitae* at the abbeys of Ghent (Saint-Bavo and Blandin) and those of Sithiu (Saint-Omer and Saint-Bertin).[49]

Epic *vitae* were also used for private devotional reading. Bede sent his verse *vita* of Cuthbert to a friend to lighten his journey.[50] Alcuin explains the purposes of his prose and epic lives of Saint Willibrord (written between 785 and 797):

> I arranged two little books, one going along in prose speech, which could be read publicly to the brothers in the church ... the other running along with a Pierian [metric] foot, which should be meditated on by only your learned men in their solitary little room.[51]

The verb *ruminare* (to ruminate, chew over) and the location *in secreto cubili* show that the epic life was intended for private meditative reading.[52] As we will see, epic lives, with their difficult language and dense allusion, were particularly suited to this kind of intensive study.

INVISIBLE EPIC

Despite the cultural importance of epic *vitae*, historians have largely ignored them. Their saintly subject matter and poetic form – the factors

---

[47] Johannes, *VR*, 1.468–489.

[48] On Charlemagne's court poets, see, Godman, *Poets*, pp. 38–92.

[49] I discuss these examples of poetic rivalry in Chapters 2 to 5.

[50] Bede, *Pref.* to *Vita Cuthberti* (metric). After Bede's death, his former student, Abbot Gutberct sent the prose and verse lives of Cuthbert to Bishop Lul for the latter's pleasure (*dilectio*). Gutberct, *Ep. Lullo Episcopo* (dated to 764), ed. Ernst Dümmler in MGH Ep. 3, p. 406.

[51] Alcuin, *Ep.*, in MGH Ep. 4, p. 175: "duos digessi libellos, unum prosaico sermone gradientem, qui puplice fratribus in ecclesia ... legi potuisset; alterum Pierio pede currentem, qui in secreto cubili inter scolasticos tuos tantummodo ruminari debuisset." I take *fratribus* as the dative ("to the brothers") rather than the ablative ("by the brothers"), because of the nonparallel construction with *inter scolasticos* in the following clause. *Puplice* is a less common variant of *publice*. Pieria was home to an ancient cult of the Muses. *Pierius pes* refers to the second *vita* having a metric foot.

[52] On *ruminatio*, Leclercq, *Love of Learning*, p. 73.

that made them so compelling to their writers and readers – have led to modern neglect. Positivist historians of the nineteenth and earlier twentieth centuries defined texts about saints as "hagiography" and either dismissed them or raided them for plausible-sounding details.[53] Later redactions were considered useless. During the last four decades, however, scholars have rehabilitated rewritings. As Felice Lifshitz has observed,

A critical trend has been to move away from bobbing for data to reconstructing mentalities and, consequently, to move from searching for the original version of each particular saint's biography to studying all extant versions, each in its particular compositional context. Instead of seeing "legendary accretions" as dross to be sifted and cleared away, scholars have seen transformations in a saint's character as crucial indicators of many different sorts of changes over time.[54]

Historians have explored how reinterpretations (along with rituals, art, and architecture) served writers, patrons, and institutions. Stories about saints enhanced authority, created legitimacy, increased prestige, and defended property.[55] Communities rewrote these narratives to express their own identities and to shape contemporary social relations with others.[56]

Despite the interest in redactions, historians have rarely considered epic lives, because they usually reproduce the basic narrative of their prose counterparts.[57] Michael Lapidge observes that Bede's early-eighth-century epic *Vita Cuthberti* has been largely ignored because

---

[53] Lifshitz, "Beyond Positivism," pp. 110–111.

[54] Ibid., p. 95.

[55] For example, Peter Brown, *The Cult of the Saints: Its Rise and Function in Latin Christianity* (Chicago, 1981); Geary, *Furta Sacra*; Gabrielle M. Spiegel, "The Cult of St Denis and Capetian Kingship," in *Saints and their Cults: Studies in Religious Sociology, Folklore and History*, ed. Stephen Wilson (Cambridge, 1983), pp. 141–168; Raymond Van Dam, *Leadership and Community in Late Antique Gaul* (Berkeley, 1985).

[56] Sharon Farmer, *Communities of Saint Martin: Legend and Ritual in Medieval Tours* (Ithaca, 1991); D. Townsend, "Anglo-Latin Hagiography and the Norman Transition," *Exemplaria* 3 (1991): 385–433; Patrick J. Geary, *Phantoms of Remembrance: Memory and Oblivion at the End of the First Millennium* (Princeton, 1994); Thomas Head, *Hagiography and the Cult of Saints: The Diocese of Orleans, 800–1200* (Cambridge, 1990); Felice Lifshitz, *The Norman Conquest of Pious Neustria: Historiographic Discourse and Saintly Relics, 684–1090* (Toronto, 1995); Amy G. Remensnyder, *Remembering Kings Past: Monastic Foundation Legends in Medieval Southern France* (Ithaca, 1995); Ugé, *Monastic Past*; Samantha Kahn Herrick, *Imagining the Sacred Past: Hagiography and Power in Early Normandy* (Cambridge, MA, 2007).

[57] Tilliette, "Poésie métrique," pp. 103–109. On the neglect of epic *vitae*, see Tilliette, "Modèles." An example of the neglect is the article in which Brennan advocates putting Fortunatus's occasional poetry alongside his *prose* hagiography for understanding the

the diction of the poem is difficult and oblique, and ... most (though not all) of the twelve additional miracles [which Bede added to the narrative] were subsequently recorded by Bede in plainer language in his prose *Vita S. Cuthberti*. I suspect that Charles Jones spoke for most historians when, in discussing Bede's hagiography, he wrote that "I have disregarded the metrical life of Cuthbert and shall continue to do so."[58]

Most scholarship on medieval epic lives examines them from a literary and philological perspective rather than a historical one.[59] Even when historians use epic lives, they tend to ignore the form.[60] The neglect reflects

poet's relationships to his patron-bishops. He omits the epic *Vita Martini*, even though it was dedicated to a bishop. Brian Brennan, "The Image of the Merovingian Bishop in the Poetry of Venantius Fortunatus," *JMH* 18 (1992): 115–139. There are exceptions. Lifshitz used the epic *Vita Romani* (BHL 7310) in her dissertation, "*The Dossier of Romanus of Rouen: The Political Uses of Hagiographical Texts*" (Columbia University, 1988), which became the basis of her monograph *Norman Conquest*. On the fifteenth and sixteenth centuries, Mario Chiesa, "Agiografia nel Rinascimento: esplorazioni tra i poemi sacri dei secoli XV e XVI," in *Scrivere di santi, Atti del II Convegno di studio dell'Associazione italiana per lo studio della santità, dei culti e dell'agiografia Napoli, 22–25 ottobre 1997*, ed. Gennaro Luongo (Rome, 1998), pp. 205–226.

[58] Michael Lapidge, "Bede's Metrical *Vita S. Cuthberti*," in *St. Cuthbert, his Cult and his Community to A.D. 1200*, ed. Gerald Bonner, David Rollason, and Clare Stancliffe (Woodbridge, Suffolk, 1989), p. 93, citing C.W. Jones, *Saints' Lives and Chronicles in Early England* (Ithaca, 1947), p. 217. Michael Lapidge is one of the scholars who has fully considered later epic *vitae* when discussing saints' cults and religious institutions. See his "Tenth-Century Anglo-Latin Verse Hagiography," pp. 249–260; "A Metrical *Vita S. Iudoci* from Tenth-century Winchester," *JML* 10 (2000): 255–306. Also, see Helmut Gneuss and Michael Lapidge, "The Earliest Manuscript of Bede's Metrical *Vita S. Cudbercti*," *ASE* 32 (2003): 43–54. Lapidge, ed., *The Cult of St. Swithun* (Oxford, 2003), contains an edition of Wulfstan the Cantor's *Narratio metrica* of Swithun (composed 990–996). Godman refers to epic *vitae* in *Poets*, pp. 175–177; and *Poetry*, pp. 57ff.

[59] Tilliette discusses epic *vitae* in "Le xe siècle dans l'histoire de la littérature," in *Religion et culture*, ed. Iogna-Prat et al., pp. 93–98; and "Un art du patchwork: la poésie métrique latine (xie–xiie siècles)," in *Théories et pratiques de l'écriture au Moyen Âge* (Paris, 1988), pp. 59–73. Articles on individual epic lives include William Charles Korfmacher, "'Light Images' in Hrotsvitha," *Classical Weekly* 37.13 (1944): 151–152; H. Walther, "Fragmente von metrischen Heiligenviten aus dem XIIten Jahrhundert," *Speculum* 6 (1931): 600–606; François Dolbeau, "Fragments métriques consacrés a S. Melaine de Rennes," *AB* 93 (1975): 115–125; Peter Christian Jacobsen, "Die Vita s. Germani Heirics von Auxerre: Untersuchungen zu Prosodie und Metrik," in *L'école carolingienne d'Auxerre de Murethach à Remi 830–901*, ed. Dominique Iogna-Prat, Colette Jeudy, and Guy Lobrichon (Paris, 1989), pp. 329–351.

[60] For example, in the discussion of the epic *vitae* of Eusebia and Rictrude in I Deug-Su, "La <<Vita Rictrudis>> di Ubaldo de Saint-Amand: un'agiografia intellettuale e i santi imperfetti," *Studi medievali* ser. 3, 31 (1990): 567–575. Thomas Head acknowledges the importance of "the distinctive literary genre of verse lives," but he devotes little more than a paragraph specifically to Rodulf Tortaire's 1,127-line epic *Passio Mauri* (BHL 5790), despite describing it as "a gem of verse hagiography," and does not consider the significance of its poetic form. Head, *Hagiography*, pp. 285, 116.

prejudices about the marginal nature of poetry as socially and politically unimportant and the ancient idea that poetry is composed of lies and is therefore not a historical source.[61] As Lifshitz characterized earlier generations of historians "bobbing for data" in the works about saints, most scholars who have consulted epic *vitae* have searched only for narrative detail, as though the format and the style were irrelevant to the work's meaning and had nothing to tell us.[62]

This is incorrect. Epic *vitae* did not have identical meanings and functions to their prose counterparts, even when they told a similar story. As Jean-Yves Tilliette observed in his 1988 call for scholarship, poets did not rewrite prose *vitae* in verse simply to improve the Latin style, because they could have achieved this end more easily through prose redactions.[63] Epic composition was a major undertaking, which thoroughly transformed the prose source, and which could only be performed by a highly educated individual.[64] The style and the myriad nonnarrative elements – digressions, poetic allusion, and authorial asides – are not mere ornament, but are part of the text's meaning and are integral to its social functions. As Michael Roberts explains, discussing Prudentius's late-fourth-century martyr poems, these "narratives cannot simply be treated as just one more ... version of a saint's legend ... form and content – poetry and the martyrs – are thoroughly interconnected."[65] When historians mine poetic works only for narrative, they overlook much of their significance.

There are several other probable causes for historians' neglect of epic lives. As François Dolbeau notes, many are unedited, so their existence tends to be known only to specialists.[66] Some are anonymously transmitted in single manuscripts and are difficult to locate and date. Because they are long and densely allusive with convoluted word order and arcane vocabulary, they can be challenging to read.[67] Some scholars find the poetry objectionable. Epic *vitae*, like much medieval Latin poetry, are criticized for being a derivative and artificial combination of the Classical

---

[61] Lifshitz, "Beyond Positivism," p. 108. An ancient Greek example of the trope is Hesiod, *Theogony*, 27–28. See Michael Roberts, "The Prologue to Avitus' *De spiritalis historiae gestis*: Christian poetry and poetic license," *Traditio* 36 (1980): 401.

[62] Lifshitz, "Beyond Positivism," p. 99.

[63] Tilliette, "Modèles," pp. 381–406.

[64] Ibid., pp. 383–384.

[65] Michael Roberts, *Poetry and the Cult of the Martyrs* (Ann Arbor, 1993), p. 6.

[66] Dolbeau, "Domaine négligé," pp. 129–131.

[67] This is highly variable. For example, *VA* has relatively straightforward word order, unlike Walter's convoluted *Passio Christophori*.

and the Christian.[68] The "hermeneutic style" characteristic of much late antique and medieval Latin verse is alien to modern tastes.[69] In discussing cathedral schools of the tenth to twelfth centuries, C. Stephen Jaeger bemoans that their main literary output was verse "in a mannerist, obscure Latin that tends to ward off careful study rather than attract it."[70] He describes the epic *Passio Christophori* as "impenetrable."[71] Baudouin de Gaiffier labels epic lives "métromanie pieuse."[72]

Modern aesthetic preferences are irrelevant to works' value as evidence. The fact that scholars often find the epic *vitae* bizarre, distasteful, or inexplicable indicates that we *should* pay attention. As Caroline Walker Bynum has pointed out, that which seems "profoundly alien to modern sensibilities" is often the most informative, and therefore, we should read puzzling medieval works seriously.[73] When we find texts (or ideas or practices) that seem anomalous, yet which were clearly important to contemporaries, we have encountered a place where modern expectations do not map onto the medieval imagination. If we cannot account for such works in our broader picture of the cultural context, then we need to question that picture, rather than brushing aside the evidence. By focusing on the problematic and the neglected, we gain new perspectives.[74]

Taking these sources seriously means not simply mining them for narrative, but paying attention to their form, style, and rhetoric. These

---

[68] Marbury B. Ogle and Dorothy M. Schullian, *Rodulfi Tortarii Carmina* (Rome, 1933), p. xxv; de Gaiffier, "Hagiographe," p. 136. Springer recounts similar charges against late antique Christian epic. See Springer, *Gospel as Epic*, pp. 7–9. Exactly what would constitute *non*-artificial poetry is unclear.

[69] Lapidge defines this style in "The Hermeneutic Style in Tenth-Century Anglo-Latin Literature," *ASE* 4 (1975): 67–111. It is characterized by "long tortuously convoluted periods, a penchant for rare and polysyllabic words, grecisms and neologisms" as well as archaic vocabulary (p. 69). On modern scholars' attitudes, see p. 102.

[70] Jaeger, *Envy*, p. 50. Cf. p. 180, "the eleventh century cannot be rescued as a text-producing age. Its strange, baroque poetry ... cannot be enjoyed as poetry.... It is best regarded as a hermetic code, hard to crack, rewarding because of what it points to, not because of what it is." Despite his antipathy, Jaeger uses cathedral-school poetry as a major source.

[71] Jaeger, *Envy*, p. 138.

[72] de Gaiffier, "Hagiographe," p. 136.

[73] Caroline Walker Bynum, "The Female Body and Religious Practice in the Later Middle Ages," in *Fragmentation and Redemption: Essays on Gender and the Human Body in Medieval Religion* (New York, 1991), p. 182.

[74] For example, Jean Claude Schmitt, *Holy Greyhound: Guinefort, Healer of Children since the Thirteenth Century*, trans. Martin Thom (Cambridge, 1983); Lester Little, *Benedictine Maledictions: Liturgical Cursing in Romanesque France* (Ithaca, 1993); Carlo Ginzburg, *The Cheese and the Worms: The Cosmos of a Sixteenth-Century Miller*, trans. John and Anne Tedeschi (New York, 1982).

are not mere embellishments to discard in the search for important information. We should read epic *vitae* as their contemporaries did, ruminatively with minds attuned to the poetic devices, tropes, themes, metaphors, and intertextual echoes that constitute their layers of meaning. Form is crucial. For medieval readers and writers, God was in the details.[75]

As a historian, I do not undertake a primarily philological reading, but rather consider the works in their settings. Because epic *vitae* were such important texts, when read in their social and cultural contexts, they provide insights that other kinds of evidence do not.[76] They give us a new perspective on the medieval classroom. They also reveal the versions of their histories that monks told for different audiences. Surprisingly, these works, which were destined for an exceptionally erudite readership, emphasize the miraculous and the memorable more and historicity less than the prose *vitae* intended for a wider public, complicating current notions of how the intended audience shaped hagiographical narrative.[77] A close reading of the highly allusive texts also illuminates how thoroughly the writers melded their Christian and Classical heritages to appeal to educated religious and lay patrons. The epic *vitae* show that the reconciliation of the two traditions was not simply a case of putting "new wine in old bottles" as the Christian apologists would have it, but a far more thorough and thoughtful synthesis.[78] Further, the exchange of epic lives around the millennium reveals the persistence of a sophisticated literary culture with its roots in the Carolingian era. The epic *vitae* emphasize connections with past poets, saints, and teachers. As a nostalgic genre, expressing continuity rather than a violent break with the past, it presents a very different picture from the narratives used to support the idea of millennial crisis and transformation. Although no less ideologically loaded than the sources that show disjunction, epic's divergent perspective reminds us that depicting continuity or rupture was an authorial choice, dependent on a text's purpose, rather than a simple reflection of social and political realities.

---

[75] Caroline Walker Bynum, "Material Continuity, Personal Survival and the Resurrection of the Body: A Scholastic Discussion in its Medieval and Modern Contexts," in *Fragmentation and Redemption*, p. 245.

[76] For example, Shopkow, "Carolingian World," pp. 19–37.

[77] Contra Aviad M. Kleinberg, *Flesh Made Word: Saints' Stories and the Western Imagination*, trans. Jane Marie Todd (Cambridge, MA, 2008).

[78] Augustine; *De doctrina Christiana*, 2.40. See Chapter 3 for tropes and attitudes about the pagan Classics.

"IN HEROIC SONG": DEFINING THE EPIC LIFE

In considering how to classify epic *vitae*, we can turn to contemporary descriptions. Poets, readers, and scribes variously called these works *vitae*, *passiones*, *gesta*, and *historiae*, the same terms used for their prose counterparts.[79] The last term is noteworthy, because saints' lives were, in the Central Middle Ages, a kind of *historia*.[80] As Lifshitz has shown, hagiography is a modern category not equivalent to a medieval genre.[81] Prose and verse works about the lives of individual saints feature many of the same tropes, themes, and features as works modern scholars have labeled historiographical.[82]

Contemporaries sometimes qualify their description of an epic *vita* or *passio* by noting that it was in metric style (*metricus stilus*) or that it had translated (*transfundere* or *referre*) a prose work into verse.[83] Milo sings the saints' deeds (*gesta*) in "sweet-sounding meter" (*metrum dulcisonum*).[84] Walafrid Strabo talks about adding "some metrical seasoning" to his prose *Vita Galli* and of putting the saint's deeds in meter (*facta ... metro referre*).[85] Some writers specify that their verse is "heroic," a synonym for *epic*.[86]

---

[79] For example, Paulinus of Périgueux describes his epic *Vita Martini* as *historia*. Paulinus, *Vita Martini*, 4.4, ed. Michael Petschenig, CSEL 16.1 (Vienna, 1888).

[80] Thomas Heffernan, *Sacred Biography: Saints and their Biographers in the Middle Ages* (Oxford, 1988), especially chap. 2.

[81] Lifshitz, "Beyond Positivism," pp. 102–103, 108–109. (The medieval *hagiographia* is not equivalent to the modern term *hagiography*.)

[82] For example, "historiographical" and "hagiographical" works (including epic saints' *vitae*) feature the same basic elements in their prefaces, including a statement that a superior requested the work, the humility topos, the plea for correction, and a claim that the work is true. Both kinds of works have moralizing intent, ascribe similar virtues to their heroes, and offer them as models for imitation. Lifshitz, "Beyond Positivism," p. 96, n. 4.

[83] *Vita Leudegarii* (BHL 4854) *Prologus*, line 33, in MGH Poetae 3, p. 6: "Nec solito lapsu decurrit scanscio metri." Paulinus of Périgueux, *Vita Martini* 4.1 calls his epic a "translatio."

[84] Milo, rubric to the *prohemium* of VA and line 16: "ut metro dulcisono canerem."

[85] Walafrid, *Vita Galli* (prose), prologue, ed. Bruno Krusch, MGH SRM 4, p. 282: "huius operis agreste pulmentum postmodum aliquibus metrorum condimentis infundam"; Walafrid Strabo, *De vita et fine Mammae monachi*, line 13, ed. in MGH Poetae 2, p. 276. Heiric, says a previous poet, "laid out the life of our holiest father Germanus in metric rule" (vitam ... sanctissimi patris nostri Germani metrica ratione digereret). Heiric, *Commendatio* to VG, p. 430.

[86] Rubrics prefacing Hilduin's epic PD and Milo's VA describe the works as "heroic song" (*carmen heroicum*). Alcuin, speaking of Bede's epic *Vita Cuthberti*, says Bede "sang his miracles in heroic verse" (heroico cecenit miracula versu). Alcuin, York Poem, line 686.

They use other generic terms for poetry, calling the lives "verses" (*versus*) or "little verses" (*versiculi*).[87] Like their Classical predecessors, they speak of verse "running," a reference to both its perceived speed (compared to prose, which "walks") and a pun on the "feet" that compose a line of poetry.[88] They often employ the terminology of song (*carmen, canere, canorus*) common to Classical and Christian poets.[89] The Classical poet's song had sacred connotations, stretching back to the mythological first poet Orpheus, son of Apollo.[90] The writers of epic lives reflect the tradition of sacred song by using the word *vates*, meaning both poet and priest, to refer to themselves and their saintly subjects.[91]

In their catalogue, the *Bibliotheca Hagiographica Latina*, the Bollandists apply the terms *vita metrica* and *passio metrica* to more than 600 medieval and Renaissance texts in Latin verse, including many short poems that are quite different from those examined here.[92] I have not

---

[87] Candid says that he wrote a pair of books on Saint Eigil, "one in prose, and the other in verses" (unum prosa, alterum vero versibus explicavi). *Ep. Modesto* in MGH Poetae 2, p. 94. Walafrid speaks of his *versiculi* in the *Praefatio* to his *Vita Mammae Monachi*, line 17; ibid., p. 265.

[88] *PD* (metric), fols. 20r–v: "It is pleasing to shape sonorous eloquence and melodious measures / For the outstanding deeds of blessed Dionysius / And the rosy triumphs with which he shone / Drawn out from the whole, let the order run more readily / So that the passion of such a great martyr shines for the world" (Eloquium vocale iuvat *modulosque canoros* / Hinc ad praecipua DYONISII gesta beati / Et quibus enituit roseos aptare triumphos / Ductus ab integro *currat* propensius ordo / Martyris ut tanti clarescit passio mundo). (My emphasis.)

[89] The most famous Classical example is the first line of Virgil's *Aeneid*: "I sing of the arms and the man ..." (Arma virumque cano ...). A few examples from the epic *vitae*: VA, *proemium*, lines 16, 43; 1.103, 386, 428; 2.1, 9, 25, 365, 397; 3.1, 181, 209, 296, 419, 4.334. In the *Versiculi Vulfai* following the VA, *carmina* is the first word and *canendo* the second last. Milo says he wrote a "life in song" (*vita carmine*) of Amand in *De sobrietate*, line 5, ed. in MGH Poetae 3, p. 613. See, also, *Carmen de sancta Benedicta* (BHL 1088), *Epilogus* 6, 12c, 15, 36c, 44; *Carmen de sancto Cassiano* (BHL 1633), 1.30, ed. in MGH Poetae 4/1, p. 182; VG, *praefatio* to book 2, line 30, 2.51; VE (metric) 1.211, prologue to book 2, line 36, 2.245.

[90] For Orpheus and medieval poets, see Chapter 1.

[91] H. Dahlmann, "Vates," *Philologus* 97 (1948): 337–353; Alice Sperduti, "The Divine Nature of Poetry in Antiquity," *TAPA* 81 (1950): 209–240, esp. p. 221; E. Bickel, "Vates bei Varro und Vergil," *Rheinisches Museum* 94 (1951): 257–314; J.K. Newman, *The Concept of Vates in Augustan Poetry* (Brussels, 1967).

[92] These short poems are copied onto the last folios of a gathering or a codex on a saint, apparently included as an afterthought to utilize leftover vellum. Examples are the 128-line life of Mary of Egypt (BHL 5421) on the last folio of Paris, BN, MS lat. 17429, fols. 107r–v (xii), the *Passio Agnetis* (BHL 164) at the end of Paris, BN, MS lat. 4214, fols. 100v–101v (xiv) and a life of Alexis (BHL 294) found in Paris, BN, MS lat. 1687, fols. 86v–89v (xii fragment at the end of a composite codex).

found the precise terms *vita metrica* or *passio metrica* used in the Central Middle Ages. I prefer the term "epic *vita*" or "epic life," both of which reflect medieval readers' and writers' own understanding of the works as *carmina heroica*, and suggest the epic features – not only meter but also length, complexity, and Classicism – that distinguish them from other *vitae* and *passiones*.[93] I employ "epic lives" or "epic *vitae*" as blanket terms that include epic *passiones*, because they possess similar features of format and style. An epic *passio*, like a *vita*, recounts the saint's life, although obviously it also emphasizes his or her heroic death.

The epic saints' lives of the Central Middle Ages share a distinctive constellation of subject matter, form, and style. Tilliette sums up their essential features:[94] they are usually based on prose saints' lives, but they are far more colorful and elaborate, enhancing the story with Classical, mythological, and historical allusions, digressions on learned subjects (such as astronomy), and long passages of direct speech.[95] They most commonly feature founding patrons who were Late Roman or Merovingian missionary bishops of local or regional importance, although some tell of female founders, abbots, martyrs, universally venerated confessors, or the recently deceased.[96] They emphasize emotional states and, in the case of martyrs, the saint's suffering and death. They also accentuate the wondrous, sometimes attributing new miracles to the saint.[97] The epic *vitae* are usually cosmic in scope, placing their protagonists in the time-frame of salvation history, beginning with Christ and the apostles and

[93] Kirsch's "hagiographische Versepik" in his *Laudes Sanctorum* is a broader category encompassing diverse poetry related to saints such as Paulinus of Nola's *Laus S. Iohannis* and Alcuin's York Poem as well as epic *vitae*. I have not employed the term "hagiographical epic," used by Roberts and Pollman, because of the problems with "hagiography" as a genre term, as discussed at length by Lifshitz, "Beyond Positivism," pp. 95–113. See Roberts, "Last Epic," p. 258; Karla Pollman, "The Transformation of the Epic Genre in Christian Late Antiquity," in *Studia Patristica* 36, ed. M.F. Wiles and E.J. Yarnold (Leuven, 2001), p. 72.

[94] Tilliette, "Modèles," pp. 388–390, 392–396.

[95] These lives reflect what Michael Lapidge, discussing tenth-century insular verse, calls the "hermeneutic style," similar to the "jeweled style" Roberts describes in late antique poetry. See Lapidge, "Hermeneutic Style," pp. 67–111; Michael Roberts, *The Jeweled Style: Poetry and Poetics in Late Antiquity* (Ithaca, 1989).

[96] Tilliette, "Modèles," pp. 388–390. Epic *vitae* about martyrs include Hilduin's *Passio Dionysii* (no BHL, see Chapter 1), and the anonymous *passiones* of Benedicta (BHL 1088), Cassian (BHL 1663), and Quentin (BHL 7010). The *Passio Cassiani* is in Paris, BN, MS lat. 12958, fols. 73r–76v; the *Passio Quintini* in Paris, BN, MS lat. 14143, fols. 74r–82v; the *Passio Benedicta* in Paris, BN, MS lat. 8431, fols. 5r–20r. They are edited in MGH Poetae 4/1, pp. 181–231.

[97] See Chapters 1 and 5.

looking forward to the judgment day, when the saint's work will reveal its full value.[98]

The epic lives are hundreds or even thousand of lines long and are often divided into books. They are usually written in dactylic hexameter, the standard verse of epic, although poets sometimes write in elegiac couplets, and they experiment with various meters in the prefatory poems.[99] Epic *vitae* often feature copious ancillary matter, including prose and verse dedications, correspondence between writer and readers, and poetic invocations to the reader, God, and the saint. Individual books may also be prefaced by such poems. The prefaces are not always clearly related to the narrative and may be allegorical.

The lives are often transmitted with a prose *vita* of the saint, sometimes by the same author. A pair of lives could be described as a "twinned work" (*opus geminatum*), a work consisting of prose and verse pieces on the same topic.[100] On the model of Hraban Maur's *In laude de sancte cruce*, Candid Brun, a monk of Fulda, wrote a twinned work on his late abbot: "I composed two books on the life of abbot Eigil ... I wrote one in prose, but the other in verse."[101] Not all authors who composed both prose and verse lives of a saint saw them as closely connected, and some wrote them at different times.[102] Candid, however, certainly saw his two lives as a unit: "I asked that they be bound together in one volume so that each might support the other in telling the story."[103]

The characteristic elaborations of the prose originals reflect Carolingian educational practices. The classroom's influence is evident in digressions

---

[98] Tilliette, "Modèles," p. 395.

[99] Rodulf Tortaire's *Passio Mauri* is composed in elegiac couplets; ed. Ogle and Schullian, *Rodulfi Tortarii Carmina*, pp. 345–387.

[100] On paired verse and prose, see Peter Godman, "The Anglo-Latin Opus Geminatum: From Aldhelm to Alcuin," *Medium Ævum* 50 (1981): 215–229; Gernot Wieland, "Geminus Stilus: Studies in Anglo-Latin Hagiography," in *Insular Latin Studies: Papers on Latin Texts and Manuscripts of the British Isles, 550–1066*, ed. Michael W. Herren (Toronto, 1981), pp. 113–133; Bill Friesen, "The *Opus Geminatum* and Anglo-Saxon Literature," *Neophilologus* 95 (2011): 123–144. For Hraban Maur's discussion of his "gemino stilo ... opera" *In laudem sanctae crucis*, see the letter ed. E. Dümmler in MGH Ep. 5, p. 384.

[101] Candid, *Ep. Modesto*, MGH Poetae 2, p. 94: "duos libros de vita Aeigili abbatis nostri ... unum prosa, alterum vero versibus explicavi."

[102] For example, as noted earlier, Alcuin indicated that his *vitae* of Willibrord had separate functions. Walafrid claimed that he would, God willing, versify his prose life of Gall, but he did not do so in his remaining sixteen years of life. Hilduin published his prose *PD* before he produced the epic version (see Chapter 1).

[103] Candid, *Ep. Modesto*, p. 94: "quos tamen ideo in unum corpus conligare rogabam, ut in rerum narratione alter alteri subsidia ferret."

on geography, astronomy, mythology, and philosophy, which emphasize the poet's erudition and provide teachers with topics for elaboration.[104] François Dolbeau observes the influence of the rhetorical exercises in which students practiced rewriting.[105] Because epic *vitae* were often written by a student at the end of his or her education, the poems employ devices learned from these *praeexercitamina*. One of the medieval rhetorical exercises, the composition of a speech from a literary character's point of view,[106] is reflected in the many monologues poets place in the mouths of saints, who express their charismatic power through thaumaturgic speech.[107] In Milo's epic *vita*, Amand uses his words to calm, convert, rebuke, advise, and persuade.[108] He is "the victor vanquishing by the weapon of the word."[109] Speeches in epic *vitae* recast the saint's charismatic and salvific oration into the poet's metrical words. This ventriloquism, which allowed the poet to speak with the saint's authority, would be even clearer when a poet-teacher was reciting his own composition in a classroom.[110]

Poets also added interjections in their own voices, including moralizing exclamations and apostrophes, which are direct addresses to absent

---

[104] Tilliette, "Modèles," p. 394, for example, the digression on astronomy in 3.817ff. of Letselin's eleventh-century *Vita Arnulfi* (BHL 708), from Saint-Arnoul in Crépy (diocese of Senlis). This epic *vita* is followed in the eleventh-century schoolbook Paris, BN, MS lat. 10851 by a *Descriptio Poli* (fols. 26v–28r) on the constellations, which echoes Letselin's pedagogical interests; ed. in *Novem vitae*, pp. 86–126. On the manuscript, F. Dolbeau, "Ancients possessions des manuscrits hagiographiques latins conservés a la Bibliothèque Nationale de Paris," *Revue d'histoire des textes* 9 (1979): 218; P. Lauer, "Les manuscrits de Saint-Arnoul de Crépy-en-Valois," *BEC* 63 (1902): 481–516.

[105] Dolbeau, "Domaine négligé," p. 137. Roberts makes the same argument for the characteristics of late antique Christian epics in *Biblical Epic*.

[106] Marjorie Curry Woods, "Weeping for Dido: Epilogue on a Premodern Rhetorical Exercise in the Postmodern Classroom," in *Latin Grammar and Rhetoric: From Classical Theory to Medieval Practice*, ed. Carol Dana Lanham (London, 2002), p. 282.

[107] "Famina divini verbi," as Johannes characterizes Amand's utterances. Johannes, *VR* 2.22. On God speaking through the saint, see Kate Cooper, "Ventriloquism and the Miraculous: Conversion, Preaching, and the Martyr Exemplum in Late Antiquity," in *Signs, Wonders, Miracles: Representations of Divine Power in the Life of the Church*, Studies in Church History 41, ed. Kate Cooper and Jeremy Gregory (Woodbridge, 2005), pp. 22–45.

[108] The pacifying effect of Amand's words was so powerful that sailors fell asleep during a storm after he told them to trust God (*VA*, 2.239–241). Combined with the appropriate gesture – the sign of the cross – his speech routed a serpent and exorcised demons (1.176–198).

[109] *VA*, 2.160: "Victor vi vincens verbere verbi."

[110] On classroom use, see Chapter 2.

persons or entities, such as the saint, a river, a city, or the reader.[111] The poets' interruptions allow for more metareferentiality and the foregrounding of the poetic persona. Particularly at the beginning and end of books, and in prefaces, the poets refer to their own work, sometimes likening it to the saint's labors.

The poets also enhance descriptions, increasing the narrative's visual and emotional impact. Poems often feature expanded ekphrastic scenes common in Classical epic (such as storms at sea).[112] Both descriptions and metaphors add color. Descriptions also increase the story's pathos and drama by emphasizing the saint's suffering and the fury of his or her adversaries.

In accordance with broader poetic trends, epic *vitae* tend to become more recondite, complex, and classicizing during the ninth and tenth centuries. The poets increasingly use Classical reminiscences, sometimes in very sophisticated ways akin to the window allusions of antique epic.[113] Writers, such as Heiric, employ lofty poetic vocabulary, using obscure Latin and even Greek words (both of which are often glossed in the manuscripts). Other features that become more pronounced are convoluted word order, and obvious Classical features, such as the appeal to the muses and Classical naming (Ceres for grain, Bacchus for wine or grapes, the "lamp of Phoebus" for the sun).[114]

The epic *vita* can be described as a genre, as long as we understand that term to designate a flexible body of ideas about style, form, and content ("the horizon of expectations," as Jauss calls it) with which a reader approaches a text, rather than as a set of precise rules.[115] These expectations, which the reader has derived from encounters with previous texts, do not constrain the author. Rather, he or she can challenge and transform the conventions in numerous ways.[116] In this way, genres evolve and mutate into others over time. As we will see, writers reformulated the epic *vita*, sometimes creating novel works that only partially resemble their antecedants. Accordingly, not all the texts I discuss are epic (which

[111] Cf. Roberts, *Biblical Epic*, pp. 179–180.

[112] Roberts, "Last Epic," p. 278.

[113] On allusion in Classical Latin verse, see Stephen Hinds, *Allusion and Intertext: Dynamics of Appropriation in Roman Poetry* (New York, 1998).

[114] *VG*, 1.112, 6.526.

[115] Hans Robert Jauss, *Toward an Aesthetic of Reception*, trans. Timothy Bahti (Minneapolis, 1982), p. 88. Roberts points out the utility of Jauss's formulation for thinking about this genre. Roberts, "Last Epic," p. 258.

[116] Jauss, *Toward an Aesthetic*, p. 88.

is to say written primarily in epic Latin verse) or *vitae* (dealing primarily with a saint's life), but they all define themselves in relation to epic lives.

Although epic *vitae* shared features of form and style, writers were free to reinterpret the tradition. So, Hilduin's epic *Passio Dionysii*, composed in the 830s, contains long passages of prose, including letters attributed to the saint. A life of Gall, perhaps composed in the late ninth century by Notker I, a teacher at the saint's eponymous abbey, comprises a dialogue between a teacher and student, written in sections of prose interspersed with different kinds verse.[117] A *vita* written around 1000 at Metz tells of Clemens's expulsion of snakes from the city and then provides a sermon, in which the hexameters are interspersed with rhythmical hymns.[118] The epic *Vita Bertini* was written in leonine (rhyming) hexameters.[119] Several *vitae* were also written in rhythmic verse.[120] Although the rhythmic *Vita Eligii* lacks many of the epic features noted earlier, its anonymous author clearly located it in epic verse tradition.[121] An anonymous author, probably from eleventh-century Saint-Amand, draws on Milo's epic *Vita Amandi*, as well as prose works on the saint and Boethius's *Consolation of Philosophy*, to write a *vita* in prose, rhythmic verse, and elegiac distichs.[122] These works

---

[117] Fragments of the *Dialogus* (BHL 3256) attributed to Notker I survive; ed. in MGH Poetae 4/3, pp. 1094–1108. See Walter Berschin, "Notkers Metrum de vita S. Galli. Einleitung und Edition," in *Florilegium Sangallense: Festschrift für Johannes Duft zum 65. Geburtstag*, ed. Otto P. Clavadetscher, Helmut Maurer, and Stefan Sonderegger (St. Gallen-Sigmaringen, 1980), pp. 17–121.

[118] Carus, *Vita Clementis* (BHL 1860f.), ed. in MGH Poetae 5, pp. 112–145. On this *vita*, see H. Müller, "The Saint as Preacher. Remarks on a Rare Motif in Late Antique and Medieval Poetry," in *Poetry and Exegesis in Premodern Latin Christianity: The Encounter between Classical and Christian Strategies of Interpretation*, ed. Willemien Otten and Karla Pollmann, Supplements to Vigiliae Christianae 87 (Leiden, 2007), pp. 285–292.

[119] *Vita Bertini* (BHL 1294), in Boulogne-sur-Mer, BM, MS 146A, fols. 1r–12r, ed. François Morand in *Vita Sancti Bertini metrica Simone Auctore. Vie de Saint Bertin, en vers composeé par Simon* (Paris, 1872).

[120] Rhythmic *vitae* and *passiones*, are ed. in MGH Poetae 4/2. The rhythmic *Passio martyrum Petri et Marcellini*, attributed to Einhard, is ed. in MGH Poetae 2, pp. 126–135.

[121] *Vita Eligii* (BHL 2478). The earliest manuscript is ninth or tenth centry. Although the poem is not in epic meter, the author locates it in the Christian epic tradition by echoing almost verbatim Sedulius's reasons for why he wished to compose in verse (*haec metrica ... componere*). See the letter appended to the *Vita*, printed in MGH Poetae 4/2, pp. 805–806. Cf. Sedulius, *Paschale carmen*, 1 5ff. in Sedulius, *Opera*, ed. Johann Huemer, CSEL 10 (Vienna, 1885). The 498-line *vita* "rethorice atque commatice expolita" contains copious allusions to Sedulius and Juvencus.

[122] This *vita*, from Valenciennes, BM, MS 412, is edited by Corinna Bottiglieri, "Oceano contigua regio Aquitanica. Una variazione ritmica sulla vita di S. Amando di Maastricht. Edizione del testo, fonti e modelli," *Hagiographica* 10 (2003): 241–297.

not only draw on the tradition of epic lives but also refer to prose *vitae* and locate themselves in broader Classical and Christian poetic traditions. Ermenric's letter to Grimald (the subject of Chapters 2 and 3), which features an appendix of prose and verse sections ostensibly on Saint Gall, Abbo's *Bella Parisiaca*, an account of the Viking attacks, and Dudo's *De moribus*, noted previously, are all examples of sui generis works, which are informed, to greater or lesser degrees by the genre of the epic *vita*.

SOURCES FOR THE EPIC TRADITION

The epic *vita* is a form with Classical and late antique Christian roots.[123] Although it is not my primary purpose to trace the genre's formation, a brief overview of its origins gives a sense of the works that influenced epic *vitae* and the synthesis of diverse literary heritages.[124]

Epic *vitae* derive their narrative structure, tropes, and some of their vocabulary from Latin prose lives. Many follow the basic arc of a saint's life, which, in the case of a male confessor, typically covers his youth, conversion, deeds (including missionary activity, exorcisms, and healings), death, and posthumous miracles.[125] The epic lives also echo standard prose *vita* tropes, which suppress individualistic characterization and assimilate the saint to a type.[126] The poets adopt the standard prose *vita*'s humility topos, in which the author professes his or her inability and claims only to have written the work out of affection for the patron who demanded it.[127] As early as the fifth century, citing his own

---

[123] A full study of their sources would consider forms of Classical poetry other than epic (particularly Horace, Juvenal, and Ovid), a broader range of Christian verse (including Ambrose's hymns, Ausonius, and Aldhelm), and the prosimetric works of Boethius and Martianus Capella. It would also examine their use of Scriptural language and ideas, especially the Psalms, and the influence of basic school texts.

[124] Kirsch's *Laude Sanctorum* traces the development of medieval religious epic verse, understood more broadly. He gives an author by author account, listing their sources and providing biographical and historical context. His second volume will cover the ninth and tenth centuries.

[125] David Townsend, "Hagiography," in *Medieval Latin*, ed. F.A.C. Mantello and A.G. Rigg (Washington, DC, 1996), p. 619.

[126] Important works on hagiography include Hippolyte Delehaye, *The Legends of the Saints: An Introduction to Hagiography*, trans. V.M. Crawford (Notre Dame, 1961 [1907]); René Aigrain, *L'Hagiographie: Ses sources, ses méthodes, son histoire*, 2nd ed., Subsidia hagiographica 80 (Brussels, 2000 [1953]); Baudouin de Gaiffier, *Recherches d'hagiographie latine* (Brussels, 1971); Réginald Grégoire, *Manuale di agioglogia: Introduzione alla letteratura agiografica* (Fabriano, 1987); Jacques Dubois and Jean-Loup Lemaître, *Sources et méthodes de l'hagiographie médiévale* (Paris, 1993).

[127] Townsend, "Hagiography," p. 620.

unworthiness, Sulpicius Severus casts his dear *patronus* ("frater carissimus") as the force behind his prose saint's life.[128] Despite these similarities, epic *vitae* are very different from their prose sources and counterparts. The distinctive features of epic *vitae* are not drawn from prose traditions, but from the antique and medieval Latin poetic heritage. Extant manuscripts, library lists, and allusions within the epic lives provide evidence of the texts available to writers.[129] Epic *vitae* of the Central Middle Ages draw on three main poetic sources: Classical epic (especially Virgil); late antique biblical epic, which appropriated its form to convey a Christian message; and early verse saints' lives, which drew in turn on biblical epic and other late antique poetry.

Because these traditions were accretive, and because poets emulated their immediate predecessors and older sources, it is not always possible to determine the models for particular aspects of the epic *vitae*. For example, "lush" description,[130] the use of pagan personifications, similes, and long sections of direct speech are all characteristic of both Classical and biblical epic. Similarly, the Classical poet Lucan's taste for learned digressions on astronomy and geography, his interest in allegory and the underlying meaning of events, his episodic structure, and his frequent intervention in the text in the form of apostrophe and moralizing are all paralleled in epic *vitae*, but these features are also found in biblical epics.[131] Highly visual imagery is characteristic of much pagan and Christian late antique verse,

---

[128] Sulpicius Severus, *Vita Martini* (BHL 5610), ed. J. Fontaine, *Vie de Saint Martin*, vol. 1 (Paris, 1967), pp. 248–317.

[129] Quotations and allusions can help establish sources, although writers drew on intermediate works, such as *florilegia* of excerpts and quotations in grammarians, as well as originals. For example, the ninth-century *florilegium*, Saint-Gall, SB, MS 870, excerpts numerous poets including Sedulius, Arator, Claudian, Ennius, Horace, Juvenal, Juvencus, Lactantius, Lucan, Lucretius, Martial, Martianus Capella, Ovid, Persius, Prudentius, Venantius Fortunatus, and Virgil. See Springer, "Sedulius," p. 186; Birger Munk Olsen, "Les Classiques latins dans les florilèges médiévaux anterieurs au XIIIe siecle I," *Revue d'histoire des textes* 9 (1979): 47–121; Eva Sanford, "The Use of Classical Latin Authors in the *Libri Manuales*," *TAPA* 55 (1924): 190–248. As Lapidge points out, identifying reminiscences is subjective. Michael Lapidge, "Knowledge of the Poems in the Earlier Period," appendix to R.W. Hunt, "Manuscript Evidence for Knowledge of the Poems of Venantius Fortunatus in Late Anglo-Saxon England," *ASE* 8 (1979): 288.

[130] Auerbach compares the "lush" description of epic with the bare bones account of the Old Testament. Erich Auerbach, *Mimesis: The Representation of Reality in Western Literature*, trans. Willard Trask (Princeton, 1953), pp. 1–20.

[131] Antony Snell, "Lucan," *Greece and Rome* 8 (1939): 86–87. On his apostrophe, see Francesca D'Alessandro Behr, *Feeling History: Lucan, Stoicism, and the Poetics of Passion* (Columbus, 2007).

including biblical epic and the works of Paulinus of Nola and Fortunatus.[132]

CLASSICAL EPIC

In language, meter, structure, and style, the poets who wrote saints' lives show themselves as the heirs to the Classical epic tradition.[133] In the influential definition of the late antique grammarian Diomedes, epic is "the presentation of divine, heroic, and human matters in hexameter verse."[134] Its heroes are closely connected with the divine sphere. Isidore (d. ca. 636), a widely read authority in the Middle Ages, explains that epic "is called heroic song because brave men's deeds and acts are recounted. For they are called heroes," he continues with a far-fetched etymology, "as if ethereal [*aerii* – literally 'of the air'] and worthy of heaven on account of their wisdom and forbearance."[135] The hero's elevated nature, virtue, and suffering were central to Isidore's definition of epic. It was a small step to envision a saintly protagonist. As Jan Ziolkowski writes, "if the central figure of epics are heroes closely related to divine beings, then saints – those distinguished imitators of Christ – were candidates for leading roles in hagiographic epics."[136] In late antiquity, epic, because it focuses "on praiseworthy actions of the individual ... becomes a form of encomiastic biography."[137] Therefore, as Roberts has observed, the saint's life became "highly appropriate material for epic treatment."[138]

Further, epics locate a hero's deeds, journeys, and battles in a grand design.[139] This cosmic vision was suited to Christian subjects. As Pollman observes, Christianity's preoccupations, God and salvation, are "epic by

---

[132] Roberts, *Jeweled Style*, pp. 124–146, for Christian contributions to that style.

[133] Some kinds of "epic encoding," which ancient poets used to signal genre, had become general poetic tropes by the ninth century. For example, compound adjectives (such as *flammivolans, doctiloquus*), which Roberts considers epic markers in Fortunatus, are poetic commonplaces in the ninth century. Roberts, "Last Epic," p. 269.

[134] Diomedes, *Ars Grammatica* 3 (Keil 1, 483f.): "carmine hexametro divinarum rerum et heroicarum humanarumque conprehensio," cited by Pollman, "Transformation of Epic," p. 63.

[135] Isidore, *Etymologiae*, 1.39.9: "heroicum enim carmen dictum, quod eo virorum fortium res et facta narrantur. Nam heroes appellantur viri quasi aerii et caelo digni propter sapientiam et fortitudinem."

[136] Jan Ziolkowski, "Epic," in *Medieval Latin: An Introduction and Bibliographical Guide*, ed. F.A.C. Mantello and A.G. Rigg (Washington, DC, 1996), p. 548.

[137] Roberts, "Last Epic," p. 267.

[138] Ibid.

[139] John O. Ward, "Medieval Epic," in *Roman Epic*, ed. A.J. Boyle (London, 1993), p. 265.

definition."[140] The lofty diction appropriate to pagan heroics was equally fitting for Christian themes.

Virgil's *Aeneid*, the core text of the curriculum, was the touchstone for writers of epic *vitae*.[141] Poets invoke Virgil as the paradigmatic pagan author, and epic based on his model remained the most prestigious literary form.[142] Reflecting broader cultural shifts, tenth- and eleventh-century poets emphasize a greater diversity of Classical sources than do their predecessors, but Virgil remains central.[143] The *Aeneid* tells of the wanderings and travails of "pious Aeneas," ancestor of the Roman people. Saints, particularly itinerant missionary bishops, could easily be fitted into this scheme. By making the protagonist a saint, the epic *vita* recasts the journey as a spiritual quest and often gives the writer's institution a foundation story to parallel Rome.

The influence of other pagan epics, such as Lucretius's *De rerum natura*, is less clear.[144] Ovid's *Metamorphoses* and the Pseudo-Virgilian mini-epic

[140] Pollman, "Transformation of Epic," p. 74.

[141] Virgil's *Georgics* and *Eclogues* were also widely read, and their language resounds in the epic *vitae*.

[142] Roberts, "Last Epic," p. 263. References to Virgil in epic *vitae* include *VA*, 2.3; Vulfaius also invokes Virgil by name in his response to the *VA*, the *Versiculi Vulfai*, line 29. Heiric names him in his *Allocutio ad librum* to his *VG*, line 20. On Virgil's medieval reception, see Domenico Comparetti, *Vergil in the Middle Ages*, trans. E.F.M. Benecke (London, 1966), and Jan M. Ziolkowski and Michael C.J. Putnam, eds., *The Virgilian Tradition: The First Fifteen Hundred Years* (New Haven, 2008).

[143] For Classical poets in the Carolingian curriculum, see Birger Munk Olsen, "Les poètes classiques dans les écoles au IXe siècle," in *La Réception de la littérature classique au Moyen Age (IXe–XIIe siècle): Choix d'articles publié par des collègues à l'occasion de son soixantième anniversaire*, ed. Karsten Friis-Jensen (Copenhagen, 1995), pp. 35–46. Lists of canonical or curriculum poets from the tenth century on are far more pagan in emphasis (see Chapter 4).

[144] Lucretius's (d. BCE 55) natural history *De rerum natura* was also written in epic form, and was known at Charlemagne's court, at Saint-Gall, and in the area around Saint-Bertin (all centers associated with epic verse) in the Central Middle Ages. It lacks an overarching story, and with its Epicurean cosmic view, it was not an obvious model for Christian poems. Heiric alludes to *DRN* 5.889 and 5.1248 (*VG* 1.96, 6.456). Ermenric, at Saint-Gall ca. 850, shows a greater familiarity with him (see Chapter 3). There is substantial evidence for Lucretius in Francia during the Central Middle Ages. Reynolds lists two ninth-century manuscripts, one associated with Charlemagne's court, and ninth-century fragments survive from Lorsch. See "Lucretius," in *Texts and Transmission*, pp. 219–220; Bernhard Bischoff, *Lorsch im Spiegel seiner Handschriften* (Munich, 1974), p. 74. A verse florilegium of Mico of Saint-Riquier, assembled at Reichenau ca. 825, and another from Saint-Gall, ca. 900 (Sankt-Gallen, SB, HS 870) both excerpt *DRN* as do two Vatican manuscripts. See U. Pizzani, "Versi Lucreziani nel Codice Vaticano Reginense Lat. 598," *Rivista di cultura classica e medioevale* 1 (1959): 399–402; Chauncey E. Finch, "Lucretius in Codex Vat. Reg. Lat. 1587," *Classical Philology* 62 (1967): 261–262. In

Culex could have provided lighter examples, leavened by humor.[145] Lucan's historical *Bellum Civile* (also known as the *Pharsalia*), written 61–65 CE, which was extremely popular from the ninth century, provided another model.[146] The impact of other Silver Age epics appears minimal.[147] Except for the *Aeneid*, the Classical tradition had less direct influence than did the late antique Christian epic.

the same century, there was also a copy at Murbach. See W. Milde, *Der Bibliothekskatalog des Klosters Murbach aus dem 9. Jahrhundert* (Heidelberg, 1968), 48, no. 318. Allusions in the *Encomium Emmae* (ed. George Pertz in MGH SS 19, pp. 509–525) imply that by the eleventh century, it was associated with Saint-Bertin, where it was catalogued in the sixteenth. See R.W. Hunt, "The Deposit of Latin Classics in the Twelfth-Century Renaissance," in *Classical Influences on European Culture A.D. 500–1500*, ed. R.R. Bolgar (Cambridge, 1971), p. 51. A gloss on Sigebert of Gembloux (ca. 1030–1112) also draws on DRN. See Manitius, *Geschichte*, vol. 3, p. 340.

[145] Ovid's *Metamorphoses* is another kind of epic, consisting of intertwined mythological stories. The work offers a less lofty version of epic, which was usually equated with serious and dignified expression and themes – kings, leaders, wars, and heroes (e.g., Horace, *Ars Poetica* lines, 73–74). As Quintilian states, "Ovid is lascivious even in heroic verses" (*Inst.*, 10.1.89: "lascivuus quidem in herois quoque Ovidius"). Ninth- and tenth-century epic lives reference the *Metamorphoses* (as well as other Ovidian works), although the manuscript tradition is lacking. See Reynolds, "Ovid," in *Texts and Transmission*, p. 276. On the Pseudo-Virgilian *Culex* (*Mosquito*), see Chapter 3.

[146] The extant witnesses suggest Lucan's popularity: from the ninth century, five complete manuscripts, one fragment, and a commentary survive. Harold C. Gotoff, *The Text of Lucan in the Ninth Century* (Cambridge, MA, 1971), p. 1; R.J. Tarrant, "Lucan," in *Texts and Transmission*, p. 214; Sanford, "*Libri manuales*," p. 199.

[147] The *Ilias Latina*, the 1,070-line Latin condensation of Homer's *Iliad* made during Nero's reign (54–68 CE), is mentioned by Ermenric (*Ep. Ad. Grimaldum*, c. 10, ca. 850) and became a popular school text (when the medieval authors discussed here mention "Homer," they are referring to this text). Statius's epics, the *Thebaid* (ca. 80–92 CE) and the unfinished *Achilleid* (94–95 CE), do not seem to have exerted a strong influence. Many Latin epic texts were virtually unknown, such as the *Punica* of Silius Italicus (d. ca. 103 CE) and the *Argonautica* of Valerius Flaccus (d. ca. 90 CE). On the *Ilias Latina*, see P.K. Marshall in *Texts and Transmission*, p. 191; Günter Glauche, *Schullektüre im Mittelalter. Entstehung u. Wandlungen d. Lektürekanons bis 1200 nach d. Quelle* (Munich, 1970); Baebius Italicus, *Ilias Latina*, ed. Marco Scaffai (Bologna, 1982), p. 15. Alcuin mentions Statius among the *auctores* at York, and Richer includes him in the curriculum that Gerbert of Aurillac taught at Rheims in the late tenth century (Richer, *Historia*, ed. Hartmut Hoffman in MGH SS 38; Glauche, *Schullektüre*, p. 63). Neither Alcuin nor Richer specifies which of Statius's works were intended, but Gerbert asks a correspondent for a copy of his *Achilleid* (Gerbert, *Ep.* 134, dated to 988, ed. Fritz Weigle, MGH Briefe d. dt. Kaiserzeit 2, p. 162, lines 4–6). Statius is also attested in the scholastic verse of Ekkehart I of Saint-Gall (d. 973) (Notker, *Carm.* 5, line 18, ed. in MGH Poetae 5, p. 548. See also, Glauche, *Schullektüre*, p. 91. The *Thebaid* survives in one ninth-century manuscript (Paris, BN, MS lat. 8051, written at Corbie), and in several tenth- and eleventh-century copies (see Reynolds, *Texts and Transmission*, p. 394). The *Achilleid*, which became a standard classroom text in the thirteenth century, is attested in the same ninth-century Corbie manuscript. See also "Silius Italicus" and "Valerius Flaccus" in *Texts and Transmission*, pp. 388–391, 425–427.

MYSTICA DONA: BIBLICAL EPIC

The fourth-century epic revival saw the production of pagan epics, such as Claudian's De raptu Proserpinae, and miniature epillya.[148] The late Latin tradition was transmitted to the Central Middle Ages largely via Christian poets, who, from the fourth to sixth centuries, appropriated epic for Scriptural narrative and explication.[149] The four "canonical" Bible epics – by Juvencus (ca. 330), Sedulius (first half of the fifth century), Arator (544), and, to a lesser extent, Avitus (544) – were often read in the classroom until at least the eleventh century.[150] Also influential was the

[148] Ziolkowski defines epillya as "narrative poems that elaborate single episodes from the heroic past and resemble epics in theme, tone, and descriptive technique." Ziolkowski, "Epic," in Medieval Latin, p. 551.

[149] Roberts, "Last Epic," p. 274. Claudian's De raptu Proserpinae (ca. 397) seems to have been little known in the Central Middle Ages, although it was a curriculum text in later centuries. It did not directly influence these epic vitae, although it may have done so indirectly via biblical epic. On Claudian's transmission, see J.B. Hall, "Claudian," in Texts and Transmission, p. 143. Claire Gruzelier, ed., Claudian. De Raptu Proserpinae (Oxford, 1993). For biography, see Alan Cameron, Claudian: Poetry and Propaganda at the Court of Honorius (Oxford, 1970), pp. 1–29.

[150] Herzog calls these four poets "die kanonischen Epiker." Reinhart Herzog, Die Bibelepik der lateinischen Spätantike: Formgeschichte einer erbaulichen Gattung I (Munich, 1975), p. xix. The three main biblical epics remained core curriculum texts until the eleventh century (Lapidge, "Versifying the Bible," p. 12). Arator was extremely popular on the Continent from the ninth century, and the glosses and manuscript context show that his De actibus apostolorum was often used as a school text. See Gernot Rudolf Wieland, The Latin Glosses on Arator and Prudentius in Cambridge Library MS GG.5.35 (Toronto, 1983), p. 4; McKinley dated twenty manuscripts of Arator to the ninth century and another four to the ninth or tenth centuries. Arthur Patch McKinley, Arator: The Codices (Cambridge, MA, 1942), p. 69. (See also his pp. 3–65 and 104–118 for MS descriptions and discussion.) Alcuin (in the late eighth century) mentions them as do Theodulf and Hraban Maur (early ninth century). Fortunatus, Vita Martini, 1.14–25, ed. F. Leo in MGH AA 4.1, pp. 295–296; Alcuin, York Poem, lines 1550–1554; Theodulf, Carmen 45, lines 13–14 in MGH Poetae 1, pp. 543; Hraban Maur, De instutione clericorum 3, 18, noted by Glauche, Schullektüre im Mittelalter, pp. 5, 10, 16. Other biblical epics, such as Claudius Marius Victorius's Alethia and the Heptateuchos attributed to Cyprian of Gaul, both from the first half of the fifth century, were less well known. Roger P.H. Green, Latin Epics of the New Testament: Juvencus, Sedulius, Arator (Oxford, 2006), p. 151. Cyprian's paraphrase of the historical books of the Old Testament in 5,250 hexameter lines (with three passages of hendecasyllables) was heavily influenced by Lucretius, Virgil, and other Classical poets (Catullus, Horace, Persius, Ovid, and Juvenal) as well as his Christian predecessors (Juvencus, Paulinus of Nola, and Prudentius). His verse stays close to his source (the pre-Vulgate Latin Bible), with less allegorical or typological interpretation than the epics of Sedulius or other later poets. Cyprian, ed. Rudolf Peiper, CSEL 23 (Prague, 1881). See D.J. Nodes, Doctrine and Exegesis in Biblical Latin Poetry (Liverpool, 1993), pp. 26–36. Claudius Marius Victorius, in Marseilles in the earlier

late-fifth-century paraphrase of Genesis, which was the first book of Dracontius's *De laudibus Dei*.[151]

From the biblical poems, *vitae* inherited a precedent and a rationale for Christian epic. Poetry, subject to suspicion as the vessel of pagan falsehood, was acknowledged, even by Christian writers, for its "sweetness" and prestige.[152] In response to criticisms of Scripture's unrefined Latin, Christian poets, starting with Juvencus, rewrote it as epic.[153] Borrowing Virgil's form, meter, and language, Juvencus, in his enormously influential Gospel poem, the *Evangelia* (ca. 330), "created the diction of Christian-Latin Biblical verse."[154] The memorability of epic imagery was not a distraction and "particular hindrance to salvation" (*speciale impedimentum salutis*), as Cassian says, but could be harnessed to benefit the reader.[155] Epic, rehabilitated with the Christian aims of "spiritual instruction, moral edification or biblical exegesis," could be salvific for both poets and readers.[156]

In appropriating epic, biblical epicists simultaneously cast themselves within and in opposition to the Classical tradition. Rejecting the "lies of the pagan poets," they offered an apologia for their use of the form: if the old poets could sing of worldly fictions, then Christians should sing of true things.[157] The topos of rejection allowed the poets to parade their Classical learning, showing themselves as heirs to the tradition they ostensibly denounced. In a programmatic statement, Juvencus explicitly locates himself in the tradition of Homer and "sweet Virgil" but claims that he will

---

fifth century, wrote a four-book commentary of Genesis in hexameter, of which three books survive in a lone manuscript, Paris, BN, lat. 7558 (ix). He amplifies his source with pagan and Platonic material, ed. P.F. Hovingh, CCSL 128 (Turnhout, 1960); White, *Early Christian Latin Poets*, p. 118. Proba's *Cento* (360s or 380s) also reworked Christian material in epic form by using Virgilian lines and half lines verbatim (or almost verbatim); ed. Charles Shenkl, CSEL 16 (Milan, 1888), pp. 568–609.

[151] Between 646 and 652, Eugenius, bishop of Toledo, revised Dracontius's *De laudibus Dei*, incorporating part of the poet's *Satisfactio*. Charles Witke, *Numen Litterarum: The Old and the New in Latin Poetry from Constantine to Gregory the Great* (Leiden, 1971), p. 173; Raby, *Secular Latin Poetry*, vol. 1, p. 149.

[152] Lactantius, *De Ira Dei*, 20. 2, calls Ovid "poeta non insuavis." Quoted by Green, *Latin Epics*, p. 144.

[153] Roberts, "Last Epic," p. 263; Pollmann, "Transformation," p. 69. For example, Augustine, *Conf*. 3, 5, 9, discussing his youthful response to the Bible's unrefined style.

[154] Lapidge, "Versifying the Bible," p. 17; Kirsch, *Laudes sanctorum*, p. 34.

[155] Cassian, *Conlationes*, 14.12 cited in Pollman. "Transformation," p. 62.

[156] Pollmann, "Transformation," p. 75; Roberts, *Biblical Epic*, p. 107; Juvencus, *praef.*, lines 22–24.

[157] K. Thraede, "Epos," *RAC* 5 (1962), cols. 997–999 for Christian criticism of epic poetry's mendacity since the third century.

celebrate the salvific deeds of Christ (*Christi vitalia gesta*), rather than falsehoods (*mendacia*) about the deeds of ancient men.[158] Christ has become the epic hero.

In the preface to his *Paschale Carmen* (first half of the fifth century), Sedulius offers a similar apologia: if the pagan poets (*gentiles poetae*) can "glorify their fictions" and create "monuments to crime," then Sedulius should not keep silent about Christ's miracles and promise of salvation.[159] The topos of rejection undermined by Classical allusions, which becomes a medieval poetic commonplace, warns us against taking hostility to the pagan tradition at face value.[160]

Epic *vitae* inherited late Latin epic features from the biblical poems, including "generic instability," that is, the tendency to absorb features from other genres, particularly panegyric.[161] Both biblical and saintly epic are encomiastic. The Bible poems employ other late Latin features,

---

[158] Juvencus, *pref.*, lines 6–10, 15–20, ed. Johannes Teumer in Juvencus, *Gai. Vettii Aquilini Iuvenci Evangeliorum libri quattuor*, CSEL 24 (Vienna, 1891). Juvencus was a Spanish priest and aristocrat, according to Jerome, *On Famous Men*, c. 84, who says he lived in the reign of Constantine. On Juvencus's origins, see Green, *Latin Epics*, pp. 1–9. Herzog discusses Juvencus at length in *Bibelepik*.

[159] Sedulius, *Paschale carmen*, lines 17–28: "Since the pagan poets endeavor to glorify their fictions (*figmenta*) in lofty-sounding measures, and with a tragic roar or with an absurd comedy or with any art of singing renew the brutal infection of unspeakable acts and in song create monuments to crime, and, through the teacher's activity, convey numerous lies in books from the Nile [i.e., of papyrus], why should I – accustomed to playing the songs of David on ten strings [of the lyre] and to standing reverently in the holy chorus and to singing the celestial psalms in soft words, why should I keep silent about the bright miracles of salvation-bearing Christ, when I am able to speak these things clearly and to revel in confessing the thunderous lord to all senses, with my whole heart" (Cum sua gentiles studeant figmenta poetae / Grandisonis pompare modis, tragicoque boatu / Ridiculove Geta seu qualibet arte canendi / Saeva nefandarum renovent contagia rerum / Et scelerum monumenta canant, rituque magistro / Plurima Niliacis tradant mendacia biblis, / Cur ego, Daviticis adsuetus cantibus odas / Cordarum resonare decem sanctoque verenter / Stare choro et placidis caelestia psallere verbis, / Clara salutiferi taceam miracula Christi, / Cum possim manifesta loqui, Dominumque tonantem / Sensibus et toto delectet corde fateri; Geta is the name of a slave in the comedies *Adelphoe* and *Phormio* by the Roman playwright Terence [d. BCE 159].)

[160] For example, Rodulf Tortaire, prologue, ed. Ogle and Schullian, *Rodulfi Tortarii Carmina*, pp. 349–351; Hilduin's epic *PD*, fols. 34v–35r (discussed in Chapter 1). Poets writing in forms other than epic also employ such apologia. For example, John Scottus, *Carmen* 2, lines 10–11, in MGH Poetae 3, p. 527.

[161] T.-C. Kevin Tsai, "Hellish Love: Genre in Claudian De raptu Proserpinae," *Helios* 34 (2007): 37; Pollman, "Transformation," p. 65; on late antique genre instability, see J. Fontaine, "Unité et diversité du mélange des genres et des tons chez quelques écrivains latins de la fin du IVe siècle: Ausone, Ambroise, Ammien," in *Christianisme et formes littéraires de l'antiquité tardive en Occident*, ed. Manfred Fuhrmann (Geneva, 1977), pp. 425–472.

such as apostrophe and episodic composition. They also represent examples of the "jeweled style," characterized by color, light, obscure vocabulary, and expression.[162] They employ varying degrees of Classical reference (from Avitus's avoidance of Classical naming conventions to Dracontius's liberal use of mythology).[163] Other aspects of epic *vitae* derived from Christian biblical epic include their length, the use of metrically distinct prefaces, and Christian invocation (replacing the appeal to the muse).[164] From late Latin, they also derive their deliberately elliptical expression and complicated syntax, which preclude a reader's easy engagement with a text.

Perhaps most significantly, biblical epics offered different models for transforming a prose source while retaining its *sensus*. Juvencus's poem is a fairly literal versification of a version of the Old Latin Bible.[165] According to Jerome, Juvencus "translated" (*transferre*) the Gospels into verse "almost word for word" (*paene ad verbum*).[166] In later biblical epic, interpretation becomes increasingly prominent. Sedulius's *Paschale carmen* contains paraphrase and exegesis.[167] He "frequently departs from the narrative in order to reflect on the typological significance of New

---

[162] Roberts, *Jeweled Style*, pp. 123–132.

[163] Michael Roberts, "The Prologue to Avitus' *De spiritualis historiae gestis*," *Traditio* 36 (1980): 399–407.

[164] The biblical poems are about 2,500 to 3,200 lines long, divided into two to five books, whereas Classical Latin epic tends to be three or four times that length. (Juvencus's epic is 3,200 lines; Sedulius, Avitus, and Arator all wrote around 2,500 lines. By contrast, the *Aeneid* contains almost 10,000 lines of dactylic hexameter in twelve books; Lucan's unfinished *Bellum civile*, comprises ten books and just over 8,000 lines of hexameter. Statius's *Thebaid* emulates the *Aeneid* in book number and overall length.)

[165] Green, "*Evangeliorum Libri*," p. 66. Juvencus rearranges passages, introduces epithets, and adds color to heighten emotional impact. Scholars have disagreed on the extent of his exegesis, explaining the text's meaning and significance. See Klaus Thraede, "Epos," in *Reallexikon für Antike und Christentum* 5 (Stuttgart, 1962), cols. 983–1042. Herzog argues that Juvencus was barely an exegete at all, whereas Fichtner sees him as no less an exegete than Sedulius. Colombi gives numerous examples of Juvencus's interpretation. Green argues that Juvencus was a "stealth" exegete, subtly interpolating his interpretations into his verse. Rudolf Fichtner, *Taufe und Versuchung Jesu in den Evangeliorum Libri quattuor des Bibeldichters Iuvencus (1. 346–408)* (Stuttgart, 1994), p. 205; Herzog, *Bibelepik*, p. 115; Green, "Evangeliorum Libri of Juvencus," esp. pp. 74–80; E. Colombi, "Paene ad verbum: gli Evangeliorum libri di Giovenco tra parafrasi e commento," *Cassiodorus* 3 (1997): 9–36.

[166] Jerome, *Liber de viris inlustribus*, ed. Ernest Cushing Richardson (Leipzig, 1896), c. 84: "quattuor evangelia hexametris versibus paene ad verbum transferens quattuor libros composuit."

[167] Sedulius, *Opera*, ed. Johann Huemer, CSEL 10 (Vienna, 1885); Springer, *Gospel as Epic*, p. 1; Lapidge, "Versifying the Bible," p. 20; Herzog, *Bibelepik*, p. xix; Green, *Latin Epics* p. xvi.

Testament events: how they were prefigured in the Old Testament, their moral, soteriological, and eschatological meaning."[168] Sedulius has been described as the Christian Virgil, but he is more akin to Virgil and Servius combined, producing a versification that incorporates its own gloss. Later, he composed a complementary prose version, the *Paschale opus*, to assist and guide readers in comprehending the *Paschale carmen*.[169] In doing so he provided the exemplar for the "twinned work" of prose and verse.

Like Sedulius, Avitus (ca. 450–518) was concerned with Scripture's hidden meanings. *De spiritalis historiae gestis* covers events from Genesis and Exodus, but the poet includes many other biblical and historical examples to draw out events' typological significance, that is, how they prefigured Christ and future Christian history.[170] As he says in his prologue, his books "graze over other matters [in addition to Old Testament events], where opportunity for including them was found."[171] His structure, which intersperses descriptions of passages with long explications of the New Testament and historical events they prefigure, subordinates narrative to "typological logic."[172] Arator surpasses Sedulius and Avitus in preferring allegorical interpretation to a paraphrase of the narrative, and exegesis all but subsumes his account.[173] His epic is less a verse redaction than a "poetic commentary."[174]

---

[168] Lapidge, "Bede's Metrical *Vita*," p. 86; Carolinne D. Small, "Rhetoric and Exegesis in Sedulius's *Carmen paschale*," *Classica et Mediaevalia* 7 (1986): 223–234.

[169] Sedulius, *Epistola ad Macedonium altera*, ed. Johannes Huemer in CSEL 10, p. 171.

[170] Avitus, *De spiritalis historiae gestis*, ed. Rudolf Peiper in MGH AA 6.2, pp. 201–294. The first five books are biblical paraphrase and commentary. The sixth and final book, *De virginitate*, addressed to his sister on the subject of chastity, possesses a separate preface. See M. Hoffmann, "Principles of Structure and Unity in Latin Biblical Epic," in *Poetry and Exegesis in Premodern Latin Christianity*, pp. 139–146, and George W. Shea, "Introduction" in *The Poems of Alcimus Ecdicius Avitus: Translation and Introduction*, Medieval and Renaissance Texts and Studies, vol. 172 (Tempe, AZ, 1997), p. 2. For Avitus's life and context, see D.R. Shanzer and I.N. Wood, *Avitus of Vienne, Letters and Selected Prose* (Liverpool, 2002), pp. 3–27. Pollman, "Transformation," p. 70.

[171] Avitus, *Prologus*: "qui licet nominibus propriis titulisque respondeant, et alias tamen causas inventa materiae opportunitate perstringunt."

[172] Pollman, "Transformation," p. 71.

[173] Arator, *Aratoris Subdiaconi De Actibus Apostolorum*, ed. Arthur Patch McKinlay, CSEL 72 (Vienna, 1951); Neil Wright, "Arator's Use of Caelius Sedulius: A Re-Examination," *Eranos* 87 (1989): 51–64 at p. 52; Lapidge summarizes Arator's composition: "the poem consists of brief paraphrases of biblical events, giving the gist of the action, ... followed by twenty-five to a hundred lines of interpretation, in which the event itself may be referred to allusively, but is rarely spelled out." (Lapidge, "Versifying the Bible," p. 20.)

[174] Lapidge, "Bede's Metrical *Vita*," p. 87.

So, several biblical epics offer a model for a kind of self-glossing text in which the poet's explication forms part of the narrative.[175] (Among the poets of epic *vitae*, Ermenric takes this tradition furthest, by creating a work that is, as I discuss in Chapter 2, almost entirely a gloss.) The popular first book of Dracontius's *De laudibus Dei* (end of the fifth century) presented a different model for elaborating Scripture.[176] His versification of Genesis contains passages of lyrical praise, rather than exegesis.

FROM BIBLICAL EPIC TO EPIC LIFE

As these poets were rewriting Scripture as epic, others employed verse to celebrate saints. Prudentius's *Peristephanon*, a late-fourth-century collection of martyr poems, was the most influential.[177] Glossed manuscripts reveal its use in the medieval classroom.[178] His hymns, the *Cathemerinon* and his mini-epic *Psychomachia*, an allegorical battle of virtues and vices, were also widely read.[179] The *Peristephanon* comprises fourteen poems of different lengths and meter, each framing a passion in a description of the place and cult of the martyr. They share features with Classical epic and epic *vitae* such as the tendency for the protagonists to give long speeches.[180] Exhibiting the ekphrastic and emotional qualities of late Latin verse, the poems "concentrate on, and glory in, the lurid details of torture and death, and the startling operation of the supernatural."[181]

Prudentius's contemporary, Paulinus of Nola provided other models for adapting Classical forms and meters to write about saints.[182] Each year from 385–409, he composed *Natalicia*, which transformed the Classical

---

[175] A New Testament precedent for the "self-glossing text," is Jesus' explanation of the parable of the sower to his disciples (Mark 4:2–32; Matt. 13:3–23; Luke 8:5–15).

[176] Ca. 650, Eugenius, bishop of Toledo, revised Dracontius's *De laudibus Dei*, incorporating part of the poet's *Satisfactio*. Witke, *Numen Litterarum*, p. 173; Raby *Secular Latin Poetry*, vol. 1, p. 149.

[177] Prudentius, *Carmina*, ed. M.P. Cunninghman, CCSL 126 (Turnhout, 1961); Anne-Marie Palmer, *Prudentius on the Martyrs* (Oxford, 1989); Roberts, *Poetry and the Cult of the Martyrs*; Kirsch, *Laudes sanctorum*, pp. 149ff.

[178] Paris, BN, MS N. A. lat. 241 is a tenth- or eleventh-century copy of Prudentius's poems (with glosses) and Paulinus of Nola's epic *Vita Martini*.

[179] The *Psychomachia* narrates an allegorical battle between personified vices and virtues. It features a metrically distinct programmatic preface in 38 lines of iambic trimeter. See Pollman, "Transformation," pp. 64–66.

[180] H. Müller, "The Saint as Preacher: Remarks on a Rare Motif in Late Antique and Medieval Poetry," in Otten and Pollmann, eds., *Poetry and Exegesis*, p. 281.

[181] Palmer, *Prudentius and the Cult*, p. 2.

[182] Paulinus was born in 353 to a wealthy senatorial family in Bordeaux. In 409, he became bishop of Nola, near Felix's shrine in Campania. On Paulinus, see Kirsch, *Laudes*

birthday poem into a celebration of the day of Saint Felix's death.[183] *Natalicia* IV, V, and VI (written 398–400), which Paulinus regarded as a set, recount the saint's life and a posthumous miracle in 1,128 lines of dactylic hexameter.[184] In some respects, these *Natalicia* anticipate the fifth- and sixth-century biblical poets. Rather than giving narrative detail, they largely consist of praise of God and the saint, addresses to the reader, digressions, and, above all, typological and moral excurses.[185] Paulinus likens the saint's deeds to Scriptural passages and draws out the moral significance of events.[186] Like Prudentius, he combines humor and gory detail;[187] on occasion, even God and the saint are amused.[188] In addition to copious references to Scripture, especially the Psalms, Paulinus draws heavily on Classical verse.[189] Prudentius and Paulinus of Nola, unlike the

---

Sanctorum, pp. 43–48; White, *Early Christian Latin Poetry*, p. 57; R.P.H. Greene, *The Poetry of Paulinus of Nola* (Brussel, 1971); D.E. Trout, *Paulinus of Nola: Life, Letters and Poems* (Berkeley, 1999); Klaus Kohlwes, *Christliche Dichtung und stilistische Form bei Paulinus von Nola* (Bonn, 1979).

[183] P.G. Walsh, *The Poems of St. Paulinus of Nola*, Ancient Christian Writers 40 (New York, 1975), pp. 4–5.

[184] Ed. W. von Hartel, *Sancti Pontii Meropii Pavlini Nolani Carmina*, CSEL 30 (Vienna, 1894). *Nat.* IV (= *Carmen* 15), *Nat.* V (*Carm.* 16), *Natalicia* VI (*Carm.* 18). On the poems as a group, *Nat.* V, lines 17ff.; *Nat.* VI, lines 70–74. The *Natalicia* describing Felix's life and posthumous miracles were transmitted together in early manuscripts. Two Northumbrian manuscripts, Vatican MS Pal. lat. 235 and Leningrad National Public Library MS Q. V, XIV (both vii–viii) contain five *Natalicia*, IV, VI, VI, X, and IX, and another poem (*Carm.* 17). See Neil Wright, "Imitation of the Poems of Paulinus of Nola in Early Anglo-Latin Verse," in his *History and Literature in Late Antiquity and the Early Medieval West: Studies in Intertextuality*, Variorum Collected Studies Series, 503 (Aldershot, 1995), Essay XII, pp. 134–135.

[185] For example, the digressions on the working of a lamp and the anatomy of the eye in *Nat.* VII, lines 129–139, 174–183.

[186] For example, *Nat.* IV, line 61, likens Felix to Abraham and lines 84ff. liken the saint and his brother to Jacob and Esau.

[187] In *Nat.* VI, Paulinus has a peasant employ lofty Virgilian language in beseeching Felix for the return of his beloved oxen (lines 260ff.). Paulinus describes the bereft *rusticus* in terms of a heartbroken lover (*amans*), inhaling the scent of the absent beasts and rubbing his entire body over their hoofprints (lines 340–345). In *Nat.* VII, the corpulent Theridius, with his eye socket impaled on a hanging lantern, is likened to a fish on a hook (lines 269–270).

[188] *Nat.* VI, lines 315–316: "audivit laetus non blando sublice martyr / et sua cum domino ludens convitia risit." The suppliant is described as "quidam homo re tenuis, plebius origine, cultu/ rusticus" (lines 219–220).

[189] Like Virgil's Dido, the peasant who lost his oxen remains awake, beset by grief and anxiety, while the rest of the world sleeps through the peaceful night. *Nat.* VI, lines 355–357: "nox medium iam vecta polum perfuderat orbem / pace soporifera, reticebant omnia terris; / solum illum sua pervigilem spes curaque habebat." Compare line 341 ("neget aegro cura quietem") with Virgil, *Aen.* 4.5 ("nec placidum membris dat cura quietem").

biblical epic poets, localize the cosmic history of salvation in the cults of particular saints. This trend is particularly important for epic *vitae*, which are usually written about a saint with regional and personal significance to the poet. In the *vitae*, epic becomes personal.[190] The poem is an expression of devotion to the saint who is addressed as the poet's *patronus* and muse. Fortunatus, especially, frames the narrative with his own experience of and relationship to the saint.[191]

Drawing on traditions of epic and poetry about saints, Paulinus of Périgueux (in the 460s) and Venantius Fortunatus (in the 570s), each wrote an epic *vita* of Saint Martin, bishop of Tours, based on the prose of Sulpicius Severus.[192] Each poet dedicated his *vita* to the current bishop of Tours (Perpetuus and Gregory, respectively), a patron invested in Martin's cult. Paulinus addresses Perpetuus in the language of *amicitia* so common in later dedications.[193]

Paulinus draws on Virgil, Ovid, Juvencus, and Sedulius.[194] His Virgilian allusions assume his readers' knowledge of the original

---

[190] Pollman, "Transformation," p. 72.

[191] Ibid.

[192] Paulinus of Périgueux, *Vita Martini* (BHL 5617), ed. Michael Petschenig, CSEL 16 (Milan, 1888), pp. 17–159; Fortunatus, MGH AA 4.1, pp. 294–370. In his first three books, Paulinus versifies Sulpicius Severus's prose *Vita Martini* (BHL 5610). Books 4 and 5 versify Sulpicius's *Dialogues* 1, 2, and 3 (BHL 5614–5616), and the sixth book is based on a *charta* of Martin's posthumous miracles. Fortunatus drew on Sulpicius's *Vita Martini* and *Dialogues* 2 and 3. For a detailed consideration of these epic lives, see Sylvie Labarre, *Le manteau partagé: Deux métamorphoses poétiques de la 'Vie de saint Martin' chez Paulin de Périgueux (Ve s.) et Venance (VIe s.)* (Paris, 1998); also, Alston Hurd Chase, "The Metrical Lives of St. Martin of Tours by Paulinus and Fortunatus and the Prose Life by Sulpicius Severus," *Harvard Studies in Classical Philology* 43 (1932): 51–76. Fontaine examines Paulinus's and Fortunatus's *vitae* in the political context of late antique Gaul. Jacques Fontaine, "Hagiographie et politique, de Sulpice Sévère à Venance Fortunat," in *La Christianisation des pays entre Loire et Rhin (IVe–VIIe siècle)*, ed. Pierre Riché (Paris, 1993), pp. 113–140. For a consideration of Fortunatus's verse and prose, see Simon Coates, "The Construction of Episcopal Sanctity in Early Anglo-Saxon England: The Impact of Venantius Fortunatus," *Historical Research* 71:174 (1998): 1–13. On Fortunatus, see also Michael Roberts, "St. Martin and the Leper: Narrative Variation in the Martin Poems of Venantius Fortunatus," *JML* 4 (1994): 82–100; and Michael Roberts, "Martin Meets Maximus: The Meaning of a Late Roman Banquet," *Revue des études augustiniennes* 41 (1995): 90–111.

[193] Paulinus, *Pref.*, p. 17. Paulinus's letter begins "Studio caritatis et dilectionis affectu oblivisci nos pudoris iubetis ..." For a discussion of which sections Bishop Perpetuus commissioned, see Raymond Van Dam, "Paulinus of Périgueux and Perpetuus of Tours," *Francia* 14 (1986): 567–73. Fortunatus addresses two additional patrons, Radegund and her fellow nun Agnes, in a metrical preface.

[194] Andy Orchard, *The Poetic Art of Aldhelm* (Cambridge, 1994), p. 181; Labarre, *Manteau partagé*, pp. 161–169. Among Classical sources, Paulinus borrows most heavily from

context.[195] Fortunatus, while familiar with Virgil, Ovid, Claudian, Statius, and other Classical *auctores*, locates himself in an exclusively Christian poetic lineage.[196] At the beginning of the *Vita Martini*, he lists his literary ancestors. After mentioning the writers of Scripture, he continues:

> For first setting out a song in an order that was easy to grasp,
> Juvencus sang a majestic work of the metric art.
> Then the tongue of outstanding Sedulius also shone,
> And Orientius bound together a few things with his flowering speech,
> And sending these holy offerings to the pious martyrs,
> The prudent man Prudentius prudently offered up their acts.
> Paulinus, powerful in lineage, heart, faith and art,
> Laid out in verse master Martin's teachings.
> What are called the deeds and acts of the apostles' fate
> The bard Arator plowed with his eloquent speech.
> What the genealogist [Moses] once set forth in a holy order,
> Bishop Alcimus [Avitus] composed with his sharp intellect[197]

All these poets, except Orientius and Prudentius, wrote biblical epic.[198] Both Paulinus of Périgueux and Fortunatus draw heavily on this

---

Virgil's *Aeneid* and *Georgics*, followed by Ovid's *Metamorphoses*. He also alludes to Virgil's *Eclogues*, other Ovidian poems, Catullus, Propertius, and Claudian. See Clemens Weidmann, "Zu Quellen des Paulinus von Petricordia," *Wiener Studien* 104 (1991): 169–182.

[195] Paulinus uses allusions to emphasize Martin's efficacy by calling to the reader's mind a scene that revealed the saint's superiority over the figures in the Classical source, for example, the sea serpents killing Lacoon (*Aen.* 2.203–211) to depict Martin's more successful encounter with a snake (5.619–636). See Thomas Gärtner, "Zur christlichen Imitationstechnik in der 'Vita Sancti Martini' des Paulinus von Petricordia," *Vigiliae Christianae* 55 (2001): 81–83.

[196] Roberts, "Last Epic," p. 259; M.L Campanale, "L'Ovidio 'eroico' di Venanzio Fortunato," in *Aetates Ovidianae*, ed. I. Gallo and L. Nicastri (Naples, 1995), pp. 133–152; Labarre, *Manteau partagé*, pp. 162–164; S. Blomgren, "De Venantio Fortunato Vergilii aliorumque poetarum priorum imiatore," *Eranos* 42 (1944): 81–88. Fortunatus also has fewer reminiscences of other Classical poets (Juvenal, Persius, Petronius, and Horace).

[197] 1.14–25: "Primus enim docili distinguens ordine Carmen / Maiestatis opus metri canit arte Iuvencus, / Hinc quoque conspicui radiavit lingua Seduli, / Paucaque perstrinxit florente Orientius ore / martyribusque piis sacra haec donaria mittens, / prudens prudenter Prudentius immolat actus. / Stemmate, corde, fide pollens Paulinus et arte /versibus explicuit Martini dogma magistri. / Sortis apostolicae quae gesta vocantur et actus, / facundo eloquio sulcavit vates Arator. / Quod sacra explicuit serie genealogus olim, / Alcimus egregio digessit acumine praesul." The reading "Alcimus" is based on an emendation (see Roberts, *Alcuin*, p. lxvii). Like Gregory of Tours, Fortunatus probably conflates the poets Paulinus of Nola and Paulinus of Périgueux. Roberts, "Last Epic," p. 261. Gregory of Tours, *Liber in gloria confessorum*, c. 108, ed. Bruno Krusch, MGH SRM 1.2, pp. 367–368.

[198] On Orientius (who wrote ca. 430–440), see Roberts, "Last Epic," p. 260. His *Commonitorium*, 1,036 lines of elegiac couplets instructing the reader on the good

tradition.[199] In length, their *vitae* are closer to biblical epics than to their Classical forebears.[200] They employ direct speech and, like Sedulius (and later poets of epic *vitae*), often interrupt the narrative with apostrophe, making exclamations and posing rhetorical questions.[201] Both embellish their texts with poetic ornament. Paulinus amplifies his narrative with paradox and other rhetorical tropes.[202] Like much late antique poetry (and later epic *vitae*), Fortunatus's *Vita Martini* is full of sparkling visual descriptions and *ecphrases* of dramatic scenes.[203] He also emphasizes emotional and affective aspects.[204] He is epigrammatic, using memorable sayings to sum up a section of the narrative.[205] In accordance with the hybrid nature of late antique epic, his epic incorporates panegyric and prayer.[206]

Despite their many similarities, Paulinus and Fortunatus augment their prose source differently. Like the biblical epic poets, Paulinus expands the prose with exegesis, explaining the significance of events and contributing moral commentary.[207] Fortunatus often gives a fairly brief paraphrase followed by his own reflections on the passage. Pollman observes that "in comparison with his predecessors ... Fortunatus avoids moralizing or exegetical meditations."[208] He is interested instead in allegorical and metaphorical elaborations that reveal Martin's heavenly power. This difference points to the poets' distinct visions. Whereas Paulinus presents Martin as an apostle and focuses on his teachings, Fortunatus shows him as a celestial patron and stresses his deeds and miracles.[209] Fortunatus frames the *vita* in the eschatological scheme of salvation history with Christ's descent and ascension with the souls of the saved.[210] Like

---

Christian life and avoiding sin to attain salvation, is ed. by Robinson Ellis in *Poetae Christiani Minores*, CSEL 16 (Vienna, 1888), pp. 205–243.

[199] Roberts, "Last Epic," p. 260.

[200] For Paulinus, 3,622 hexameters in six books; 2,243 hexameters in four books for Fortunatus.

[201] Roberts, "Last Epic," p. 265.

[202] Chase, "Metrical Lives," p. 58.

[203] Roberts, "Last Epic," p. 277.

[204] Ibid., p. 279.

[205] Ibid.

[206] Labarre, *Manteau partagé*, p. 120. Fortunatus, *Vita Martini* 1.123–145 is an *encomium* of Saint Hilary in metaphorical, highly visual language.

[207] Labarre, *Manteau partagé*, p. 159; Roberts, "Last Epic," p. 262.

[208] Pollman, "Transformation," p. 73.

[209] Roberts, "Last Epic," p. 262.

[210] Fortunatus, *Vita Martini*, 1.1–9; Labarre, *Manteau partagé*, p. 120.

Sedulius's *Paschale carmen*, his *Vita Martini* is highly episodic, privileging the message's repetition over the story's continuity.[211]

Fortunatus's poem, which was far more influential than Paulinus's, stands at a pivotal point in the genre's development.[212] It has been described as both "the last epic of Antiquity" and the prototype for the verse saint's life.[213] Fortunatus simultaneously looks back to epic traditions and establishes the core features of medieval epic lives.

We find the next verse lives in England, where the influence of biblical epics was particularly strong:[214] Bede's early-eighth-century *vita* of Cuthbert and Alcuin's *vita* of the Anglo-Saxon missionary Willibrord written toward the end of that century.[215] Bede and Alcuin, like Sedulius, wrote prose counterparts to their verse.[216]

Bede shows familiarity only with Virgil among Classical authors, but draws heavily on the three main biblical epics, especially Arator, whom he also uses in his commentary on Acts, and other Christian poets, including

---

[211] Ibid., p. 159; Roberts, "Last Epic," p. 265.

[212] On Fortunatus's influence, see M. Manitius, "Poetarum posteriorum loci expressi ad Fortunatum," in MGH AA 4.2, pp. 137–144.

[213] Tilliette, "Modèles," p. 382; Roberts, "Last Epic," pp. 257–285; Pollman, "Transformation," p. 72.

[214] A fragment of Arator from England may date to the sixth century. The English poets Aldhelm (ca. 639–ca. 709) and Bede (ca. 672–735) use biblical epics heavily in their verse and their educational treatises. Arator was very popular in England. See Lapidge, "Versifying the Bible," pp. 23–24; Michael Lapidge, "The Study of Latin Texts in Late Anglo-Saxon England," in *Latin and the Vernacular Languages in Early Medieval Britain*, ed. N.P. Brooks (Leicester, 1984), p. 102; Andy Orchard, "After Aldhelm: The Teaching and Transmission of the Anglo-Latin Hexameter," *JML* 2 (1992): 96–133.

[215] Bede, *Vita Cuthberti*, BHL 2020 (metric) and 2021 (prose), in *Two Lives of Saint Cuthbert: A Life by an Anonymous Monk of Lindisfarne and Bede's Prose Life*, ed. Bertram Colgrave (New York, 1969); and Werner Jaager in *Bedas metrische Vita Sancti Cuthberti* (Leipzig, 1935), respectively. Lapidge identifies an early version of the epic *vita*, composed ca. 705, which Bede later corrected into the standard version. Lapidge explains that Alcuin is incorrect in stating that Bede wrote the prose first. See Michael Lapidge, "Bede's Metrical *Vita*," p. 78; Gerald Bonner, "Saint Cuthbert – Soul Friend," in *Church and Faith in the Patristic Tradition: Augustine, Pelagianism, and Early Christian Northumbria*, ed. Gerald Bonner (Aldershot, 1996), Essay IX:23–42. On Bede's *aemulatio*, see Kirsch, *Laudes sanctorum*, p. 405. Alcuin, *Vita Willibrordi* BHL 8937 (prose) and 8938 (metric), ed. W. Levison in MGH SRM 7, pp. 13–41; and MGH Poetae 1, pp. 207–220.

[216] Bede says, "I wrote the life of the holy father bishop Cuthbert, earlier in heroic meter and later in plain speech" (Vitam sancti patris monachi simul et antistitis Cudbercti, et prius heroico metro et postmodum plano sermone, descripsi). Bede, *Historia ecclesiastica gentis Anglorum*, ed. Betram Colgrave and R.A.B. Mynors (Oxford, 1969), book 5, c. 24. In the prologue to his prose *Vita Cuthberti* (ed. Colgrave, p. 146), he refers to the work "I previously published in heroic verses" (heroicis dudum versibus edidi).

Prudentius and Paulinus of Nola.[217] It is unclear if he knew Fortunatus's *Vita Martini*.[218] His epic *Vita Cuthberti* employs Arator's exegetical methods. Short prose *capitula* summarize an event from his source (an anonymous prose life), omitting details, then twenty to fifty verse lines interpret its significance.[219] Like Scripture, the saint's life is part of God's *historia*, the full significance of which can only be extracted by reading beneath the surface of events for moral allegorical meanings. Bede's language forces the reader to grapple with it: "because of its allusiveness and compression it is often extremely difficult, and was clearly intended to be so. Bede's poem was intended as a meditation on the life and significance of Cuthbert."[220]

Alcuin (ca. 735–804) also wrote prose and verse *vitae*. Like his predecessors, he begins his verse *vita* with a personal appeal to the saint (in a metric preface), and he intervenes in the text to address the reader.[221] In other ways, however, it lacks epic elements. Its syntax is straightforward and, unusually, the verse is shorter than its prose counterpart, presenting an abbreviated version of events.[222] Unlike his other poems, it is largely devoid of rhetorical ornamentation and Classicism.[223] One of Alcuin's students wrote a verse *vita* and *miracula* of bishop Ninian, which Lapidge describes as "a virtual cento of lines from classroom *auctores*."[224] The eighth-century poets did not engage with epic traditions to the extent

---

[217] M.L.W. Laistner, "Bede as a Classical and a Patristic Scholar," in *The Intellectual Heritage of the Early Middle Ages* (New York, 1966), pp. 96–99; Lapidge, "Bede's Metrical *Vita*," p. 87. Most of Bede's Classical reminiscences derive from grammarians' examples and Isidore's *Etymologies*. Bede's first commentary on Acts, roughly contemporary with his epic *Vita Cuthberti*, is ed. M.L.W. Laistner, *Bedae Venerabilis Expositio Actuum Apostolorum et Retractio* (Cambridge, MA, 1939). Bede transformed Paulinus of Nola's verse *Life of Felix* into prose. See Laistner, "The Library of the Venerable Bede," in *Intellectual Heritage*, p. 123.

[218] Lapidge, "Knowledge of the Poems," pp. 291–292.

[219] Lapidge, "Bede's Metrical *Vita*," pp. 89–90.

[220] Ibid., p. 93.

[221] Alcuin, *pref.* to *Vita Willibrordi*, in MGH Poetae 1, p. 208. Addresses the reader: c. 13, 33, 34.

[222] In c. 13, Alcuin refers the reader to the prose for a fuller account.

[223] References to muses (c. 13 and 34) and wine as "pocula Bachi" (c. 20). The direct speech attributed to the visiting angel (c. 4), who is merely mentioned as appearing in a dream in the prose (c. 7), likens it to the classical winged messenger figure. The dream-vision of the saint's mother, taken from the second chapter of the prose and appended in a separate meter to the end of the metric *vita* (c. 33–34), is the only section that employs the visual metaphors and ornate language of the epic tradition.

[224] Lapidge, "Appendix: Knowledge of the Poems," p. 294, n. 2. *Miracula Nynie episcopi* (BHL 6240b), ed. in MGH Poetae 4/3, pp. 944–961. This work drew on Bede but not Fortunatus. See Kirsch, *Laudes Sanctorum*, vol. 1, pt. 2, pp. 418–419; W. Levison, "An

Fortunatus had in producing a saint's life. Nonetheless, their works were influential in promoting the idea of the epic life and the "twinned work" in England and on the Continent in the following centuries.

These Classical and Christian antecedents formed a rich and diverse tradition, which justified the writing of Christian epic verse and offered models for the form, style, and elaboration of the original. It was not until the ninth century that poets fully utilized their literary heritage to create a corpus of epic saints' lives.

EPIC *VITAE* IN THE CENTRAL MIDDLE AGES

The Central Middle Ages, from the early ninth to the eleventh centuries, was a time of great cultural transformation and innovation.[225] These centuries form a coherent unit in terms of attitudes toward patron saints, the main subject of the epic *vitae*.[226] It was also the genre's golden age; Tilliette counts over seventy extant examples from Francia in this period.[227] I conclude the current study before the beginning of the "long twelfth century," because the dramatic educational transformations, which included a plethora of new didactic-poetic works, displaced the epic *vita* from its centrality. The manuscripts reflect the change. In the ninth and tenth centuries, we find epic *vitae* most often in teacher's books and in *libelli*, collections of writings on a particular saint or saints. After the tenth century, they are copied less often in schoolbooks. In the twelfth century, they appear occasionally in large lectionaries, accompanying a prose life of the same saint.[228]

Both Bede and Alcuin influenced the flowering of epic *vitae* on the Continent.[229] Alcuin, who left York for Charlemagne's court, may have

---

Eighth-century Poem on St. Ninian," *Antiquity* 14 (1940): 280–291; Orchard, "After Aldhelm," pp. 96–133.

[225] Geary, *Furta Sacra*, p. 15.

[226] Ibid.

[227] Tilliette, "Poésie métrique," p. 103. On the era's modest resurgence of historical epic, see Ebenbauer, *Carmen historicum*, esp. pp. 101–211.

[228] For example, Douai, BM, MS 836 (xii²), which includes one epic *vita* (Johannes, *VR*) with dozens of prose texts, and Douai, BM, MS 840 (xii), which includes the anonymous epic *VE* in a similar context.

[229] Lul, archbishop of Mainz, had asked the abbot of Wearmouth-Jarrow for Bede's lives of Cuthbert, and in 764 the abbot sent him "the little books composed in meter and prose." See *S. Bonifatii et Lulli Epistolae*, ed. Michael Tangl in MGH Epistolae Selectae 1, p. 251. Fulda had a copy of the epic life by the second half of the eighth century. More than twenty manuscript witnesses of Bede's epic *vita* survive. See Lapidge, "Bede's Metrical *Vita*," p. 78.

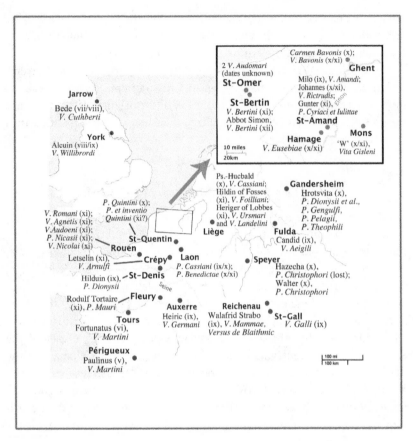

FIGURE 6. The Composition of Epic Lives in Western Francia (map)

If an author is not given, the life is anonymous. The centuries are given in Roman numerals following the BHL number. For the anonymous lives, the dates are approximate.

provided the impetus for the widespread production of epic *vitae* in the ninth and tenth centuries, because many of the poets were his intellectual descendants, particularly through his student Hraban Maur (ca. 780–856). The provenance of extant lives from the Central Middle Ages suggests networks of readers and writers associated with the closely linked abbeys of Fulda (where Hraban was abbot), Reichenau, and Saint-Gall (see the map in Figure 6). Writers from those abbeys included Walafrid Strabo, Candid,

Ermenric, Notker I, and an anonymous writer of Saint-Gall.[230] Flanders, a
site of intense literary creativity in these centuries, also produced a large
number of epic lives. Writers included Milo, Johannes, and Gunter of Saint-
Amand and poets from Saint-Bavo in Ghent, Saint-Bertin, Saint-Omer, and
houses around Liège.[231] England also continued to be a source of epic lives; a
number of tenth-century examples were associated with the school at
York.[232]

Despite writers' experimental approaches, and a general trend toward
more hermeneutic poetry, the uses, manuscript contexts, and form of the
epic *vita* remained fairly stable. The consistency, however, belies the social,
political, and cultural transformations of those centuries. By looking at
works from the ninth-century Carolingian Renaissance and others from
the late tenth and early eleventh centuries, we can examine how epic *vitae*
were written and read in different contexts. I examine texts from several
points within the Central Middle Ages. My study begins at the court of
Louis the Pious in the 830s, and then picks up, in Chapters 2 and 3, in the
mid-ninth century, at the monastery of Saint-Gall, which was by then part
of Louis the German's kingdom. The following century and a half saw the
dissolution of the Carolingian kingdoms and the rise of the Capetians in
France and the Ottonians in Germany and the ascendency of local authorities, such as counts and castellans. Throughout the ninth and tenth
centuries, epic *vitae* were sent to important patrons, but with the fragmentation of Carolingian power, the patterns of patronage changed. In
Chapters 4 and 5, I look at epic *vitae* from Flanders, close to the border
of Lotharingia, where the counts of Flanders, the French and German
rulers, the bishop, the local castellan, and abbots all sought to exercise
power in the late tenth and early eleventh centuries. Both the political and
cultural landscape had changed since the ninth century. The rise of the
cathedral schools and the imperial episcopate had challenged the monasteries' cultural centrality. Saint-Amand, once a Carolingian royal abbey,
was now culturally, politically, and geographically peripheral. The epic

---

[230] Anonymous, *Vita Galli*, in MGH Poetae 2, pp. 428–473; Candid, *Vita Aeigili*, in MGH
Poetae 2, pp. 96–117. For Ermenric's putative *Vita Galli*, see Chapters 2 and 3.

[231] This group also includes anonymous poets who composed passions of Benedicta (BHL
1088) and Cassian (BHL 1633), as well as the eleventh-century poet Gunter of Saint-
Amand. On the passions of Benedicta and Cassian, see John Contreni, *The Cathedral
School of Laon from 850 to 930: Its Manuscripts and Masters* (Munich, 1978), p. 144.
For the intellectual genealogies at Auxerre, see Louis Holtz, "L'école d'Auxerre," in
L'École carolingienne, ed. Iogna-Prat et al., pp. 131–133.

[232] See Michael Lapidge, "Aediluulf and the School of York," in *Lateinische Kultur im VIII.
Jahrhundert*, ed. Albert Lehner and Walter Berschin (St. Ottilien, 1989), pp. 161–78.

vitae from Flanders around the millennium share many formal features with the ninth-century texts, but they operated in a very different world.

Although I bring in other epic *vitae* as ancillary examples, I concentrate on a small number of works because the texts are so rich, complicated, and interconnected that each warrants an in-depth study. Close readings of the *vitae* and responses to them reveal the creative strategies their authors used and the social functions of the works in a way a survey would not.[233] By undertaking several close readings, rather than giving a broad survey or focusing on a single time or place, I can both demonstrate the range of functions and creativity of the epic lives and examine specific ways individuals used these texts. My approach allows me to consider each as a poet's response to particular circumstances.

Epic *vitae* were part of broader programs of aggrandizement, self-promotion, and education. In each case, I establish the work's historical and cultural contexts, using codicological and sometimes archaeological evidence in addition to textual sources. I examine the *vitae* in different milieux, including the monastic classroom, the imperial court, a royal abbey, and a small monastery struggling for survival. I have chosen to focus on epic *vitae* that provide useful and diverse insights. These examples implicate a wider set of texts and illustrate aspects of their thought and culture including notions of patronage, poetry, sanctity, creativity, competition, and uses of the past.[234] Each one illuminates a different aspect of monastic and learned culture in the ninth, tenth, and eleventh centuries.

*

In Chapter 1, "Forging Sanctity: Hilduin of Saint-Denis and the Epic *Passio Dionysii*," I consider the epic life of Saint Dionysius from the 830s. This work (which is unpublished) was part of a massive undertaking by Hilduin, abbot of Saint-Denis and former archchaplain, to enhance his own prestige, and that of the saint and abbey. Hilduin merged his abbey's patron, the martyred bishop of Paris, with an earlier Greek saint of the same name, a minor Scriptural figure and, supposedly, a mystical theologian. He embroidered the saint's passion with an unprecedented miracle in which the decapitated martyr picked up his head and, accompanied by a

---

[233] Other intriguing lives include the nun Hrotsvita's epic passions, Walter's adolescent epic on Christopher, the dog-headed saint, the competing verse hagiographies of the monasteries of Sithiu, and Heiric of Auxerre's accomplished *VG*. Nor do I look at the place of epic lives in versified liturgy, which has been studied by specialist musicologists. See Jonsson, *Historia*; Björkvall and Haug, "Performing Latin Verse," pp. 278–299.

[234] Cf. McKitterick, *History and Memory*, p. 24.

choir of angels, carried it to his burial site. In response to detractors who doubted his story, Hilduin produced many pieces of falsified evidence, a prose *Passio Dionysii* dedicated to Emperor Louis the Pious, and the epic version. These works contain competing and ambivalent notions of history, evidence, truth, and poetry. The prose life establishes a biography for the newly confected martyr, whom Hilduin casts as the emperor's particular friend, companion, and protector. The epic adds luster to the implausible saint and unifies the narrative by employing poetic metaphors to imbue the text with the saint's brand of mysticism and to prompt the reader to contemplative salvific modes of reading. Like other Carolingian poets, Hilduin engages in literary in-jokes and one-upmanship, but these games, far from being playful, are mechanisms of serious political rivalries. The epic life provides insight into the role of literature in these machinations and shows how poetry, self-promotion, and patronage worked at the highly factionalized court of Louis the Pious.

Chapters 2 and 3 look not at an epic *vita* but at the only sustained piece of writing about such a work. Around 850, the monk Ermenric sent his prospective patron a letter asserting his intention to complete an epic life of Saint Gall. Scholars have dismissed this letter as a series of rambling digressions, when in fact, properly understood, it is an excellent source for early medieval education and the role of epic *vitae* in the curriculum. While other sources mainly provide information about pedagogical theory, this letter takes us inside the Carolingian schoolroom to observe the teacher at work. In Chapter 2, "Glossing the Imaginary: Epic *Vitae* in the Classroom," I examine how Ermenric presents himself as a teacher addressing different levels of students. His letter shows how teachers could use epic lives and how the advanced students' rhetorical exercises could lead to the composition of such texts. The lives, often produced by students at the end of their education, were reincorporated into the curriculum that had produced them, and inspired new generations of students to emulation.

In Chapter 3, "Classical Nightmares: Christian Poets and the Pagan Past," I examine Ermenric's letter and his putative epic *vita* in their larger context. Surrounded by backbiting monks, Ermenric was part of a competitive culture of composition, in which poets vied for patronage. By writing about an epic life of Gall, Ermenric cast himself as heir to the renowned poet Walafrid Strabo, whose untimely demise had thwarted his intention to write such a work. Examining Ermenric's nightmare of Virgil and another pagan vision, I explore the role of the Classics in Carolingian education and in the composition of epic lives. Ermenric's demonic specter of Virgil draws on a rich tradition of disturbing Classical visions experienced by Christian monks. Despite its apparent condemnation of the pagan poet, the incident in fact reveals a nuanced approach to the Classics. Understanding the apparition and integrating the Classics were a rite of passage in becoming a writer of epic lives and a teacher for advanced students. The anti-Classics sentiment expressed in the Middle Ages was often a rhetorical trope, and Ermenric's literary hauntings show the utility of the monks' engagement with pagan writers. The confrontation of Classical and Christian was a creative tension that necessarily underlay the composition of epic lives – saints' lives in a classicizing form – and monastic learning as a whole.

Chapter 4, "Bishops, Monks, and Mother Bees: An Epic *Vita* at the Millennium," examines a less hostile literary contest between writers and readers of epic saints' lives. Johannes's life of Rictrude, written at Saint-Amand and the monk Rainer's reply reveal a flourishing literary culture in western Francia around the year 1000. With its emphasis on continuity rather than change, the *vita* offers a different perspective on the transformations of that era. Further, Rainer's dense Christian and Classical allusion shows a thorough synthesis of traditions and belies the writers' disavowal of pagan literature. Their protestations were a trope drawn from biblical epic tradition, rather than a true expression of anxiety, and these writers and readers harbored far less ambivalence to Classical learning than they professed.

Chapter 5, "Mothers and Daughters: Affiliation and Conflict in the Lives of Rictrude and Eusebia," examines a literary contest in which a community's very survival was at stake. The abbeys of Marchiennes and Hamage cast themselves as mother and daughter houses, symbolically represented by their warring mother and daughter patron saints, Rictrude and Eusebia. Piecing together Hamage's neglected history from charters, archaeology, and other sources, I establish a context for the production of the epic *vita* of Eusebia. In the tenth and early eleventh centuries, Marchiennes threatened to annex Hamage. The residents of these houses expressed the conflict through saints' lives that vindicated the righteousness of their respective patrons. I argue that the brothers of Hamage, bereft of other resources, used an epic life of Eusebia in which she defied her violent mother to stake a claim against their oppressive mother house.

Epic saints' lives were tokens in the economy of advancement within a monastery and beyond its walls. Exchanged between teachers and students, monks of different houses, and poets and patrons, the epic *vitae* linked their authors, donors, and recipients into real and imagined networks. Poets flattered their imperial and episcopal patrons by sending them long, erudite, highly classicizing poems. They demonstrated to their teachers and colleagues that both writer and recipient were members of a dynamic literary and pedagogical culture that encompassed Classical *auctores*, Christian poets, and future students and emulators. As the miniatures illustrating Milo's *Vita Amandi* show, the composition and exchange of an epic life was key to establishing networks of friendship and patronage.

Forging Sanctity: Hilduin of Saint-Denis and the Epic *Passio Dionysii*

In the later 830s, Hilduin, abbot of Saint-Denis and perfidious former archchaplain of Louis the Pious, sought to enhance his own prestige, and that of his abbey and its patron, Saint Dionysius, by composing an epic *passio*, which told a highly embellished version of the saint's life.[1] This *Passio Dionysii* and its prose counterpart were part of an ambitious scheme comprising architecture, liturgy, ritual, miracle stories, and the creation of numerous historical documents. Hilduin merged his abbey's traditional patron, the martyred first bishop of Paris, with a Greek scriptural figure known as Dionysius the Areopagite. In 827, Louis had sent the abbey a codex of works misattributed to the Areopagite, and Hilduin excerpted these Pseudo-Dionysian writings in his passions of the composite saint. He further embroidered the saint's story with a miracle in which the decapitated martyr picked up his head and, accompanied by a choir of angels, carried it to his chosen burial site. Hilduin forcefully defended the veracity of his controversial saint, critiquing contrary evidence and citing his own spurious sources. He incorporated the originally discrete saints' biographies into an overarching narrative, which he first elaborated in the prose passion.

The epic *Passio Dionysii* that followed is almost twice as long, conveying the same story in ornamented and convoluted language. Hilduin produced the epic version to take advantage of the functions of verse among the erudite churchmen of the court. Literature, especially poetry, was a serious game for the Carolingian intellectuals who proved their

---

[1] This epic passion was identified by Lapidge, "Lost Passio."

membership in an elite group by producing complex and creative texts replete with allusions and inside jokes. Poetic composition represented the culmination of liberal education and was an ideal medium for asserting culture and learning among patrons and rivals. A poem on Christian themes was an especially appropriate gift for Emperor Louis, who famously disdained pagan verse.[2]

Hilduin, as archchaplain, had been one of the most powerful figures at court until his betrayal of Louis in 829. In writing the epic passion, Hilduin sought to assert his place in court culture and reingratiate himself with the emperor. As a former *familiaris* of the emperor, he understood how intercessors could be used to restore favor.[3] Excluded from the human realm of patronage, he invoked a celestial mediator, the emperor's *patronus peculiaris* Dionysius, to work in his stead.

Further, the formal characteristics of lofty epic allowed Hilduin to infuse the verse *passio* with symbolism and to create a text that enacted the principles of Pseudo-Dionysius's Neoplatonic teachings about language and the approach to God. Accordingly, the epic passion's language both hides meaning and leads the reader to it. Hilduin exploited poetry's capacity for the obscure and imagistic to create an epic that works as a spiritual exercise for the reader while underscoring the new identity of the saint and Hilduin's role as his intermediary. The epic passion combined the power of the Carolingian patron saint with the prestige of Christian epic verse, imbued with Pseudo-Dionysian theology. It allowed Hilduin to disseminate the otherwise inaccessible teachings while glorifying the saint. The first part of this chapter examines the historical context, narrative, and themes shared by the prose and epic *passiones*. The second section considers the latter's distinctive features and functions.

To understand Hilduin's composition of the *passiones*, we must turn to the tumultuous dynastic politics of the 820s and 830s and the operation of patronage at court. Louis's reign (814–840) was punctuated by revolts, fueled by dynastic rivalries and the resentments and opportunism of ecclesiastical

---

[2] Hraban Maur dedicated his *In honorem sanctae crucis* to Louis; see CCCM 100, ed. M. Perrin (Turnhout, 2000). On Louis and the pagan songs (*poetica carmina gentilia*) of his youth, see Thegan, c. 19.

[3] Gerd Althoff, "(Royal) Favor: A Central Concept in Early Medieval Hierarchical Relations," in *Ordering Medieval Society: Perspectives on Intellectual and Practical Modes of Shaping Social Relations*, ed. Bernhard Jussen and trans. Pamela Selwyn (Philadelphia, 2001), pp. 246–247. See also Gerd Althoff, "Friendship and Political Order," in *Friendship in Medieval Europe*, ed. Julian Haseldine (Stroud, 1999), pp. 91–105.

and lay magnates. After his accession, Louis had exiled relatives and courtiers he suspected of treachery from court.[4] His division of empire in 817 resulted in his nephew Bernard's swiftly quashed rebellion.[5]

The birth in 823 of Charles (later Charles the Bald) to Louis and his second wife, Judith, posed a greater problem for the imperial partition. In August 829, Louis redivided the kingdom, promising Charles territories including Alemannia and Alsace, previously designated for his eldest son Lothar.[6] Lothar and his brother Pippin rebelled against their father. Counts Hugh of Tours and Matfrid of Orléans, deprived of their positions after a failed military campaign, joined them.[7] The rebels accused Judith of adultery with Louis's chamberlain and sent her to a convent.[8] The emperor's third son, Louis the German, supported his father, who was soon reconciled with Lothar and Pippin.[9] The peace was short-lived. Louis the Pious deposed Pippin and bestowed Aquitaine on Charles.[10] In response, the three older sons united against their father in a second rebellion. In June 833, Louis's allies deserted him on the "field of lies" in Alsace.[11] Lothar took his father to Metz and then to the abbey of Saint-Médard at Soissons, to be kept under close guard.[12] Judith was exiled to Tortona in Italy, and Charles to the monastery of Prüm.[13] Lothar had his father deposed, forcing him to perform public penance in a ritual at the abbey of Saint-Médard.[14] Louis placed his royal armor (*cingulum militiae*) before the

---

[4] McKitterick, *Frankish Kingdoms*, p. 134.

[5] The *Ordinatio Imperii*, dividing the kingdom among his sons after his death, designated Aquitaine for Pippin, Bavaria for Louis the German, and the bulk of the kingdom for Lothar, who was crowned co-emperor. Nelson, "Frankish Kingdoms," p. 112; *Ordinatio imperii*, ed. Alfred Boretius in MGH Capitularia 1, no. 136, pp. 270–273. On the revolt, see Thomas Noble, "The Revolt of King Bernard of Italy in 817: Its Causes and Consequences," *Studi medievali*, 3rd ser., 15 (1974): 315–326. On Louis's penance for his harsh punishment of Bernard, see Mayke de Jong, "Power and Humility in Carolingian Society: The Public Penance of Louis the Pious," *EME* 1 (1992): 31, 49.

[6] Nelson, "Frankish Kingdoms," p. 117.

[7] Ibid.

[8] Ibid.; Thegan, c. 36, p. 222.

[9] Nelson, "Frankish Kingdoms," p. 117.

[10] Ibid.

[11] Astronomer, c. 48; de Jong, "Power and Humility," p. 30.

[12] Astronomer, c. 48.

[13] Ibid.; Mayke de Jong, *The Penitential State: Authority and Atonement in the Age of Louis the Pious, 814–840* (Cambridge, 2009), p. 48.

[14] Louis Halphen, "La pénitence de Louis le Pieux à Saint-Médard de Soissons," *Bibliothèque de la Faculté des Lettres de Paris* 18 (1904): 117–185; de Jong, "Power and Humility," p. 29. The bishops and Agobard claim that Louis's penance was voluntary;

altar of Saints Medard and Sebastian, symbolically relinquishing his role as soldier of Christ and defender of the realm.[15] Louis, then imprisoned at Aachen, resisted his captors' pressure to take monastic vows.[16] Pippin and Louis the German, meanwhile, came to their father's assistance. Louis's biographer, "the Astronomer," writes that Lothar moved his father from Aachen to Saint-Denis, where he joined Charles, brought from the monastery of Prüm.[17] Lothar, threatened by his brothers' armies, fled, and Louis and Charles were freed. In March 834, bishops at Saint-Denis reinvested Louis with his royal robes and weapons.[18] So, a ceremony at Hilduin's abbey reversed the deposition that had occurred at Saint-Médard. Lothar finally surrendered in September 834.[19] Louis was re-crowned at Metz in February 835, his penance was overturned, and Archbishop Ebbo of Rheims, who had overseen his deposition, was forced to publically confess his sins.[20] Louis sent Lothar back to Italy.[21] The remaining years of Louis's reign were eventful. After Pippin of Aquitaine died in 838, Louis granted the kingdom to his own son, Charles.[22] Pippin's son Pippin II resisted. Meanwhile, Louis the German, who had fallen from favor, rebelled against his father.[23] Louis the Pious died in June 840, with these conflicts uresolved.

As a leading courtier and churchman, Hilduin found his life bound up in the vicissitudes of Louis's reign. Born around 785, probably of Frankish origin, he rose to prominence when, in 814, he was appointed abbot of

---

the Astronomer and the *Annals of Saint-Bertin* disagree. *Relatio episcoporum* and Agobard, *Cartula de poenitentia*, ed. Alfred Boretius and Victor Krause in MGH Capitularia 2, nos. 195 and 196, pp. 51–58; cf. Astronomer, c. 49; *Annales Bertiniani*, ed. C. Dehaisnes, *Les annales de Saint-Bertin et de Saint-Vaast* (Paris, 1871), for 833.

[15] In 826, as abbot of Saint-Médard, Hilduin had translated Saint Sebastian there. Astronomer, c. 40, and *Translatio Sebastiani* (BHL 7545), ed. O. Holder-Egger in MGH SS 15/1, pp. 377–391. On the armor's significance, see Elizabeth Sears, "Louis the Pious as Miles Christi: The Dedicatory Image in Hrabanus Maurus's *De laudibus sanctae crucis*," in *Charlemagne's Heir: New Perspectives on the Reign of Louis the Pious (814–840)*, ed. P. Godman and R. Collins (Oxford, 1990), pp. 605–628.

[16] De Jong, "Power and Humility," p. 44; Thegan, c. 43; *Annales Bertiniani* for 834.

[17] Astronomer, c. 50, 52; *Annales Bertiniani* for 834; Nithard, *Historiae*, book 1, c. 6, ed. Ernst Müller in MGH SRG 44.

[18] *Annales Bertiniani* for 834; Astronomer, c. 51; Courtney Booker, *Past Convictions: The Penance of Louis the Pious and the Decline of the Carolingians* (Philadelphia, 2009), p. 25.

[19] Thegan, c. 55; Astronomer, c. 55.

[20] *Annales Bertiniani* for 835; de Jong, "Power and Humility," p. 42.

[21] Booker, *Past Convictions*, p. 25.

[22] *Divisio imperii* of 839, ed. in MGH Capitularia 2, no. 200, p. 58.

[23] Nelson, "Frankish Kingdoms," p. 119; Eric Goldberg, *Struggle for Empire: Kingship and Conflict under Louis the German, 817–876* (Ithaca, 2006), p. 86.

Saint-Denis.[24] Saint-Denis outside Paris had long been a prosperous royal abbey.[25] Although its monks' propensity for invention obscures much of its past, it seems that the Merovingians, especially Dagobert, had supported the community.[26] The Carolingians, like their predecessors, made Saint-Denis their mausoleum.[27] Charters show their largesse to the abbey.[28] When Hilduin became abbot, Saint-Denis housed about 150 residents.[29] In accordance with Louis's zeal for reform, Hilduin attempted to impose a stricter lifestyle on the inhabitants, about half of whom, in protest, left for a cell on the Oise River.[30] They remained there for the next decade and were only reconciled through synods in 829 and 832.[31] Louis also appointed Hilduin abbot of several other important monasteries:

---

[24] On Hilduin's origins, see Léon Levillain, "Wandalbert de Prüm et la date de la mort d'Hilduin de Saint-Denis," *BEC* 108 (1949/1950): 21, n. 1; Lapidge, "Lost Passio," p. 57. According to Lapidge, two charters of December 814 name Hilduin as abbot. The charters are noted by Jules Tardif, *Monuments historiques, cartons des rois* (Paris, 1866), p. 77, nos. 105 and 106.

[25] According to her *vitae*, Saint Genevieve first built a church outside Paris dedicated to Dionysius. *Vita Sanctae Genovefae* (BHL 3334), c. 4, and *Alia vita* (BHL 3336), c. 4, in AASS Jan. vol. 1, 139–140, 144–145.

[26] *Gesta Dagoberti*, c. 42, ed. Bruno Krusch in MGH SRM 2; J.M. Wallace-Hadrill, *The Long-Haired Kings* (London, 1962), pp. 53, 224–225. The *Gesta Dagoberti*, which record Dagobert's largesse and his desire to be interred at Saint-Denis, were composed at Saint-Denis during the reign of Louis, possibly by Hilduin, and so, like the charters, are, contrary to Wallace-Hadrill's assertion, not "above suspicion." McKitterick describes them as a "revisionist work" (*History and Memory*, p. 214). The *Gesta*'s language, in which Dagobert refers to the church "domni Dyonisii peculiaris patroni nostri, in qua ipse pretiosus martyr cum suis sociis corpore quiescit" sounds suspiciously like Louis's letter to Hilduin. Other sources on Dagobert's relations with Saint-Denis are Fredegar, *Chronicae*, book 4, c. 79, SRM 2, p. 161, and *Vita Eligii* (BHL 2474), in MGH SRM 4, pp. 688–689.

[27] On Saint-Denis, F. d'Ayzac, *Histoire de l'abbaye de Saint-Denis en France*, 2 vols. (Paris, 1858); Julien Havet, "Questions mérovingiennes. V: Les origines de Saint-Denis," *BEC* 51 (1890): 5–62; Léon Levillain, "Études sur l'abbaye de Saint-Denis à l'époque mérovingienne," *BEC* 82 (1921): 5–116; Sumner McKnight Crosby, *The Abbey of St.-Denis* (New Haven, 1942); Jules Formigé, *L'abbaye royale de Saint-Denis: recherches nouvelles* (Paris, 1960); Jean Cuisenier and Rémy Guadagnin, eds., *Un village au temps de Charlemagne, moines et paysans de l'abbaye de Saint-Denis, du VIIe siècle à l'an mil* (Paris, 1988), and, in that volume, especially, Karl Ferdinand Werner, "Saint-Denis et les Carolingiens," pp. 40–49.

[28] Werner, "Saint-Denis," pp. 40–49.

[29] Charter in Michel Félibien, *Histoire de l'abbaye royale de Saint-Denis en France* (Paris, 1706), p. lxxii; Crosby, *Abbey of St.-Denis*, p. 95.

[30] Robert Berkhofer, *Day of Reckoning: Power and Accountability in Medieval France* (Philadelphia, 2004), pp. 13–14; Georges Tessier, *Recueil des actes de Charles II le Chauve* (Paris, 1943–1955), vol. 2: 65, no. 247.

[31] Berkhofer, *Day of Reckoning*, pp. 13–14.

Saint-Germain-des-Prés in Paris, Saint-Médard in Soissons, Salonnes, and probably Saint-Ouen in Rouen.[32] In 819, Hilduin became head of the palace chaplains and part of the royal inner circle.[33]

Examining Hilduin's role as archchaplain we see a court culture in which power was wielded through personal relationships rather than through institutional channels. At court, *amicitia* (political association couched in the language of friendship) functioned through the exchange of the patron's favor, manifested in symbolic and material rewards, for the dependent's service, loyalty, and expressions of devotion. The ruler's closest friends benefited above all from his *familiaritas*.[34] Access to and influence with the king, "Königsnähe," was power, and his closest associates, *familiares*, in turn became patrons of others.[35] Agobard of Lyon complained of the corruption the system engendered.[36] According to Einhard, even God's own messenger, the archangel Gabriel, needed a patron to convey a message to Louis.[37] The archchaplain, as one of the men closest to the king, exercised a great deal of power.

Hilduin's protégé Hincmar, in his *De ordine palatii*, describes the archchaplain's role during Louis's reign. Writing in the 880s, he presents an exaggerated picture of the archchaplain's power, probably influenced by Hilduin, whom he cites as an example.[38] Hincmar glorifies the office, which he calls the *apocrisiarius*, attributing its creation to Constantine[39] and labeling it one of the two most powerful positions in the palace.[40] The

---

[32] On Hilduin's abbeys, Fleckenstein, *Hofkapelle*, p. 53; The *Annals of Saint-Germain-des-Prés* list him as abbot in 826, ed. George Pertz, in MGH SS 3, p. 167; Depreux, *Prosopographie*, p. 251. Saint-Germain housed about 120 monks. Berkhofer, *Day of Reckoning*, p. 13; Wilhelm Levison, *England and the Continent in the Eighth Century* (Oxford, 1946), p. 217.

[33] Fleckenstein, *Hofkapelle*, p. 52; McKitterick, *Frankish Kingdoms*, p. 125. The earliest evidence for Hilduin as archchaplain comes from May 819. Depreux, *Prosopographie*, p. 251.

[34] Althoff, "(Royal) Favor," p. 245.

[35] The term was coined by Gerd Tellenbach, *Königtum und Stämme in der Werdezeit des Deutschen Reiches* (Weimar, 1939).

[36] Agobard, *Ep.* 10 (written between 818 and 828), in MGH Ep. 5, pp. 201–203; Stuart Airlie, "Bonds of Power and Bonds of Association," in *Charlemagne's Heir*, p. 195.

[37] Einhard, *Translatio Marcellini et Petri* (BHL 5233), Book 3, c. 13, ed. G. Waitz in MGH SS 15/1, p. 253.

[38] Hincmar, *De ordine palatii*, c. 15, ed. Maurice Prou, *Hincmari Epistola de Ordine Palatii* (Paris, 1885).

[39] H. Löwe, "Hinkmar von Reims und der Apocrisiar. Beiträge zur Interpretation von 'De ordine palatii,'" *Festschrift für Hermann Heimpel zum 70. Geburtstag*, v. 3 (Göttingen, 1972), pp. 197–225.

[40] *De ordine palatii*, c. 19. The other was the *comes palatii*.

apocrisiarius supervised ecclesiastical matters, overseeing palace chaplains, directing religious service in the palace, and exercising spiritual care for courtiers.[41] He also attended the major assemblies of the king and his magnates.[42] Hincmar emphasizes the *apocrisiarius*'s role as intermediary, controlling access to the king.[43] Even when cases were brought before the ruler, the *apocrisiarius* and his secular counterpart, the *comes palatii*, would exercise their influence, briefing the ruler in advance, so he would respond appropriately.[44]

Hincmar's aggrandizement of the archchaplaincy probably reflects his mentor's ambitions. Hilduin employed increasingly lofty terminology to emphasize the distance between himself and the other chaplains: to the title *summus sacri palatii capellanus* was added the new *sacri palatii archicapellanus* in 823.[45] Odilo's *Translatio Sebastiani*, which was based on sources from Hilduin's time as abbot of Saint-Médard and probably reproduces his self-presentation, portrays him in superlative terms as "a very modest man endowed with every kind of righteousness and wisdom and industry, outstanding in justice, shining in holiness" and presents him as Louis's most trusted advisor, whom the emperor had appointed as "archchaplain for the whole empire."[46]

Sources for Hilduin at Louis's court support Hincmar's picture. Hilduin was almost always at the palace.[47] Charters show he accompanied Louis to Aachen, Compiègne, and Ingleheim and on a military expedition in

---

[41] c. 19–20.

[42] c. 32.

[43] c. 19–20: preventing petitioners from disturbing the king, the *apocrisiarius* and *comes palatii* would determine whether a matter required royal consultation. No religious matter was to be presented without the *apocrisiarius*'s *consilium*, lest something "less useful or unworthy" (*minus utile aut indignum*) trouble the king.

[44] c. 19, p. 50.

[45] Fleckenstein, *Hofkapelle*, p. 52.

[46] Ibid. Odilo (d. after 930), *Translatio S. Sebastiani* (BHL 7545), c. 1, ed. Oswald Holder-Egger in MGH SS 15/1, p. 380. "Among all the leading men of the empire, whose advice he consulted, he loved and esteemed to such an extent the venerable abbot Hilduin – a very modest man endowed with every kind of righteousness and wisdom and industry, outstanding in justice, shining in holiness – that he would entrust to him specifically whatever must be handled more discreetly, and he appointed him archchaplain of his whole empire" (Hic inter cunctos imperii sui primates, quos consilio suo asciverat, Hilduinum abbatem reverentissimum, virum quoque omni probitatis genere permodestum omnique sagacitate et industria praeditum, iustitia conspicuum, sanctitate praeclarum, in tantum amavit et extulit, ut ei specialius quicquid secretius tractandum esset committeret eumque archicapellanum in omni imperio suo constitueret).

[47] Agobard, *Epistola* no. 6, ed. E. Dümmler, MGH Ep. 5, p. 179.

Brittany in 824.[48] The poet Ermold Nigellus, in 826, presents him as Louis's right-hand man, and three years later, in another poem, Walafrid Strabo portrays him as Aaron to the emperor's Moses.[49]

Einhard's description of Hilduin waiting outside Louis's chamber first thing in the morning (*primo mane*) shows both Hilduin's closeness to Louis and the extent to which he controlled access to him.[50] Correspondents asked Hilduin to relay matters to Louis.[51] Agobard appealed to Hilduin and Wala, abbot of Corbie, in flattering terms as "the emperor's most Christian helpers."[52] Frothar, bishop of Toul, presented his case to Hilduin because the latter was accustomed to bringing requests before Louis.[53] Hilduin's *familiaritas* with the emperor meant that petitioners invoked him as their own patron and protector.[54]

Because the ruler often granted favor (*gratia*) based on personal ties, the person who presented a matter before the emperor could be key to gaining a favorable decision.[55] Even those who had access to the emperor, therefore, might prefer to employ an intermediary. Louis had ordered Frothar and Smaragdus to report to him on the conflict between the abbot and monks of Moyenmoutier.[56] Instead of sending the report directly to Louis, Frothar sent it to Hilduin, with a request that he deliver it and champion the monks.[57] The letter to Hilduin is far more ingratiating than the one addressed to Louis. The extent of Hilduin's influence is suggested by Frothar's appeal that he intervene in an inheritance dispute with a woman from the emperor's *familia*.[58] Clearly Frothar thought Hilduin might sway the emperor against the woman.

[48] Depreux, *Prosopographie*, p. 252.

[49] Ibid., p. 251; Ermold Nigellus, *In Honorem Hludowici*, book 4, line 413, in MGH Poetae 2, p. 69; Walafrid Strabo, *De imagine Tetrici*, lines 209–220, MGH Poetae 2, pp. 376–377.

[50] Einhard, *Translatio et Miracula Marcellini et Petri*, book 2, c. 1.

[51] Frothar, *Ep.* no. 21, pp. 290ff.

[52] Agobard, *Ep.* no. 6, MGH Ep. 5, p. 179.

[53] Depreux, *Prosopographie*, p. 255; Frothar, *Ep.* 17, MGH Ep. 5, pp. 287–288.

[54] Frothar appealed to Hilduin directly, invoking the "protection of your oversight" (vestri regiminis tutela). The clergy of Sens addressed him as "most reverent lord" (reverentissime domine) and protector. See, Depreux, *Prosopographie*, p. 254; Frothar, *Ep.* no. 9, ed. K. Hampe, MGH Ep. 5, p. 282; Ep. 13, p. 285. Particularly fawning examples are *Ep.* 17, p. 287, and *Ep.* 20, pp. 289–290.

[55] Althoff, "(Royal) Favor," p. 244; Depreux, *Prosopographie*, pp. 253–54.

[56] Frothar, *Ep.* no. 22, MGH Ep. 5, pp. 290–91.

[57] Ibid., pp. 291–92.

[58] Ibid., p. 290.

Letters and charters reveal Hilduin's considerable autonomy in deciding church matters.[59] Their wording sometimes shows Hilduin presenting matters to the emperor as faits accomplis.[60] A comparison of letters that the clergy of Sens sent to Hilduin, Einhard, and Judith in the first half of 829 shows the power they attributed to him. Whereas they appealed to Hilduin to intervene in a problematic archiepiscopal election directly, they asked the others to bring the problem before Louis, implying that Hilduin had the power to decide this important matter without consulting the emperor.[61] Hilduin was probably also involved in the church councils of 825 and 829.[62] Influential churchmen sought his advice.[63]

Hilduin used his position at court to further the interests of his abbeys and saints, as the many charters benefiting Saint-Denis in the 820s attest.[64] He must have also used his closeness with Louis to familiarize him with his preferred version of Dionysius, as the emperor clearly subscribed to the identification of martyr and Areopagite; in 827, when the Byzantine emperor Michael II sent Louis a codex containing Greek works attributed to the Areopagite, Louis gave the book to Saint-Denis. Hilduin orchestrated the book's arrival during the night office of the saint's feast, a perfect setting for a display of saintly *virtus*. In his letter to Louis, Hilduin recalls that the book's advent, like a relic's *translatio*, prompted a spate of miracles.[65]

The culture of patronage and favor bred competition and envy, and the court was rife with animosity.[66] The palace *capellani* were particularly

---

[59] Depreux, *Prosopographie*, p. 254.

[60] Ibid., p. 252; B.M. 782 (757), ed. *Doc. Dipl. Rhin. moyen*, no. 55, pp. 61ff.; B.M. 789 (764), ed. *Recueil des hist.* 6, no. 124, p. 538.

[61] Frothar, *Ep.* 13, 14, 15, pp. 285–286.

[62] Lapidge, "Lost Passio," p. 59.

[63] MGH Ep. 5, pp. 179 (Agobard writes to Hilduin and Wala), 282, 287, 291–292 (Frothar seeks Hilduin's intercession), 247 (Amalarius writes to him on a religious matter), 520 (a letter from Fulda groups Hilduin with the bishops on ecclesiastical matters), 528 (Hraban Maur consults him about Gottschalk), 401 (Hraban sends him a copy of his commentary on the book of Kings); MGH Poetae 2, p. 383 (Walafrid Strabo sends him a poem).

[64] Johann Friedrich Böhmer, *Regesta imperii*, vol. 1, *Die Regesten des Kaiserreichs unter den Karolingern 751–918* (Hildesheim, 1966): BM 727 (703); 729 (705); 746 (721); 803 (779); 844 (818); 846 (820).

[65] Hilduin, *Rescriptum*, c. 4. Sigebert, presumably drawing on Hilduin or another Saint-Denis source notes the healings, as does the Saxon Annalist, who also places them in 824. Sigebert, *Chronica* for 824, ed. D.L.C. Bethmann, MGH SS 6, p. 338; *Annalista Saxo*, for 824 ed. D.G. Waitz, MGH SS 6, p. 573.

[66] Althoff, "(Royal) Favor," p. 251.

rebuked for their greed.[67] Depictions of Louis's court, seething with intrigue and immorality, come from very partisan sources, but the competition was real, as the exiles show.[68] Rebellions gave factions opportunity to malign their rivals, and the court poets' pleas to patrons to protect them from envy are not empty rhetoric.[69] Literature was a means of attracting patronage and of attacking one's enemies, as Theodulf's verse from Charlemagne's rule exemplifies.[70] In the 820s, for all his power, Hilduin was not beyond poetic reproach. In an ostensibly flattering picture, written in 829, Walafrid hints at his excess and treachery.[71] Walafrid's poem, subtly disparaging his probable patron, illustrates the court's competitive and underhanded poetic culture.

Walafrid's implications were confirmed when Hilduin supported the princes' first rebellion.[72] As a result, Louis stripped him of his abbacies and archchaplaincy and exiled him to Paderborn.[73] From there he went to Corvey.[74] According to Flodoard, Hincmar voluntarily accompanied his abbot into exile and then importuned Louis for his return.[75] Hilduin's return may have been part of a wider amnesty in spring 831.[76] By 832, Louis had recalled Hilduin and reinstated him as abbot of Saint-Denis and possibly Saint-Germain-des-Prés, but not as archchaplain.[77]

Hilduin's role in Louis's sons' second rebellion (833–834) is unclear. According to Flodoard of Rheims, Hilduin ordered Hincmar to accompany

---

[67] Airlie, "Bonds of Power," p. 194; Lupus of Ferrières, i,16; Walafrid Strabo, *Visio Wettini*, lines 327ff., in MGH Poetae 2, p. 314; Paschasius Radbertus, *Epitaphium Arsenii*, c. 4–5.

[68] Paschasius Radbertus *Vita Walae* Book II, 8, 9, 12. Louis exiled Theodulf in 818 and Ermold Nigellus.

[69] Theodulf, who was part of the rebellion against Louis in 818, refers to "consuming jealousy" (*livor edax*) and likens the situation to that of Ovid, "made an exile out of envy" (*factus exul ob invidiam*). Theodulf, *Rescriptum Modoini* 73 in MGH Poetae 1, pp. 569–573, discussed by Godman, "Louis the Pious and his Poets," pp. 250–251.

[70] Godman, *Poetry*, pp. 12–13.

[71] On Walafrid's representation of Hilduin, see my "Books, Bodies, and Bones: Hilduin of Saint-Denis and the Relics of Saint Dionysius," in *The Ends of the Body; Identity and Community in Medieval Culture*, ed. Suzanne Conklin Akbari and Jill Ross (Toronto, 2013).

[72] Thegan, c. 36.

[73] Astronomer, c. 45. Fulk, abbot of Saint-Wandile and Saint-Remigius, became archchaplain. After his restoration in 834, Louis installed his own half brother Drogo, bishop of Metz, as archchaplain. McKitterick, *Frankish Kingdoms*, p. 125.

[74] On Hilduin at Corvey, *Translatio Viti*, c. 12; MGH SS 2, p. 580.

[75] Flodoard, book 3, c. 1.

[76] *Annals* of Saint-Bertin for 831, and Astronomer, c. 46 (neither mentions Hilduin).

[77] Crosby, *Abbey of St.-Denis*, p. 167; "Hilduin, archichapelain de Louis le Pieux et abbé de S.-Denis," in *DHGE* 24, col. 519. Flodoard says Hilduin was restored to two of his abbacies, but does not specify which ones (book 3, c. 1). On intercession to regain a ruler's favor, see Althoff, "(Royal) Favor," p. 246.

him to Lothar's camp, but Hincmar refused.[78] Flodoard's tenth-century account is unreliable, but other sources hint that Hilduin remained sympathetic to the prince.[79] Lothar's charter granting a *beneficium* to Saint-Denis implies conversation between the two, and his decision to imprison his father and Charles at Saint-Denis in early 834 suggests confidence in its abbot.[80] On the other hand, Louis took no sanctions against Hilduin on his return to power. Perhaps, like other churchmen of the era, Hilduin had avoided clear expressions of partisanship. Louis may have considered his loyalties ambiguous, since, in 837, he made Hilduin, alongside Count Gerard of Paris, swear an oath of loyalty to Charles.[81] On Louis's death in 840, Nithard reports that Hilduin and Gerard immediately defected to Lothar.[82] Hilduin, therefore, lost Saint-Denis, which became part of Charles's West Frankish Kingdom.[83] Before the twentieth century, historians put Hilduin's death in the early 840s, but since then, others have argued that he continued his career under Lothar and died in the later 850s.[84]

The immediate context for Hilduin's prose and epic passions of Dionysius was his return from exile and Louis's restoration. Hilduin was no longer an insider in the court. Théry observes that in the first half of the 830s, his activities were not political or diplomatic, but monastic and Dionysian.[85] In Hilduin's absence, the monks of Saint-Denis had become even more troublesome, and he was compelled to persevere in the

---

[78] Janet Nelson, *The Frankish World, 750–900* (London, 1996), p. 46. Nelson accepts Flodoard's version of events.

[79] Flodoard is biased toward Hincmar, who would become archbishop of Rheims.

[80] Lothar states that Hilduin had "suggested" to him that he make the gift to Saint-Denis. Schieffer dates the charter to October 833. Ed. Theodor Schieffer, MGH Dipl. Karol. 3, no. 13, pp. 78–80. Tardif, *Monuments*, p. 94 (no. 139), dates the charter to 841.

[81] Nithard, book 1, c. 6; Frank Reiss, "From Aachen to Al-Andalus: The Journey of Deacon Bodo (823–76)," *EME* 13 (2005): 131–157 at p. 133.

[82] Nithard, book 2, c. 3.

[83] He also would have lost Saint-Germain-des-Prés, if he had resumed its abbacy in 831. Fleckenstein, *Hofkapelle*, p. 143.

[84] See Ferdinand Lot, "De quelques personnages du ixe siècle qui ont porté le nom de Hilduin," *Le Moyen Âge* 16 (1903): 268–274 (cf. Fleckenstein, *Hofkapelle*, pp. 122–123). For the historiography, see Lapidge, "Lost Passio," p. 62, n. 39. On Hilduin's possible later career, see Robert Parisot, *Le royaume de Lorraine sous les Carolingiens, 843–923* (Paris, 1899), pp. 743–746; charter ed. Schieffer, DD Kar. 3 no. 100, pp. 239ff. Ernst Tremp, *Studien zu den Gesta Hludowici imperatoris des Trierer Chorbischofs Thegan*, MGH Schriften 32, p. 20; *DHGE* 24, col. 511. For his death, see Depreux, *Prosopographie*, p. 250; Levillain, "Wandalbert de Prüm," p. 35.

[85] P.G. Théry, "Hilduin et le première traduction des écrits du Pseudo-Denis," *Revue d'histoire de l'Église de France* 9 (1923): 30.

reform.[86] He also continued using saints to promote his monasteries (and by extension, himself) and in 832 completed a new, gem-encrusted *crypta* for the martyrs at Saint-Denis.[87]

The emperor's own diminished prestige in the wake of his sons' rebellions provided further opportunites.[88] Louis's deposition and humiliation of 833 may have permanently undermined his royal legitimacy.[89] His unprecedented second investiture at Saint-Denis in 834, preceding his coronation at Metz, implies both the emperor's need for the ritual renewal of power and his recognition that the ancient royal patron Dionysius could buttress his authority.

Like the emperor and the abbot, the saint himself faced threats to his standing. The relic trade had brought an influx of popular Roman martyrs (such as those Hilduin translated to Saint-Médard), and the Gallic saints needed an infusion of power. Hilduin accordingly promoted an improved Dionysius, a "sacred bricolage" that combined Eastern and Western saints.[90] As Michael Lapidge writes, "from ... disparate sources Hilduin was able to confect a saint who represented an amazing amalgam of originally distinct figures."[91] Excluded from the innermost circles of power, Hilduin drew on the saintly capital of the emperor's personal patron and the literary language of *amicitia* – poetry – as well as his own erudition and imagination to regain his standing at court.

A NEW DIONYSIUS

From our perspective, Hilduin's Dionysius is a conflation of at least three separate personas – a Scriptural figure, a fifth-century theologian, and the martyr-bishop of Paris. The first piece of the composite saint is a minor

[86] Robert F. Berkhofer, *Day of Reckoning*, p. 14; Flodoard, book 3, c. 1.

[87] Lapidge, "Lost Passio," p. 59. The crypt was consecrated on November 1, 832. See Félibien, *Histoire*, p. clxviii. On Hilduin's earlier relic-related activity, Odilo, *Translatio Sebastiani*, in MGH SS 15/1, pp. 380–391; Depreux, *Prosopographie*, p. 251. On his involvement in the underground relic trade, see Geary, *Furta Sacra*, p. 46.

[88] David Luscombe, "Denis the Pseudo-Areopagite," in *Tradition and Change: Essays in Honour of Marjorie Chibnall Presented by her Friends on the Occasion of her Seventieth Birthday*, ed. Diana Greenway and Christopher Holdsworth (Cambridge, 2002), p. 118.

[89] Nelson, however, claims that this conventional view underestimates Louis's efficacy during his last years. Janet L. Nelson, "The Last Years of Louis the Pious" in *Charlemagne's Heir*, pp. 147–160.

[90] Head borrows the term from Levi-Strauss. Thomas Head, "Art and Artifice in Ottonian Trier," *Gesta* 36 (1987): 76, citing C. Levi-Strauss, *The Savage Mind* (London, 1966), p. 21.

[91] Lapidge, "Lost Passio," p. 67.

figure mentioned in Acts, Dionysius the Areopagite, whom Paul converted on the Areopagus Hill in Athens.[92]

Around the fifth century, a Greek writer adopted the Areopagite's persona to compose letters and theological works. This pseudonym connected the writer's mystical theology with the subject of Paul's preaching on the Areopagus, in which the evangelist claimed that the "unknown god" to whom the pagan Athenians had built an altar was actually the Christian God.[93] The writer, whom scholars call Pseudo-Dionysius, addressed personal letters to prominent first-century figures, so later Christians inherited a biography that elevated his importance. He was revered as an authority in the West, although little was known of his writing before 827.[94] The Greek writer's claim to be the Areopagite was generally accepted in the Middle Ages.[95]

The attempt to conflate the Areopagite with a third figure, Saint-Denis's patron saint, was more controversial. It is unclear whether Hilduin was the first to amalgamate the Eastern and Western saints and the first to add the cephalophory or if he adopted existing ideas. The Western Dionysius was based on a long Latin prose tradition. Hilduin's verbal echoes suggest he knew the earliest extant passion (BHL 2171), the *Gloriosae*, initially composed around the fifth century.[96] The *Gloriosae*'s Dionysius has no Eastern connection and is not a cephalophore.[97]

---

[92] Acts 17:34.

[93] J. Vanneste, "Echte of onechte mystiek bij Pseudo-Dionysius?" *Bijdragen. Tijdschrift voor filosofie en theologie* 24 (1963): 154–169 at p. 167, and J. Vanneste, *Le mystère de Dieu*, pp. 14, 181, both cited in Gerben Groenewoud, "The Unknowable God: An Essay on the Theology of Pseudo-Dionysius the Areopagite," *Stoicheia: Tijdschrift voor historische wijsbegeerte* 3 (1988): 53.

[94] The "geometry, orthography, and grammar" sent from Pope Paul I to King Pippin the Short around 760 were apocryphal additions to the Pseudo-Dionysian corpus. Paul, ed. K. Hampe, MGH Ep. 5, pp. 32–33. Gregory the Great and Pope Hadrian I praise Dionysius. Gregorius Magnus, *Homiliae in Evangelia*, CCEL 141, ed. Raymond Étaix (Turnhout, 1999), 1.12, 34; Hadrian, *Ep.* 2, c. 36, ed. K. Hampe, MGH Ep. 5, pp. 32–33.

[95] Suspicions about the author's identity date to at least 532 in the East. See David Luscombe, "Denis the Pseudo-Areopagite in the Middle Ages from Hilduin to Lorenzo Valla," in *Fälschungen im Mittelalter*, MGH Schriften 33, p. 133, n. 2; I. Hausherr, "Doutes au sujet du 'Divin Denys,'" *Orientalia Christiana Periodica* 2 (1936): 488–489; Jaroslav Pelikan, "The Odyssey of Dionysian Spirituality," in *Pseudo-Dionysius: The Complete Works* (New York, 1987), pp. 11, 13, 21.

[96] *Gloriosae* (BHL 2171), ed. Bruno Krusch in MGH AA 4.2, pp. 101–105. Changes (primarily the naming of previously anonymous characters) may have been made to the *Gloriosae* as late as the eighth or early ninth century. See Levillain, "Études," pp. 17, 25.

[97] Another early source, the *Vita Genovefae* (BHL 3334), written around 520, mentions the Western Dionysius (c. 18ff.), but contains no hint of Greek origins. In MGH SRM 3, pp. 221ff.

Another passion of Dionysius (BHL 2178) with the incipit *Post beatam et gloriosam* conflates the saints and recounts the cephalophory, but it is unclear if it informed or followed Hilduin's writings.[98] Regardless of whether Hilduin invented the idea of merging the Dionysii, he was the most energetic proponent of the idea and of the enhanced saint. The *Post beatam et gloriosam*, which was clearly not written at Saint-Denis, combines the saints perfunctorily, dispatching the Greek portion of the biography in only three chapters of eighteen and omitting any mention of his writings.[99] The saint is far less spectacular than is the Dionysius of Hilduin's passions.

MANUSCRIPTS AND AUTHORSHIP

Hilduin's popular prose *Passio Dionysii* (BHL 2175) is transmitted in at least 130 manuscripts,[100] many of which contain three prefatory letters: Louis's epistle to Hilduin requesting works on Dionysius (BHL 2172), Hilduin's reply (BHL 2173), and Hilduin's address to "all the sons" (*omnibus filiis*) of the church (BHL 2174).[101] Tenth-century copies of the

---

[98] Scholars variously date *Post beatam et gloriosam* from the eighth to the early tenth centuries. Loenertz, who places it in 826, insists it was composed first, whereas Théry claims priority for Hilduin's prose *passio*. The dating of the *Post beatam et gloriosam* is complicated by its close relationship to the Greek panegyric of Dionysius (BHG 554), probably composed in 810, which is either a translation of the *Post beatam et gloriosam* or its source, leading scholars to argue about whether the conflation of the two Dionysii derived from an Eastern tradition. See P.G. Théry, "Contribution à l'histoire de l'Aréopagitisme au IXe siècle," *Le Moyen Âge*, 2nd ser., 25 (1923): 124ff.; Loenertz, "Légende parisienne," pp. 228ff.; Luscombe, "Denis ... Middle Ages," p. 138. Alcuin provides ambiguous evidence for an older identification of the Areopagite with the Western martyr. His poem on the Parisian Dionysius notes the "little books" (*libelli*) preserved "in the heavenly citadel" (*caelesti in arce*), suggesting that he identified his subject as a writer, but the books may be metaphorical. Alcuin, *Carmen* 19 in MGH Poetae 1, p. 316.

[99] BHL 2178, printed in AASS October 4, vol. XX, pp. 792–797. For the sake of clarity, I refer to this anonymous passion by its incipit "Post beatam et gloriosam" and BHL 2175 as Hilduin's prose passion (rather than by its incipit "Post beatam et salutiferam"). Levillain gives *Post beatam et gloriosam*'s geographical errors as evidence that it was written outside Paris. Levillain, "Études," p. 58. It does not emphasize Saint-Denis as the saint's final earthly destination.

[100] Camilla Weltsch notes 130 manuscripts. Lapidge, "Lost Passio," p. 66, cites her unpublished dissertation, "Der Einfluß der 'Vita S. Dionysii Areopagitae' des Abtes Hilduin von St. Denis auf die hagiographische Literatur" (Munich, 1922), pp. 19–23. Of the 100 copies for which I have information, one is from the ninth century, thirteen from the tenth, three from the tenth or eleventh, eighteen from the eleventh, one from the eleventh or twelfth, twenty-five from the twelfth, eighteen from the thirteenth, ten from the fourteenth, and eleven from the fifteenth century. I have drawn information on these manuscripts from the *BHL*, the library catalogues it cites, and the edition of the letters, MGH Ep. 5, p. 325.

[101] The best edition of the letters is by E. Dümmler in MGH Ep. 5, pp. 326–337.

passion, usually in *libelli* containing works on several saints, are commonly transmitted with all three letters or with the third alone.[102] Many eleventh-century copies are transmitted with only this letter.[103] In the twelfth and thirteenth centuries, the *passio* was copied in large lectionaries of prose lives, few of which include the prefatory letters.[104] Other configurations are rare.[105] Several fourteenth- and fifteenth-century codices, which transmit Hilduin's prose life and all three letters, appear to be from Saint-Denis.[106]

---

[102] At least three of the thirteen tenth-century copies transmit all three letters with the prose *PD*: Chartres, BM, MS 193 (507 5/B), fols. 300v–311v; Paris, BN, MS lat. 2873 A, fols 1r–41r; Paris, BN, MS lat. 10866, fols. 81r–150v. Another four tenth-century copies transmit Hilduin's prose *PD* with his letter *omnibus filiis*: Milan, BA, MS P. 113 Sup., fols. 136v–153r; Paris, BN, MS lat. 13345, fols. 88v–114v; Paris, BN, MS lat. 18298, fols. 99r–122v; Paris, BN, MS N.A. lat. 2164, fols. 1r–10v. Another tenth-century manuscript, Paris, BN, MS lat. 10846, fols. 1r–14r and 21v–75v, contains both Hilduin's letters and his prose *PD*.

[103] Two of eighteen eleventh-century manuscripts transmit three letters. Paris, BN, MS lat. 10847, fols. 1r–23r, contains the prose *passio* and all the letters, and Vatican, Archivio del Capitolo di San Pietro, MS A. 4 (Alias C), fols. 231v–238v, appears to contain the three letters and other texts on Dionysius, but not Hilduin's prose *passio*. Paris, BN, MS lat. 11751 contains BHL 2172 and 2174, and Hilduin's prose *passio*, but not BHL 2173 (Hilduin's letter to Louis). Six eleventh-century copies transmit the passion and Hilduin's letter *omnibus filiis* (BHL 2174) but no other letters. (Paris, BN, MS lat. 17627, fols. 236r–260r; Paris, BN, MS lat. 18305, fols. 62r–62v; Paris, BN, MS lat. 18300, fols. 1r–32v; Paris, BN, MS lat. 12600, fols. 213v–236v; Paris, BN, MS N.A. lat. 2179, fols. 322r–323v; Paris, BN, MS lat. 15436, fols. 29v–42r.)

[104] Only two out of twenty-five twelfth-century manuscripts and one out of eighteen thirteenth-century manuscripts contain all three letters and Hilduin's prose *PD*: Rouen, BM, MS U2, fols. 96–110v (xii); Paris, BN, MS lat. 2445A, fols. 2r–28r (xii); Zwettl, ZS 14, fols. 28v–37r (xiii¼). According to the BHL, Brussels, KBR, MS 9290 (3223), fols. 81r–85v (xii), includes the three letters, but not the prose passion.

[105] Douai, BM, MS 363, fols. 182r–188v (xii), contains the three letters, but not the prose *PD*, at the end of a manuscript of Hugh of Saint Victor's *Expositio super Dionisium Ariopagitam de tribus hierarchiis*. (Dehaisnes, "Catalogue," pp. 196–197, omits the third letter.) Brussels, KBR, MS 11550–11555 (3233), fols. 157v–166v (xii¹) apparently contains Louis's letter and other works on Dionysius, but neither Hilduin's letters nor his *PD*. (See J. Van den Gheyn, *Catalogue des manuscrits de la Bibliothèque Royale de Belgique*, vol. 5 [Brussels, 1901–1948], p. 227.) Two manuscripts of the prose *PD*, Paris, BN, MS lat. 10846, fols. 1r–14r, 21v–75v (x), and London, BL, MS Add. Misc. 22793, fols. 1–29 (xii), contain both Hilduin's letters but not that attributed to Louis. Paris, BN, MS lat. 10847 fols. 1r–23r (xi) and Paris, BN, MS lat. 11751, fols. 1r–50v (xi²/⁴–³/⁴), contain Hilduin's prose *PD*, Louis's letter, and Hilduin's *omnibus filiis*, but not Hilduin's letter to Louis. Cheltenham, MS 16339 Libri 626 [ix] may contain the same configuration (this manuscript is cited by the MGH Ep. edition, but I have been unable to locate additional information). Paris, BN, MS lat. 17631, fols. 32r–60v (xiv) contains Hilduin's letter to Louis and the prose *PD*.

[106] A larger proportion of fourteenth- and fifteenth-century copies transmit all the letters (three out of ten and two out of eleven, respectively): Paris, BN, MS lat. 2447 (xiv); Paris, BN, MS N.A. lat. 1509 (xiv); Paris, BN, MS lat. 2873B (xiv); Erpenburg, Schl, B 7 (xv³/⁴) and Melk, SB, M. 7 (xv²). Two of these, Paris, BN, MS lat. 2447 (xiv) and Paris, BN, MS lat. 2873B (xv), also contain a *vita* of Sanctinus and Antoninus (BHL 7488), bishops of Meaux and

The unpublished epic passion (no BHL) is known from a single copy titled "Passio beati Dionysii sociorumque eius heroico carmine edita" on folios 1–37 of the late-eleventh-century manuscript Oxford, Bodleian, MS Bodley 535 (S.C. 2254).[107] Although no author is named, Lapidge has identified it as Hilduin's epic passion of Dionysius, seen by Sigebert of Gembloux in the twelfth century and Aubert Le Mire in the seventeenth.[108] Sigebert writes that "Hilduin, abbot of Saint-Denis of Paris wrote to the Emperor Louis in each style, that is in prose and meter, the life of this Dionysius."[109] Sigebert here refers to a twinned work, comprising prose and verse on the same topic.[110]

The passions' intense similarities substantiate Sigebert's claim of their common authorship.[111] Rarely is the language so alike in the pieces of a twinned work. The poet draws vocabulary from the prose and adds rhetorical flourishes, such as Classical allusions and metaphors, creating a longer more involved text (the prose was clearly written first).[112] The versifier follows the content and order down to the smallest detail. So, the poet excerpts identical sections of the Pseudo-Dionysian writings. Both

supposed witnesses of Dionysius's passion, whose feast was celebrated at Saint-Denis after 1259 when parts of their bones were translated there. Both manuscripts contain a large number of works on Dionysius. The other fourteenth-century codex with all three letters, Paris, BN, MS N.A. lat 1509, does not include the *vita* of Sanctinus and Antoninus, but, like Paris, BN, MS lat. 2873B, it contains the *Iter Hierosolymitanum* (BHL 1587), following a similar set of texts on Dionysius. Lauer identifies the same hand as copying Paris, BN, MS lat. 2447 (which was written at Saint-Denis, according to a comment on fol. 238) and Paris, BN, MS N.A. lat. 1509. See Ph. Lauer, *Bibliothèque nationale, Département des manuscrits. Catalogue général des manuscrits latins*, v. 2 (Paris, 1940), pp. 461–462. On the translation of Sanctinus and Antoninus, see William C. Jordan, *A Tale of Two Monasteries: Westminster and Saint-Denis in the Thirteenth Century* (Princeton, 2009), p. 34.

[107] Falconer Madan and H.H.E. Craster, *Summary Catalogue of Western Manuscripts in the Bodleian Library at Oxford*, vol 2, pt. 2 (Oxford, 1922), pp. 280–281.

[108] Lapidge, "Lost Passio," pp. 67–68. Lapidge cites Robert Witte, ed., *Catalogus Sigeberti Gemblacensis monachi de viris illustribus*, Krit. Ausgabe, Lat. Sprache und Literatur des MA.s 1 (Bern, 1974), 76, 132 (§ 82); and Aubert Le Mire, *Liber de Ecclesiasticis Scriptoribus in Bibliotheca ecclesiastica* (Antwerp, 1639), p. 71. The *explicit* labels the work "exametro decurrens passio versu magni cum sociis Dyonisii" (fol. 37r). According to Le Mire, a manuscript containing abbot Hilduin's prose and verse passions of Dionysius existed at Gembloux in the seventeenth century. The verse passion Le Mire notes, like that found in the Oxford manuscript, comprised four books.

[109] Sigebert *Catalogus* 76, 132: "Hilduinus abbas de Sancti Dionysii Pariensis scripsit ad Ludowicum imperatorem utroque stilo, id est prosaico et metrico, vitam ipsius Dionisii," quoted by Lapidge, "Lost Passio," p. 67.

[110] Ibid. On "twinned works," see the Introduction.

[111] The twelfth-century *Poleticum* of Marchiennes incorrectly attributes the anonymous verse and prose *vitae* (BHL 2736 and 2737) of Saint Eusebia to the same author (see Chapter 5).

[112] Lapidge, "Lost Passio," p. 72.

passions unusually include the *capitula* (chapter titles) of the theological works.[113] They break the *capitula* of the *Divine Names* into the same four sections (which are not self-evident divisions), interspersed with discussion at exactly the same points. It is hard to imagine a poet in the culture of competitive composition following another writer's prose life in such minute detail. Even other twinned epic *vitae* show less fidelity to their sources.[114] Hilduin, as we shall see, painstakingly crafted his narrative of the composite saint, and having done so, he adhered to it.

The poet's affiliation with Saint-Denis is consistent with Lapidge's attribution of authorship. Most *vitae* and *passiones* were written at or for the abbey that claimed the titular saint's relics, because that institution was most interested in promoting the saint, and this was particularly true of epic renditions, which required a great investment of resources. A *vita* or *passio* not written at or for the saint's cult center would downplay its foundation, but the epic *Passio Dionysii*, like Hilduin's prose, glorifies it by telling how the saint made his miraculous posthumous journey (with angelic accompaniment) to his divinely chosen resting place: he walked "until he came to that place that conceals his body and, in accordance with divine will, rightly covers his grave."[115]

Lapidge dates the poem to the ninth or tenth century stylistically and shows that it must have been written before 960, due to reminiscences in Hrotsvita of Gandersheim's *Passio S. Dionysii egregii martyris*.[116] We can place the poem's *terminus ante quem* a century earlier. A satirical poem by Sedulius Scottus (fl. 848–859) apparently alludes to it.[117] Further, the epic

---

[113] Occasionally *capitula* are included in a manuscript without their accompanying text. For example, Lucan's *capitula* are included in the eleventh-century Paris, BN, MS lat. 9345, which contains poems by other Classical authors. See Eva Matthews Sanford, "The Use of Classical Latin Authors in the *Libri Manuales*," *TAPA* 55 (1924): 220.

[114] Other pairs of lives by the same author differ far more than the two *passiones* of Dionysius (e.g., Alcuin's *vitae* of Willibrord, Candid's *vitae* of Eigil, Walter's *passiones* of Christopher). The anonymous epic *VE* is heavily based on the prose (by another author), but adds features to the story (see Chapter 5).

[115] *PD* (metric), fol. 33v: "donec ad usque locum venit qui corpus obumbrat/ numine divino digne tegit atque sepultum." Cf. *PD* (prose), c. 32.

[116] BHL 2186. Lapidge, "Lost Passio," pp. 73, 75. The Office for Dionysius's *translatio*, composed at Saint-Emmeram in 1049, may also depend on the epic *PD* rather than on the prose. Ed. Roman Hankeln, *Historiae Sancti Dionysii Areopagitae, St Emmeram, Regensburg, ca. 1050/ 16. Jh.* (Ottawa, 1998), p. 2. The Hymn *Alma lux sideram* recounts the cephalophory: "Qui portans proprium caput abscisum / cantu angelico, venit subito / ductus ..." Cf. the rubric on fol. 33v of the epic: "quomodo caput proprium angelico ducto portavit."

[117] Sedulius, *Mock Epyllion on a Gelded Ram*, ed. Godman, *Poetry*, pp. 293–301. See, Taylor, "Books, Bodies, and Bones," pp. 42–44.

passio was written before John Scottus Eriugena's translation of Pseudo-Dionysius appeared around 860. Eriugena's version, made at Emperor Charles the Bald's behest, rapidly replaced Hilduin's flawed translation, which the prose and verse passions excerpt.[118] It is highly unlikely that a writer of an erudite poem working after 860 would quote Hilduin's obscure translation, which Charles had deemed inadequate, rather than Eriugena's version.

Verse composition was time-consuming, so Hilduin, writing the prose *vita* and other works and continuing his reform and building projects, probably took several years to complete the epic.[119] Although no dedication survives, it was probably sent to the emperor as Sigebert claims. As monumental undertakings that demonstrated the author's erudition while flattering the recipient's culture and intellect, verse texts were gifts fit for a king.[120]

AUDIENCE

Prose and verse lives had different audiences. The writers of prose lives refer to both *auditores* and *legentes*.[121] They stress that their works are for both the devoted and the disdainful (the *studiosi* and the *fastidiosi*) and seek to balance these groups' competing needs.[122] The writers claim that the short attention spans of the *fastidiosi* and the threat of boredom

---

[118] John Scottus Eriugena, letter to Charles the Bald, ed. Ernst Dümmler, in MGH Ep. 6, pp. 158–161. On this translation, see the letter of 862 from Anastasius the librarian, ed. E. Perels and G. Laehr, in MGH Ep. 7, pp. 430–434, and Édouard Jeauneau, "L'abbaye de Saint-Denis introducatrice de Denys en occident," in *Denys l'Aréopagite et sa postérité en Orient et en Occident. Actes du Colloque international, Paris, 21–24 septembre 1994*, ed. Ysabel de Andia (Paris, 1997), p. 366. On Hilduin's translation of Pseudo-Dionysius, see Théry, who identified it in the manuscripts Paris, BN, lat. 15645 and Brussels KBR 756–757. Théry, "Hilduin et la première traduction," pp. 23–39. Hilduin's translation is printed in Théry, *Études Dionysiennes*.

[119] Heiric claims his epic *VG* took a decade (MGH Poetae 3, p. 429).

[120] Charles the Bald was the recipient of both Milo's *VA* and Heiric's *VG*.

[121] Hilduin mentions the prose passion's *auditores* and *lectores* (*Rescriptum*, c. 2). Other references to *auditores* for prose *vitae* are from the ninth-century *Vita Melanii Episcopi Redonici* (BHL 5887), c. 1, in MGH SRM 3, p. 372; *Prefatio* to Hincmar's *Vita Remigii* (BHL 7152–7162), in ibid., p. 254; the *Vita Caesarii* (BHL 1509), book 2, c. 1, in ibid., p. 484.

[122] In his *Vita Remigii*, Hilduin's student Hincmar uses symbols to distinguish excerpts suitable for a rarified readership from those appropriate for liturgical readings (*Prefatio, Vita Remigii*, pp. 262–263). Ionas explains that he divides his *Vitae Columbani Abbatis Discipulorum eius* (BHL 1898) into two books to lessen the boredom (*fastidium*) of some readers (MGH SRM 4, p. 63).

(*tedium*) compel them to truncate their works.[123] Some exhibit a style suitable for aural comprehension. The audience's limitations are invoked as a humility topos excusing the writer's style.[124]

The prefatory letters to Hilduin's prose *Passio Dionysii* lay out its intended readership. Louis's letter asks Hilduin to render the sources on Dionysius into one work so "they can be made known in a brief form to the faithful, and so that they might allay the boredom of reading for the contemptuous, or the less competent, or for the zealous, and equally that they might provide edification for all."[125] The composition is to be beneficial for all people, regardless of their capacities and enthusiasm. Hilduin claims, "we shall set out for all readers and listeners, the story, in order, gathered into one work."[126] How comprehensible an uneducated ninth-century Frankish audience would have found Hilduin's prose is unclear, but he addresses his work to "all the sons" of the church. Because prose *vitae* provided readings for a saint's feast day, they communicated the narrative to a wide audience including the illiterate majority.[127] In deference to this intended audience, says Hilduin, the prose *passio* is "written in a straightforward manner" (*scripta simpliciter*).[128]

Prose and verse lives had different audiences. Alcuin writes that his prose life of Willibrord was to be "read publically to the brothers in church," whereas its verse counterpart "should be meditated upon by

---

[123] For *fastidium* see *Vita Bavonis* (BHL 1049), c. 1, in MGH SRM 4, p. 535, and the *transitus* appended to the *Vita Aridi* (BHL 666), in MGH SRM 3, p. 609.

[124] Alcuin explains that for this reason his prose *Vita Richarii* is "simple and less polished" (*simplex et minus polita locutio*). *Pref.* to *Vita Richarii* (BHL 7223–7227), in MGH SRM 4, p. 389.

[125] Louis, *Ep. Hilduino*, p. 327: "devotis compendiosius valeant innotesci, et fastidiosis minusve capacibus vel studiosis lectionis possit tedium sublevari pariterque omnibus aedificationis utilitas provideri."

[126] Hilduin, *Rescriptum*, c. 2: "ordinem igitur historiae, sicut vestra iussit dominatio, in unum congestum et singillatim postea plenitudinem eius discretam, cunctis legentibus atque audientibus pandemus."

[127] Hincmar designates sections of his *Vita Remigii* as readings and homilies of the saint's feast days. Hincmar, *Praefatio* (BHL 7152) to *Vita Remigii*, in MGH SRM 3, p. 258.

[128] Hilduin, *Omnibus filiis*, p. 336. The letters also refer to a collection of works appended (*subiungere*) to the prose *passio* and to an *alter volumen* of Dionysius's writings. The appendix, which includes hymns and the night office for the feast, is for the same audience as the *passio*, which would include churchmen who performed the liturgy and, indirectly, a wider public. The liturgical pieces would be useful for priests in abbeys or parishes outside Saint-Denis who celebrated the Feast of Dionysius. Excerpts from the prose *passio* could provide material for the readings on the saint's feast as well as other occasions (such as the *lectio* at meal times in a monastery). The *alter volumen*, a collection of works by the saint, is specifically to facilitate the emperor's personal relationship with Dionysius (*Ep. Hilduino*, p. 327).

only your learned men in their private cell."[129] Unlike prose lives, epic *vitae* were intended exclusively for literate consumption.[130] Hilduin also posits different readerships for his *passiones*. He explains that he excerpts the saint's letter to Demophilus in his prose passion "because it is useful to readers who might not get their hands on the entire letter."[131] He iterates a point from his letter to Louis: that the prose *passio* provides texts that readers would otherwise lack.[132] Introducing the letter to Demophilus in the epic passion, he addresses himself to a different readership, the wise reader (*sagax lector*).[133] *Sagax* and the related noun *sagacitas*, terms common in Carolingian epistolary flattery, connote a discerning, critical mind, for whom verse is appropriate.[134] The epic *Passio Dionysii*, like other Carolingian verse, was intended for a highly educated readership. It was fitting, then, for the emperor and the *lectores sagaces* of Hilduin's milieu. It was a prestigious form that flattered the recipients' intellect and impressed on them the poet's erudition. It also asserted Hilduin's place in the literary culture and displayed the shared textual culture of the writer and the reader. In this way, its functions differed from those of the prose life *scripta simpliciter*.

THE SAINT'S STORY

Hilduin's narrative of Dionysius falls into three distinct thematic sections. (The division of the verse into four books is a later imposition.)[135] The first section (prose, c. 1–8; verse fols. 1r–10r) recounts his youth as a noble Athenian. He traveled to Egypt with his fellow student Apollophanius to

---

[129] Alcuin, *Ep.* 120, in MGH Ep. 4, p. 175, quoted in the Introduction.

[130] Hucbald, *VR*, prologue. Hucbald of Saint-Amand, in 907, describes writing his prose *vita* for the edification of *audientes* or *legentes*.

[131] *PD* (prose), c. 15: "quam hic ob utilitatem ista legentium, in quorum manus fortasse plenitudo ipsarum non perveniet litterarum, narrare censuimus."

[132] Hildiun, *omnibus filiis*, pp. 336–337: "one who cannot find them elsewhere will benefit from reading our humble writings ..." (si ... et alibi ea invenire nequiverit, litterarum nostrae parvitatis ... lectione valebit).

[133] *PD* (metric), fol. 16r.

[134] Hilduin characterizes Dionysius's mind as *sagax* in the verse *passio* (fol. 7) when he grasps Paul's teachings: "unrolling such great things in his wise mind, Dionysius was discerning the true and highest teaching of salvation" (Tanta DIONYSIUS replicans sub mente sagaci / Doctrinam veri cernens summaeque salutis). Louis's letter describes Hilduin's zeal for translating Greek (*sagax studium*) (*Ep. Hilduino*, p. 327), and Hilduin describes Louis's "sagacitatis vestrae prudentia" in searching for Dionysius's acts and writings (*Rescriptum*, c. 1).

[135] The epic *PD* was divided into four books before Sigebert saw it in the twelfth century.

learn astrology and, witnessing the eclipse that signaled Christ's death, correctly interpreted its meaning, although he was a pagan. On his return from Egypt, he encountered Paul on the Areopagus, and, after their debate, Paul converted him (and his wife, Damaris, who is barely mentioned) and later ordained him bishop of Athens.

The second section (c. 9–16; fols. 10r–20r) does not recount the protagonist's deeds (*gesta*), as we would expect at this point of a saint's life, but his writings. Hilduin summarizes the Pseudo-Dionysian theological treatises and lists the *capitula* of the *Celestial Hierarchy*, the *Ecclesiastic Hierarchy*, the *Divine Names*, and the *Mystic Theology*. Hilduin briefly mentions the theological letters (#1–6 and 9 in the Pseudo-Dionysian corpus), but focuses on those containing biography. He paraphrases the letter to Polycarp (#7) and appends to it the entire apocryphal letter to Apollophanius (#11). He gives a partial summary of the letter to Demophilus (#8) from which he excerpts the vision of the holy man Carpus. He incorporates the entire letter to John on Patmos (#10), in which the writer foretells the Baptist's return from exile. In the epic passion, the letters to Apollophanius and John are reproduced in prose, so they, like the *capitula*, visually and metrically interrupt Hilduin's text with the saint's own voice.

The third section of each passion (c. 17–36; fols. 20r–37r) covers Dionysius's apostolate and death. He evangelized through the Greek world, then, hearing of the persecutions, went to Rome seeking martyrdom. There, Pope Clement appointed him missionary to Gaul. Dionysius's successes in the West provoked the Roman emperor Domitian, who ordered the prefect to imprison him with his companions Rusticus and Eleutherius. He was beaten, stripped, flogged, put on an iron bed, "cooked like a fish," thrown to the beasts, placed in an oven, and tied to a pillory.[136] Throughout his ordeals he addressed his companions and the prefect, prayed, and sang. While the martyrs were imprisoned, Christ appeared with angels and gave them communion. When Dionysius was finally decapitated, he collected his head and, accompanied by an angelic chorus, walked to the site of his future church. A pious woman, Catulla, collected the bodies of Rusticus and Eleutherius and hid them so that they too were preserved. The saints were revered by the pious, a church was built, and the requisite healing miracles occurred.

Throughout, Hilduin supplements the biographical information of the Pseudo-Dionysian letters and Latin *vitae*, with details such as Paul's

---

[136] *PD* (metric), fol. 29v: "in morem piscis adurit."

ordination, Christ's visitation, and the angelic retinue. Even if he derives the identification of his saint with the Areopagite and the cephalophory from an earlier tradition, he greatly elaborates both of these aspects. His inclusion of summaries and excerpts from the writings underline the saint's status as a theologian and apostolic correspondent. By having Paul ordain him bishop of Athens, Hilduin gives Dionysius direct apostolic transmission and emphasizes his origins in the most renowned center of learning and philosophy.[137]

Hilduin strengthens the identification of the Eastern and Western saints and unifies the narrative by using themes and concepts from his translation of the Pseudo-Dionysian corpus.[138] The passions' tripartite structure echoes Pseudo-Dionysius's preoccupation with triads. Hilduin incorporates the theologian's interest in angels in the *Celestial Hierarchy* by adding heavenly hosts to the narrative.[139] Linguistic echoes in both versions remind the reader of Hilduin's description of the *Celestial Hierarchy*.[140]

Hilduin also recalls the *Ecclesiastical Hierarchy* by having Dionysius and his fellow martyrs embody the triad of initiators: bishop, priest, and deacon. He makes all three "arch officials," just as he had named himself the "archicapellanus."[141] He also iterates Pseudo-Dionysius's emphasis on the sacraments, which he employs at pivotal moments in the plot.[142] Dionysius's execution echoes a hierarch's consecration, in which he kneels and has the Scripture laid upon his head, symbolizing his role as a teacher (*EH* 5.2, 5.3.8). Similarly, the submersion of his companions'

---

[137] M.M. Delaporte, "He Darkens Me with Brightness: The Theology of *Pseudo-Dionysius* in Hilduin's *Vita* of Saint Denis," *Religion and Theology* 13 (2006): 226.

[138] Ibid., p. 222. Delaporte observes that Pseudo-Dionysian theology permeates Hilduin's passions.

[139] Christ appears to the imprisoned martyrs with a heavenly crowd (*cum multitudine angelorum*; prose, c. 26, 29); and a host of hymn-singing angels (*comes multitudo coelistis exercitus* in the prose, *chorus sacer* in the verse) accompanies the saint's cephalophory (prose, c. 32; metric, fols. 33v–34r).

[140] PD (metric), fol. 10r: "orders of angels distinguished by ranks, who justly render melodious hymns to God" (Scilicet angelicos distantes ordine caetus / Hymnos reddentes deitati iure canoros).

[141] Hilduin makes Dionysius, Rusticus, and Eleutherius archbishop, archpriest, and archdeacon, respectively. PD (prose), c. 18, 25; Elizabeth A.R. Brown, "Saint Carpus, Saint Denis, and Benign Jesus: The Economy of Salvation at Saint-Denis" (forthcoming). See also Elizabeth A.R. Brown, "*Gloriosae*, Hilduin, and the Early Liturgical Celebration of St. Denis," in *Medieval Paradigms: Essays in Honor of Jeremy du Quesnay Adams* (New York, 2005), pp. 39–82. The *Gloriosae* had called Eleutherius "archidiaconus" and the *Post Gloriosam* calls Eleutherius an archdeacon and Rusticus a presbyter.

[142] In addition to Dionysius's baptism, Hilduin adds Paul's ordination of Dionysius as bishop of Athens and Christ's administering of the Eucharist to the martyrs.

bodies in the river is reminiscent of baptism, in which the body's immersion signifies its concealment in the earth after death (*EH* 2.3.7). As we will see, Hilduin further infused his verse *passio* with a more profound Pseudo-Dionysian mysticism.

HILDUIN'S EVIDENCE

Not everyone accepted the composite apostolic-era saint. Hilduin repeatedly refers to the muttering (*garrulitas*) of unnamed critics.[143] These "gossips" (*susurrones*) are the "worst kind of men" (*pessimmi generis hominum*); foolish, impious, and perverse, they use "slander and the threat of gossip" (*detractione et famae minoratione*) and read with one eye open.[144] Their dullness, *hebetudo*, is etymologically akin to the executioners' blunted axes (*hebetatae secures*).[145] Whoever continues to doubt after the truth is discovered, "inquires out of a zeal for lies," and will rightfully be judged "the companion and student of ... the father of lies."[146] The terms *scioli* (learned men) and *cavillationes* (sophistries) hint at the conflict's scholastic milieu;[147] the men "are quarrelsome in this case ... out of stolen wisdom, because they wish to be seen as learned (*scioli*)."[148] Although detractors are a Carolingian literary topos, Hilduin did not invent the criticisms; even at Saint-Denis, his Areopagite-martyr was not completely accepted.[149] He defended his Dionysius through the two passions, the three prefatory letters, and a plethora of documents that supported the composite saint's historicity.

The prose passion's prefatory letters provide a context for reading that work and therefore its verse redaction. The first letter, ostensibly from Louis to Hilduin, requests works on Dionysius, lists the kinds of sources Hilduin should gather, and specifies certain documents. Hilduin's reply

---

[143] Hilduin, *Rescriptum*, c. 8.

[144] Ibid., c. 9, 14, 15.

[145] Ibid., c. 14, 16; *PD* (prose), c. 31; (metric), fol. 32v.

[146] Hilduin, *Rescriptum*, c. 13. "ex studio mendacium quaerit, comes et discipulus eius, qui ab initio mendax et pater mendacii extitit." (With an allusion to John 8:44.)

[147] Ibid., c. 15; cf. See also, Boniface, letter to the bishops of Gaul: "astuta cavillatio eorum, qui versutis agendum credunt esse consiliis nunquam innocentiae nomen accipit," cited in MGH Conc. 2.2, Aev. Kar 1, p. 840, n. 7.

[148] Hilduin, *Rescriptum*, c. 9: "ut in hoc iure contentiosi ... ex usurpata sapientia, quia videri se scioli volunt."

[149] For example, Hilduin's devoted student Hincmar avoided conflating the saints for many decades. See Luscombe, "Denis ... Middle Ages," pp. 140–142. On *detractores*, see Godman, *Poets*, p. 78.

gives the sources in more detail, explaining the information each provided. Many of these works turn out to be created by Hilduin. It would be incredibly convenient if the emperor had listed the precise sources Hilduin used (including the falsified ones), thereby vouching for the existence of works that, by Hilduin's admission, the readers would have never encountered and, therefore, for the validity of the composite Dionysius.[150] Rather than accepting the emperor's letter at face value, we must consider it within the framework of Hilduin's enthusiasm for manufacturing evidence.

Loenertz considers that Hilduin wrote, solicited, or rewrote Louis's letter.[151] Audacious as it seems for Hilduin to speak for Louis, writing in the emperor's voice was established practice among Carolingian courtiers.[152] How much of the letter Hilduin composed is unclear. Louis may have written to request works on Dionysius; his choice of Saint-Denis for his reinvestiture shows his attachment to his family's *patronus peculiaris*, and his desire to strengthen his position by association with him.[153] Louis may have sent Hilduin a letter, but at the very least Hilduin redacted portions of it, shaping the emperor's words to suit his own agenda.

Although we cannot confidently use the letter as a source for Louis's thoughts, we can see it and the other letters as the framework Hilduin provides for reading the narrative. In addition to establishing the purpose and audience of his works, Hilduin argues for his Dionysius's veracity and lays out the evidence.

Louis's letter summarizes the sources: mentions of Dionysius in Greek histories (*notitia ex Grecorum hystoriis*) and other Greek texts, which Hilduin and his team have been translating at Louis's command, Latin codices, the *libellus* of the saint's passion, and very ancient charters (*cartae vetustissimae*), which Hilduin had discovered in the *armarium* of Saint-Denis (*in cartis vetustissimis armario Parisiacae ecclesiae*) and shown to Louis. Hilduin is to "render these into one body and assemble a uniform text" (*in corpus unum redigas atque uniformem textum exinde componas*) and to append additional works to this volume:

---

[150] Hilduin could have familiarized the emperor with these fabricated Dionysian sources during his time at court (presuming that he had begun creating them ahead of time), but nonetheless the emperor's inventory of these works is suspiciously convenient.

[151] Loenertz, "Légende," p. 228.

[152] For example, Alcuin, *Disputatio de rhetorica et de virtutibus sapientissimi regis Carli et Albini magistri, The Rhetoric of Alcuin and Charlemagne*, ed. and trans. Wilbur Samuel Howell (Princeton, 1941); Walafrid Strabo, *Carmen* 30, in MGH Poetae 2, p. 384. Godman, *Poets*, pp. 53ff., provides further examples by Peter of Pisa and Alcuin (*Carm.* 33, 34).

[153] *Annales Bertiniani* for 834. For examples of Louis's devoion to Saint-Denis, see Nelson, *Frankish World*, p. 114.

We wish that you also attach the revelation shown to blessed Pope Stephen in the church of the same most holy Dionysius, just as he told it, and the deeds that were added to it, together with the hymns you have about this most glorious martyr and priest, and the Night Office.[154]

Louis's overview of the sources sets up Hilduin's lengthy discussion of his evidence.

The two prefatory letters Hilduin writes in his own name are characterized by their insistence on the truth: "we took care to gather these things *truthfully* from the *true* historians and pages of histories – since the *truth*, which supplies its own evidence, does not need to be supported by our falsehood – whatever produces the *truest* witnesses, which it supplied, attests to *true* things" (my emphasis).[155]

A highly defensive tone pervades these two letters. Hilduin appeals to divine support for his Dionysius by describing how the Areopagite's writings (the Greek Pseudo-Dionysian codex) and the martyr's relics at Saint-Denis celebrated their reunion by performing healing miracles.[156] Mostly, however, Hilduin uses textual evidence. He employs a three-pronged strategy in order to refute the doubters and substantiate his story. First, he discounts the contrary evidence through source criticism. Second, he cites *notitiae* from authorities. Third, to support his most contentious points, he appeals to evidence that his detractors had not encountered: that which was newly uncovered or translated.

Authoritative writers (*auctores*) contradicted Hilduin's narrative by making the Areopagite bishop of Corinth rather than Athens and by attributing his episcopal ordination to Pope Clement rather than to Paul. Luscombe shows how Hilduin undermines the inconvenient evidence through source criticism.[157] Distance and linguistic barriers explain why

---

[154] "Volumus, ut revelationem ostensam beato papae Stephano in ecclesia eiusdem sanctissimi Dionisii, sicut ab eo dictata est, et gesta quae eidem subnexa sunt, una cum ymnis, quos de hoc gloriossimo martire atque pontifice habes, et officium nocturnale subiungas." The MGH prefers the reading *subnixa*, but at least one manuscript, the tenth-century Oxford, Bodleian, MS 1276 (Laud. misc. 549), contains the variant *subnexa*.

[155] Hilduin, *Rescriptum*, c. 16. "haec ... veraciter ex veracibus hystoriographis et hystoriarum paginis colligere procuravimus, quoniam veritas ... nostro mendatio adstipulari non indiget, quae suo sibi testimonio suffigit, quaeque testes veracissimos quos repleverit tesitificantes veracia efficit."

[156] Hilduin, *Rescriptum*, c. 4.

[157] Luscombe, "Denis ... Middle Ages," pp. 147–148. Hilduin characterizes Gregory of Tours as a man of holy simplicity rather than cleverness (*non calliditatis astu*) who relied on inferior oral tradition rather than on the oldest histories (*Rescriptum*, c. 12). Hilduin claims that Bede was deceived when he says the Areopagite was bishop of Corinth. In a

Greek and Latin sources fail to connect the Eastern and Western saints. The Greek writers do not record his martyrdom "because it remained unknown to them, since their lands were far away."[158] Fortunatus omits the saint's national origin and episcopal ordination in his hymns because he could not read the Greek sources.[159] Hilduin applies the principles of Carolingian textual criticism to undermine inconvenient readings in an ancient *passio* of Dionysius. Readers who asserted that Clement had ordained Dionysius bishop erred, says Hilduin, in using corrupt manuscripts.[160] Discounting the evidence of some authorities, Hilduin appeals to others, such as Basil, Ambrose, Augustine, and John Chrysostom, who substantiate the conventional parts of his narrative, lending authority to the overall picture without actually endorsing his novel assertions.

To support the controversial elements, Hilduin refers to works that his detractors had not read. He repeatedly invokes a shadowy set of conveniently discovered documents. As he describes them, they appear antique (as shown by their authorship and format), cohering with Hilduin's principle that oldest sources are best.[161] Most were in Greek, a language that few of his readers knew. One, an ancient Byzantine martyrology crumbling with age (*tanta vestutate dissolvitur*), allegedly told of Dionysius's Athenian episcopate.[162] Another, the letter of the otherwise unknown Aristarchus to Onesiphorus,[163] *primercerius* of Athens,

---

statement, whose irony skeptical readers must have appreciated, he claims that Bede had conflated Dionysii from two different eras: "this reasoning is completely ridiculous since those two Dionysii are separated by many aeons" (quantae absurditati ratio sit ista obnoxia, cum inter hos duos Dionysios tam plura discreta sint tempora; p. 332).

[158] Hilduin, c. 10: "quia propter longinquitatem terrarum transitus ipsius penitus eis mansit incognitus."

[159] Ibid., c. 12: "de natione autem eius et ordinatione episcopatus mentionem non facit, quia lingua Grecae penitus expers fuit."

[160] Ibid., c. 11.The *Gloriosae*, the best surviving candidate for the *libellus antiquissimus*, indeed has an extremely variable manuscript tradition, but none of the extant manuscript families contains the information that Hilduin claims to derive from it, namely, the saint's cephalophory and angelic retinue (nor does any other text that could be considered ancient by Hilduin's day; *Rescriptum*, c. 5).

[161] Hilduin, *Rescriptum*, c. 12.

[162] Ibid., c. 10.

[163] Onesiphorus, Aristarchus's addressee and another minor Pauline disciple, has a similar profile in the New Testament and the Apocrypha. Paul praises him for his steadfastness in visiting him in prison and blesses him and his house (Onesiphorus: 2 Timothy 1:16–18, 4:19). Like Dionysius and Aristarchus, Onesiphorus acquires a fuller biography in later works. In the apocryphal *Acts of Peter and Paul* from a Bodleian Manuscript, Onesiphorus is a wealthy convert of Paul. In the *Acts of Paul and Thecla*, Onesiphorus and his family are converted and abandon worldly things to follow Paul. Onesiphorus:

supports Hilduin's controversial claims about Dionysius, including his ordination.[164] Aristarchus is, like Dionysius, a minor Scriptural figure associated with Paul.[165] As Luscombe observes, he was an imaginary historian Hilduin invented.[166] The surviving fragment of his letter (BHL 2182), which only exists in Latin, closely paraphrases Hilduin's prose *passio*.[167]

Dionysius's letter to Apollophanius, included in full in both Hilduin's passions (c. 14; fol. 14v), appears in no prior sources.[168] In his canonical letter to Polycarp, Pseudo-Dionysius says he wrote to Apollophanius and that the reader can fill in the details himself.[169] Hilduin apparently took the invitation literally and composed the letter to Apollophanius.[170] This "pseudo-pseudo-Dionysian" letter elaborates on the information contained in the letter to Polycarp and substantiates Dionysius's biography presented earlier in the passions (c. 5; fol. 4v).

Hilduin also cites "previously lost" Latin works, including missal books almost destroyed by age, and a hymn attributed to Eugenius of Toledo,

---

Acts of Paul and Thecla, in *Fathers of the Third and Fourth Centuries,* ed. and trans. A. Cleveland Coxe (1886) pp. 487, 489. In the *Acts of Peter and Andrew,* printed in the same volume, the arrogant Onesiphorus is being converted by miraculous means at the point at which the manuscript ends (p. 527).

[164] Hilduin, *Rescriptum,* c. 3.

[165] Aristarchus of Thessalonica was a companion and fellow prisoner of Paul (Colossians 4:10; Philemon 24; Acts 20.4, 27.2). He also appears twice in Timothy and in the Apocrypha.

[166] Luscombe, "Denis . . . Middle Ages," p. 138.

[167] Ibid., p. 138. AASS IV October, cols. 704Aff.; the BHL cites a lone eleventh-century manuscript, Milan, BA, MS. B. 055 inf (fols. 170v–173r), which contains a large number of hagiographic works. A *passio* (BHL 2178) and *laudatio* (BHL 2187) of Dionysius precede Aristarchus.

[168] Hilduin, *Rescriptum,* c. 3; *PD* (prose), c. 13 and (metric), fols. 15r–15v. Letter 11, labeled "spuria" in PG 3, 1119–1122.

[169] Ep. 7 in PG 3, col. 1081. Pseudo-Dionysius's original letter to Polycarp concludes, "we have expressed these things sufficiently in this letter. You can fill in what is lacking and finally bring that man who is clearly wise in many things to God; perhaps he will not despise learning mildly and humbly the truth beyond wisdom of our religion" (Τοσαῦτα ὡς κατ' ἐπιστολὴν ἡμῖν εἰρήσθω. Σὺ δὲ ἱκανὸς καὶ τὰ ἐλλείποντα προσαναπληρῶσαι καὶ προσαγαγεῖν τελέως τῷ Θεῷ τὸν ἄνδρα σοφὸν τὰ πολλὰ ὄντα καὶ ἴσως οὐκ ἀπαξιώσοντα πράεως μαθεῖν τὴν ὑπέρσοφον τῆς θρησκείας ἡμῶν ἀλήθειαν).

[170] Théry, "Aréopagitisme," p. 123. On composing in the voice of a literary character as a classroom exercise, see Marjorie Curry Woods, "Weeping for Dido: Epilogue on a Premodern Rhetorical Exercise in the Postmodern Classroom," in *Latin Grammar and Rhetoric: From Classical Theory to Medieval Practice,* ed. Carol Dana Lanham (London, 2002), p. 282. If we could date the earliest of Hilduin's *passiones* to the end of the 830s, I would suspect a reference to Bodo, who had been Hilduin's fellow student and who notoriously converted to Judiasm (Hilduin makes Apollophanius into Dionysius's fellow student in this letter and rebukes his religious choices).

which, according to Théry, is another of Hilduin's forgeries.[171] He also refers to "very ancient charters" found in the church.[172] Saint-Denis was a major producer of self-serving charters,[173] and the *Conscriptio Visbii* (BHL 2183), which survives in a Paris manuscript with other works on Dionysius, is one of them.[174] Visbius, who appears briefly in Hilduin's passions, seems to be another imaginary figure.[175] Levillain argues that Hilduin also composed the ostensibly eighth-century *Revelatio* and *Dedicatio altaris*, which are among the works requested in Louis's letter.[176] Along with a third short piece, the *Clausula de unctione Pippini*, they stress the saint's power and the connections among the papacy, Carolingian royal legitimacy, and Saint-Denis.[177] They also emphasize the saint's spiritual glory: in the *Revelatio*,

[171] Hilduin, *Rescriptum*, c. 5 ("nimia pene vetustate consumpti"), c. 7; *PD* (prose), c. 7; Théry, "Aréopagitisme," p. 122; *Hymnus Eugenii Episcopi de Sancto Dionysio*, ed. F. Vollme in MGH AA 14, p. 282.

[172] Louis, *Ep. Hilduino*, p. 327: "in cartis vetustissimis armario Parisiacae ecclesiae." The emperor conveniently vouches for the existence of these *cartae*, saying that Hilduin has already shown them to him and explained their context: "for our serene intellect to look upon, you had shown them according to what you knew concerning their agreement on matters, causes, and times" (obtutibus sollertiae nostrae serenitatis ostenderas secundum quod rerum, causarum etiam et temporum, convenientiam noveris).

[173] The abbey had Merovingian papyrus diplomas, which forgers erased and reused to provide a convincing support for false documents. For a discussion of eleventh-century forgeries at Saint-Denis, see Hartmut Atsma and Jean Vezin, "Les faux sur papyrus de l'abbaye de Saint-Denis," in *Finances, pouvoirs et mémoire: Mélanges offerts à Jean Favier*, ed. Jean Kerhervé and Albert Riguadière (Brest, 1999). With the caveat that this analysis is exclusively linguistic rather than paleological, see W.H. Stevenson, "The Old English Charters to St. Denis," *EHR* 6 (1891): 736–742. Havet has identified a recycled papyrus pseudo-Merovingian charter. See Julian Havet, "Questions mérovingiennes," pp. 42–43, n. 2.

[174] Paris, BN, MS lat. 3851A, fols. 54r–v (x), a manuscript that includes a collection of hagiographical sources. The *Conscriptio Visibii* (BHL 2183) follows the *Revelatio* of Pope Stephen (BHL 2176) on fols. 53v–54r.

[175] *PD* (prose), c. 21–22, 27, 33 and *PD* (metric), fols. 23v, 34v.

[176] Ed. G. Waitz in MGH SS 15/1, pp. 1–3. Levillain claims Hilduin wrote the *Revelatio*. He asserts that the *Dedicatario altaris* is essentially a historical (by which he presumably means accurate) account. Léon Levillain, review of M. Buchner, *Das Vizepapstum des Abtes von St. Denis* in *Le Moyen Age*, 2nd series 30 (1929), pp. 85–95. Many copies of the *Revelatio* and *Dedicatio* survive (the BHL lists 46). They are often transmitted with other works relating to the saint, including Hilduin's prose *PD* and the prefatory letters (BHL: http://bhlms.fltr.ucl.ac.be; accessed May 5, 2010).

[177] These pieces relate Pope Stephen II's healing by Dionysius at Saint-Denis, his dedication of an altar, and his anointment of Pippin, the first Carolingian king there in 754. On the dating and authenticity of the *Clausula de unctione*, preserved in a single witness, a late-tenth-century manuscript of the *Miracula* of Gregory of Tours (Brussels, KBR, MS 7666–7671, fols. 96v–97r), see M. Buchner, *Die Clausula de unctione Pippini: eine Fälschung aus dem Jahre 880* (Paderborn, 1926); Léon Levillain, "De l'authenticité de la Clausula de unctione Pippini," *BEC* 88 (1927): 20–42; Thomas Noble, *The Republic of St Peter: The Birth of the Papal*

Dionysius appears shiny-haired and magnificently attired in a purple under-shirt and a pallium ornamented with gold stars.

Hilduin counters potential objections to his obscure sources by suggest-ing that the critics examine them in the archive.[178] The *curiosus* "can even borrow the Greek sources from which we drew this."[179] He can make this offer because, as their survival attests, he had not only imagined his sources, but had also written them or overseen their production. The archives were full of Dionysius's newly created past. The creation of so much evidence represents a vast effort. Together with the works openly produced by or under Hilduin (such as the *Annales Regni Francorum*, Dionysius's *Miracula*, and the translation of the Pseudo-Dionysian corpus) as well as liturgy and building projects, we can see the energy that Hilduin invested in shaping, supporting, and promoting his patron saint.[180]

TRUTH AND SANCTITY

Hilduin's insistence on the saint's veracity and his use of supporting evidence are extreme by contemporary standards.[181] We can see his efforts

State, 680–825 (Philadelphia, 1984), p. 87; Rosamund McKitterick, "Power in the Carolingian Annals," *EHR* (2000): 7–8; McKitterick, *History and Memory*, p. 141; I. Haselbach, *Aufstieg und Herrschaft der Karlinger in der Darstellung der sogenannten Annales Mettenses priores* (Lübeck, 1970), pp. 193–200. The *Revelatio* claims to be a letter from Pope Stephen and is quoted as such in the *Saxon Annals* for 753 (ed. D.G. Waitz, in MGH SS 6, p. 556).

[178] Hilduin, *omnibus filiis*, p. 337: "for if one does not deign to believe it, nonetheless if he sets out without any arrogance, he shall readily discover for himself where, in what manner, and in what order all the aforementioned things occurred. If he does not have the full contingent of books, he will be able to borrow them from our Church archive" (Nam et si eis credere dignatus non fuerit, ille sibi tamen sine quolibet supercilio prodet [corrected from *prodent*], ubi haec universa, et qualiter ac quo ordine dicta manifeste reperiat. Ipsorumque librorum plenitudinem, si indiguerit, mutuare ab archivo ecclesiae nostrae quibit).

[179] Hilduin, *Rescriptum*, c. 3: "curiosus autem ex Grecorum fontibus, unde et nos illam sumpsimus, poterit mutuare."

[180] E.A.R. Brown, "Saint Carpus, Saint Denis, and Benign Jesus: The Economy of Salvation at Saint-Denis" (forthcoming); McKitterick, *History and Memory*, p. 103. On Hilduin's contributions to liturgy at Saint-Denis, see Michel Huglo, "Les chants de la <<missa graeca>> de Saint-Denis," in *Essays Presented to Egon Wellesz*, ed. Jack Westrup (Oxford, 1966), pp. 74–83, at p. 74. Huglo suggests that the liturgy of Dionysius from the late-ninth-century Compiègne antiphonary is Hilduin's. The hymn from this antiph-onary is printed in René-Jean Hesbert, *Corpus Antiphonalium Officii*, Rerum ecclesias-ticarum documenta (Rome, 1963), pp. 312–314, and PL 78, cols. 807–808. Théry, noting the parallels of the hymn *Coeli cives adplaudite* with Hilduin's prose *PD*, argues that Hilduin speciously attributed his own composition to Eugenius.

[181] We find later examples of scholars falsifying the archives to support the new version of history. Hincmar followed in his master's footsteps, creating documents, such as a letter from Saint Benedict to Remigius. Hincmar, *Praefatio* to *Vita Remigii* (BHL 7152–7162),

as an example of "Carolingian historical-mindedness," but writers before and after him saw no need for such elaborate evidence and argumentation.[182] Writers do not usually preface lives with repeated truth claims and lengthy source description and analysis. (The best parallel we find for Hilduin's method is in his student Hincmar's prose *Vita Remigii*.)[183] When writers mention source analysis at all, it is in general terms, asserting their rejection of falsehoods in favor of the truth, but rarely explaining the principles used to distinguish the two.[184] Writers also assert the lack of reliable sources and describe the creative ways they supplemented them, relying on divine inspiration or their own imagination.[185] The commonly

---

ed. Bruno Krusch, MGH SRM 3, pp. 250ff.; see Michael Moore, "Prologue," *Teaching and Learning in Northern Europe, 1000–1200*, ed. Sally Vaughn and Jay Rubenstein (Turnhout, 2006), p. 30. On Bishop Gerard I creating supporting documentation for the *Gesta Episcoporum Cameracensium* in the eleventh century, see Robert M. Stein, *Reality Fictions: Romance, History, and Governmental Authority, 1025–1180* (Notre Dame, 2006), p. 18.

[182] McKitterick, *History and Memory*, p. 273.

[183] Hincmar, *Vita Remigii*, pp. 250ff.

[184] The following examples are from prose works. The writer of the *Vita sanctorum abbatum Acaunensium* complains about the *confusae fabulae* that he had to omit and insists that in order to edify believers "it is necessary to impress the truth in letters" (necessarium litteris est veritatem adsignari; c. 1, MGH SRM 3, p. 174). The author of the *Vita Carileffi* (BHL 1568) in a tenth-century manuscript did not want to be a "fabricator of deception" (fallendi … artifex), and so did not use false works, but only those "found written in ancient volumes or by the inhabitants of the place where the holy man was converted" (quae aut in antiquis repperi scripta voluminbus aut ab incolis loci illius, in quo sanctus vir conversatus est; c. 1 in ibid., p. 389). The *Vita Leutifredi* (BHL 4899) uses material "from ancient records and mostly related to us by the elders" (ex antiquariis monumentis partimque relatione maiorum nobis; c. 1 in MGH SRM 7, p. 8). The author of the *Miracula Martini Vertavensis* (BHL 5568) says that fire had destroyed the book of the saint's life at Thouars and that he had drawn on the surviving *volumen exiguum* containing *carmina* including a short rhythmic life (*praef.*, MGH SRM 3, p. 567). The author of the *Vita Desiderii* (BHL 2148) vouches for his sources by noting the antiquity of the parchment on which they were written: "I transcribed these things, full of truth, just as I saw them entered in the more ancient parchments for you" (plena veritate, sicut in membranis antiquioribus insertum vidi, … transposui; c. 7, ibid., pp. 647–648). Others claim to rely on their own experience or eyewitnesses. Balther, in his *Vita Fridolini* (BHL 3170), c. 22, says witnesses had seen the miracles or they had related them from an older tradition that they knew to be true (how they knew this, he does not say; ibid., p. 364). The author of the *Vita Caesarii* (BHL 1508) names his two leading witnesses in c. 1 (ibid., p. 457). The author of the late-eighth-century *Vita Eucherii* (BHL 2260) claims to have consulted the most truthful of the saint's peers (*praef.*, MGH SRM 7, p. 46).

[185] Hucbald of Saint-Amand, in 907, in his preface to the *VR*, claims to draw on nuns' recollections of a source, a lost text mediated by oral tradition, that is simultaneously ancient and unverifiable. In the mid-ninth century, in the preface to his prose *Vita Maximini* (BHL 5824), Lupus of Ferrières laments that there are few pieces of evidence "and among these are found some resembling fables" (et in his ipsis quaedam fabulosis inveneniuntur similia). He says that he set aside the things that could impugn the

stated purpose of prose lives (including Hilduin's), to provoke admiration and imitation, is unrelated to the narrative's historical accuracy.[186] Underlying motivations for writing (such as the aggrandizement of the author, saint, and abbey) are similarly unaffected by the specific historical truth, narrowly understood, as opposed to the message's broader divine truth.[187] Even stories far outside the audience's experience of the world, such as Jerome's *vita* of the apocryphal desert father Paul with its mythical beasts, or the passions of the dog-headed Christopher, did not demand such support.[188]

Given that saints need not be criticized for implausibility (miracles are by definition contrary to everyday experience), it seems that the rejection of the revamped Dionysius was not theological but political, directed at Hilduin, who must have made enemies among both Louis's and Lothar's partisans by supporting the son in the first rebellion but, not overtly, in the second. As a means for the abbot's self-promotion, the upstart Areopagite would have attracted his enemies' hostility.[189]

On closer inspection, Hilduin undermines his insistence on the truth and hints that he expects more educated readers to see beyond his fervent proclamations. In the epic passion, Hilduin introduces the apocryphal letter to Apollophanius (which he leaves unversified), saying, "it is preserved in its own speech for all to read, so that I might not seem [or be seen] to have transgressed and to boldly attack with other words this thing, which is made from the saint's utterance."[190] The subjunctive in this negative purpose clause *ne videar* is ambivalent ("lest I seem" *or* "lest

---

credibility of the rest and, hampered by too little evidence, relied on divine grace rather than on his own intellect. Ed. Bruno Krusch in MGH SRM 3, p. 74; cf. *Gloriosae*, c. 1.

[186] Hilduin, *omnibus filiis*, p. 336: "gesta bene viventium elementa sunt vitam volentium et exempla martyrum exortationes sunt martyriorum" (the deeds of the living, accomplished well, are the first principles of those wanting life and the examples of the martyrs provide the incitement to martyrdom).

[187] Richard Landes, *Relics, Apocalypse, and the Deceits of History: Ademar of Chabannes, 989–1034* (Cambridge, MA, 1995).

[188] On Jerome's *Vita Pauli* (BHL 6596, written ca. 374) and other outlandish narratives, see Aviad Kleinberg, *Flesh Made Word: Saints' Stories and the Western Imagination*, trans. Jane Marie Todd (Cambridge, MA, 2008), pp. 151–163. Patricia Cox Miller, "Jerome's Centaur: A Hyper-Icon of the Desert," *Journal of Early Christian Studies* 4 (1996): 209–233.

[189] Similarly the objections of the monks of Blandin about the proliferation of Saint-Bavo's saints, discussed in Chapter 5, are political rather than theological.

[190] Fols. 14v–15r: "Quam ne transgressus aliis invadere verbis / Audacter videar constructam famine sancti, / Servatur proprio cunctis sermone legenda." More literally it reads "So that, having transgressed, I would not seem with other words to attack (or take possession of) ..."

I be seen"), and grammatically it is not clear that the past participle *transgressus* is negated. So, Hilduin can be read as saying that he had transgressed, but did not wish it to appear so. Hilduin actually describes his pseudo-pseudo-Dionysian letter accurately – Latin prose is indeed "its own speech" (because it had never existed in a Greek original), and, because it draws heavily on the canonical letter to Polycarp and Hilduin's translation of Pseudo-Dionysius, it is "built out of the saint's words" although not written by him. Only someone familiar with the Greek codex of Pseudo-Dionysius (presumably a small circle at Saint-Denis) would know that it did not contain this letter and would see that Hilduin had taken literally Pseudo-Dionysius's rhetorical suggestion that his reader fill in the details.

The *Clausula de unctione Pippini* also uses the subjunctive of *videri* in an ambivalent statement about the text's origin: "if you wish, reader, to know in what times this little book *would seem* to have been written or produced for the precious praise of the holy martyrs, you will find it in the year seven hundred and sixty seven from the birth of our lord. . . ."[191] The text does not actually say it was written in 767, but only that this would *appear* to be the case.[192]

Few readers would have seen that Hilduin undermined his own truth claims. Because, however, Carolingians privileged the cryptic, such subtle tactics redounded to a writer's reputation. Carolingian literature worked on multiple levels, providing different messages to readers and audiences depending on how much culture and education they shared with the writer. A work intended to persuade some readers could contain inside jokes for others.

Whether or not Hilduin self-consciously undermined his arguments for a select audience, the evidence for his Areopagite saint seems unlikely to have convinced the intransigent critics. The tradition of separate saints was well established (they had different feast days and were reputed to have lived centuries apart) and supported by authorities. Perhaps, however, Hilduin's aim was not necessarily to persuade the most educated readers of his saint's authenticity, as much as to impress them with his rhetorical abilities and sophistical skill in dissecting and creating evidence. Another

---

[191] *De unctione Pippini regis nota monachi S. Dionysii*, ed. G. Waitz in MGH SS 15/1, p. 1: "si nosse vis, lector, quibus hic libellus temporibus videatur esse conscriptus vel ad sacrorum martirum preciosam editum laudem, invenies anno ab incarnatione Domini septingentesimo sexagesimo septimo. . . ." As McKitterick points out, it then spends a disproportionate amount of time establishing the date (*History and Memory*, p. 140).

[192] Hilduin imitates Pseudo-Dionysius in ironically undermining his own assertions. See the following on the *Visio Carpi*.

way of impressing the readers was by infusing the passions with Pseudo-Dionysian theology.

PSEUDO-DIONYSIAN PASSIONS

Pseudo-Dionysius was a Neoplatonist who used complementary kataphatic, symbolic, and apophatic theologies to discuss how the soul could rise toward the divine. Contemplation of things perceived could lead to the contemplation of abstract ideas. In Pseudo-Dionysian mysticism, human approach to the divine could begin with the senses and proceed by the intellect, but ultimately, it must transcend language and cognition (*super sermonem enim et mentem*).[193] Pseudo-Dionysius, as befits his Scriptural persona, draws on Paul's teaching on God's ineffability.[194] The hierarch assisted this ascent by presenting his superior understanding to others in symbolic terms. In the *Divine Names*, Pseudo-Dionysius discusses the possibility and limitations of contemplating God with the symbols of Scripture and hymns given to humankind through revelation. He explains that the best symbols do not resemble their object. We might mistake a similar symbol for its object, but there is no such risk in contemplating a dissimilar symbol, such as a worm for God in *Psalms*.[195] Dissimilar symbols shield true meaning in paradox or in troubling images that demand the reader's attention. Their incongruity goads the reader to ponder them (*CH* 2.3, 2.5), and in this way they are both concealing and uplifting.[196]

Ultimately, however, human understanding and language cannot grasp God, and union with the divine is shrouded in a mystical darkness. The apophatic way (*via negativa*) to God, the subject of the *Mystical Theology*, requires the negation of all categories, even negation. Hilduin plays with this negation of apophatic expression, saying that in the *Mystical Theology*, Dionysius "established these things through kataphasis and not through apophasis."[197]

Although few of Hilduin's Western contemporaries had read Pseudo-Dionysius, they could have encountered references to his writings. Gregory the Great invokes him as an authority (*antiquus videlicet et venerabilis Pater*) on the ranks of angels, although implies that he has not read him

---

[193] *DN* 1.1, cf. *DN* 11.2.
[194] Rom. 1:33, 2 Cor. 9:15, Phil. 4:7, all quoted in Ep. 5.
[195] *CH* 2.2, Ps. 22:6.
[196] *CH* 1.2; *CH* 2.3, in Hilduin's translation: "excitans autem quo sursum ducitur anima."
[197] *PD* (metric), fol. 13r: "per cataphasin illa struit nec non apophasin."

(fertur vero Dionysius Areopagita ...).[198] Writers referred to him during the eighth- and ninth-century iconoclasm debates. At the council of Rome in 769, Pope Stephen quotes his letter to John to discuss images: "in truth, images are clearly visible invisible things."[199] He also includes a translation from the *Celestial Hierarchy*:

For the aforementioned incorporeal ranks are depicted in diverse colors and compositions, which he relates through various colors, so that we ourselves might go, if quietly and with a pious mind, through the most sacred likenesses to the single and incorporeal things; since it is impossible with our mind to reach *(pertingere)* toward these incorporeal things in imitation of the heavenly army and the vision, unless we will be able, through visible elements, to perceive the invisible and most beautiful likeness and the visible and fragrant images show the invisible, conveyed in a manner open to reason.[200]

In 825, the Council of Paris used identical citations.[201] So, the concept of perceptible things as symbols for the imperceptible was associated with the theologian, as was the idea that the ascension from the former to the latter required a quiet and pious mind. Since Hilduin summarizes and excerpts his own translations of the Pseudo-Dionysian writings, a reader without prior knowledge of the theology could discern many of his passions' subsequent allusions, which then operate as a kind of instant intertextuality.

As Pseudo-Dionysius's theology prescribes, Hilduin employs symbolism to teach about the divine. The cephalophoric saint is a dissimilar symbol. Carrying its head like a war trophy *(exuvia)* in its dangling arms

---

[198] Gregorius Magnus, *Homiliae in Evangelia*, ed. Raymond Étaix, CCSL 141 (Turnhout, 1999), 1, 12, 34. Pope Hadrian writes to Charlemagne in 791: "Sanctus Dyonisius Areopagita, qui et episcopus Athiniensis, valde nimirum laudatus est a sancto Gregorio papa, confirmans eum antiquum patrem et doctorem esse. Iste sub temporibus apostolorum fuit, ut in actibus apostolorum monstratur" (ed. K. Hampe, MGH Ep. 5, p. 32).

[199] "In veritate et manifeste imagines sunt visibiles invisibilia." *Concilium Romanum*, A. 769, fragment g, ed. Albert Werminghoff, in MGH Concilia 2.1, p. 91. See Andrew Louth, "Truly Visible Things are Manifest Images of Invisible Things: Dionysios the Areopagite on Knowing the Invisible," in *Seeing the Invisible in Late Antiquity and the Early Middle Ages*, ed. Giselle de Nie, Karl F. Morrison, and Marco Mostert (Turnhout, 2005), p. 16.

[200] "Predicta enim incorporea agmina diversis coloribus effigurantur, et conpositionibus variosas per colores tradidit, quatenus si tacite nosmet ipsas per sacratissimas effigies ad simplices et incorporales pia mente transeamus; etenim impossibile est nostra mente ad incorporea illa pertingere caelestis militiae imitatione visionemque, nisi per elementorum poterimus per visibilem ad invisibilem pulcherrimamque attingi effigiem et visibiles odoriferasque imagines rationali traditione invisibiles prefulgi ..." The reference is to *Celestial Hierarchy* 1.3. The Latin grammar is not entirely clear.

[201] *Consilium Parisiense*, ed. Albert Werminghoff, MGH Concilia 2.2, p. 512.

(*brachia pendula*), it is a jarring image for spiritual perfection.[202] As such, it is the best sort of image – one that disturbs the readers and forces them to work to understand it. In Hilduin's passions, the separation of the head (which, for Pseudo-Dionysius, signifies the mind) from the body symbolizes the final mystical union of the saint and God.[203] The body immediately rose from the ground, signifying its own ultimate resurrection (*EH* 1.7, 7.I.2). The eloquent orator passed beyond the powers of human cognition.

In death, the saint became a paradoxical speaker of the ineffable. Finally, he was not a practitioner of kataphasis, the outpouring of language, which Pseudo-Dionysius discusses in the *Divine Names*: ordinary language cannot express God; Scripture and Hymns are the appropriate language of praise. As soon as their heads hit the ground, the souls of Dionysius and his fellow martyrs returned to God (*animas retulere tonanti*).[204] Nonetheless, they appeared to continue speaking: "although they had been decapitated, their tongues were thought still to confess the Lord Jesus Christ."[205] The saints, like the angels of the *Celestial Hierarchy*, did not verbalize their experience of the divine, but rather resorted to standard praises and hymns. The angelic chorus sang "Alleluia," which Pseudo-Dionysius alludes to in the *Ecclesiastical Hierarchy*.[206] Singing, Dionysius picked up his head and walked to his resting place. The missionary and writer who had possessed the "excessive eloquence of evil old age," as the prefect characterized him, was silenced, but in his place the perfected saint sang the ultimate praises.[207] Dionysius uttered the language of the dead; God spoke through Dionysius's body.

Accompanying the kataphasis is its inverse, apophasis. Hilduin takes the worn *topos* that a saint's countless miracles defy the writer's capacities and gives it an apophatic twist: "not only is speech unable to recount the signs of these miracles, but they cannot even be grasped by human

---

[202] *PD* (prose), c. 32.
[203] *DN.* 9.5. If the incorporeal soul were considered in terms of a body, the head would represent the intellect. In Hilduin's translation: "et caput quidem mentem ... dicimus."
[204] *PD* (metric), fol. 33r: "returning their bodies to the earth, they bore their blessed souls to heaven" (reddentes terrae corpora, beatas caelo animas intulerunt; c. 31).
[205] *PD* (prose), c. 31: "amputatis capitibus adhuc putaretur lingua palpitans Jesum Christum Dominum confiteri." *Gloriosae*, c. 25; Ovid, *Metamorphoses* 6, 558–560. Hilduin borrows the morbid Ovidian allusion to Philomela's writhing dismembered tongue from the *Gloriosae*. Maurice Coens, "Nouvelles recherches sur un thème hagiographique: la céphalophorie," *Recueil d'études bollandiennes par Maurice Coens* (Brussells, 1963), p. 26.
[206] *PD* (prose), c. 10, 32; (metric), fols. 11v, 34r.
[207] *PD* (prose), c. 26: "pessimae senectutis nimia eloquentia."

minds."[208] An unspeakable light (*lux ineffabilis; lux haud effabilis ulli*) shines on the cephalophore.[209] The songs of the angelic choruses also illustrate Pseudo-Dionysian ideas about the limits of human understanding: some can be perceived by the senses (*sensualiter Alleluia concinere*) and others by the intellect.[210] Others exist on a higher level: "they were singing these and other things that are not able to be perceived by the mind."[211]

Hilduin uses dissimilar symbols, kataphasis, and apophasis in both his passions, but the distinctive nature of epic verse allows him to enact another Pseudo-Dionysian teaching, leading the reader, through the contemplation of perceptible things, to the imperceptible. He uses dense, allusive, difficult poetic language to create an anagogic text.

JEWELED VERSE

Epic *vitae* were made colorful and challenging to exhibit the writer's skill and to impress, amuse, and edify the *sagax lector*. As Walafrid Strabo says, versifying a life spices up the rustic prose dish (*aliquibus metrorum condimentis*).[212] The epic *Passio Dionysii*, like much Carolingian poetry, is written in an erudite "hermeneutic" mode that features lofty and obscure vocabulary, including Greek words and copious allusions to Classical and Christian sources.[213] It is similar to the "jeweled style" of late antiquity, with its interlocking word order, rhetorical ornamentation, and vivid imagery.[214]

The augmentation (*amplificatio*) of texts, like the transformation of prose into verse, was an exercise taught in the monastic classroom, and poets supplemented their prose sources in various ways.[215] Works translated into heroic verse usually expand on the prose originals, as Hilduin acknowledges:

---

[208] *PD* (prose), c. 36: "Quorum miraculorum insignia, non solum sermo non pravalet enarrare; verum nec ipsis queunt humanis mentibus comprehendi"; *PD* (metric), fol. 33v.

[209] *PD* (prose) c. 32; (metric), fol 33v.

[210] *PD* (prose), c. 10.

[211] Ibid., c. 32: "haec et alia, quorum intellectus non potuit percepi concinebat."

[212] Walafrid, preface (BHL 3246t) to prose *Vita Galli* (BHL 3247), MGH SRM 4, p. 282.

[213] Michael Lapidge, "The Hermeneutic Style in Tenth-Century Anglo-Latin Literature," *ASE* 4 (1975): 67–111.

[214] Michael Roberts, *The Jeweled Style: Poetry and Poetics in Late Antiquity* (Ithaca, 1989).

[215] Michael Roberts, *Biblical Epic and Rhetorical Paraphrase in Late Antiquity* (Liverpool, 1985); Dolbeau, "Domaine negligé," p. 137.

I'm allowed to tell the full course of the matter so that on the winding path
The appointed line of the deeds recount
Nothing more or less than the matter requires
Nonetheless, this verbose tragic actor is able to capture the themes
And to stretch out the full scenes with songs of lament.[216]

The verse *Passio* follows its source closely, but as is typical of epic *vitae*, amplifies it with Classical mythological allusions, asides to the reader, addresses to the saint, and poetic metaphor.[217] Like other epic lives, it emphasizes the marvelous and the heroic, stressing the saint's suffering (Dionysius is often called *heros*), and the cephalophory.[218]

A comparison of corresponding passages illustrates differences between the *passiones*.[219] The prose introduces the *Divine Names* with barely any description, incorrectly equating it with the lost or apocryphal *Symbolic Theology* and noting the precision and orthodoxy of the theologian's argument.[220] The verse takes more than twice as many words:

The father, conspicuous in piety and eloquent in speech,
So that he might justly double the talents handed over
And build the temples of God with collected teachings,
Did not refrain from completing his gracious labor
And with these writings he repeatedly enriches the faithful man of God.
So, he sent to nurturing Timothy the third book,
Which he calls *On Symbolic Theology*
In which, in a series of teachings, as a greening crop,
he argues from orthodoxy, proceeding in an exact manner.[221]

---

[216] Fol. 34v: "Quod super est narrare libet ne tramite flexo/ Linea gestorum plenum sortita tenorem / Quid minus aut supra quam res petit ipsa reponat / Thema loquax tamen hic posset captare tragedus / Cantibus et querulis amplas distendere scenas."

[217] Approximately 18,000 and 10,000 words, respectively.

[218] Tilliette, "Modèles," p. 393.

[219] For another comparison of the verse and prose, see Lapidge, "Lost Passio," pp. 70–72.

[220] PD (prose), c. 11: "[Dionysius] also composed a third volume of these, *On the Divine Names*, which he also calls *On Symbolic Theology* arguing in it with precision and according to orthodoxy as he was able" (Tertium quoque ipsi conscripsit tomum de divinis nominibus, quem et apellat de symbolica theologia, examussim et orthodoxe, ut sufficit, in eo disputans). The *Symbolic Theology* is one of several texts Pseudo-Dionysius mentions that was either lost or never written.

[221] Fols. 11v–12r: "Insignis pietate pater facundus et ore / Ut sibi congeminet contradita iure talenta / Edificetque dei collato dogmate templa / Haud parcit scriptis gratum praestare laborem / Hisque virum crebro domini ditare fidelem / Tertius unde liber Timotheo mittitur almo / Quem de symbolica prescribit theologia / In cuius serie doctrinae fruge virente / Disputat orthodoxe examussimque retractans."

The verse draws language from the prose (e.g., pairing *examussim, ortho-doxe*), but drastically inflates the material. The first five lines add no information.

The poet adds a botanical (and Scriptural) metaphor "frux virens" to characterize Dionysius's work.[222] Visual imagery is one way that the poem augments and ornaments its source. For example, the prose uses a brief floral metaphor to describe the saint's selection of Scriptural passages: "he wrote a useful letter, fragrant with examples and witnesses from the Scriptures, in the manner of a wreath, gathered from the bountiful field of holy Writ."[223] The verse elaborates the trope of Scripture as flowers:

> Fragrant with the scent of virtue, it was offered to that man.
> Clearly blossoming with the flowers of sacred Scripture,
> The wreath flourishes as with violets and shining privet,
> Which the little field of the holy word once adorned.[224]

Ager in the prose becomes the poetic diminutive *agellus*, and the field bursts into bloom with purple and white flowers. Hilduin's verse employs other visual language, especially, as we will see, numerous images of light and dark.[225]

USE YOUR ALLUSION

Hermeneutic poetry is highly allusive. The references make the work more dense and subtle by invoking material that only a highly educated reader would recognize. The epic *passio* alludes to the canonical authors of the Carolingian classroom:[226] Cicero, Virgil, Ovid, Lucan, and Horace among the Classical sources and Fortunatus, Prudentius, Prosper of Aquitaine, Paulinus of Nola, Bede, and Aldhelm among the Christian.[227] The epic

---

[222] See the Conclusion to this book for a discussion of the Scriptural trope of the sower.

[223] *PD* (prose), c. 15: "utilem scripsit epistolam, exemplis ac Scripturarum testimoniis in modum serti, de agro pleno sacrae Scripturae . . . collecti redolentem."

[224] Fol 16r: "Est porrecta viro virtutis odore redolens / Floribus et sacrae scripturae sane virescens / Floret uti sertum violis nitidisque ligustris / Quod sacri quondam verbi decorauit agellus."

[225] Examples of other metaphors include the flower-scented book (*redolenti flore volumen*, fol. 11r) and the characterization of martyrdom as rosey or rose red, for example, *rosea . . . palma* (fol. 1v); *rosei triumphi* (fol. 19v); *rosea corona* (fol. 21r). The snake stands for the persecuting emperor Domitian (fols. 24r–26r).

[226] Lapidge, "Lost Passio," p. 76, lists Christian and Classical sources.

[227] Hilduin borrows Eulalia's angelic retinue for describing the vision of Carpus; cf. "angelico comitata choro" (Prudentius, *Peristephanon* 3.48) and "Angelicusque chorus Ihesum comitatus" (fol. 18v).

uses more Classical allusion, vocabulary, tropes, and imagery than does the prose.[228] Hilduin litters the poem with Virgilian phrases such as *fama volat* (fol. 27r) and *mirabile dictu* (13v). Like earlier Christian poets, he co-opts pagan religious terms: God is called *Tonans* (the Thunderer, an epithet of Jupiter), Christ is depicted as Apollo, wine is personified as Bacchus, heaven is Olympus, and hell is Tartarus or Erebus.[229]

The passions pun on the similarity of the saint's name to that of the Greek god of wine, Dionysus (Hilduin's letters also play on this through the recurrent wine metaphor).[230] By characterizing the saint's persecutors raging like *bacchantes* (female followers of Dionysus),[231] Hilduin likens the saint to the mythical Greek poet Orpheus. According to Classical sources, Orpheus was torn apart by *bacchantes* and, like the saint's fellow martyrs Eleutherius and Rusticus, he was thrown into a river.[232] A temple was founded where his singing head washed ashore on Lesbos, and pilgrims visited it to hear oracular pronouncements.[233]

---

[228] For example, the poet uses the particularly Virgilian line ending "mirabile dictu" on fol. 13v; for example, Virgil, *Georgics* 2.30; 3.275; *Aeneid* 1.439, 2.174, 4.182, 7.64, 8.252.

[229] Christ as Phoebus, fol. 14r; Bacchus, 1r; Olympus and Erebus, 1r, 29v, 28v; Tartarus, 29v.

[230] Hilduin says Dionysius was not from "Semele or Deucalion," in reference to the god Dionysus's mother and a Greek mythological figure who refounded humanity after the flood, respectively (c. 5, fol. 5r). The verse line begins "non inquam Semele" (fol. 5r), cf. Ovid, *Fasti*, III. 715 on the *Liberalia*, a feast of Bacchus / Dionysius, "nec referam Semelen." Hilduin, in his letters, uses images of the wine-press, wine measure, toasting, and drunkenness (*Rescriptum*, c. 2; *omnibus filiis*, p. 336).

[231] *PD* (metric), fols. 26r ("Progrediturque celer bachantum more per orbem") and 27r ("Dirus et ipse furor bachantum sane uirorum"); *PD* (prose), c. 24 ("Persecutionis ergo publicat sententia, iniquorum gaudens turba in omnem mundi partem bacchando progreditur"). Cf. Horace, *Odes* 3.3, lines 53–55 ("quicumque mundo terminus obstitit . . . qua parte debacchentur ignes"). The lovesick Dido is likened to a bacchante in Virgil, *Aeneid*, 4.301ff.

[232] Virgil, *Georgics*, 4.453–527, ed. Fredericus Arturus Hirtzel, *P. Vergili Maronis Opera* (Oxford, 1900); Ovid, *Metamorphoses*, ed. R.J. Tarrant (Oxford, 2004), 10.1–142, 11.1–66. On Orpheus in the Middle Ages, see André Boutemy, "Une version médiévale inconnue de la légende d'Orphée," in *Hommages à Joseph Bidez et à Franz Cumont* (Brussels, 1949), pp. 43–70; Peter Dronke, "The Return of Eurydice," *Classica et Mediaevalia* 23 (1963): 253–294; Klaus Heitmann, "Orpheus im Mittelalter," *Archiv für Kulturgeschichte* 45 (1963): 253; John Block Friedman, *Orpheus in the Middle Ages* (Cambridge, MA, 1970); E. Irwin, "The Songs of Orpheus and the New Song of Christ," in *Orpheus: The Metamorphoses of a Myth*, ed. John Warden (Toronto, 1985), pp. 51–62; and, in the same volume, P. Vicari, "Sparagmos: Orpheus among the Christians," pp. 63–84; C. Stephen Jaeger, "Orpheus in the Eleventh Century," *MJ* 27 (1992): 141–168; Jaeger, *Envy*, pp. 143ff.; chap. 1, "Orpheus among the Barbarians," in Godman, *Poets*.

[233] On Orpheus's oracular head, see W. Déonna, "Orphée et l'oracle de la tête coupée," *Revue des études greques* 38 (1925): 44–69. On decapitated heads as "accoutrements" for prophesy, see Alice Sperduti, "The Divine Nature of Poetry in Antiquity," *TAPA* 81 (1950): 22, n. 54.

The poet makes the parallels of Dionysius and Orpheus more explicit. Like Orpheus, Hilduin's Dionysius is an *oraculum*, both a priest and a prophet, who utters divine pronouncements (*mystica orsa*) and prognostications.[234] Hilduin similarly describes the saint as a *vatis* (meaning both priest and poet).[235] The verse contains eight lines (unparalleled in the prose) explaining that a prediction Dionysius sang (*canere*), came true.[236] *Canere*, as Servius states in his *Aeneid* commentary, means "to sing about," "to praise," and "to prophesize."[237] The emphasis on Dionysius singing – also more pronounced in the verse (as befits a *carmen*) further likens the saint to the first poet Orpheus and the poet Hilduin. The verse also borrows from Virgil's description of Orpheus's death to create a hellish synthesis of the Roman and Christian underworlds.[238]

The first poet of Classical tradition – who can move stones and trees with his song and even evoke compassion from the rulers of the dead – is an appealing figure for the priest-poet Hilduin. Orpheus provides a literary ancestor akin to his Christian forefather Dionysius.[239] As Ovid uses the divine poet Orpheus to frame tales of ill-fated love, Hilduin uses the saintly writer Pseudo-Dionysius to embed stories by excerpting the saints' letters.[240] Unlike Ovid, and unlike other epic *vitae*, which typically feature long speeches, the epic *Passio Dionysii* emphasizes the *written* nature of the protagonist's communication.[241] In this way also, Hilduin implicitly likens the saint to himself as a writer. So, like Pseudo-Dionysius and Orpheus, Hilduin is a *vatis*, a priest-poet whose words transcend death.

---

[234] *PD* (prose), c. 16–17; (metric), fols. 10v, 20r.

[235] Ibid., fol. 19v. On the Classical association of prophesy, priesthood, and poetry, see Sperduti, "Divine Nature," pp. 209–240. Medieval Christian poets adopted the religious terminology for poetry (such as *vates* and *carmen*) from the Augustan poets, including Virgil and Horace.

[236] *PD* (metric), fols. 19v–20r.

[237] Servius, *Comm. In Aen.* 1.1; Irvine, *Textual Culture*, p. 133.

[238] Hilduin, in the epic, uses *Tartarus* and *Styx* and mentions the *Eumenides* (furies) with their *angues* (snakes). In Virgil (*Georgics* 4.470, 480–484), Cerberus the dog of Hades is agape (*inhiare*), whereas in Hilduin Tartarus itself gapes (*hiscare*, fol. 29v).

[239] Fortunatus, *Praefatio*, in MGH AA 4.1, ed. F. Leo, p. 2. Fortunatus describes himself as a new Orpheus (*novus Orpheus lyricus*). See also his *Carmen* 7.1.1, which begins with Orpheus (ibid., p. 153). Orpheus (or the "Thracian priest") appears in Carolingian verse as a generic poet, for example, Alcuin 18 (MGH Poetae 1, p. 240); Sedulius Scottus, *Carmina* II, VI, and XLIX (MGH Poetae 3, pp. 172–174, 211).

[240] Ovid, *Metamorphoses*, 10.

[241] In the epic, Hilduin (fol. 19r) states that "the *documents* conveyed to Demophilus establish such things" (talia Dimofilo constant documenta relata). The corresponding prose (c. 15), reads "these things were *spoken* to Demophilus" (Haec ad Demophilum dicta sunt).

Many features that distinguish Hilduin's epic *passio* from his prose are the characteristic ornamental elements of Carolingian poetry, but Hilduin does not use them simply for embellishment. Rather, by drawing on the difficult and imagistic qualities of poetry and the ways a reader approached verse, the epic enacts a central principle of Pseudo-Dionysian mysticism in which the teacher leads the initiate to higher understanding (*DN* 1.4). Hilduin draws on the medium's potential to imbue the saint's entire story with Pseudo-Dionysian meaning and purpose.

CONTEMPLATING SALVATION

As the only piece of canonical Pseudo-Dionysian prose that Hilduin versi-fies in the epic passion, the vision of Carpus from the letter to Demophilus provides insight into the functions of prose and verse. The *visio* tells of the holy Carpus who, bitter at apostates from his flock, had a vision of the men in a snake-infested pit. When Carpus refused to help, Christ rescued them and rebuked Carpus for lacking charity. Pseudo-Dionysius prefaces the account by admonishing his addressee Demophilus to be in the right frame of mind and not laugh, tacitly acknowledging that the story could seem ridiculous. Nevertheless, he insists it is true. In the verse *passio*, Hilduin paraphrases the theologian's introduction to the episode:

> "If," he [Dionysius] said, "you have good will towards me in your soul,
> This divine vision will now be conveyed openly to you.
> It was shown, once upon a time, to a holy man.
> You will not be able to absorb it properly, if you are snickering
> Although evidently I speak true things and I do not pursue trifles."[242]

Pseudo-Dionysius (in the original Greek letter and in both Hilduin's Latin versions) begins by saying that he heard the story while in Crete, thus appealing to the ancient stereotype that Cretans were notorious liars, and immediately undermining his claim about the story's veracity.[243]

---

[242] Fol. 17r: "Est, ait, est animo tibimet si grata voluntas / Visio tradetur iam nunc divina patenter / Est ostensa viro quodam quae tempore sancto / Quam dignam nulli poteris aptare cachinno / Nimirum cum vera loquar nec frivola secter."

[243] The mendacious Cretan of Latin and Greek literature is most famously used by Dionysius's putative mentor Paul who, in Titus 1:12–13, quotes a Cretan saying "all Cretans are liars" and then asserts the truth of this Cretan's statement. (This is the famous "liar paradox.") Pseudo-Dionysius similarly asserts the truth of his tale. Greek examples of the trope include Odysseus's fabrication of a Cretan background (*Odyssey* 13.256ff.; 14.191ff.; 19.165ff.; see Adele J. Haft, "Odysseus, Idomeneus and Meriones: The Cretan Lies of 'Odyssey' 13–19," *Classical Journal* 79 [1984]: 289–306), and Callimachus,

Hilduin is similarly ambivalent about the story's truth. In his introduction to the excerpt in the prose, he explains, "I would not say [it is] a fable, but a spiritual matter, which happened spiritually."[244] Thus, he indicates that the vision is not exactly a tall story, but neither should it be read literally: rather, it is to be understood as it happened, *spiritaliter*. Employing a Pseudo-Dionysian phrase, Hilduin says the vision occurred before the "eyes of the mind." In the corresponding section of the epic, he is similarly ambiguous: the *visio* is "not some fable, but truly a thing conveyed by holy speech."[245]

Hilduin continues, explaining why he versifies the *visio*: "We decided that we would express it according to the pleasing metrical rule / So that whoever is a wise reader and seeks the gates of heaven / Would profit from seizing the prudent harvest."[246] In the epic, Hilduin implies that he leaves other Pseudo-Dionysian excerpts in their own speech (*proprius sermo*) for greater authenticity (fol. 15r). He versifies this excerpt so it might better induce the wise reader's soul "seeking the gates of heaven." The unversified *visio* of Carpus in Hilduin's prose *passio* is, by contrast, merely described as useful for readers who would not have access to it otherwise (c. 15). Therefore, his passage is particularly salvific for the wise reader because it is versified.[247] What is it about verse that makes it so salutary for this kind of reader? The reader was trained to approach verse differently from prose, and the peculiarities of its style demanded a certain kind of reading.

Verse was suited to this salvific function for several reasons. As noted, it was thought to be both more appealing and more memorable than prose. Epic lives also tend to focus more on inner states and the saint's heroism.

Hymn 1.8, which uses the same phrase as Paul's Greek "Κρῆτες ἀεὶ ψεῦσται." Latin sources, which would have probably been familiar to Hilduin include Ovid, *Amores* 3.10.19 ("Cretes erunt testes – nec fingunt omnia Cretes"), *Ars Amatoria* 1.298 ("Quamvis sit mendax, Creta negare potest"), and *Metamorphoses* 8.123 ("generis falsa est ea fabula!"); Arator, *De actibus*, 2.1107–1110, ed. Arthur Patch McKinlay, *Aratoris Subdiaconi De Actibus Apostolorum*, ed. CSEL 72 (Vienna, 1951).

[244] c. 15: "cui hanc quoque, non dicam fabulam, sed rem spiritalem spiritaliter gestam subiungit."

[245] Fol. 16r: "... non fabula quaevis / Res equidem sancto flatu dictante peracta." The phrase *sancto flatu dictante* is similar to that which Hilduin uses to introduce his own forged Dionysian letter to Apollophanius (see earlier discussion).

[246] "Quam modo quo valeat sapidos hinc capere fructus / Lector quisque sagax ac caeli claustra requirens / Censuimus grata metri depromere lege."

[247] If, as Delaporte argues, the *Visio*'s message of mercy and forgiveness was specifically aimed at Louis, then it was especially relevant for the wise reader. Delaporte, "He Darkens Me," p. 234. On the significance of the compassionate Christ here, see Brown, "Saint Carpus."

This epic *passio*, with its description of intense emotions – the saint burning with divine love and his enemies boiling with rage – and its elaboration of the saint's tortures, is a goad to *compunctio*.[248] In this way, too, verse more strongly impresses its message on the reader. Further, poetic language is suitable for conveying abstract spiritual meaning that pushes against the limits of expression, because it is frequently symbolic and proceeds by metaphor and analogy, rather than by logic and explanation.

Verse is a better medium than prose for prompting contemplation. Alcuin says that the *scolastici* should read his epic *vita* to themselves and ruminate (*ruminari*) on it.[249] The verb implies meditative reading, the kind that imprints the text on the heart. The reader chews the words (subvocalizing them) and digests them.[250] For the *Visio Carpi*, a quasi-fabula, that must be understood on a spiritual level, the *lector* also needed to engage in contemplative, meditative reading with an open heart (*anima ... grata voluntas*; fol. 17r).

Verse lends itself to careful contemplation because it is difficult (which means it takes time to read and cannot be entirely understood without reflection). Michael Roberts describes how confusing wordplay and intractable grammatical constructions operate in Fortunatus's epic *Vita Martini*: "[Fortunatus's] formulation ... privileges verbal play over referential content, with a disorienting effect on the reader, who has difficulty following the sequence of syntax because of the distractions of the self-advertising verbal surface that demands his or her attention."[251] The effort needed to interpret figurative difficult language impresses the subject's

---

[248] For example, "aestuat et magno mentis fervescit amore" (fol. 20v); "festinabat enim casto succensus amore" (fol 21r); "mens hominum rabidis eheu suffusa medullis" (fol. 30r); "fervore calescens" (fol. 28r).

[249] Alcuin, *Letter to Bishop Beornrad*, in MGH Ep. 4, p. 175. Alcuin uses the metaphor of words speaking in the heart to describe reading in another letter (MGH Ep. 4, p. 109): "as often as you read this, know that I am speaking in your heart" (quotiescumque eam perleges, me loquentem in corde tuo agnosce). The prose *Vita Eligii* (BHL 2474) describes how the words are imprinted on the heart through *ruminatio*: "ibi ex divinis scripturis recitabantur, aurem libenter accommodans, avidissime hauriebat atque ita in cordis sui memoriam recondebat ut etiam, cum absens esset, ea quae didicerat meditatione intentissima ruminaret" (MGH SRM 4, p. 671). See also the *Vita Gangulfi*, ed. W. Levison. MGH SRM 7, p. 157: "qui puerulus ... favos divini eloquii ab eorum ore suscipiens, catholicas ruminare sententias et in ventrem memoriae trahicere non desistebat, adeo ut in tenero ipsius pectore inpressam cerneres imaginem sanctitatis, et ... normae ecclesiasticae sitienti indesinenter epotabat pectore."

[250] I discuss this metaphor in Chapter 4. On meditative reading see, in particular, Leclercq, *Love of Learning*, pp. 15–17 and 72–75.

[251] Michael Roberts, "The Last Epic of Antiquity: Generic Continuity and Innovation in the *Vita Sancti Martini* of Venantius Fortunatus," *TAPA* 131 (2001): 281.

importance on the reader. Isidore, drawing on the *Ars maior*, explains one of the functions of metaphor: "these and other tropes are covered with figurative clothes with reference to the things that are to be understood so they may exercise the reader's understanding and not be considered worthless by being bare and readily grasped."[252] The challenging nature of poetic language requires the reader's effort. Like dissimilar symbols, the obscurity of poetry "force[s] the reader to push beyond the surface meaning of the text."[253] This is crucial, because, in Pseudo-Dionysian thought, meaning could not be gleaned from superficial reading. Truth necessarily did not appear on the surface or indeed in words at all, but could only be understood through the experience they prompted.[254] By definition, since the divine can never be fully expressed in language, a text can only point the reader toward it. For those who paid attention only to the surfaces of words, they were devoid of meaning.[255]

Students were trained to read poetry in ways that extracted truth. Allegorical interpretation, like numerological analysis, employed intellect and recollection of linguistic and conceptual echoes to decode hidden messages. Even pagan poetry could yield truth, if approached correctly. Speaking of Virgil and Ovid, the Carolingian poet Theodulf says, "Although there are many worthless things in their words / Beneath a false covering are hidden many true things."[256] The meanings of Christian poetry, too, could be highly obscure. Verse, with its difficult and figurative language and concealed meaning, needed to be approached like Scripture or, in Pseudo-Dionysius's view, the *enigmata* of the sacraments. (As we shall see in the next chapter, poetry was such a useful part of the monastic curriculum because it was used to teach such methods of reading.) In the *Ecclesiastical Hierarchy*, Pseudo-Dionysius appends to his description of each of the sacraments, contemplations (*theoria*) on their meaning. As Hilduin summarizes it,

> Laying out beforehand the mystic sacraments
> And in such a way, joining certain contemplations to each,
> With the robe of the hidden mysteries receding from the peaks,

---

[252] Isidore, *Etymologiae*, 1.37.2: "sed hac atque aliae tropicae locutiones ad ea, quae intellegenda sunt, propterea figuratis amictibus obteguntur, ut sensus legentis exerceant, et ne nuda atque in promptu vilescant." Trans. Irvine, *Textual Culture*, p. 229.

[253] Louth, "Truly Visible Things," p. 21. See also *EH* 5.I.2

[254] Thus, the Old Testament offered truth through images (*EH* 3.5).

[255] *DN* 4.11.

[256] Theodulf, *Carmen* 45, MGH Poetae 1, p. 543, line 20: "In quorum dictis quamquam sint frivola multa, / Plurima sub falso tegmine vera latent."

> In these things the wise man shows, as it were, openly all things,
> Which take place in the holy cults and mysteries
> Of the Church . . .[257]

Pseudo-Dionysius and Hilduin stress that Scriptural images for the divine need to be contemplated with the "eyes of the mind" to reveal their meanings and to allow the ascent of the reader.[258] Thus, poetry facilitated the contemplative reading that was necessary for the revelation of meaning, leading ultimately to union with the divine.[259]

Allegorical readings required intellectual engagement, yet ultimate understanding was beyond the grasp of the human mind and knowledge itself. The soul needed to transcend the intellectual and interpretive altogether. Pseudo-Dionysius's approach to knowledge and the divine used a different kind of presentation and interpretation. The surface of the epic passion, like a Pseudo-Dionysian symbol, conceals and reveals the inner truth and draws a reader toward a divine it cannot disclose (*CH* 2.2). Through metaphor and imagery, poetic expression could lead the reader toward an understanding beyond his or her current abilities and even beyond the powers of language itself.

SHADOW AND LIGHT

One of the epic *Passio Dionysii*'s most striking features is the prevalence of light and darkness metaphors derived from Pseudo-Dionysius's theology. Pseudo-Dionysius is an intensely visual writer, who uses metaphors of suns, lamps, shadows, and fog.[260] In describing the soul's journey toward

---

[257] *PD* (metric) fol. 11r: "Ante sacramenta ponens sat mystica clare / Sicque theorias subiungens quasque quibusque / Verticibus refluo clausarum syrmate rerum / In quibus ostendit ceu prudens cuncta patenter / Quae sacris in cultibus mysteriisque / Ecclesiae . . ." I translate this passage differently from Delaporte, who takes *vertices* as "whirlpools," as a metaphor for difficulty. I understand it as "peaks," in accordance with the Pseudo-Dionysian idea of the hidden peaks of mystical experience (cf. Delaporte, "He Darkens Me," p. 240).

[258] Hilduin translates *DN* 5.7: "ex obscuris imaginibus ad causam ascendentes, supermundialibus oculis contemplari omnia cause . . ." Also, *CH* 1.2, 2.4; *EH* 2.3.

[259] Although Hilduin's emphasis is on the revelation of the mysteries, Pseudo-Dionysius equally emphasizes the necessity of concealing them. Echoing Paul, he iterates that truths must be veiled, cloaked in riddle, both to present them in ways that readers can grasp and to hide them from the uninitiated, who would mock them (e.g., *DN* 1.7; *MT* 2; *CH* 2.2, 2.5; *EH* 1.4, 7.3.1, 7.3.10). Thus, for Pseudo-Dionysius, the symbolic veil of language enacts both revelation and concealment (*CH* 2.2). (In Acts 17:32, Paul speaks of those who mock the idea of the resurrection of the dead: "cum audissent autem resurrectionem mortuorum quidam quidem inridebant.")

[260] Louth, "Truly Visible Things," p. 18.

union with the divine, Pseudo-Dionysius both uses and inverts the usual polarity of darkness as ignorance and light as revelation. He characterizes the divine as a superabundant light and uses a mystical darkness to symbolize the soul's ascent into an "unknowing" (ἀγνωσία) that is beyond sense and intellect and thus apophatic, beyond the descriptive powers of language.[261] In the fifth letter to Gaius (summarized by Hilduin in both passions), Pseudo-Dionysius characterizes the divine as both an overflowing light and an encompassing darkness (fol. 14r). Hilduin's description of the letter to Dorotheus provides another example:

> Let him learn to despise the inner illusions of his mind
> And to truly contemplate the brilliant rays of light. . . .
> For now he set his pen to writing on high
> Almost as if drawing forth deep knowledge from the mouth of God.
> Certainly, he writes, that the darkness of God is very deep. . . .
> Let there be the golden light that is inaccessible to all while they breathe
> Where God alone dwells continually and without end.[262]

God here is a light that transcends mental illusions, a light unseen by the living, and a great darkness.

Pseudo-Dionysius also employs a more straightforward use of the symbolism, in which light represents knowledge, spiritual ascent, and godliness, and darkness stands for ignorance and superstition. Drawing on the tradition of Plato's *Republic*, Pseudo-Dionysius uses the sun as an image of the superabundant Good, which shines its light on all (*DN* 4.1–5, 4.4). The Good illuminates everything and repels shadows and so light is one of the names by which one can praise God.[263] Because the perceptible world is the product of the imperceptible cause, and all being participates in the Good to some degree, visible symbols such as light are not simply metaphors, but reflections and emanations of the ultimate transcendent Good (*DN* 5.8).

---

[261] This is the theme of *MT*; *Ep.* 1 and 5 to Gaius; *Ep.* 9. It also recurs frequently in *DN*.

[262] Fol. 14r: "Internos discat mentis contemnere fucos / Et vere radios lucis spectare choruscos / Miro namque modo calamum defixit in altum / Vix velut eliciens deitatis ab ore profundum. . . . / Nempe dei caligo refert quod valde profunda / Lux sit inaccessa cunctis spirantibus aura / Qua deus inhabitet iugiter sine limite solus."

[263] *DN* 4.4–5; Jan A. Aertsen, "The Triad <<True-Good-Beautiful>>. The Place of Beauty in the Middle Ages," in *Intellect et imagination dans la philosophie médiévale* (Turnhout, 2006), pp. 415–435 at p. 421; C.C. Putnam, *Beauty in the Pseudo-Dionysius* (Washington, DC, 1960); U.R. Jeck, "Philosophie der Kunst und Theorie des Schönen bei Ps.-Dionysios Areopagites," in *Documenti e studi sulla tradizione filosofica medievale* 7 (1996): 1–38.

Hilduin's metaphors are mostly of this conventional kind. As Delaporte notes, the prose *passio* contains significant light and darkness imagery, especially in the story of the eclipse, which each passion recounts three times.[264] The use of light as a metaphor, however, is far more pervasive throughout the whole epic *passio*. A comparison with Hilduin's translation of the Pseudo-Dionysian theology shows that he incorporates its terminology of light (such as *lux, lumen, illuminare, splendor*) and shadow (such as *tenebra, caligo*) into his epic passion.

The images suffuse the epic *passio* with a Pseudo-Dionysian mystical sensibility, appropriately reflecting the Neoplatonic symbol of overflowing light emanating from God, which is one of Pseudo-Dionysius's most pervasive images. Visual images function as uplifting signs of invisible reality, and the most prevalent of these images, in Pseudo-Dionysius, is light, particularly the sun (*DN* 4.1, 4.4). Hilduin's epic passion coruscates with *lumina* and *radii*, especially in descriptions of apostolic activity. Initially the poet uses this language to describe Paul. Lit by a heavenly glow (*caeleste lumen*), he came to people "drowning in deep gloom" (*alta caligine mersae*; cf. *DN* 4.5) and banished the shadows (*tenebrae*) of pagan superstition with the light of his luminous doctrine.[265] (Pseudo-Dionysius uses similar imagery for Paul's teaching in *DN* 7.1.) This luminosity characterizes Dionysius after Paul has ordained him; the disciple inherits his master's radiance as a mark of apostolic succession. Dionysius's "lamp of teaching" (*doctrinae lampas*) allowed people to see the glittering rays of light (*radii lucis ... chorusci*).[266] He is "shining with a brightness more dazzling than any snow."[267] Light also characterizes learning, and the saint's passion; heated up on the iron bed, "Dionysius glows more radiant than molten gold."[268] Light imagery in the epic *Passio Dionysii* adorns learning, teaching, and martyrdom.

[264] Delaporte, "He Darkens Me," pp. 239–240, 236.

[265] *PD* (metric), fol. 4r–v: "doctrina ... lumine plena"; also fol. 12v: "Paulo caelesti luce chorusco."

[266] Fols. 25v, 26v, 14r.

[267] Fol. 27v: "Candidiorque nitens omni candore nivali."

[268] Fols. 2v (pagan learning at Athens), 30r: "splendidior cocto prodit DIONYSIUS auro." Hilduin borrows Virgil's language. Cf. Aeneas's divinely manufactured armor, including a shield of "unspeakable fabric" in *Aen.* 8.623–625 ("solis inardescit radiis longeque refulget; / tum levis ocreas electro auroque recocto"); also Fortunatus, *Vita Martini*, 1.127 ("pulchrior electro, ter cocto ardentior auro"), ed. F. Leo in MGH AA 4.1, p. 299; Theodulf 25, line 13 ("cocto clarior auro"), in MGH Poetae 1, p. 483.

In neither Pseudo-Dionysius's writings nor Hilduin's verse is the imagery mere window dressing. "This visual luxuriance savoured in words is not ... there for its own sake: its purpose is to draw human kind, and indeed the whole cosmos, towards the radiance that shines through it and bestows on it the quality of beauty."[269] Images (which are emanations as well as reflections of the ultimate Good) are anagogic, leading the reader's spiritual ascent. Few minds can grasp or be moved by the purely conceptual. Rather, they must be prompted to higher, spiritual understanding by contemplation of the perceptible. From there, the reader can move to comprehension of the invisible and abstract (*CH* 1.3). The initiate moves beyond sense perception to the intellect (*mens, ratio* in Hilduin's language), and finally beyond all language and knowing to God. From the multiple and varied material world, the soul is raised to contemplation of the unitary. The soul turns inward and its contemplation moves from the material to the immaterial (*DN* 4.9), from "obscure images" to the divine Cause (*DN* 5.7).

Hilduin conveys this idea of anagogic imagistic language in his summary of Pseudo-Dionysian thought in the central section of each passion. Translating the letter to John on Patmos, he repeats a favorite quotation from the iconoclasm controversies: "from visible things they draw out the image of the invisible."[270] Because the epic passion describes the writings at much greater length, it emphasizes this central idea more strongly, preparing the reader to comprehend the function of the imagery in later sections. The language of light and shadow in Hilduin's epic passion is not merely decorative, but both an emanation and an anagogic symbol to draw the reader's mind toward the divine.

As noted, Hilduin recounts the eclipse Dionysius witnessed three times in each passion, clearly signaling its importance. The last of these accounts is contained in the apocryphal letter to Apollophanius transmitted in virtually the same prose form in both passions.[271] This letter, which Hilduin composed, contains a commentary on the correct discernment of visual signs (specifically those of light and darkness) and the appropriate spiritual response. It pertains to the central Pseudo-Dionysian themes of the interpretation of symbols and the limits of human understanding. In the letter, the saint recalls that when he and Apollophanius observed the

---

[269] Louth, "Truly Visible Things," p. 20.
[270] *PD* (prose), c. 16: "ex visibilibus invisibilium praetendunt imaginem"; Louth, "Truly Visible Things," pp. 15–24.
[271] Ibid., c. 14, *PD* (metric), fol. 15r–15v.

eclipse, they consulted an astronomical work.[272] When that failed to explain it, Dionysius "still ignorant of so great a mystery" (*adhuc nescius tantae rei mysterium*) asked his learned friend, a "mirror of teaching" (*speculum doctrinae*), to interpret the event's hidden meanings (*haec secreta*). Apollophanius was, briefly, divinely inspired: "and you replied to me, with a divine omen, and speech not born of human perception, 'These things, O good Dionysius, are divine recompenses.'"[273]

In the other accounts of the eclipse, Dionysius's prophetic pronouncement is noted, but Apollophanius's is not. In the earlier passages, Hilduin shows that Dionysius discerned the eclipse's meaning, and a little spark (*scintilla*) was lit (*relucere*) within him, although he was still mired in darkness (*adhuc fuerat mens caeco mersa profundo*).[274] Only when he heard Paul preaching, did he understand fully: the sun, the Neoplatonic symbol for the One, darkened and returned demonstrating Christ's death and resurrection.

In the apocryphal letter, Hilduin notes Apollophanius's interpretation and his subsequent failure to act upon the "signs of shadows" (*signa tenebrarum*) (fol. 14v). At the eclipse, both men grasped at the symbolism of light and dark and the divine truth behind it. Apollophanius, however, missed the point. Although perceiving with "non humani sensus" that the eclipse had divine significance, he rejected Paul's teachings. He did not want to reach "from material things toward the immaterial."[275] As a "mirror of teaching," Apollophanius, like the mirrors described by Pseudo-Dionysius – the saints and angels – should have reflected and transmitted divine light (cf. *CH* 3.2; *EH* 3.3.9).

The eclipse episode is full of ironies underscoring the theme of reading light. Hilduin draws attention to the meaning of Apollophanius's name – literally, "the appearance of Apollo," the pagan sun god – by dividing it into its constituent parts.[276] Apollophanius indeed experienced a kind of theophany, in recognizing the eclipse as a divine sign, but continued to be a devotee of the sun (*cultor solis*), revering the creation (*creatura*) rather than

---

[272] For speculations about the identity of this work, see Franz Cumont, "Regula Philippi Arrhidaei," *Isis* 26 (1936): 8–12; Otto Neugebauer, "Regula Philippi Arrhidaei," *Isis* 50 (1959): 477–478.

[273] c. 14; fol. 15r: "ad quae mihi tu inquiens omine divo, et non humani sensus sermone: 'Ista, o bone Dionysi, divinarum retributiones sunt rerum.'"

[274] "Nec frustra tenebris cernens involuier orbem" (fol. 6v).

[275] *PD* (prose), c. 14; *PD* (metric), fols. 15r–15v: "de materialibus ad immaterialia non velle suscipere."

[276] *PD* (metric), fol. 5v: "Nomen Apollo cui compactum fanius extat," and again when he is reintroduced into the narrative in the central section of the epic, 14v: "Hinc et Apollo facit fanii memorabile."

the Creator. A further irony is that (in one of Hilduin's additions to the story), the pair had gone to Heliopolis to study astrology, the pagan art of interpreting celestial signs.[277] Apollophanius, insanely (*demens*) devoted to that misguided way of reading heavenly symbols, remained unenlightened.

Dionysius and Apollophanius provide positive and negative examples for the interpretation of visual symbols. The eclipse stands for the images of light and darkness that the reader encounters. Hilduin employs his verse, with its visual imagery and obscurity, to impress a similar experience on the readers, leading them to "the gates of heaven" (*caeli claustra*; fol. 16r). An image is a starting point, but the meaning may only later be revealed or illuminated (as it was to Dionysius by Paul), based on contemplation and initiation into the mysteries.

LITERATURE AS RELIQUARY

Hilduin's poem, with its color and light, encourages the reader to move from sense perception to the contemplation of the conceptual and beyond. Roberts's description of Fortunatus's epic language applies to Hilduin also:

> The impression is akin, in visual terms, to the brilliance of heaven ... that dazzles normal perception and signifies the otherworldly splendor of the divine.... Arguably such language serves the same purpose in Fortunatus' poem as the profusion of brilliant visual detail ... that is, it communicates the special status of the saint, who can transcend normal worldly constraints, as the preciousness of Fortunatus' language foregrounds a gorgeous verbal surface that defies normal categories of grammatical and syntactical understanding.[278]

The verse works like a jeweled reliquary, which dazzles the eyes, and prompts the viewer to meditate on what it conceals (the saint) and what it signifies (divine power and mystery, salvation, eternal life). Reliquaries are literally ostentatious, taking unremarkable looking bones and showing their meaning to the onlooker. The jeweled surfaces can be read. As Pseudo-Dionysius explains, precious stones have allegorical meanings that the viewer can decode.[279] The reliquary's shining exterior also mirrors the incorruptible glory of the saint within, which itself prefigures the

---

[277] Ibid., fol. 5v, describes Apollophanius: "Arte mathematica cupiens pollere magister / Voto discendi stellarum rite meatus."

[278] Roberts, "Last Epic," p. 281.

[279] Pseudo-Dionysius, *CH* 15.7; Stock, *Implications*, pp. 68–69; Schmitt, "Reliques et les images," in *Les Reliques. Objets, cultes, symboles*. Actes du colloque international de l'Université du Littoral-Côte d'Opale (Boulogne-sur-Mer), 4–6 septembre 1997, ed. Edina Bozóky and Anne-Marie Helvetius (Turnhout, 1999), pp. 52–53; Revelation 21:18–21.

transformed bodies of the end days when, Pseudo-Dionysius says, the incorrupt body will reunite with the soul.[280] The richly ornamented reliquary ensures that the bones are understood as saints' relics and precious objects, despite their grim resemblance to the bones of the ordinary dead.

In the twelfth century, Abbot Suger of Saint-Denis, drawing on his abbey's Pseudo-Dionysian theological tradition, articulated the idea of beautiful things – in this case, his church – leading a viewer to higher contemplation.

> Thus, when – out of my delight in the beauty of the house of God – the multicolored loveliness of the gems has called me away from external cares, and worthy meditation has induced me to reflect on the diversity of the sacred virtues, transferring that which is material to that which is immaterial, then I seem to see myself, by God's grace in an anagogical manner, able to be transported from the inferior to the higher world.[281]

According to Suger, the architecture's color, splendor, and variety lead to inward reflection, understanding, and spiritual ascent. The light from the cut and polished surfaces encourages the viewer toward a mystical experience. Hilduin too appreciated the salutary value of shiny things. His contemporary, the Irish poet Dungal, describes the jeweled chapel Hilduin had constructed for Dionysius and his co-martyrs: "As the triple tombs sparkle / . . . the metal is glowing red, / They are appropriately adorned with gleaming marble columns."[282]

Writing could be likened to gold and gems in revealing the splendor of its subject matter: "golden letters are painted on purple pages . . . God's eloquence shining with worthy glow . . . the teachings of God written in precious metals."[283] In fact, writing was superior to gems, because it was

---

[280] *EH* 2.3.7, 7.1.2–3, 7.3.9; Schmitt, "Reliques et images," p. 153. Shortell describes the gilding of Saint Quentin's skull as "covering the bones with new flesh in a more perfect material, not subject to decay." See Ellen M. Shortell, "Dismembering Saint Quentin: Gothic Architecture and the Display of Relics," *Gesta* 36 (1997): 38.

[281] Panofsky's translation. "Unde, cum ex dilectione decoris domus Dei aliquando multicolor gemmarum speciositas ab extrinsecis me curis devocaret, sanctarum etiam diversitatem virtutum, de materialibus ad immaterialia transferendo, honesta meditatio insistere persuaderet, videor videre me . . . ab hac etiam inferiori ad illam superiorem anagogico more Deo donante posse transferri." Suger, *De Administratione*, 62–65 in *Abbot Suger: On the Abbey Church of St.-Denis and its Art Treasures*, ed. and trans. Erwin Panofsky, 2nd ed. (Princeton, 1979).

[282] Dungal, *Carm.* 17 in MGH Poetae 2, pp. 664–665: "busta ut trina coruscant. / . . . rutilante metallo/ Fulti marmorei decorantur rite columnis."

[283] Dagulf, *Ad Moulinum* (late viii), in MGH Poetae I, p. 94; Godman, *Poets*, p. 46: "Aurea purpureis pinguntur grammata scedis . . . Eloquiumque dei digno fulgore choruscans. . . . doctrina dei pretiosis scripta metallis."

immortal.[284] Hilduin's language suggests that he thought of the epic passion as the literary equivalent of a chapel or a reliquary – a glorious structure for holding the saint's remains.[285] The terminology of poetry and relics coincides when he explains that he enshrines the saint's story in verse:

> How the triumphant martyr then bore the shining banners,
> Arising as a pall bearer of these things after death
> Now it is permitted to sing and *to compose* (*claudere*) in confined verse
> The body of the saint, while it was mutilated, with his neck cut,
> His holy mind was already received into the lap of heaven.[286]

Claudere here is a pun meaning both "to enclose" and "to compose." Elsewhere the verb is used for interring a saint's body in a tomb, but here the corpus ("body," "body of work") is shut up in the *strictus versus*.[287] Hilduin's poem is a metaphorical tomb to encase the martyr. He uses forms of *claudere* frequently in the verse *passio* (although only rarely in the prose).[288] He pairs the closing with an opening or revelation, such as the curing of blindness, or the explanation of the mysteries of the sacraments.[289] The most obvious use of such a pair is Paul's quotation from Apocalypse while preaching to the Athenians: "what he alone closes, no power opens / What he alone opens, no power closes."[290] So, *claudere* has connotations not just of enclosing, but also of locking away and of hiding things that will be revealed. Accordingly, Hilduin's verse is the metaphorical tomb in which the martyr is not only enclosed or hidden, but also revealed.

---

[284] Godman, *Poets*, p. 61.

[285] A gospel produced at Tours, ca. 820–830 (London, British Library, MS Add. 11848), is literally a reliquary, with saints' bones embedded in its jeweled cover.

[286] Fol. 33v: "Quam praeclara dehinc tulerit vexilla triumphans / Martyr post obitum existens baiulus horum / Iam cantare libet, ac stricto claudere versu / Corpus dum sancti deciso vertice truncum / Caelorum gremio sacra iam mente recepta."

[287] Fol. 28v: "clausum ... sepulchrum," and a similar usage on fol. 32r. Cf. the inscription on Bernhard's tomb in Thangmar's prose *Vita Bernhardi*, c. 57, ed. G. Pertz in MGH SS 4, p. 782: "hac tumuli fossa clauduntur praesulis ossa / Bernwardi ..."

[288] Paul's citation from Apocalypse: "qui claudit, et nemo aperit; aperit, et nemo claudit" and a description of blindess (*clausi oculi*) are the only uses of *claudere* in the prose (c. 6, 8).

[289] Fol. 11r. He also uses the term for blind eyes (*clausae fenestrae*, fol. 8v; *reserantur claustra genarum*, fol. 36r), for prisons, both real (fols. 31v, 20v) and metaphorical (fol. 8v), and for the persecution unleashed by Domitian (fol. 26v). The cognate *claustrum* describes the gates of heaven (fol. 16r) and those of death broken by Christ at his resurrection (fol. 1r, 28v). It is of course also the word for cloister.

[290] Fol. 7v: "Solus et hic claudit aperit quod nulla potestas / Solus et hic aperit claudit quod nulla potestas." Apoc. 3:7. The prose *PD* quotes straight from the Vulgate: "qui claudit, et nemo aperit; aperit, et nemo claudit."

Hilduin literally encloses the saint's theological corpus, or at least fragments of it, in his epic, just as he placed the relics of Dionysius and his
companions in the *martyrium*. There are pieces of Pseudo-Dionysius's
literary body (the *capitula* and two prose letters) incorporated into the
central section of the *passio*. The letters are not obviously out of place in
the prose *passio* (other prose *vitae* include letters), but they and the *capitula*
are striking in the verse life, breaking the hexameter lines' metrical flow
and visual consistency. Hilduin presents the excerpted letters as
Dionysius's original words, translated and embedded in the text. They
should stand out because – as pieces of the saint's corpus, encased in
Hilduin's *strictus versus* – they are qualitatively different from the surrounding material. Hilduin's epic *passio* functions like a reliquary for the
saint's literary remains, presenting them to the readers and providing
meaning and context, while also hiding them in a jeweled poetic form
that promoted contemplation.

In identifying books and texts with relics, Hilduin draws on a long
Christian and Classical tradition.[291] He elsewhere equates writings and
relics: he describes writings at Saint-Denis entombed in their boxes
(*sepulta ... scriniis*), as if they were human remains.[292] The volume of
Pseudo-Dionysian theology is called a *pignus* (literally, a pledge, a term
often applied to relics), with which the emperor might pray and commune.[293]

THE HIERARCH

In mediating the theology to his readership, Hilduin fulfils the Pseudo-
Dionysian role of hierarch, the apex of the earthly church, who grasps
higher mysteries and communicates them to an audience who could not
otherwise comprehend them (*CH* 12.2; *EH* 1.4–1.5). The hierarch, says
Pseudo-Dionysius, may rightly be called an angel, because his understanding is closest to the level of the angels.[294] He presents the higher truth in

---

[291] See my essay "Books, Bodies, and Bones."

[292] Hilduin, *omnibus filiis*, p. 336.

[293] Louis's letter explains the need for this book (*Ep. Hilduino*, p. 327): "since we believe
that we have the greatest and very sweetest token of the desired presence of this our very
lord and benefactor, wherever we may be, if, in prayer, recitation, or reading we speak
with him or about him or in words by him" (quoniam maximum valdeque dulcissimum
pignus desiderabilis presentiae ipsius domini et solatiatoris nostri, ubicumque simus,
habere nos credimus, si cum eo vel de eo aut ab eo dictis oratione, conlatione sive
lectione conloquimur).

[294] *CH* 12.1–2; *PD* (prose), c. 9.

symbols, such as ritual (the sacraments) and by using parable and image like a good teacher.[295] The hierarch is simultaneously a priest and a teacher. He should not simply explain the text, but, as the character of Symmachus says in Macrobius's *Saturnalia*, approach "the sacred places of the poem" (*adyta sacri poematis*), and reveal to the learned its "secret meanings" (*arcanorum sensuum*) and "innermost shrines" (*reclusa penetralia*).[296] It is the teacher's role to uncover the "secret treasury" (*thesaurus occultus*) of "concealed wisdom" (*sapientia abscondita*) and open it to the minds (*sensus*) of those less enlightened "so they understand holy Writ."[297] Hilduin's passions show the saint working in this capacity as writer, missionary, and teacher of doctrine, comprehending hidden truths (mysteries) and conveying them to others:

Employing a divine style and shining speech, showing himself by his word to be filled with the bread upon which the angels live, with conspicuous eloquence and the deepest and most admirable intelligence, as if he had truly placed his own mouth in heaven, he spoke about heavenly matters, where he was abiding in heart and way of life.[298]

By composing the epic passion, Hilduin, a priest and writer like the saint, also embodies the role. By expressing theological ideas in metaphorical and symbolic form, he transmits angelic knowledge to his audience and presents it in ways they can grasp and, in the epic passion, in an imagistic mode that encourages contemplation.

Hilduin, like Dionysius, both reveals and conceals. He lays open (*patere*) the vision of Carpus for the wise reader.[299] He uncovers the

---

[295] EH 5.1.6. Pseudo-Dionysius's idea coincides with anthropologist Harvey Whitehouse's claim that ritual "helps the religious grasp the hard ideas underlying the religion." See Kate Douglas, "Religion is Based on Ritual," *New Scientist* 204, issue 2739, December 19, 2009, p. 63. Harvey Whitehouse, *Arguments and Icons: Divergent Modes of Religiosity* (Oxford, 2000). Whitehouse draws his distinction between imagistic and doctrinal modes from Max Weber and William James.

[296] "Sed arcanorum sensuum investigato aditu doctorum cultu celebranda praebeamus reclusa penetralia." Macrobius, *Saturnalia*, 1.24.13, cited and trans. Irvine, *Textual Culture*, p. 145.

[297] Gisla and Rotruda, *Ad Alcuin* in MGH Ep. 4, p. 324: "aperuit illis sensus ut sanctas intellegerent scripturas." Charlemagne's sister and daughter, Gisla and Rotruda (writing in 800) address Alcuin as a teacher, asking him to write a commentary on John, because Augustine's is too difficult and obscure.

[298] PD (prose), c. 9: "divino usus stylo, fulguranti sermone, se eiusdem panis verbo quo vivunt angeli repletum ostendens ... insigni intelligentia, sicut revera is qui in coleo os suum posuerat, cum de coelestibus loquebatur, ubi corde et conversatione degebat." Paul is also presented in this manner, as "a wise man, who uncovered the holy secrets of the mystery" (Mysterii qui sacra sagax archana retexit). PD (metric), fol. 6v.

[299] PD (metric), fol. 15v.

obscure and brings it to light. His prefatory letters are full of metaphors of unearthing (*eruere*) and revealing (*propalare*) hidden (*obtecta*) documents:

> It seemed to me that, with Christ as my helper, I should bring to light references to the series of events of blessed Dionysius's conversion, prophesy, and arrival at Rome, or his triumphal martyrdom, which are mostly contained in the Greek histories, with a considerable amount preserved, hidden among the Latin writings, buried in the boxes of the ancients.[300]

In bringing a well-hidden volume (*in tomo satis superque abdito*) to light, Hilduin is the agent of divine will (*nutu inventa*).[301] Like sacred mysteries, the documents are brought forth in due time; God "did not wish all things to be revealed (*revelari*) at the same time or to all people at once."[302] Hilduin brings his readers divinely revealed texts "they would not be able to find otherwise."[303] Because Dionysius has joined "the company of angels," it is Hilduin's duty to convey his spiritual message to those below. Hilduin controls access to the saint as the keeper of his relics, as the translator of his corpus (literary and physical), and as the hierarch-figure who mediates the angelic understanding to others – through poetry and symbolism – so that they too might gain spiritual understanding.

This poem suggests a different picture of Hilduin than his career implies, showing his profound engagement with the mystical philosophy of Pseudo-Dionysius along with his incessant politicking. Although his Latin translation was lacking in many respects, his interpretation shows him wrestling with making the difficult Greek text meaningful to his audience. Spirituality and self-interest were not mutually exclusive.

*

In Hilduin's works on Dionysius we find competing ideas of truth, fiction, and poetry. In the prefatory letters to the prose *Passion*, he insists on the veracity of his composite saint, supporting him with fabricated sources. Much of the evidence for Dionysius is invented, redacted, reframed, or strategically dismissed by Hilduin. The epic passion conveys a different kind of truth. Like Pseudo-Dionysius's mystical writings, it is an anagogic text, which can draw the reader upward via contemplation of its

---

[300] Hilduin, *omnibus filiis*, p. 335: "visum est mihi ... ut notitiam de ordine conversionis et praedicationis atque adventus Romam seu trumphalis martyrii beatissimi Dionysii, quae maxime Grecorum continetur hystoriis et quae sepulta antiquorum scriniis apud Latinos non modica portione servabatur obtecta, in luce Christo iuvante reducerem."

[301] Hilduin, *Rescriptum*, c. 5.

[302] Hilduin, *omnibus filiis*, p. 336: "simul noluit revelari cuncta vel cunctis in semel ..."

[303] Ibid., pp. 336–337: "alibi ea invenire nequiverit."

images. Verse is expected to operate on multiple levels and therefore is especially suited to conveying a deeper meaning that is only partially apparent on the surface. Hilduin draws on the Pseudo-Dionysian idea of language that both conceals and reveals, proceeding through kataphasis, apophasis, and symbol and drawing one toward a divine, which words cannot express.

The verse *passio* functions as a Neoplatonic text, drawing a reader from the visible to the invisible. For Pseudo-Dionysius, symbols are not decorative elements or simply metaphors, but a means the hierarch employs to induce the intellect to rise toward (and eventually beyond) knowledge of God. The vivid visual imagery, the emphasis on suffering and inner states, and the beauty of verse all provide goads to the senses and emotions. Hilduin draws on poetry's imagistic potential and deploys it for more than ornamentation, to reflect, rehearse, and even prompt the mystical ascent that is a theme of Pseudo-Dionysian theology. In doing so, he shows himself to be the heir of both Pseudo-Dionysius and Orpheus, the poet-priest whose compelling words take the reader beyond comprehension and transcend death. Hilduin utilizes the distinctive features and expectations of epic verse to create a text that, while conveying the same narrative as the prose, operates in different ways, appealing to the reader on emotional, cognitive, and perceptual levels.

By promoting Dionysius, Hilduin added to the prestige of the emperor and Saint-Denis, while demonstrating his own piety and poetic prowess. Hilduin's epic functions on multiple levels, appealing to Louis the Pious by integrating the narrative and the mystical writings of his personal patron into a meditative poetic work for the the devout emperor. By revealing the hidden and leading the reader, Hilduin positioned himself as a hierarch like Dionysius himself. No longer an intermediary between Louis and his petitioners, as he had been as archchaplain, Hilduin made himself the mediator of the saint and his salvific message. In this new role, he presented himself continuing to oversee the spiritual well-being of emperor and kingdom.

2

Glossing the Imaginary: Epic *Vitae* in the Classroom

Around 850, the monk Ermenric sent a long strange letter to Grimald. This work meanders among topics without obvious rationale, alighting on Scriptural exegesis, Latin prosody, the nature of the soul, allegorical readings, Classical mythology, and the monk's recent experiences at the abbey of Saint-Gall, of which Grimald was abbot. It has no overarching structure, and the links between sections are tangential at best. Ermenric closed the letter with an appendix containing prose and verse passages (in several meters) excerpted from an epic *vita* he claimed to be writing about the abbey's eponymous patron.

Ermenric likens his progress through the letter to a drunk falling off a path, and modern readers have largely agreed.[1] Some scholars have dismissed his work as nonsensical ravings, and others have doubted whether the parts of the texts are programmatically related. Yet such judgments miss the central logic of Ermenric's work and the rare window it provides into ninth-century monastic culture. Ermenric proposes three reasons for writing his letter: to satisfy Grimald's desire for an introduction (*exordium*) to a theological topic, to educate a wider second readership, and to garner Grimald's patronage for composing an epic life of Gall.[2] The relationship of these three purposes is not readily apparent, nor is it clear why Ermenric would attempt to combine them into a single letter. The short appendix, which he calls the "calx epistolae," set down hastily, as he describes it, on a few scraps

---

[1] Ermenric, c. 19. For a negative portrayal of Ermenric, see F. Brunhölzl, *Histoire de la littérature latine du moyen âge 1/2 l'époque carolingienne*, trans. H. Rochais (Turnhout, 1991), p. 122.
[2] c. 19.

of parchment (c. 30–36), appears to be an afterthought, yet Ermenric claims that the epic *Vita Galli*, which it represents, is his main reason for writing. If the *calx* represents the *Vita Galli* and the preceding twenty-nine chapters are its prefatory letter, the relative lengths are anomalous, as is the inclusion of the didactic material, which necessitates Ermenric's frequent protestations that he is not condescending to his erudite prospective patron. Further, the letter's chatty and informal tone is inappropriate in a letter addressed to a social and ecclesiastical superior.

The relationship among Ermenric's three professed purposes – social, didactic, and poetic – provides the key to comprehending this letter and in turn offers insight into the contexts and functions of epic *vitae*. The letter's many riddles are resolved when we understand its premise: Ermenric presents himself as a teacher in an imaginary classroom in which the reader is a student undergoing a crash course in intermediate and then advanced language arts. In the first section of the letter (c. 1–29), Ermenric depicts himself glossing a text, probably the epic *Vita Galli* that he claims to be writing. In the final section, the *calx* (c. 30–36), he models elements of that *vita* being used as *progymnasmata* – rhetorical composition exercises – in his virtual classroom. Although his claim to compose a *Vita Galli* appears peripheral to the rest of Ermenric's epistle, it is actually central since he depicts himself teaching from the epic life.

By framing the epic *Vita Galli* as his absent teaching text, Ermenric combines his pedagogical purpose with a bid for poetic patronage. As we have seen, epic *vitae* were appropriate gifts for patrons. As a text composed at the culmination of education, they showcased the writer's proficiency (proving his or her qualification for teaching) and represented a high level of cultural prestige while celebrating the abbey's saint and glorifying God. Poetry was the language of elite *amicitia* and the currency of intellectual rivalries.

Understanding the role of the epic *vita* in Ermenric's letter gives us an unprecedented view inside the Carolingian classroom unparalleled in any other source. Suerbaum has noted that the letter provides evidence for Carolingian education and the role of the Classics within it.[3] When the letter is understood in its social and didactic contexts, it also reveals the functions of an epic life in the school and the wider monastic community.

---

[3] Werner Suerbaum, "Ein heidnischer Klassiker als 'Dünger' christlicher Bildung. Quellen und Bedeutung des Vergil-Bildes bei Ermenrich von Ellwangen (um 850)," in *Panchaia: Festschrift für Klaus Thraede*, ed. Manfred Wacht, Jahrbuch für Antike und Christentum 22 (Münster, 1995), pp. 238–250.

After sketching the political context of Ermenric's letter, I turn to the manuscript and the letter itself to show how it works and what it tells us about educational practices.

ERMENRIC'S WORLD

Ermenric's letter belongs to the years following the tumultuous civil wars among the heirs of Louis the Pious. It is grounded in the lives of the three main figures it represents – Ermenric, the writer; Grimald, the recipient; and Walafrid Strabo, whose death occasioned its composition and who acts as Ermenric's role model, precedent, and poetic forebear. These men were associated with Fulda, Reichenau, and Saint-Gall, three important and closely linked East Frankish abbeys.[4]

Although Ermenric wrote his letter within two decades of Hilduin's epic *Passio Dionysii*, the political landscape had changed immensely. When Hilduin wrote during the mid-830s, the Frankish *regna* were still combined (however precariously) into the empire Charlemagne had forged. At the time of Louis's death, his son Louis the German, who had fallen from favor, had been in open rebellion against him.[5] After the emperor's death in 840, Louis the German and Charles the Bald allied against Lothar and Pippin II. The fighting between Louis and Lothar concentrated on the Rhine and the lands to its east, so the civil wars particularly affected the East Frankish abbeys.[6] In 840, Louis took the abbeys of Reichenau and Saint-Gall and replaced the abbots with his own supporters.[7] Around 841, he deposed Hraban Maur, the abbot of Fulda, who had supported Louis the Pious and then Lothar.[8] Hraban

---

[4] Scholars, manuscripts, letters, and prayers were exchanged among these abbeys. Grimald, abbot of Saint-Gall, was educated at Reichenau. Walafrid Strabo and his friends Lupus of Ferrières and Gottschalk traveled among them as students. The former two maintained their connection with the abbot of Fulda, Hraban Maur, whereas Gottschalk entered into a decades-long struggle with him (see, for example, Walafrid Strabo, *Carm.* 9, in MGH Poetae 2, p. 358). Hraban wrote to Tatto, Walafrid's teacher at Reichenau, and Gozbert, abbot of Saint-Gall. Hraban addressed a poem to Grimald at Saint-Gall (*Carm.* 6, MGH Poetae 2, pp. 169–170). Around 800, a prayer fraternity is recorded between Saint-Gall and Reichenau. See Dieter Geuenich, "The St. Gall Confraternity of Prayer," in *The Culture of the Abbey of St. Gall: An Overview*, ed. James C. King and Werner Vogler (Stuttgart, 1990), p. 29.

[5] Eric Goldberg, *Struggle for Empire: Kingship and Conflict under Louis the German, 817–876* (Ithaca, 2006), p. 86; *Annals of Saint-Bertin* for 838.

[6] Goldberg, *Struggle for Empire*, p. 86.

[7] Ibid., p. 96.

[8] Ibid.

retired to Fulda's mountain hermitage and remained there until after the treaty of Verdun of 843.[9]

After several years of strife, the brothers divided the Carolingian kingdoms among themselves. In the partition of 843, Charles acquired the West Frankish kingdom (including Neustria, Aquitaine, and Septimania).[10] Lothar received the middle kingdom, including Aachen and the regions of Frisia, western Austrasia, Alsace, eastern Burgundy, Provence, and his kingdom of Italy.[11] Louis acquired all the territory east of the Rhine and, on its west bank, Mainz, Worms, and Speyer.[12] His realm, therefore, included the abbeys of Ermenric's milieu. For the rest of the 840s, Louis and Charles remained allied, and tensions with Lothar continued.

The conflicts and negotiations among the brothers had major consequences for Grimald and Walafrid, as important political figures, and for Ermenric, as a monk associated with Fulda, Reichenau, and Saint-Gall. Grimald was the nephew of archbishop Hetti of Trier and a relative of Wettin, the *magister* of Saint-Gall.[13] He became a student and then a teacher at Reichenau, the island abbey on Lake Constance.[14] As a chaplain at the court of Louis the Pious in the 820s, he would have been under the authority of archchaplain Hilduin.[15] Under the name Homer, Grimald appears as an important member of that emperor's entourage in Walafrid's *De imagine Tetrici*, written in 829.[16] Walafrid and Hraban Maur dedicated works to him.[17]

---

[9] The reconciliation of Hraban and Louis, leading to Hraban's appointment as archbishop of Mainz in 847, represented the rapprochement of the king and the East Frankish churchmen. Lynda L. Coon, "Historical Fact and Exegetical Fiction in the Carolingian *Vita S. Sualonis*," *Church History* 72 (2003): 5–6; Goldberg, *Struggle for Empire*, pp. 96, 159–160. (Coon gives 842 as the date of Hraban's retirement from the abbacy of Fulda; Goldberg states that he was exiled over the winter of 840–841.)

[10] Goldberg, *Struggle for Empire*, p. 114.

[11] Ibid.

[12] Ibid.

[13] Stuart Airlie, "Bonds of Power and Bonds of Association," in *Charlemagne's Heir*, pp. 196–197; Fleckenstein, *Hofkapelle*, pp. 89, 170; Walafrid Strabo, in the *Praefatio* to *Visio Wettini*, dedicating it to Grimald, refers to "Wettinus propinquus vester." MGH Poetae 2, p. 301.

[14] Bischoff, "Bücher," p. 192.

[15] Walafrid calls him *capellanus*. Walafrid Strabo, *Praefatio* to *Visio Wettini*, in MGH Poetae 2, p. 301.

[16] Walafrid, *De imagine Tetrici*, lines 227ff., in MGH Poetae 2, p. 377.

[17] Walafrid, *Visio Wettini*, note 13; Hraban dedicated his *Martyrology* to Grimald whom he addresses as "dulcissmo fratri ac revertissmio abbati Grimoldo." Hraban, *Carmen 6*, MGH Poetae 2, pp. 169–170.

During the early 830s, Grimald was loyal to Louis the Pious.[18] Between August 830 and November 833, he received from that emperor the abbacy of Wissembourg.[19] Around this time, Grimald became one of the most important figures at Louis the German's court. (Louis the Pious had sent his namesake son to Bavaria to rule as subking in 825.)[20] He is first attested as the head of the younger Louis's chancellery in October 833.[21] During the last years of the elder Louis's reign, Grimald's career suffered from the conflict between father and son. His actions and loyalties are obscure, but he was deposed from both his abbacy (between the autumn of 838 and January 840) and his position at court (between 837 and 840).[22] Depreux suggests that his refusal to choose a side may have provoked the hostility of both parties.[23] After the emperor's death, Grimald regained his standing with Louis the German, who made him abbot of Saint-Gall in 841 and reappointed him as abbot of Wissembourg in 847 (the identity of a third abbacy he held is unknown).[24] In the following years, his importance at court was paramount, and he succeeded Baturich of Regensburg as Louis's archchaplain, probably in 848.[25] As had been the case at Louis the Pious's court, the archchaplain was one of the men closest to the king, and therefore one of the most important people at court. The archchaplain's role at the younger Louis's court included supervising the chaplains and the palace school where young nobles were educated, overseeing ceremonies,

---

[18] As Depreux notes, receiving the abbacy of Wissembourg during these years, during which Louis the Pious's sons revolted twice, implies Grimald's loyalty to the emperor, as does his inclusion on the mission sent by Louis the German in January 834 to his father, whom Lothar had imprisoned at Aachen. Depreux, *Prosopographie*, pp. 221–222; Thegan, c. 47.

[19] He is first mentioned as abbot in Doc. Dipl. Wissembourg, no. 158, ed. Karl Glöckner and L. Anton Doll, *Traditiones Wizenburgenses. Die Urkunden des Klosters Weissenburg, 661–864* (Darmstadt, 1979), pp. 36off. noted in Depreux, *Prosopographie*, p. 221.

[20] *Ann. Reg. Franc.* for 825, ed. F. Kurze, MGH SRG 6, p. 168.

[21] Fleckenstein, *Hofkapelle*, p. 168. A charter of October 19, 833 notes "advicem Grimaldi" (*Dipl. regum Germ.* 1, no. 13, ed. P. Kehr, *Die Urkunden Ludwigs des Deutschen*, MGH diplomata regum Germaniae 1, pp. 15–16); his predecessor Gozbald was last attested on May 27, 833 (MGH, Dipl. regum Germ. 1, no. 11, pp. 13–14); documents cited by Depreux, *Prosopographie*, p. 222.

[22] Depreux, *Prosopographie*, p. 222.

[23] Ibid.

[24] Ratbert, *Casus Sancti Galli*, c. 7, ed. I. von Arx, MGH SS 2, p. 67; Depreux, *Prosopographie*, p. 222.

[25] Bischoff, "Bücher," p. 193. According to Depreux, the first mention of Grimald as archchaplain is April 21, 857 in MGH, Dipl. regum Germ. 1, no. 80, pp. 116–117 (cited in *Prosopographie*, p. 222). Fleckenstein gives 854 as the first time he is called "archicapellanus" (*Hofkapelle*, p. 171).

and providing counsel to the king.[26] Grimald resumed his position as head of the chancellery by mid-854.[27] He was a poet, a builder, a book collector, and an avid promoter of East Frankish saints' cults.[28] Clearly, he was an important figure for the aspiring scholar Ermenric to cultivate. Because Grimald was an educator and a poet with an interest in saints, an epic *vita* of his abbey's patron, as Ermenric promised, would be ideal for acquiring his *amicitia*.

Like Grimald, Walafrid (808/809–849) was a courtier of Louis the Pious, and, like him, he was adversely affected by the conflict following the emperor's death.[29] Walafrid, nicknamed "Strabo" ("Squinty"), was an oblate of humble birth from Alemannia, educated first at Reichenau and then, from 826–829, at Fulda.[30] At these abbeys, he became friends with two other luminaries of his era, Lupus of Ferrières and the rebel theologian Gottschalk.[31] He was renowned as a poet from a young age, composing the *Visio Wettini* in 827.[32] In 829, he was taken to court, perhaps to be the tutor of the young Charles (later Charles the Bald), and there he enjoyed Empress Judith's favor.[33] In the turbulent 830s and 840s, Walafrid

---

[26] Thegan, *Vita* c. 47. The Grimalt codex (St. Gallen, SB 397) contains information on royal ceremonial (see Goldberg, *Struggle for Empire*, p. 209).

[27] His reappointment as head of the chancellery is first documented in a diploma of July 22, 854, MGH, Dipl. regum Germ. 1, no. 69, pp. 96–99, cited by Depreux, *Prosopographie*, p. 222.

[28] On Grimald as a poet, Godman, *Poets*, p. 94, and Walafrid, *De imagine Tetrici*, lines 230–232, in MGH Poetae 2, p. 377; Bischoff, "Bücher," pp. 196–200, 210–211; Goldberg, *Struggle for Empire*, pp. 169–170. Gall is one of the saints whose feast is listed in the "Grimalt codex," and Grimald oversaw the translation of Otmar to Saint-Gall.

[29] Depreux, *Prosopographie*, pp. 393–394, no. 270.

[30] Wesley M. Stevens, "Walahfrid Strabo – A Student at Fulda," in Wesley M. Stevens, *Cycles of Time and Scientific Learning in Medieval Europe* (Aldershot, 1995), X, pp. 13–20; Irmgard Fees, "War Walahfrid Strabo der Lehrer und Erzieher Karls des Kahlen?," ed. M. Thumser, A. Wenz-Haubfleisch, and P. Wiegand, *Studien zur Geschichte des Mittelalters: Jürgen Petersohn zum 65. Geburtstag* (Stuttgart, 2000), pp. 42–61 (pp. 42–47 on Walafrid's youth).

[31] C. Lambot, *Oeuvres théologiques et grammaticales de Godescalc d'Orbais* (Louvain, 1945), p. 504.

[32] On Walafrid's verse, see Alf Önnerfors, "Walahfrid Strabo als Dichter," in *Die Abtei Reichenau. Neue Beiträge zur Geschichte und Kultur des Inselklosters*, ed. Helmut Maurer (Sigmaringen, 1974), pp. 83–113; Peter K. Stein, "Poésie antique et poésie néo-antique sous les règnes de Charlemagne, Louis le Pieux et Louis le Germanique: l'exemple de Walahfrid Strabo," in *La représentation de l'antiquité au moyen âge. Actes du Colloque des 26, 27 et 28 mars 1981*, ed. Danielle Buschinger and André Crépin (Vienna, 1982), pp. 7–27.

[33] Walafrid, *Carm.* 23a, MGH Poetae 2, pp. 379–380; and *Carmen ad Ruadbern* (*Carm.* 38), pp. 388ff.; Elizabeth Ward, "Caesar's Wife: The Career of the Empress Judith, 819–829,"

cultivated patrons and friends across the political spectrum, including Hilduin, Adalhard, and Thegan.[34]

In 838, Louis the Pious appointed him abbot of Reichenau, his beloved home abbey, although the monks claimed the right to elect their own abbot.[35] In 840, Louis the German ousted him, and he spent two years in Speyer.[36] During his exile, he addressed a poem to Louis's older brother Lothar, in which he relates his expulsion and places his hope in Lothar's reunification of the Carolingian kingdoms.[37] When Louis and Charles defeated Lothar at the battle of Fontenoy in 841, Walafrid's attempt seemed foiled, but his connections spanned political divisions, and he was able to invoke the assistance of one of Louis's partisans, his most important patron, Grimald.[38] He may have composed his verse *De cultura hortulorum*, dedicated to Grimald, in this context.[39] After he was reinstated as abbot of Reichenau in 842, Walafrid sent verse to Louis.[40] Peter Godman summarizes his career: "[p]oetry remained the consistent means with which Walahfrid spun the web of his allegiances and ambitions."[41] His corpus included two saints' lives in verse, the *Vita Blaithmaic* and the *Vita Mammae*.[42] According to the preface to his prose *Vita Galli*, he had

in *Charlemagne's Heir*, pp. 221–224; Friedrich von Bezold, "Kaiserin Judith und ihr Dichter Walahfrid Strabo," *Historische Zeitschrift* 130 (1924): 377–439.

[34] Godman, *Poets*, pp. 145–146, gives a long list of Walafrid's contacts. Walafrid dedicated a poem to Hilduin, *Carm.* 29, MGH Poetae 2, p. 383. See also his *Carm.* 65, p. 407. Contra Walafrid as Charles's tutor, see Fees, "War Walahfrid Strabo der Lehrer," pp. 42–61. On Adalhard, see Courtney M. Booker, "*Imitator daemonum dicor*: Adalhard the Seneschal, Mistranslations, and Misrepresentations," *Jahrbuch für internationale Germanistik* 33 (2001): 124–126; Walafrid's poems to Thegan, *Carm.* 2 and 3, MGH Poetae 2, pp. 351–353. Other contacts included Drogo, bishop of Metz (*Carm.* 5, p. 253), Ebbo of Rheims (*Carm.* 1, pp. 350–351), and Bodo (*Carm.* 34, p. 386). On Bodo, see Frank Riess, "From Aachen to Al-Andalus: The Journey of Deacon Bodo (823–876)," *EME* 13 (2005): 131–157.

[35] Alice L. Harting-Correa, *Walahfrid Strabo's Libellus de Exordiis et Incrementis Quarundam in Observationibus Ecclesiasticis Rerum: A Translation and Liturgical Commentary* (Leiden, 1996), pp. 8–10; David A. Traill, *Walahfrid Strabo's Visio Wettini: Text, Translation, and Commentary* (Frankfurt am Main, 1974), pp. 5–6; Eleanor S. Duckett, *Carolingian Portraits: A Study in the Ninth Century* (Ann Arbor, 1962), pp. 136–137.

[36] Courtney M. Booker, "A New Prologue of Walafrid Strabo," *Viator* 36 (2005): 84.

[37] *Carm.* 76, MGH Poetae 2, pp. 413–415; Godman, *Poets*, p. 146.

[38] Godman, *Poets*, pp. 146–147.

[39] Walafrid, *De cultura hortulorum*, MGH Poetae 2, pp. 335–350; Goldberg, *Struggle for Empire*, p. 170; Godman, *Poetry*, p. 38. The poem's date is uncertain. Goldberg dates it to his exile, Godman to his abbacy at Reichenau.

[40] Walafrid, *Carm.* 71, MGH Poetae 2, pp. 410–411.

[41] Godman, *Poets*, p. 146.

[42] Walafrid, *Vita Mammae* and *Vita Blaithmaic* both printed in MGH Poetae 2, pp. 275–296 and 297–301. Discussed by Martin Brooke, "The Prose and Verse Hagiography of

intended to versify that work as well.[43] In 849, he died crossing the Loire on a mission from Louis to Charles.[44]

The dynastic conflict affected the career of a less important monk in different ways. Ermenric (ca. 814–874) was originally from Ellwangen and probably received his earliest education at that cloister.[45] His parents and social origins are unknown, and there is little evidence of his early years.[46] By 839 he was a deacon and, a decade later, a priest.[47] He studied at Fulda in Saxony (under its *magister* Rudolf and its famous abbot Hraban Maur), Reichenau, and Saint-Gall, but the chronology is obscure.[48]

Between 839 and 841, Ermenric visited his friend and former fellow student, Hraban's nephew Gundram, whom Louis the German had sent to Fulda's isolated hermitage at Solnhofen.[49] Gundram had been a courtier and a deacon at Louis's court, and Ermenric implies that the king had sent him to Solnhofen to ensure Hraban's compliance while the latter was still abbot of Fulda.[50] At his exiled friend's request, Ermenric composed a

---

Walahfrid Strabo," in *Charlemagne's Heir*, pp. 551–564. The *Vita Blaithmaic* is only 172 lines long. The *Vita Mammae* comprises 733 lines of hexameter, with opening and closing verses in other meters. Brooke convincingly argues that the *Vita Blaithmaic* is a juvenile work, whereas the *Vita Mammae* is a product of Walafrid's adult life.

[43] Walafrid, *Pref.* to *Vita Galli*, ed. B. Krusch in MGH SRM 4, p. 282.

[44] Booker, "New Prologue," p. 84.

[45] Suerbaum, "Ein heidnischer Klassiker als Dünger," p. 238. For a summary of Ermenric's education, see Wilhelm Forke, "Studien zu Ermenrich von Ellwangen," *Zeitschrift für Württembergische Landesgeschichte* 28 (1969): 5–11. He is listed in prayer confraternity records among the brothers of Ellwangen. Based on the minimum age for a deacon, and the fact that he must have been younger than his teacher Walafrid, Ermenric must have been born between 810 and 814 (see Forke, pp. 4–6). On Ermenric, also see H. Löwe, "Ermenrich von Ellwangen," in *Lexikon des Mittelalters*, vol. 3 (Zürich, 1986), p. 2157; F.J. Worstbrock, "Ermenrich von Ellwangen," *Verfasserlexikon: Die deutsche Literatur des Mittelalters*, vol. 2 (Berlin, 1978/1979), col. 610.

[46] Forke, "Studien zu Ermenrich," p. 4.

[47] Ibid., p. 5. In 839, he is included in the Saint-Gall confraternity records among the deacons (*diaconi*), which coheres with his description of himself in the letter prefacing the *Vita S. Suoli*. In his *Vita Hariolfi*, written around 849, he describes himself as a *presbiter*. On these two prose *vitae*, see the following discussion.

[48] Forke, "Studien zu Ermenrich," pp. 5–6; Coon, "Historical Fact," p. 4; Ermenric, *Epistola*, MGH SS 15/1, p. 155. From references in Ermenric's writing, Forke suggests that following his study at Fulda, he spent time at Louis the German's court and returned to Ellwangen. See Forke, pp. 8–11.

[49] Coon, "Historical Fact," p. 6.

[50] *Vita Sualonis* (BHL 7925–7926), c. 10, ed. O. Holder-Egger, MGH SS 15/1, p. 161.

prose *vita* of Solnhofen's founder, Sualo.[51] Foreshadowing Ermenric's letter to Grimald, the life barely mentions its supposed subject (an Anglo-Saxon hermit and follower of Boniface), concentrating instead on allegorical interpretation.[52] Lynda Coon has shown how Ermenric, emphasizing Fulda's significance, and expressing respect for both Carolingian royalty and Hraban, negotiates the tense relations between Fulda's abbot and Louis the German.[53] He dedicated the *Vita Sualonis* to his teacher Rudolf.[54]

Before 849, he also composed a prose *vita* of Hariolf, founder of the abbey of Ellwangen.[55] The life takes the form of a dialogue between Ermenric and a certain Mahtolf, whom he addresses as a teacher.[56] The work is dedicated to Gozbald, bishop of Würzburg (842–855), who was related to Hariolf, was a highly ranked courtier, and sometime archchancellor, of Louis the German.[57]

In the letter to Grimald, which he wrote between 849 and 855, Ermenric says that he had been studying at Reichenau (*Augia felix*), Walafrid's abbey.[58] Although they were near contemporaries, Ermenric describes Walafrid as his "most blessed instructor" (*beatissimus praeceptor meus*). In 849, Grimald had ordered Ermenric to leave Reichenau for Saint-Gall "for the sake of lingering and learning."[59] Ermenric's initially cordial relations with the monks there soon soured. The deacon Gozbert, nephew of the former abbot of Saint-Gall of the same name (d. 837), asked him to write an epic *vita* of Gall, but then transferred his patronage to another.[60] This, then, is the context for Ermenric's letter. Although we do not have Grimald's reply, the fact he had it copied into a teaching collection shows that he valued it, so presumably Ermenric's cultivation of his patron was rewarded. He may have become a chaplain of Louis's court at Ratisbone at this time.[61]

---

[51] Coon, "Historical Fact," p. 4.

[52] Ibid., p. 8.

[53] Ibid., p. 23.

[54] Ermenric, *Epistola*, MGH SS 15/1, p. 155.

[55] Coon, "Historical Fact," p. 4; ed. G. Pertz, MGH SS 10, pp. 11–15. The DHGE (vol. 15, col. 759) dates it to 848–854.

[56] Ermenric desribes himself as "vester alumnus."

[57] Goldberg, *Struggle for Empire*, p. 171. Gozbald was also abbot of Niederaltaich, which had been founded by monks from Reichenau. Ermenric mentions Gozbald in c. 30.

[58] Ermenric discusses sending works to the bishop Gozbald whose death in 855 therefore provides a *terminus ante quem* for the letter. Goullet, p. 232.

[59] Ermenric, c. 27: "commorandi et discendi gratia."

[60] Ibid., c. 27.

[61] Fleckenstein, *Hofkapelle*, pp. 184, n. 133; DHGE 15, col. 759.

Little is known of Ermenric's later years.[62] In 866, Louis appointed him bishop of Passau and, the following year, sent him as an emissary to Kahn Boris of the Bulgars.[63] In 870, Bavarian bishops including Ermenric tried the Greek missionary Saint Methodius at Regensberg, and, according to the complaints of Pope John VIII, Ermenric threatened the saint with violence.[64] The bishops sentenced Methodius to three years in prison. In response, in 873, John VIII suspended Ermenric from performing mass and summoned him to Rome.[65] Ermenric died the following year.

Grimald, Walafrid, Ermenric, and their East Frankish abbeys were connected to Hilduin and Louis the Pious's court, discussed in the previous chapter.[66] In addition to Grimald and Walafrid's familiarity with Hilduin, there are many other personal ties among the milieux. Epistolary exchanges and literary echoes reveal the intersecting circles. Hilduin's epic *Passio* and Walafrid's poems exhibit reminiscences, although the direction of borrowing is impossible to ascertain.[67] The anonymous epic *Vita Galli* composed at Saint-Gall in the mid-ninth century also borrows

---

[62] Forke, "Studien zu Ermenrich," p. 22 (for a summary of the arguments for the identity of Ermenric of Ellwangen with Ermenric of Passau, see pp. 24ff.).

[63] Goldberg, *Struggle for Empire*, pp. 172, 280–81; *Annals of Saint-Bertin* for 866; *Annals of the Franks* for 867. Heinz Löwe, "Ermenrich von Passau, Gegner des Methodius: Versuch eines Persönlichkeitsbildes," in *Der Heilige Method, Salzburg und die Slawenmission* (Innsbruck, 1987), pp. 221–241.

[64] Goldberg, *Struggle for Empire*, p. 300; *Fragmenta registri Iohannis VIII papae*, nos. 21–22, ed. E. Caspar MGH Ep. 7, pp. 284–86. In this letter, the pope accuses Ermenric of menacing Methodius with a horsewhip.

[65] *Struggle for Empire*, pp. 300, 319; MGH Ep. 7, pp. 283–286.

[66] Hilduin's predecessor at Saint-Denis, Waldo, had also been abbot of both Saint-Gall and Reichenau. See Werner Vogler, "Historical Sketch of the Abbey of St. Gall," in *The Culture of the Abbey of St. Gall: An Overview*, ed. James C. King and Werner Vogler (Stuttgart, 1990), p. 12. If Hilduin of Saint-Denis is the same Hilduin who was later abbot of Bobbio, then the inclusion of Bobbio in Saint-Gall's prayer confraternity in 846 suggests another link between the author of the epic *PD* and Ermenric's milieu. See Dieter Geuenich, "The St. Gall Confraternity of Prayer," in *Culture of the Abbey of St. Gall*, p. 29. Sedulius Scottus (associated with Saint-Gall) addressed a poem to one Hildwinus, possibly Hilduin, former abbot of Saint-Denis. See Sedulius Scottus, *Carm.* lxxvi, MGH Poetae 3, pp. 226–227, discussed by Lapidge, "Lost Passio," p. 63, n. 48. Einhard, Hilduin's rival in relic acquisition, had been educated at Fulda. Hraban Maur, abbot of Fulda, sent his prose and verse versions of his poem on the cross to the brothers at Saint-Denis (Hraban Maur, MGH Poetae 2, p. 162). Hraban communicated with Hilduin (and Hilduin's student Hincmar of Rheims) on the problem of Gottschalk and sent him his commentaries on the book of Kings (MGH Ep. 5, pp. 528, 424).

[67] Lapidge, "Lost Passio," p. 73. Lapidge shows hexametrical formulae used in the same places in lines of Walafrid's *Visio Wettini* (of 826), *De imagine Tetrici* (of 829), and *Vita Mammae* and in Hilduin's epic *PD*.

from Hilduin's epic.[68] The Pseudo-Dionysian reminiscences in Ermenric's letter indicate an intellectual connection with Saint-Denis, because, at this time, Hilduin's was the only translation of the theological works.[69]

The connections and correspondence of Grimald, Ermenric, and, particularly, Walafrid illustrate the continuing importance of patronage in the politics of these turbulent years, and the role of poetry in acquiring, maintaining, and utilizing such *amicitia*. The composition of poetry and the profession of piety remained the defining features of courtiers and, therefore, epic *vitae*, which expressed the latter through the former, continued to be an effective claim to patronage. Like his father, Louis the German surrounded himself with learned churchmen. A poet himself, he cultivated an erudite court culture.[70] Eric Goldberg describes its operation:

In this milieu of learned churchmen around Louis's court, the composition and dedication of works of literature became profoundly political. Books, literary works, and poetry served to reinforce ties of patronage and *amicitia* between churchmen and the palace and to heal political rifts caused by the civil war.[71]

The sources of literary patronage were shifting from kings to churchmen,[72] and the dedications reflect this change. While Hilduin sent his epic *passio* to the emperor, Ermenric directed his putative epic *vita* to Grimald. Ermenric, self-appointed protégé of Grimald and Walafrid, attempted to follow in their footsteps as courtiers. His two earlier prose *vitae* show his concern for patronage. His letter to Grimald represents his most ardent attempt at using saints and literature to gain favor. I turn now from the historical context to a consideration of the letter's codicology and contents.

THE MANUSCRIPT

The letter, eighty-nine pages long, is preserved in one medieval manuscript, St. Gallen, Stiftsbibliothek, MS 265, from the second half of the ninth century.[73] Ermenric's letter, the first text in this plain and utilitarian codex,

---

[68] Lapidge, "Lost Passio," p. 73.

[69] Francesco Mosetti Casaretto, "Intuere cælum apertum: l'esordio dell' 'Epistola ad Grimaldum abbatem' di Ermenrico de Ellwangen fra Ilduino di Saint-Denis e Giovanni Scoto," in *History and Eschatology in John Scottus Eriugena and his Time* (Leuven, 2002), pp. 203–225.

[70] Louis, *Ad Baldonem*, MGH Poetae 1, pp. 643–644.

[71] Goldberg, *Struggle for Empire*, p. 170.

[72] Godman, *Poets*, p. 166.

[73] The manuscript is paginated rather than foliated. Gustav Scherrer, *Verzeichniss der Handschriften der Stiftsbibliothek von St. Gallen* (Halle, 1875), pp. 99–100: Bischoff,

is followed by a letter of Pseudo-Hippocrates (also found in Walafrid's *vademecum*), which gives symptoms of disease and recommends simple practical treatments, such as radish and cardamom, mustard seed in honeyed wine, and cabbage.[74] The remaining texts are metrical works by Bede: the verse *vita* of Saint Cuthbert (BHL 2020), the *carmen* to Saint Etheldrida (BHL 2633), and metrical versions of Psalms 41 and 112.[75] (For a description of this codex, see Appendix A.)

The manuscript's physical properties and contents show that it was a teacher's book of excerpts for classroom use and consultation.[76] The medical letter contains practical information for its readers and is written in straightforward Latin. Many of Bede's texts are found in other schoolbooks.[77] Ermenric writes that his letter could have educational value, standing in for a teacher: "its utility as much as its authority is conspicuous for them in the varied manner of a teacher."[78] A note in the manuscript written above the work's title in a slightly later hand shows that this copy of Ermenric's letter indeed fulfilled a didactic function: "monk, burning to gain a thorough knowledge of the study of grammar, you can consult it in this outstanding book."[79] The editor Goullet notes that "ce qui montre que

"Bücher," pp. 200–201. An electronic facsimile and description of this manuscript have been published at http://www.e-codices.unifr.ch/en/description/csg/0265 (accessed August 21, 2009); Augusti Beccaria, *I codici medicina del periodo presalernitano* (ix, x, et xie s.) (Rome, 1956), no. 132, pp. 371–372. There is also a sixteenth- or seventeenth-century copy of Ermenric's letter in fols. 301–368 of the manuscript discussed in Mosetti Casaretto, "Ermerico di Ellwangen, Epistola ad Grimaldum abbatem, MS München, Bayerische Staatsbibliothek, Oefeleana 147: fisionomia di un 'descriptus,'" *Filologia mediolatina* 6/7 (1999–2000): 201–214.

74 Walafrid's *vademecum* is St. Gallen, SB, MS 878, and the letter is found on pp. 327–331; see Stevens, "Walahfrid Strabo," p. 16.

75 The metric Psalms are labeled XLI and XXII, respectively. Helmut Gneuss and Michael Lapidge, "The Earliest Manuscript of Bede's Metrical *Vita S. Cudbercti*," *ASE* 32 (2003): 53.

76 Bischoff, "Bücher," p. 200.

77 There are twenty copies of Bede's metric *Vita Cuthberti*. Michael Lapidge, "Bede the Poet," *Jarrow Lecture for 1993*, p. 12. Ed. in *Bedas metrische Vita sancti Cuthberti*, ed. Werner Jaeger (Leipzig, 1935). Bede's *De arte metrica* and other works are copied in numerous schoolbooks. See Harry Bober, "An Illustrated Medieval School-Book of Bede's 'De Natura Rerum,'" *The Journal of the Walters Art Gallery* 19/20 (1956/1957): 64–97; Springer, "Sedulius," p. 32.

78 Ermenric, c. 8: "tam utilitas quam auctoritas in eis magisterii vario modo eniteat."

79 St. Gallen, SB, MS 265, p. 3: "grammaticae studium monachos pernoscere fervens / potes adhibuisse hoc libro egregio." The end of the note seems to read "[on the left] read this as pentameter" ([sinistr]e hunc pentametrum legas) referring to the fact that, with creative use of vowel quantities, the annotator's previous two lines can be read as an elegiac couplet (one line of dactylic hexameter followed by one line of pentameter). The reading *sinistre* is uncertain. Cf. Goullet, p. 36, n. 70.

pour les lecteurs médiévaux, la lettere de Grimald était perçue avant tout comme un traité grammatical" and "par un traité didactique contribue au bien collectif mieux que par un texte hagiographique de command."[80]

Bischoff has shown that St. Gallen, SB, MS 265 belongs to a group of manuscripts made for Grimald. The extant version of the letter is therefore not Ermenric's autograph, but probably a direct copy of it.[81] Clearly, then, Grimald thought enough of the letter's didactic properties to have it included in his *vademecum*, a miscellany of useful and educational materials.

As mentioned earlier, Ermenric gives three reasons for writing the letter. At the beginning, he claims to write in response to Grimald's request for an *exordium* on the first two commandments, love of God and neighbor, on which, says Ermenric, all the other commandments hinge. The notion of *caritas* (particularly toward one's *proximus*) recurs throughout the work.[82] By writing this letter, itself a kiss (*basium*) of charity, Ermenric hoped to earn Grimald's *amicitia* (friendship, patronage).[83] Ermenric needed Grimald's support for the composition of an epic *Vita Galli*, which he finally reveals as his real reason for writing. Gozbert and other monks had asked Ermenric to write the epic life of their patron saint, to fulfill a task that Walafrid, author of the prose *Vita Galli*, had promised to complete. Gozbert, however, grew impatient with Ermenric's slow progress and turned to Ermenric's rival, a "new Homer" (*Homerus . . . novus*), who composed verse more swiftly.[84] Having lost his original patron and apparently mired in a snake pit of enmities, Ermenric appealed to Grimald's higher authority.[85]

Ermenric also claims that he writes to educate a wider readership. He repeatedly refers to readers who are unlearned and slow.[86] In lamenting the shortage of teachers (*docentium raritas*), he alludes to the English writer Aldhelm, showing his own erudition while opining its lack in

---

[80] Goullet, pp. 36, 377.

[81] Bischoff, "Bücher," pp. 200–201.

[82] c. 1 and passim; Casaretto, "Iter caritatis," passim.

[83] c. 28.

[84] Ibid., c. 29

[85] Ermenric alludes to these enmities in c. 5 and 27.

[86] c. 17, 19. He reiterates the slowness (*tarditas*) of these readers and the cheapening (*vilescere*) of learning in several passages: "scio enim, quod quibusdam minus studiosis vel insciis haec coram exposita et cum auctoritate prisca confirmata vilescunt, vel quia hactenus haec ignorauerunt, vel quia in talibus alium usum habuerunt" (c. 17). See also c. 24, in which he says he offers a taste for the *infantes* "who are uninformed or slow at reading" (qui nesciunt, vel qui ad legendum tardi sunt).

others.[87] Acknowledging that some of his material is too long and boring for the learned such as Grimald, he insists that his didactic explications are for the edification of this wider audience. The teachings that Ermenric has "heaped up" (*conglobare*)

are especially necessary for the ignorant. Out of love for them, although they are absent, I proceed by expounding these matters in such a long progression, so that they might know them, since I desire to have the grace of God in common with them, in knowledge of art and in spiritual understanding.[88]

Because liberal monastic education was religious education, necessary for the interpretation of Scripture, this absent readership was in spiritual as well as intellectual peril and Ermenric's teaching was thus an act of *amor*, a term that Ermenric uses interchangeably with *caritas*.[89] He offered a "heavenly treasure" (*thesaurus caelestis*) to the willing and the unwilling. In return, he hoped that the readers would pray for his soul.[90] So, Ermenric envisioned his teaching as salvific for both writer and reader.

THE LETTER

The text consists of a letter on myriad topics (c. 1–29) and what Ermenric refers to as the *calx epistolae*, literally, "the heel of the letter" (c. 30–36) excerpted, he says, from his epic *Vita Galli*. (The chapter divisions employed in the printed editions are modern.) The first section, the letter proper, comprises discussions on a wide number of subjects. The first six chapters form the *exordium* on the first two commandments.[91] Subsequent chapters contain discussions on theology, the divisions of dialectic and rhetoric, aspects of prose and verse prosody, orthography, and allegory (c. 7–19). He draws on many sources, which reflect the monastic

---

[87] Aldhelm, *Ep.* to Leutherius, ed. Rudolf Ehwald in MGH AA 15, p. 477. Discussing his own education, including that in metrics, Aldhelm uses similar language to describe a slightly different problem: "cuius rei studiosis lectoribus tanto inextricabilior obscuritas praetenditur, quanto rarior doctorum numerositas reperitur."

[88] c. 15: "precipue necessaria sunt ignorantibus. Ob quorum etiam amorem, licet absentium, haec tam, longa serie prosequar exponendo, ut sciant quod communem habere cum eis gratiam Dei desidero, in scientia artis et intellectu spirituali."

[89] c. 21, another example of the link between salvation and learning.

[90] c. 15.

[91] Toward the end of this section, Ermenric refers back to his discussion in the perfect tense, and in c. 22, he refers back to his *exordium* in which he spoke about the *ratio* of the soul, showing that he uses the word *exordium* to mean the beginning of the letter, not just the introduction to the subject.

curriculum at Saint-Gall and other elite abbeys,[92] including pagan and Christian poets (including Lucan, Virgil, Horace, Ovid, and Prudentius), and the grammars of Alcuin and Gottschalk. He takes a long passage verbatim from Gregory's *Commentary on Ezekiel*. The quotations are carefully chosen to cohere with his thematic interests. So, the excerpts from Gregory (c. 21, 23) discuss topics he had touched on earlier, namely, the allegorical reading of Noah's ark (c. 5) and the *anima* (c. 2, 6). Ermenric next recounts a personal anecdote about being haunted by Virgil and then discusses Classical literature (c. 24–25). A short autobiographical interlude follows describing his experiences at Saint-Gall and providing the context and rationale for composing the epic *Vita Galli* (c. 27–29). Ermenric says he has attached a work on the foundation of the monastery, which he had already sent to Bishop Gozbald (this work is not transmitted in the manuscript), and materials excerpted from his *vita* of Gall. He asks Grimald to receive them,

although I am lowlier than the poets named above and have been spurned on account of their sufficiently urbane wit, because I declare myself neither a poet nor an acolyte of the muses, nonetheless, at your command, you whom little things delight, I excerpt small things about [*or* from] the great. . . .[93]

The *calx epistolae* (c. 30–36) is an appendix of prose and verse excerpts from his *Vita Galli*: "my teacher and most beloved master, in the end of this letter I earnestly request that your holiness receive these trifles of my eloquence, just as I rightly trust in your paternal authority."[94] He repeats the idea a few chapters later in verse: "now I pick certain flowers of my mind concerning saint Gall."[95] The verse passages are in several meters and include acrostics. The topics in this final section include invocations to God and the saint, discussions of the Trinity, geographical description, allegorical interpretation, and the conflict between Ermenric and his rival poet.

---

[92] Goullet, p. 47.

[93] c. 29: "quapropter licet supra nominatis poetis sim abiectior, et ob ipsorum facetam urbanitatem satis spretus, quia nec poetam nec amusoterum me esse profiteor, tamen vestra auctoritate iubente, quibus parva delectant, de magnis parva excerpo ..."

[94] c. 30: "ceterum, mi magister et domine amabillime, in calce huius epistolae sanctitatem vestram obnixe deposco, ut nugas praesentes eloquii mei ita suscipiatis, veluti optime confido in paternitatem vestram." He also says, c. 30, that he appends a "little work" on the foundation of the monastery, which he had previously written, but it is not attached to the letter (Adiunxi autem et huic operi breve opusculum quod de incoeptione nostri coenobii et fratrum ibidem Deo olim famulantium vita conscripsi).

[95] c. 33: "mihi nunc mentis floscellos carpere quosdam / De sancte Galle."

Where many scholars have seen only chaos and disorder in Ermenric's assortment of topics, Mosetti Casaretto has shown that he returns to certain themes and images.[96] The metaphor of light in the letter's opening compresses and presages the work's concerns, and the themes of *caritas* (especially as it pertains to the love of God and neighbor) and *amicitia* recur throughout.[97] Ermenric also returns to other apposite themes such as the loyalty to princes, the active and contemplative life, and the virtues.[98] He also returns to (and mixes) a number of metaphors including the four wheels of the apostles and the airborne *quadriga* (four-horse chariot) of the virtues.[99] The first two commandments are envisioned as a pair of wings that allow one to fly to heaven.[100] He varies the traditional image of grammar as a forest.[101] Rivers, both metaphorical and literal (in

---

[96] Goullet also argues that the letter is in fact quite structured. See Goullet, p. 33. Francesco Mosetti Casaretto has written several articles on themes in the letter: "L'Epistola di Ermenrico di Ellwangen: identità e destinazione, scopo, tipologia redazionale," *Studi medievali* ser. 3, 38 (1997): 647–677; "Iter caritatis: forma e metaforma dell'enciclopedismo epistolare di Ermenrico di Ellwangen," *Studia monastica: Commentarium ad rem monasticam investigandam* 40.2 (1998): 265–279; "Santità virtuale e "petitio" agiografica nell'*Epistola ad Grimaldum* di Ermenrico di Ellwangen," *Hagiographica* 5 (1998): 49–84; "L'*amicitia*, chiave ermeneutica dell' 'Epistola ad Grimaldum abbatem' di Ermenrico di Ellwangen," *Revue Bénédictine* 109 (1999): 117–147; "L'esordio mistico dell'*Epistola ad Grimaldum abbatem* di Ermenrico de Ellwangen: immaginario, fonti dirette e indirette," *MJ* 36 (2001): 205–233; "'Intuere coelum apertum': l'esordio dell'epistola ad Grimaldum abbatem' di Ermenrico di Ellwangen fra Ilduino di Saint-Denis et Giovanni Scoto," in *History and Eschatology in John Scottus Eriugena and his Time*, Proceedings of the Tenth International Conference of the Society for the Promotion of Eriugenian Studies, Maynooth and Dublin, August 16–20, 2002, ed. Michael Dunne and J.J. McEvoy (Leuven, 2002), pp. 203–225; "Sole e luna nell' *Epistola ad Grimaldum Abbatem*. Il cielo ripiegato di Ermenrico di Ellwangen," *Micrologus* 12 (2004): 291–321.

[97] Casaretto, "Iter caritatis"; "L'*amicitia*"; "Sole e luna."

[98] *Vita contemplativa* and *vita activa* (c. 19, 20); love of one's neighbor (c. 19).

[99] For example, the *quadriga* of virtues appears in c. 2, 6, 8, 19, 24; the apostolic wheels in c. 6, 22, 24.

[100] c. 1, 6, 21.

[101] Forest and foliage metaphors for grammar: c. 8, 9, 16; similarly, sea metaphors: c. 8, 11, 24. Goullet, p. 199, notes sources for these images. Ermenric uses many of the terms from Aldhelm's image of the forest of grammar. Aldhelm, *De metris*, c. 8, ed. Rudolf Ehwald in MGH AA 15, p. 78: "nor in such a dense forest of all of Latin and among the wooded groves of syllables, where, according to the ancient tradition of the elders, many small branches of rules spring forth from single roots of words, is this matter easily grasped by the uncultivated, especially those deficient in or ignorant of the art of meter" (Neque enim in tam densa totius latinitatis silva et nemorosis sillabarum saltibus, ubi de singulis verborum radicibus multiplices regularum ramusculos pululasse antiqua veterum traditio declarat, rudibus facile negotium deprehenditur et praesertim metricae artis disciplina carentibus et nescientibus ...).

questionable taste, given Walafrid's death), and venomous snakes occur throughout.[102]

Despite the recurring themes and images, the letter lacks a coherent overarching structure. The relationship of the body of the letter (c. 1–29) to the *calx epistolae* (c. 30–36) is unclear. Ermenric claims that he composed the *calx* in a hurry (c. 30), which makes it seem like an afterthought, but he also says that the composition of the epic life, which the *calx* represents, is his main reason for writing (c. 28).[103] Ermenric's text can be read as a comic inversion of the conventional epic *vita*, in which a short dedicatory letter is followed by a long verse life.[104] If this is the case and the main body of the letter is a very long dedicatory epistle, then the second set of dedications at the beginning of the *calx* (c. 30–30a) are puzzling. The body of Ermenric's letter does contain some conventional features of a dedicatory letter, such as flattery of the patron and an account of the work's composition, but the lengthy didactic digressions are alien to such a work. Further, it is unclear why Ermenric would have combined his bid for Grimald's patronage with a didactic text. Although the passages on grammar, prosody, orthography, and allegory showcase his erudition, they also require him to repeatedly and awkwardly apologize to his addressee, insisting that he is not patronizing Grimald's intellect when he explains things that the older man already knows.

The structure within each of the two main parts also presents difficulties. Individual subsections of the letter (such as the discussion of prosody), have internal coherence but connections between thematic sections are unclear. Ermenric proceeds from one subject to the next tangentially and then abruptly breaks off and changes topics, with variations of "that's enough about that."[105] Curtius explains that medieval writers and readers judged digressions stylistically pleasing,[106] but this fact does not explain the strange combination of the tangential and sudden transitions.

Another difficulty is the letter's tone, which is quite distinct from the customary formality of Carolingian letters written to superiors who were not also friends. Although Ermenric presents his relationship with Grimald as hierarchical and provides no evidence of familiarity, such as that Alcuin enjoyed with his former students and Charlemagne, the letter's tone is casual and personal, featuring joking asides to the addressee. At one point,

---

[102] Rivers: c. 1, 14, 16, 36; snakes: c. 5, 14, 35, 36.
[103] Casaretto, "Epistola ad Grimaldum," pp. 647–677; Goullet, p. 37.
[104] Goullet, p. 37.
[105] Ermenric, c. 24: "de istis iam dicta sufficient"; cf. 7, 10, 11, 31.
[106] Curtius, *European Literature*, pp. 501–502.

amid a discussion of technical aspects of a class of verbs, Ermenric suddenly requests Grimald's assistance in escaping from the grammatical explication in which he is ensnared:

because I walked into the densest forest of the verb, I cannot get out by myself. Father, give me your hand and lead me out of these thorn bushes – they are making me bleed. But while you reach out your hand too slowly, a certain branch drags me back into the word "sapio," about whose perfect tense the authors disagree ..."[107]

Despite his gratuitous flattery of Grimald, the entire letter has a flippancy that we do not see in the prefatory letters that usually accompany saints' lives or other texts to prospective patrons.

THE IMAGINARY CLASSROOM

The peculiar way Ermenric fulfills his didactic purpose explains these puzzling features. Ermenric states that he writes for a second readership who lack teachers and therefore education, but clearly this work, with its range of specialized topics, is not a conventional or systematic textbook, such as Bede's *De arte metrica* or Alcuin's grammar (both of which he used).[108] Ermenric, like other Carolingian writers, was an original thinker unconstrained by genre expectations, and he created new forms to suit his needs. (His *Vita Hariolfi* is a prose saint's life in dialogue form and his *Vita Sualonis* is almost saint-free.)[109] In his letter to Grimald, he educated his readers (*legentes*) in an innovative way, by presenting himself as if he were a *magister* in the classroom, orally glossing aspects of a text for intermediate students. Ermenric's novel premise – he depicts himself as a teacher at work – accounts for the letter's content, tone, and ostensible lack of structure.

It is likely that Ermenric was in fact a teacher at this stage. In addition to references to the letter's readers (*legentes*), who require education, Ermenric mentions *infantes* and *infantuli* whom he taught. Ermenric

---

[107] c. 16: "quia in silvam verbi densissimam ingressus sum, nec valeo per memet egredi, mitte pater manum et educ me de vepribus istis: valde enim cruentant me. Sed dum manum tardius prebes, retrahit me ramnus quidam in verbum 'sapio', cuius preteritum auctores varie protulerunt ..."

[108] c. 19; cf. c. 17: "ad utilitatem legentium"; c. 24.

[109] Ermenric, *Vita Hariolfi* (BHL 3754), ed. G. Pertz, MGH SS 10, pp. 11–15; Ermenric, *Vita Sualonis*, written 839–842, ed. O. Holder-Egger, MGH SS 15, pp. 151–163. On this *vita*, Coon, "Historical Fact," pp. 1–24.

establishes that he educated the young monks, preparing them for Grimald's more exalted instruction. Drawing on Aldhelm,[110] he writes,

> I know you are eloquent in teaching, most beloved master, and although I am slower than a tortoise, I follow you in such dense material, especially when your little ones signal to me that I should not stay quiet. But these kernels gleaned from the authorities should suffice for them for now, until they acquire the strength for perceiving more things and then finally return to the very source and drink where I slaked my thirst until their ears resound.[111]

He presents himself as a junior teacher at Saint-Gall, introducing the *infantuli* to the core of the curriculum and preparing them for their more advanced lessons given by the senior *magister*, nominally Grimald (although it seems unlikely that Grimald, as bishop and abbot of three houses was still teaching). Ermenric appears to have been one of the *magistri adolescentes*, attested at Saint-Gall, such as Ratpert, who had been a *magister scolarum* there "ab adolescentia."[112] Evidence from other abbeys shows the presence of such figures and gives us some idea of their duties. Thangmar depicts a youth who acted in this capacity and helped the younger students.[113] Abbo of Fleury, according to the *vita* by his contemporary Aimoin (later tenth century), taught reading and chanting (that is, the very beginning of the curriculum) at a young age.[114] Unlike the *legentes*, whom he presents as an absent and passive audience for his letter, Ermenric depicts the *infantuli* as his actual students and characterizes his communication with them as oral (*ut non sileam*) rather than written. These *infantuli* make requests of him (*mihi innuant*), he says, and he responds.

A comparison of the letter with glosses in contemporary teachers' books shows that Ermenric is depicting himself glossing a text. The glosses transcribed in schoolbooks are usually highly abbreviated, providing information in attenuated form, acting as mnemonics to remind the teacher to raise

---

[110] Ermenric paraphrases Aldhelm, *De metris*, c. 8, ed. Rudolf Ehwald, MGH AA 15, pp. 77–78.

[111] c. 16: "puto argutus es in educendo, preceptor amabillime, et ego tardior testudine te sequor in hac spissitudine, precipue cum infantuli vestri mihi innuant, ut non sileam. Sed haec enucleatim ab auctoribus excerpta eis ad tempus sufficiant, usque quo ad maiora percipienda convalescant, et tunc demum recurrant ad ipsum fontem, unde haec hausi et bibant, usque quo eis aures sonent."

[112] Ekkehard IV, *Casus S. Galli*, c. 34. For the junior *magistri* and an excellent discussion of education at Saint-Gall, see Grotans, *Reading*, pp. 65–68 and Chapter 2 in general.

[113] Thangmar, *Vita Bernwardi* (BHL 1253), c. 1, ed. George Pertz MGH SS 4, p. 758.

[114] BHL 3, PL 139, 390; Lutz estimates that Abbo was sixteen or younger. See Cora E. Lutz, *Schoolmasters of the Tenth Century* (Hamden, CT, 1977), p. 43.

a point or ask a question, or referring the teacher to another work. Such glosses are concise, since they are usually copied out between the lines or in the margins (some more prolix commentaries, such as Servius's commentary of Virgil, are transmitted separately). Ermenric's letter reads not like a series of abbreviated glosses, but like the transcription of a loquacious teacher employing them in the classroom; Ermenric presents a mock transcription of himself at work.

This first section of Ermenric's letter (c. 1–29) – a written version of a teacher glossing a literary text – contains a "complex interplay between orality and literacy."[115] Although he refers to his readers (almost always addressing the recipients of his teachings as *legentes*, rather than the *auditores* who would be present in a classroom), he maintains the fiction of an extemporaneous performance, whose unpredictability requires him to adapt his course as he goes: "because I unexpectedly leapt into the verb, the principle part of speech after the noun, I must keep quiet about the noun and touch on a few things about this part of speech."[116]

The premise of the first portion of the letter, that it represents a teacher at work, explains its fragmented structure. This portion of the work lacks organization because glosses do not usually proceed logically, one to the next, but are generated from the text they annotate. That is, the narrative of the glossed text provides the framework for its glosses, and without it, they will appear as a random assortment of notes. Although some glossators are particularly interested in certain themes, most elucidate aspects of the text in a nonsystematic way. Topics are discussed as the text's story, allusions, vocabulary, meter, language, and stylistic features present opportunities. The nonlinear nature of glosses explains the digressive and fractured character of the first section, in which Ermenric wanders tangentially from one topic to another and then abruptly changes tack. The teacher, glossing the text, launches into an explanation of a feature and then digresses to cover similar or contrary examples, to expound the underlying principles, or to touch on peripherally related matters. As Ermenric explains, likening his progress to that of a stumbling drunk, "as if inebriated I leave the path and wander into other arts, touching

---

[115] Grotans, *Reading*, pp. 7, 102. Grotans notes that the tenth-century works *De definitione* and *De syllogismis* contain oral elements that suggest they are notes taken by Notker's students at Saint-Gall.

[116] c. 11: "quia sic inprovise in verbum, principalem post nomen partem orationis, prosilui, silendum est de nomine et de ista parte pauca tangenda." Grotans, *Reading*, p. 42, notes the extemporaneous appearance he projects.

upon something from them and explaining it so it is understood."[117] He apologizes to his addressee for wandering off topic and worries that Grimald will "hate him like a cicada that never shuts up."[118]

The flow that runs through a series of chapters, as Ermenric moves tangentially from one topic to the next, is broken when he brings himself back and changes tack: "enough of that!"[119] With such a statement, he moves to the next feature of the text he wishes to gloss. This new topic may be completely unrelated to the preceding one (for example, one line of the glossed text might require metrical explication, the next mythological background). It is not at all clear from his letter why he "now must say a few words" about a new topic at a particular place.[120] The necessity of Ermenric's meanderings is not apparent, because they are not prescribed by any internal logic of the letter but rather by whatever required explication in the text.

The first section of Ermenric's letter strongly resembles the depiction of imaginary pedagogy in Fulgentius's sixth-century *Continentia Virgiliana*, an interpretation of Virgil's *Aeneid*.[121] Fulgentius was a familiar source for pagan mythology.[122] Laistner shows that Ermenric knew Fulgentius's *Mitologiae*, and the correspondences between Ermenric's letter and the *Continentia* show that he was also familiar with the latter work.[123] In the *Continentia*, Fulgentius summons Virgil from the dead and, adopting

---

[117] c. 19: "quasi ebrius, via coepta relicta, in alias partes etiam devolvor tangendo quaedam ex his et ad intellegendum exponendo."

[118] c. 6: "neque me pro cycada numquam silenti abhorreas."

[119] c 24: "sed et de istis iam dicta sufficient."

[120] For example, c. 31: "clearly before I touch upon the life of Saint Gall, I must say a few things about the essence or substance or the Holy Trinity" (Sane antequam de vita sancti Galli aliqua tangam, de sanctae Trinitatis essentia vel substantia pauca dicam).

[121] Fulgentius, *Expositio Virgilianae continentiae secundum philosophos moralis*, in *Fabii Planciadis Fulgentii Opera*, ed. Rudolf Helm (Leipzig, 1898), pp. 83–107.

[122] Carolingian poets, including writers of epic verse lives, such as Milo, Heiric, and the anonymous authors of the *Carmina* of Cassian (BHL 1633), Lambert (BHL 4682), and Benedicta (BHL 1088) all draw on Fulgentius's works. M.L.W. Laistner, "Fulgentius in the Carolingian Age," in *The Intellectual Heritage of the Early Middle Ages* (New York, 1966), p. 209. Laistner cites as examples from the *Carmina* of Cassian, Lambert and Benedicta in MGH Poetae 4/1, p. 182, line 25; p. 143, c. 1; p. 211, line 17, respectively. The glosses to the *VG* (probably by Heiric) name Fulgentius as a source. Laistner, "Fulgentius in the Carolingian Age," p. 209; *VG*, p. 436.

[123] Laistner, "Fulgentius in the Carolingian Age," pp. 207, 209. See also Robert Edwards, "The Heritage of Fulgentius," in *The Classics in the Middle Ages: Papers of the Twentieth Annual Conference of the Center for Medieval and Early Renaissance Studies*, ed. Aldo S. Bernardo and Saul Levin (Binghamton, NY, 1990), p. 141. Goullet, p. 218, posits the possibility of an intermediary source between Fulgentius and Ermenric. The works have many similarities: both depict dead Virgil in a humorously unpleasant manner. In each,

the role of a humble student, asks him to teach him "light things, which the grammar teachers draw out for their young audience in return for their monthly paycheck."[124] Fulgentius envisions a classroom setting. Twice he uses the term *timor magistrianus* (fear of the teacher) to describe a student's experience at school.[125] Continuing the adversarial picture of the classroom, Fulgentius's Virgil reads the boxing match of Entellus and Dares (in *Aeneid*, book 5) as an allegory for the interaction of teacher and student.[126] The *magister* calls on the student, asking him to summarize book 1, to check he has done the reading.[127] The shade of Virgil gives an allegorical reading of the *Aeneid*, and the student responds with questions and requests for clarification.

The correspondences between Ermenric's pronouncements and Fulgentius's ghostly *magister* further show that Ermenric's text likewise depicts a teacher explicating a text. In explaining the first line of the *Aeneid*, Fulgentius's Virgil demonstrates just how far a commentator can wander from the lines of the page and how rambling and disconnected a disembodied gloss can appear. Ermenric and the spectral Virgil cover similar topics, including substance and accidence and the "Samian Y" (the idea attributed to the philosopher Pythagoras of Samos, that a young person was faced with a choice of the kind of life to live).[128] Like

the writer (Fulgentius, Ermenric) addresses a teacher (Virgil, Grimald) in similar ways, expressing both respect toward him ("vates clarissime," p. 87, "Maro doctissime," p. 97) and contempt or condescension. Both draw imagery from *Aeneid*, book 6, and share metaphors and images, such as branches, forests, fountains, and cicadas. Thematically, they also overlap, giving *caritas* as the reason for writing and emphasizing allegorical interpretation.

[124] Fulgentius, *Continentia*, p. 86: "illa ... levia, quae mensualibus stipendiis grammatici distrahunt puerilibus auscultatibus." See J.W. Jones, Jr., "Vergil as Magister in Fulgentius," in *Classical, Mediaeval and Renaissance Studies in Honor of Berthold Louis Ullman*, ed. C. Henderson, Jr., vol. 1 (Rome, 1964), pp. 273–275.

[125] Fulgentius, *Continentia*, pp. 101, 103

[126] Ibid., p. 95; Andrew Laird, "The Poetics and Afterlife of Virgil's Descent to the Underworld: Servius, Dante, Fulgentius and the Culex," *Proceedings of the Virgil Society* 24 (2001): 60.

[127] Fulgentius, *Continentia*, p. 89.

[128] Ermenric, c. 19. The Samian Y is glossed in Heiric's *VG*. Paris, BN, MS lat. 13757, fol. 13v, printed in MGH Poetae 3, p. 441. The *Vita Arnulfi* contains a reference to the "twofold branches of the Samian" (*Samii bivios ... ramos*), printed in *Novem vitae*, p. 91. In the metric *Vita Gisleni* "ramus" (branch) is glossed "pitagorea littera" (*Novem vitae*, p. 151). Vienna, Österreichische Nationalbibliothek, Codex Vindobonensis Palatinus 969, a tenth-century manuscript containing Aldhelm's *De virginibus* and *Poema de octo principalibus vitiis*, along with Cato's *Distichs*, Seneca's *Proverbs*, and other useful school texts, includes an explanation of the Pythagorean letter, on fol. 55v, which begins "Y Samius ad exemplum vitae humanae primus formavit. Cui virgula subtilior primam

Ermenric, the shade introduces quotations (from Juvenal, Petronius, and his own works) and a sprinkling of Greek.

Modern scholarly responses to the *Continentia* echo the criticisms of Ermenric, underlining the similarities between the two. Comparetti calls it "violent and incoherent."[129] Coffin characterizes it as "a distorted product of misapplied industry" in accordance with his dim view of the early Middle Ages in which learning was practically a dark art.[130] To him, "there is no order or balance in the arrangement of material; several pages are devoted to the elucidation of a few phrases. ... Not infrequently the course of the exposition is broken by long digressions."[131] Such a description could equally apply to Ermenric's letter.

Ermenric's odd combination of obsequiousness and levity is also explained by the letter's dual nature, as a bid for patronage and a pedagogical work. The letter's praise of Grimald is conventional for an appeal to a patron, whereas its conversational and informal tone reflects a teacher before a class. Humor was an established element of early medieval pedagogy.[132] Ermenric intersperses informative passages with direct address and humorous asides. In addition to his histrionic claims to be drowning in the sea of the prophets, or ensnared in the branches of grammar, there are jokes scattered through the text. For example, Ermenric says that if people were to employ archaic pronunciation, only the learned and the mice would understand the latter presumably because of their propensity for squeaking.[133] He achieves comic effect by using puerile examples from the Roman satirists alongside the lofty words of Scripture, epic, and Classical orators.[134]

---

aetatem significat incertam ..." On the Samian Y, see M.A. Dimier, "La lettre de Pythagore et les hagiographes du moyen âge," *Le Moyen Âge* 60 (1954): 403–418.

[129] Domenico Comparetti, *Vergil in the Middle Ages*, trans. E.F.M. Benecke (Princeton, 1997 [1895]), p. 112.

[130] Harrison Cadwallader Coffin, "Allegorical Interpretation of Vergil with Special Reference to Fulgentius," *Classical Weekly* 15 (1921): 34–35: "we have the first indication in Christian Latinity of the regular medieval type of wise man, who in his demeanor and character partakes of the darkness in which all knowledge is shrouded. Learning had become so rare that its possession was an occult attribute; the scholar was not to be distinguished from the war-lock who held unholy communion with spirits and gained his wisdom through his control over the mysterious forces of nature."

[131] Ibid., p. 35.

[132] Carin Ruff, "Desipere in Loco: Style, Memory and the Teachable Moment," in *Anglo-Saxon and Old Norse Studies for Roberta Frank*, ed. Antonia Harbus and Russell Poole, Old English Series 13 (Toronto, 2005), pp. 91–103.

[133] Ermenric, c. 13. In c. 9, he also brings up mice: If we break up nouns into syllables, the individual parts have no meaning or a different one, so *domus* (house) is divided into *do* (I give) and *mus* (mouse), the "animal frugibus infestum" (animal dangerous to grain).

[134] For example, to illustrate the formation of third conjugation verbs in –*io*, he quotes Persius: "Depict two snakes: boys, the place is sacred, urinate outside" (Pinge duos

Ermenric's inclusion of larger and smaller sections of other writers' works, quoted or paraphrased, also reflects the fictional classroom setting. Glosses could direct teachers to other works, which they could discuss from memory or pick up and read.[135] For example, the glosses of a ninth-century Irish master on a manuscript of Servius refer the user to other writers, including the ninth-century theologian and Hellenist John Scottus Eriugena (abbreviated as "Ioh"), although they do not specify passages.[136] This presupposes either that the teacher – presumably the glossator himself in the case of the Bern manuscript because the notes are too cryptic to be used easily by anyone else – had these other books on hand and knew his way around them or that the marginal notes were enough to prompt his memory of the relevant passage.[137]

In chapters 20 through 23, Ermenric quotes at length from Gregory's *Commentary on Ezechiel*. The chosen passages cohere with the letter's themes, including the *anima* and mystical reading. We can imagine that here Ermenric has opened Gregory's commentary to read out the relevant passages. The section is not simply a block of Gregory's text. Rather, it is peppered with Ermenric's asides, which link the long quotations together and bend them to his overarching purpose. So, between several quotations from Gregory on the grades of the soul in its contemplation of God, he inserts a few words of his own and a paraphrase of Isidore.[138] He explains his choice of topic: "this love compels us, by which we are ordered to love God with our entire soul and our neighbor just as ourselves."[139] In this way, he subordinates Gregory's discourse to his own central theme of *caritas* and the second commandment.

Ermenric, in typically obscure fashion, does not name the text from which he teaches. Ermenric's commentary, with its long discussion on prose and verse prosody, could gloss one of the metric or prosimetric curriculum works he cites, such as Virgil's *Aeneid*, Ovid's *Metamorphoses*, Martianus Capella's *De nuptiis Philologiae et Mercurii*, Prudentius's *Psychomachia*, Sedulius's *Paschale carmen*, or a less common work, such

---

angues: pueri, sacer est locus, extra / Miete) (c. 13, Persius, *Satire* I.113–114), followed by a scatological quotation from Horace (*Satires* I.8, 37–38, c. 13).

[135] John J. Contreni, "The Irish in the Western Carolingian Empire," in *Carolingian Learning*, p. 772.

[136] Bern Burgerbibliothek MS 363. Contreni, "Inharmonious Harmony: Education in the Carolingian World," in *Carolingian Learning*, p. 88; Contreni, "Irish in Empire," p. 770.

[137] Contreni, "Irish in Empire," p. 772.

[138] Dümmler, p. 560, cites Isidore, *Diff.*, II.17,27,28, 30.

[139] Ermenric, c. 22, "dilectio ipsa compellit, qua Deum ex tota anima et proximum sicut nos ipsos diligere iubemur."

as the satires of Persius.[140] The *Aeneid*'s central place in medieval education and its author's guest appearance in chapter 24 make that work a plausible candidate, as does the similarity of Ermenric's glosses to those of Fulgentius's *Virgiliana Continentia*. The glossed work could also be an epic *vita*, possibly Ermenric's own putative *Vita Galli*. If this is the case, it would tie together the first part of the letter and the final six chapters, which purport to represent this *vita*.

READING EPIC LIVES IN THE CLASSROOM

It is possible that Ermenric, in the first part of his letter, depicts himself glossing his own epic *Vita Galli*. As we will see, he certainly shows himself using his own epic poem in the classroom in the final chapters. It is unclear, however, whether it is the text being glossed in the main body of the work. Because we have, at best, fragments of his incomplete verse *Vita Galli* (represented in c. 30–36), it is hard to compare its content with those of the glosses in the previous chapters. Nonetheless, we know that teachers employed their own works, including epic poems, in their classrooms,[141] and there is sufficient coincidence between the material of the two sections to make the suggestion plausible. Goullet describes portions of the *calx* (c. 31 and the beginning of c. 32, on the Trinity) as a gloss of an earlier discussion (c. 18), but we could equally describe the earlier chapter as a gloss on the more succinct material of the later chapters.[142] Other intra-textual resonances suggest that the first section (c. 1–29) could comprise explications of the epic life represented in the *calx*.[143] The poem of dedication to Grimald (c. 30a) of the *calx* revisits many of the letter's themes and images in concise form, including the metaphor of drinking from a river, the four virtues, *caritas*, the chariot, envious enemies, and the pairing of language arts with theology. Similarly, the topics and themes in the verse of chapter 32 – rivers, venom, wings of virtue, the Classics, and

---

[140] Ermenric may have borrowed some of these examples from grammarians and collections of excerpts (*florilegia*), so we cannot be sure that Ermenric had read all the texts he cites.

[141] The irate student in an English poem claims that his pretentious teacher's verse – which is clearly epic since the teacher compares himself to Virgil, Homer, and Statius – should not even be read by schoolboys. *Altercatio*, lines 35–36 from Camb. Uni. Lib., MS Kk. 5.34, 71rff., ed. and cited in Michael Lapidge, "Three Latin poems from Æthelwold's's School at Winchester," *ASE* 1 (1972): 85–137.

[142] Goullet, p. 42.

[143] The discussion of dialectic in c. 7 could explain c. 31 (and vice versa). Aristotle's accidence and substance, which first come up in c. 9, are also revisited in c. 31, as are that philosopher's ten categories (c. 7), the ineffability of God, shining garments (c. 1), and celestial ascension.

numerological interpretation – are all subjects explicated in earlier passages.[144] Many of the Classical figures such as Orpheus and Eurydice whose stories are noted in chapters 24 and 25 recur briefly in chapter 36. In most cases, the material is discussed in a more comprehensive and detailed manner in the first section of the letter than in the *calx*, suggesting the earlier chapters constitute a gloss on the more succinct passages of the final section (rather than vice versa). It seems strange that glosses would precede the glossed text, because in a classroom, the core text would be read aloud and then glossed. Yet, this is not simply another example of Carolingian literary inversion. For Ermenric's readers, it makes sense to absorb more detailed discussions of the material before they encounter briefer references to it. The readers are able to understand the difficult material of the *calx*, because they have already been given the necessary background.

An epic life, such as Ermenric's *Vita Galli*, would be appropriate for intermediate students. The material in the first part of the letter is similar to that found in teaching glosses aimed at students of at least an intermediate level. (Most glossed schoolbooks belong to teachers, not students.)[145] The discussions reflect a teacher's instruction of a group already proficient at the basics of Latin. He discusses technical points of the language arts and interpretation, whereas more elementary education focuses on the mechanics of reading Latin, for instance, by construing word order and building vocabulary.[146] Sophisticated glosses, which parallel the subjects in Ermenric's letter, deal with more advanced grammar, allusion, interpretation, rhetorical devices, theology, philosophy, and mythology.[147]

---

[144] Rivers: c. 1, 14, 16; snakes: c. 5, 14, 35, 36; wings: c. 1, 6, 21; Classics: c. 24–25; numerological interpretation: c. 19, 20.

[145] Gernot Wieland, "The Glossed Manuscript: Classbook or Library Book?" *ASE* 14 (1985): 153.

[146] Glosses helped beginning readers with the basic grammar by indicating more natural word order, showing word agreement, and supplying subjects for verbs. On teaching reading, levels of education, and the role of glosses, see Grotans, *Reading*, chapter 2, and the introduction to *The St. Gall Tractate*, ed. Anna A. Grotans and David W. Porter (Columbia, SC, 1995). For basic glosses, see Tony Hunt, *Teaching and Learning Latin in Thirteenth-Century England*, 3 vols. (Woodbridge, 1991); for glosses generally, see Robert Black, *Humanism and Education in Medieval and Renaissance Italy: Tradition and Innovation in Latin Schools from the Twelfth to the Fifteenth Centuries* (Cambridge, 2001).

[147] For examples of such glosses, see G.R. Scott, "Persius MSS," *Classical Review* 4 (1890): 241–247; J.P. Elder, "A Medieval Cornutus on Persius," *Speculum* 22 (1947): 240–248; James E.G. Zetzel, *Marginal Scholarship and Textual Deviance. The "Commentum Cornuti" and the Early Scholia on Persius* (London, 2005).

Epic *vitae* were appropriate texts for classroom *lectio* for several reasons. They were useful for intermediate students because they covered a range of material that reflected the monastic curriculum. With their learned digressions, they were appropriately didactic texts. Because they reconfigured the conventions of Latin epic poetry in Christianized form, they were excellent supplements to the Classical poetry taught in the medieval classroom. Unlike Virgil, whose recitation the epic poet Milo derides, the saint's *vita* offered an edifying Christian exemplum, even when read *literaliter*.[148] Because students started reading literally, not allegorically, works with manifestly Christian content would be easier to teach than would those whose most immediate meanings were pagan.

Epic *vitae*, like other classicizing Christian verse, were also useful because they contained many of the aesthetic pleasures of pagan poetry. As Sedulius states, readers prefer the delights of worldly literature.[149] In the letter, which prefaces many copies of his *Paschale carmen*, a popular school text, he explains the rationale of composing Christian verse: the sweetness of the poetry would cause readers to return to it enthusiastically and therefore remember it better.[150] Sacred literature, sweetened with poetic trappings could lure them into reading more avidly and often, and so they would store its content in their memories. Because what was read in youth was most deeply imprinted in the heart, the moral import of this material was key. A *vita* of Virgil, explaining why young students read him, draws on Augustine and quotes Horace to convey this idea.[151] If youthful reading was indelibly inscribed in the memory, then the epic *vita* offered a Christian alternative.

Finally, because monks and canons usually composed verse about their regional patrons and early saints, epic lives often provided the students

---

[148] *VA*, 2.10–13.

[149] Springer, "Sedulius," p. 10, n. 27.

[150] Carl P.E. Springer, *The Gospel as Epic in Late Antiquity: The Paschale Carmen of Sedulius*, Supplements to Vigiliae Christianae 2 (Leiden, 1988), c. 2.

[151] A *vita* of Virgil (the *Vita Noricensis* II) in a ninth-century manuscript (St. Paul in Lavanttal MS Samblasianus 86, fols. 1r–1v) excerpts Augustine's statement about the memorability of Virgil learned in youth: "Virgilium nempe propterea parvuli legunt, ut videlicet poeta magnus omnium praeclarissimus atque optimus teneris ebibitus animis non facile oblivione possit aboleri, secundum illud Horatii: 'Quo semel est imbuta recens, servabit odorem testa diu'" (Augustine, *De civitate Dei* 1.3, quoting Horace, *Epistles* 1.2.69–70), printed in Jan M. Ziolkowski, Michael C.J. Putnam, eds., *The Virgilian Tradition: The First Fifteen Hundred Years* (New Haven, 2008), pp. 280–281. See Suerbaum, "Heidnischer Klassiker," p. 249. On the lifelong influence of Augustine's reading of Virgil, see Sabine MacCormack, *The Shadows of Poetry: Vergil in the Mind of Augustine* (Berkeley, 1998).

with their house's foundation story, couched in the grandiose and memorable form of classical Virgilian epic. Along with lessons in grammar and metrics, the young monks and canons would have imbibed the story of their spiritual family's origins.

Contemporary writers and readers note the pedagogical context of epic *vitae*. After checking its dogma and meter, Haimin guided others through the verse *Vita Amandi*.[152] Milo's repudiation of the Virgil-belching teachers (surely ironic in a work sent from one teacher to another) also perversely confirms the place of *epic lives* in the classroom.[153] In an address to the reader, he writes,

> I do not send this work to be recited by the teachers of the world,
> Whose speech flows like a rushing stream,
> Who, belching out the grandiose words of thunder-mouthed[154] Virgil,
> Bring forth the singing of the swan's voice from their throat
> All of them, while comparing their own song to the sweet muses,
> Show it to be empty and capable of no gain.
> Therefore I do not send out my verses to be performed by them,
> But by monks, in whose mouths lies quietly the health-giving treasure,
> The Psalms and hymns or songs for Christ,[155]
> Which they sing through the temple,
> Shouting from their mouth just like thunder.[156]

It is unclear whether Milo objected to all teachers using his work, or only the garrulous teachers who were "belching out Virgil." Regardless, his complaint implies that the reader would expect teachers to recite (*recitare, citare*) this epic life.

Codicological evidence shows that epic lives functioned as schoolbooks. For example, a ninth-century collection of *carmina*, often with teaching

---

[152] Haimin, *Rescriptum*, in MGH Poetae 3, pp. 566–567.

[153] Later in this passage and at the beginning of book 3, he maligns the work of poets (in a contrived poetic style). *VA*, 2.20–21; 3.27–31.

[154] "Thunder-mouthed" is my conjecture for the meaning of the word *oritoni*. Jennifer Ebbeler has suggested that it might be a form of *orisoni* meaning "spine-tingling." Jennifer Ebbeler, personal communication, June 2, 2006.

[155] Paul F. Gehl, "Competens Silentium: Varieties of Medieval Silence," *Viator* 18 (1987): 138. The idea of Psalms and hymns reposing quietly (*requiescit*) in the monks' mouths accords with Gehl's description of singing the Psalms as "a common, wordy silence."

[156] *VA*, 2.10–19, p. 579: "Non opus hoc orbis recitandum mitto magistris, / Quorum sermo fluit torrentis gurgitis instar, / Grandia qui oritoni ructantes verba Maronis / Vocis olorinae concentum gutture promunt / Quique suum carmen, dum Musis suavibus aequant, / Ostendunt vanum nullisque aptabile lucris. / Non his ergo meos versus transmitto citandos, / Sed monachis, quorum requiescit in ore salubris / Thesaurus, psalmi et hymni seu cantica, Christo, / Quae per templa canunt tonitrus velut ore boantes."

glosses, includes the anonymous verse *Passio Quintini.*[157] A tenth-century copy of Bede's verse *Vita Cuthberti* has interlinear glosses such as grammatical examples and notes on *computus* that suggest classroom use.[158] Other schoolbooks include a glossed eleventh-century codex containing Letselin's verse *Vita Arnulfi* and the twelfth-century codex containing the verse *Vita Eustachii.*[159] The anonymous verse *Vita Agnetis*, marked with the rhetorical categories *propositio, invocatio, enarratio, apostrophus,* and *allusio,* may also have been used in the classroom, although the surviving manuscript is not a schoolbook.[160] The earliest manuscript of Heiric's *Vita Germani*, from the ninth century, with notes transcribed in the same hand as the main text, seems to be a teacher's copy.[161] Its copious

---

[157] Paris, BN, MS lat. 14143 containing *Passio Quintini* (BHL 7010), ed. in MGH Poetae 4/ 1, pp. 197–208.

[158] Glauche, *Schullekture im Mittelalter*, p. 30. Paris, BN, MS lat. 2825 containing Bede's *Vita Cuthberti* (BHL 2020), which is ed. Werner Jaager, *Bedas metrische Vita Sancti Cuthberti* (Leipzig, 1935). For catalogue information, Bibliothèque nationale, *Catalogue général des manuscrits latins*, vol. 3 (Paris, 1952), pp. 118–119. On schoolbooks featuring Bede's verse and prose *Vitae Cuthberti*, see Fred Robinson, "Syntactical Glosses in Latin Manuscripts of Anglo-Saxon Provenance," *Speculum* 48 (1973): 463–644.

[159] Paris, BN, MS lat. 10851 containing (among other works), the *Vita Arnulfi* (BHL 708) ed. in *Novem vitae*, pp. 86–126. As is always the case, the print edition obscures the codicological evidence of the classroom text. On the manuscript of the verse *Vita Eustachii* (BHL 2768), Paris, BN, MS lat. 11341, see Léopold Delisle, *Inventaire des manuscrits latins conservés à la Bibliothèque nationale sous les numéros 8823–18613*, vol. 2 (Paris, 1863–1871), pp. 627–628. This codex, which also contains the *Speculum prelatorum* and the *Vita monachorum*, appears to be a verse compilation for monks.

[160] BHL 161, ed. in *Novem vitae*, pp. 38–51, and MGH Poetae 6/1, pp. 108–120. Dolbeau identifies the manuscript of *Vita Agnetis*, Paris, BN, MS lat. 14145, as a schoolbook, but this copy, with its expensive vellum, fine script, pristine condition, and lack of annotations (other than the rhetorical categories written in the scribal hand), is not a school copy. (The codex is composite codex, so the other contents do not provide information on function.) An individual epic life could be put to a range of uses, so the fact that the surviving copy of the *Vita Agnetis* was not used in a classroom does not discredit Dolbeau's observation that the rhetorical categories suggest a classroom use. See Dolbeau, "Domaine négligé," p. 136. Letselinus's metric *Vita Arnulfi* in Paris, BN, MS lat. 10851, which was clearly once part of a schoolbook, is also marked with such categories.

[161] Jeaneau argues that this manuscript, Paris, BN, MS lat. 13757, was Heiric's autograph copy, but other scholars disagree, based on comparison with the collection of excerpts written in Heiric's hand, which Bischoff has identified. See Bernhard Bischoff, "Palaeography and the Transmission of Classical Texts in the Early Middle Ages," in *Manuscripts and Libraries in the Age of Charlemagne*, trans. Michael Gorman (Cambridge, 1994), p. 127. See also Édouard Jeauneau, "Heiric d'Auxerre disciple de Jean Scot," in *L'école carolingienne d'Auxerre de Murethach à Remi 830–901*, ed. Dominique Iogna-Prat, Colette Jeudy, and Guy Lobrichon (Paris, 1989), pp. 356–357; G. Billanovich, "Dall'antica Ravenna alle biblioteche umanistiche," *Annuario dell' Università cattolica del Sacro Cuore. Anni accademici (1955/1956–1956/1957),*

marginal and interlinear glosses elucidate points of grammar, meter, Classical mythology, and history. The notes also translate Greek words (preserving the grammatical case), provide synonyms, explain mythological references, and explicate the poem's meaning, drawing on Augustinian and Pseudo-Dionysian theology.[162] Another glossed schoolbook containing an epic *vita* is a tenth-century manuscript, which includes Sedulius's *Paschale carmen* along with the verse *Vita Verenae* (BHL 8543), the verse *Passio Mauritii* (BHL 5751), and Walafrid Strabo's verse *Visio Wettini*. It features interlinear and marginal glosses (including some in German).[163] Finally, Grimald's teaching book, which includes Ermenric's letter, also contains Bede's verse *Vita Cuthberti*.

As we will see, the verse *Vita Galli* is key to the educational scheme Ermenric develops over the entire course of the letter. Even if it is not the glossed text imagined at the heart of the letter, Ermenric certainly shows himself using it in the later chapters (30–36) to teach the more advanced students.

THE READER AS STUDENT

Ermenric's explanations all assume a basic working knowledge of Latin, but he does not pitch his discussion at the same level throughout the letter. Rather, he moves from simpler to more advanced material, often putting the earlier lessons to use. This letter does not reflect, then, the content of one class session, or a summary of a student's education, but an "iter studiorum."[164] It is a whirlwind journey through intermediate and advanced training in the language arts, with the reader touching down at strategic points for an occasional lesson. The letter is a kind of "distance learning," in which the reader experiences being Ermenric's student, traveling through the curriculum at superspeed.

The reader, the imaginary student, traces a broad, upward arc from dialectic to composition over the course of the letter. Ermenric refers to the

pp. 73–107. Iogna-Prat argues that Paris, BN, MS lat. 13757 was written at Auxerre under Heiric's direction. Manitius thinks it was either written by Heiric or under his supervision. Dominique Iogna-Prat, "Heiric d'Auxerre, *Vie de saint Germain*, 873–875," in *Abbaye Saint-Germain d'Auxerre*, p. 70; Manitius, *Geschichte* v. 1, p. 504.

[162] Paris, BN, MS lat. 13757, contains the most complete version of these notes, which Traube prints as footnotes in MGH Poetae 3, pp. 432–437.

[163] Munich, Bayerische Staatsbibliothek, MS Clm 18628. Springer, "Sedulius," p. 72. On tenth-century German glosses, see Grotans, *Reading*, chap. 3.

[164] Cassaretto, "Intuere coelum apertum," p. 206.

beneficiaries of his teachings, in the first main section, as the very young (*infantuli*). He excerpts and summarizes works for these students in preparation for the fuller training that they will receive later: "even if I do not give them everything, I offer, nonetheless, a taste of some essentials to those who are ignorant of them or who are slow at reading."[165] After the *exordium* on the first two commandments, which Grimald had requested, Ermenric embarks on his discussion of language by dividing up philosophy into its component parts and focusing on the fundamental language arts *dialectica* and then *rhetorica*. Next, he draws on Priscian to define the noun, which is also a basic principle, although he introduces more advanced material, combining grammar and theology (as he had in the *exordium*) and using the Aristotelian concepts of substance and accidence to discuss the nature of God in chapter 9.

The subsequent chapters (10–18) focus on prosody, that is, comparing syllable lengths used by writers of prose and verse (giving instances in which the latter employ "poetica licentia" due to the exigencies of meter), and orthography. This is not the basic information transmitted in the standard textbook on meter, Bede's *De arte metrica*, but more advanced material, preparing students for the next level of their education. Ruff notes that "there is a large gap between mastery of the formula" students learned in textbooks "and the writing of Latin hexameter verse."[166] Bede's *De arte metrica* prepares students to scan verse, but students required further education in order to produce it. Ermenric's discussions provide preparation for metric verse composition.

The passages on orthography and pronunciation are, like those on prosody, not fundamental for reading Latin. Rather, they hone one's knowledge of technical details and correct misconceptions.[167] The

---

[165] c. 24: "si non omnia, non tamen gustum ex aliquantis necessariis porrigo illis, qui nesciunt, vel qui ad legendum tardi sunt." In 800, Charlemagne's sister and daughter, Gisla and Rotruda, similarly asked Alcuin for a commentary on John appropriate for their intellects since Augustine "multo obscuriores maiorque circumlocutione decoratas, quam nostrae parvitatis ingeniolo intrare valeat." They, like Ermenric's students, required a smaller taste: "Scis enim optime parvis parva sufficere, nec ad mensam magnatorum pauperum turbam accedere posse." John J. Contreni, "The Irish Contribution to the European Classroom," in *Carolingian Learning: Masters and Their Manuscripts* (Hampshire, 1992), p. 82; MGH Ep. 4, ed. Ernst Dümmler, p. 324. Hilduin similarly offers a "taste" (*gustum*) of materials on Dionysius to those who would otherwise not have access to them. Hilduin, *Omnibus filiis*, ed. Dümmler, MGH Ep. 5, p. 336, discussed in detail in Chapter 1.

[166] Carin Ruff, "The Place of Metrics in Anglo-Saxon Latin Education: Aldhelm and Bede," *Journal of English and Germanic Philology* 104 (2005): 149–170.

[167] c. 17.

material that Ermenric assembles, such as his discussions on syllable length and verb formation, is fairly specialized. This information is pitched at a higher level than is the explication of dialectic and rhetoric. In the chapters that follow, he turns from looking at individual words to interpretation (*enarratio*), which is also the domain of the more advanced student.[168] He draws heavily on his sources, such as grammars, throughout, but in the earlier sections he predigests them, breaking them down into smaller sections and combining them with one another and his own explication.[169] Later in the work (c. 20–23), in describing how to read typologically (*typicare*), he employs large sections of Gregory's *Commentary on Ezechiel* verbatim, implying that his readers can now grapple with the *auctor* independently.[170]

Through his selection of material, Ermenric allows the readers, like students in an effective program, to build on what they have already learned. Despite the diversity of the subject matter, Ermenric revisits topics, themes, and images. In this way, he teaches by accretion and repetition. Circling back to certain subjects, he impresses them on the readers' minds through "imprégnatio par répétition."[171] He uses the verb *replicare*, noting that he is returning to a subject he addressed at the beginning (*exordium*) of his letter (c. 22). When he revisits an earlier topic, such as the Trinity, accidence and substance, *caritas*, or the Virtues, he does not repeat himself, but puts it in a new context, refers to it in passing, or approaches it differently.[172] He also employs unusual words that he has already provided as exempla.[173]

Directing his lessons at an increasingly educated readership, he presupposes a deeper level of engagement from the reader as the text progresses. When discussing correct grammatical usage in later chapters, he raises principles, gives examples, and asks the students to consider them, or even to produce the answers for themselves (c. 17). He challenges his readers to recall and use what they have learned. Ermenric does not just convey information to the *legentes*, but also teaches interpretive skills. For example, he assists the reader with the recognition of allusion, a skill essential for reading the Classics, decoding Carolingian learned literature, or, most importantly, reading Scripture. His description of the infernal

---

[168] Grotans, *Reading*, p. 97.
[169] Goullet, p. 31.
[170] Ibid.
[171] Ibid., p. 42.
[172] Ibid.
[173] For example, *putto*, c. 13, 29.

Virgil as "a certain shadowy and entirely horrible monster" approaching the sleeping Ermenric echoes a passage from the *Georgics*, in which the enraged goddess Juno persecutes Io who has been turned into a cow.[174] An educated Carolingian reader, well versed in allusion and intertext, would recognize the line's origin (and presumably appreciate Ermenric likening himself to the sleeping bovine being attacked by a gadfly). Because Ermenric wished to enlighten the slow readers (*qui tardi sunt ad legendum*), whom he has just mentioned, he provides some assistance for them. A little later (the next page in the manuscript), listing Virgil's stories about the gods, Ermenric quotes the precise passage from which he draws the Io allusion.[175] So, if the *tardi* readers (unlike their learned counterparts) did not initially recognize Ermenric's playful use of his source – that he describes the Virgilian specter with a Virgilian allusion – they would recognize it now. Not only does Ermenric contribute material to the reader's repertoire, but more significantly, by echoing the words he has recently used and therefore bringing their previous context to mind, he also makes the reader practice the allusive cross-referential reading central to Carolingian comprehension. Other examples of Ermenric echoing passages in his own text are further apart, requiring more of the reader.[176]

THE *CALX EPISTOLAE*: BEYOND GLOSSING

The material appended to the "heel" of the letter is an assemblage of verse and prose passages (c. 30–36), which Ermenric describes as "certain flowers of my mind about Saint Gall."[177] Following his account of Gozbert's rejection of his epic composition and the saint's comforting appearance, he says he sends Grimald "small things from the great" or "about the great."[178] So, the "clouds of eloquence" (*nugae eloquii*) that Ermenric appends represent excerpts of his epic life, but they do not exactly resemble one, because they are partially in prose and because they barely mention the saint. These last chapters form a prose address to Grimald (c. 30), a verse address to him in elegiac meter (c. 30a), a diagram (c. 31), a verse *invocatio* to the Trinity (c. 32), an acrostic verse to the Trinity and

---

[174] c. 24 "monstrum quoddam fuscum, et per omnia horribile."

[175] Virgil, *Georgics* 3.152–153: "hoc quondam monstro horribilis exercuit iras / Inachiae Iuno pestem meditata iuvencae."

[176] Goullet, p. 41, gives several examples.

[177] c. 33: "mihi ... mentis floscellos ... quosdam / De sancte Galle."

[178] c. 29: "de magnis parva excerpo."

Gall (c. 33), a second acrostic to the saint in another meter (c. 34), a prose description of Ireland's geography (c. 35), an allegorical interpretation of it, and, finally, a verse section, which starts with another geographical description, before wandering into other topics. This last poem ends on an autobiographical note, with Ermenric returning to the conflict with his rival. The saint is only mentioned in passing. Twice, claiming that he must touch on other matters, Ermenric puts off beginning the actual saint's life and never gets around to narrating it (c. 31, 35).

Although the material in these chapters seems extraneous to a life of Gall, it parallels (albeit with much more prose) the openings of the most-learned ninth-century epic lives, which feature prose dedicatory letters, and verse in different meters invoking God or the saint or discussing theological points. Heiric's epic *Vita Germani* completed ca. 875, provides a close parallel to the final section of Ermenric's letter. Heiric prefaces the *vita* with a letter to Emperor Charles the Bald dedicating the work and explaining its genesis.[179] This is followed by two poems, the first of which is an *Invocatio*. Like Ermenric, Heiric helpfully informs the reader of an unusual meter (Phalaecian).[180] The *Invocatio* contains very similar topics to those of Ermenric's six final chapters: the Trinity and the qualities of God. Like Ermenric's verse *Oratio ad Sanctam Trinitatem* (c. 33), it features several words and lines of Greek. Heiric's second poem prefacing the *vita* is a seventy-two-line *Allocutio ad Librum*, which, like Ermenric's last chapter (c. 36), touches on Classical topics, beginning with mythological and Virgilian references. Apart from the fact that Heiric does not intersperse these verses with prose, the contents are remarkably similar to those of Ermenric's *calx*. In Heiric's work, as in Ermenric's letter, Greek words are glossed with a Latin translation in the correct case, meaning that a reader (or a teacher) could comprehend the passage even without any knowledge of Greek.[181]

The opening sections of Milo of Saint-Amand's *Vita Amandi*, although written in a less ornate style, also have several similarities to the content of Ermenric's *calx*. The most elaborate version is prefaced by a similar

---

[179] Heiric, VG (BHL 3458), pp. 428–517.
[180] Paris, BN, MS lat. 13757, note on fol. 6v. A marginal gloss explains the meter: "Faulleucius versus constat spondeo dactilo tribus trocheis" (MGH Poetae 3, p. 432). See Dag Norberg, *An Introduction to the Study of Medieval Latin Versification*, trans. Grant C. Roti and Jacqueline de La Chapelle Skulby (Washington, DC, 2004), pp. 71–72.
[181] For example, on fol. 6v., *ELLHNAC* is glossed *grecos* and *KATA* is glossed *iuxta*. Heiric's glosses are more accurate and helpful than are Ermenric's. He was clearly more proficient at Greek (perhaps having learned it from John Scottus Eruigena).

assortment of poetry and prose: two acrostics by Hucbald dedicating the work to Charles the Bald, Milo's letter to his teacher, Haimin's reply, and a fifty-line verse preface to the work.

Gall's virtual absence from this last section of Ermenric's letter also reflects a convention in ninth- through eleventh-century epic lives, which may spend many lines on geographical, historical, and religious context before introducing their protagonist. They often place the saint in the broad historical scheme of salvation history, starting with Christ and relating the history of the Franks from their mythical foundation by the Trojans (these features also occur in prose *vitae*, although less extensively). Both prose and verse *vitae* can include lengthy geographic descriptions as well.[182] An extreme example of the delayed saint occurs in the late-tenth-century verse *Passio Christophori* from the cathedral school at Speyer, in which the poet spends the entire first book giving an overview of the topics of his *own* education, with nothing about the saint at all.[183]

It seems, therefore, that the diverse materials of the *calx* represent excerpts from the beginning of the *Vita Galli*. Ermenric's inclusion of only these sections from his epic life was informed by classroom practice. The beginnings of works were often the most useful for teaching reading or composition, because their introductory letters and poems exhibit a greater variety than the later sections. Prefatory poems allowed discussions of meters and poetic forms, peculiarities of verse prosody and distinctive features of verse, such as poetic vocabulary, acrostics, complex word order, and stylistic features. In addition, religious invocations, such as those to the Trinity, provided opportunity for theological explication. The dedicatory letters could launch discussions of epistolary conventions. The beginning of the epic life proper gave the student a sampling of classicizing epic verse and often features a range of topics, such as the evangelists, the mythical Trojan origins of the Franks, and the saint's geographical origins. Some classroom copies of texts, including certain manuscripts of epic lives, have only the initial sections copied or glossed, showing that these sections could be the focus of teaching.[184]

---

[182] The delayed introduction of the protagonist also occurs in some prose *vitae*, especially where the writer lacks information about the saint, such as Hucbald's VR and Ermenric's own *Vita Sualonis* (BHL 7925–7926). On the VR, see Chapter 4.

[183] Walter, *Passio Christophori* (BHL 1776) in MGH Poetae 5/1, pp. 1–78.

[184] For example, teaching glosses on Heiric's VG are heavily concentrated on the prefatory material and earlier sections of book 1. The worn copy, Paris, BN, MS lat. 17302, contains glosses on the prefatory *Commendatio* as well as the *Vita* itself. These additional notes are Latin synonym glosses or short explanations. The scribe only copied the introductory

Some modern scholars contend that the strange mix of verse and prose in these chapters shows that Ermenric intended to compose a prosimetric saint's life. Although the presence of both forms could indicate that Ermenric was composing an early example of such a *vita*, the prosimetric format by itself would not account for other unusual features, such as the diagram in chapter 31.[185] Rather, what accounts for the unique format of this final section is that Ermenric simultaneously presents pieces of his epic *Vita Galli* and, as in the earlier chapters, depicts himself at work in the classroom. The inclusion of a diagram, a common teaching tool, indicates the setting is still pedagogical, as do the directions peppered throughout these chapters and the content.

The magisterial voice is less prominent than in the preceding section, but Ermenric continues to instruct the *legentes*, albeit in a new manner appropriate to their more advanced level. The readers Ermenric posits in this final section are not the slow, confused, and inadequately educated readership of the earlier chapters, but advanced students capable of writing epic verse. When Ermenric addresses the readers in the *calx*, it is to challenge them to undertake poetic composition of their own (c. 32).

In this section, he undoubtedly uses his *Vita Galli* as the basis for his teaching. The *calx* does not contain the polished or finished *Vita Galli*, but shows the work being used with students in a classroom. Ermenric notes, "I expressed these things neither in wax or on a tablet, but *just as if dictated onto the present scraps of parchment*."[186] He earlier characterizes himself

materials and the life up to 2.40 (empty ruled lines in the second column of folio 8v show the book was not mutilated but was left incomplete). Similarly, the partial copy of Heiric's *vita* in Paris, BN, MS lat. 6400B, folios 80–85v, contains only two prefatory poems and the first 151 lines of book 1. Only folios 80r–82v, those containing the *Invocatio*, are glossed. This copy of the life was never completed (the gathering contains another two folios). Another example of the concentration of glosses in the opening sections is the Persius in Vatican, BAV, MS Reg. Lat. 1562, in which the scribal hand has made copious glosses on fols. 2–3v, but few on later folios. The poems of Persius in Vatican, BAV, MS Reg. lat. 1424 follow the same pattern. On these manuscripts, see Dorothy M. Robathan, "Two Unreported Persius Manuscripts," *Classical Philology* 26 (1931): 288, 294.

[185] For a summary of the discussion of whether Ermenric's *Vita Galli* (or Walafrid's prospective version) was intended to be prosimetric, see Goullet, pp. 222–223. Contra Goullet's assertion that there are no known ninth-century prosimetric lives, is Hilduin's metric *PD*, which is effectively a prosimetric *vita*, because it contains several passages of prose. The prosimetric dialogue life of Gall sometimes attributed to Notker I of Saint-Gall may be from the late ninth century (ed. in MGH Poetae 4/3, pp. 1094–1108). Ninth-century literature defies neat genre categories, and so we need not posit a hard-and-fast division between metric and prosimetric lives. Predominately prose lives could incorporate verse (for example, in introductory dedications), and predominately metric lives (such as Hilduin's), could include prose.

[186] c. 30: "nec in cera vel in tabula haec expressi, sed sicut in presentibus scedis dictata sunt."

as a slow poet, so he does not mean he threw together the poetry off the top of his head. Rather, he indicates that he is providing something akin to a transcription of his speech, as if copied down by another (*sicut . . . dictata sunt*) on *scedae* (scraps of parchment, such as those a student might use to preserve a copy of class work). The contents of the *calx* are something like notes taken in class, comprising dictation given by the teacher and, as we shall see, compositional and interpretive exercises.

The *calx* differs from the first twenty-nine chapters because instead of glossing a text for the readers, Ermenric here models *exercitamina* or *progymnasmata*, classroom composition exercises inherited from the ancient schools of rhetoric.[187] These included a series of graded exercises prescribed by Priscian, in his popular *Praeexercitamina*.[188] In this section, Ermenric is not glossing a text for the students but is leading them through exercises based on his material on Gall. The reason, then, for the strange format of the *calx*, written in both prose and verse and returning to the same topics in different form, is that rather than appending excerpts from a finished version of the epic life, Ermenric presents a second classroom scenario, in which advanced students practice exercises based on passages they are given. That verse lives were used to teach exercises, *progymnasmata*, is suggested by manuscript annotations marking sections with Priscian's rhetorical categories.[189] The *calx*, which also includes an allegorical interpretation of a narrative description (the geography of Ireland), presents teachers and students at work on *progymnasmata*, including allegorical interpretation and *conversio*.

Conversio, the rewriting of prose in meter and vice versa, was a standard exercise.[190] Thangmar, in the *vita* of his former student Bernward, written after 1022, describes such exercises:

---

[187] Marjorie Curry Woods, "Weeping for Dido: Epilogue on a Premodern Rhetorical Exercise in the Postmodern Classroom," in *Latin Grammar and Rhetoric: From Classical Theory to Medieval Practice*, ed. Carol Dana Lanham (London, 2002), pp. 282–294.

[188] Grotans, *Reading*, p. 54, n. 26; p. 77. Priscian, *Opuscula*, ed. Marina Passalacqua, vol. 1, *De figuris numerorum; De metris Terentii; Praeexercitamina* (Rome, 1987), pp. xxix–xxx. Passalacqua identifies many manuscripts of the *Praeexercitamina*, including one from the late eighth century, twelve from the ninth century, three from the tenth century, and two that belong to either the tenth or eleventh centuries.

[189] *Vita Agnetis*, Paris, BN, MS lat. 14145, mentioned previously, and likewise, Letselin, *Vita Arnulfi* in Paris, BN, MS lat. 10851.

[190] Quintilian *Inst. Or.* Book 1, 9.2–4 describes the former. Discussed in Roberts, *Biblical Epic and Rhetorical Paraphrase*, p. 15.

For often we spent the whole day studying at our drills, now by reading no less copiously in our spare time, than if we had come to this in school, now by writing poetry, we composed in meter. Then, by turns, we undertook the exercises of the prose gymnasium. Sometimes we discussed reason in a simple scheme, often we sweated over sophistic syllogisms.[191]

Students might rewrite passages from the *Aeneid*, or they could compose works on topics supplied by a teacher.[192] This rewriting was not simply a matter of choosing and arranging words according to a particular meter, but also of transforming the tenor of the passage.

The alternating sections of prose and verse in Ermenric's *calx* reflect a similar exercise of *conversio*, with the verse sections redacting and transforming the prose that precedes them. On three occasions in Ermenric's *calx*, prose passages are followed (directly or indirectly) by verse rewritings. It is characteristic of the verse sections that they begin with the basic subject of the prose and then wander afield, encompassing different details (often echoing earlier themes of the letter) and adding copious adornment. Accordingly, the verse *invocatio* to Grimald that follows the prose address begins with the well-worn praises of Grimald's virtues and learning and repeats Ermenric's call for patronage, but also encompasses rhetorical flourishes, including three lines of Greek.[193] The prose passage labeled "De vera essentia deitatis ..." is reiterated in part in the verse *invocatio* based on the preceding sections ("Unde supra invocatio sive repeticio dictantis SSS"). The next two pieces of verse are clearly marked as acrostic, which is a favorite Carolingian form. The second is in the unusual catalectic tetrameter (labeled "metro tetrametro accatalecto").[194] Therefore, chapters 30 through 36 do not represent the completed introduction to the epic

---

[191] *Vita Bernhardi*, ed. G. Waitz, MGH SS 4, p. 758: "Nam saepe totum diem inter equitatum studendo attrivimus, nunc legendo non minus prolixam lectionem, quam si in scolis ad hanc vacaremus, nunc poetizando per viam metro collusimus, inde ad prosaicam palaestram exercitium alternantes, interdum simplici contextu rationem contulimus, saepe syllogisticis cavillationibus desudavimus." *Scola* had a range of meanings including a group of children for school, but also a group more generally, or the place in the monastery where the children resided. See Grotans, *Reading*, p. 53.

[192] Scott C. McGill, "Other Aeneids: Rewriting Three Passages of the Aeneid in the Codex Salmasianus," *Vergilius: The Journal of the Vergilian Society* 49 (2003): 84–113; Grotans, *Reading*, p. 78. Ekkehard IV reports using poems, written at his teacher Notker's request, "so that I might encourage our youths in this same endeavor." Ekkehard IV, *Liber Benedictionum*, ed. Egli, p. 279, cited by Grotans, *Reading*, p. 78: "ut iuvenes nostros in id ipsum adortarer."

[193] c. 30a, lines 31, 33, and 35.

[194] c. 33, 34: "invocatus sub istis litteris versus incipientes"; "sub litteris ipsius versus."

Vita Galli, but prose pieces and the verse being generated from them in an illustration of *conversio*.

The nature of this section – prose sources and the exercises based on them – explains some of Ermenric's otherwise displaced signposting comments. Ermenric appeals to the saint's help in writing verse: "Now, giving songs (*carmina*), help me," leading us to expect he will embark on a poetic composition, but the passage that follows is in prose, and only later is the topic of this passage – the geographical origins of the saint – rendered in verse.[195] There the muse finally "breaks out."[196] It makes sense for the poet to invoke the saint's help for *carmina* in chapter 34, at the beginning of a prose section, if the prose is included as part of that composition process. The prose that follows is the material that the saint will help him transform into verse. Similarly, at the end of chapter 31, he states "enough has been said about the essence or substance of God,"[197] implying that he will change topics, yet the verse in the following chapter is labeled *Unde Supra novatio sive repeticio dictantis SSS* and iterates some of the same issues. This signposting also only makes sense when the verse is understood as the prose transformed, rather than a new exploration of the issue.

READING ALLEGORICALLY

In addition to modeling *conversio* and several kinds of verse, the *calx* demonstrates the key skill of Scriptural reading, allegorical interpretation, which was also taught in classroom exercises. Once again, Ermenric calls on the reader's experience, acquired in the earlier section of the letter. After describing the geography of Ireland in a literal manner, he adds "of course, we are able to read the mystical meanings in these things allegorically."[198] The first person plural here is not merely rhetorical, since the reader has already learned about allegorical interpretation in the first part of the letter (c. 5, 21).

Ermenric again encourages active participation from the reader. Just as in the earlier section, he leaves clues to encourage allusive reading, here he gives the reader the information to decode another level of meaning and therefore offers practice in allegorical interpretation. In describing the geography of Ireland literally, he notes that the place is free of snakes

---

[195] c. 34: "Nunc succurre mihi carmina donans."
[196] c. 36: "Hinc iam musam diu inclusam iuvat exclamare!"
[197] c. 31: "Haec de essentia sive substantia deitatis dicta sufficient."
[198] c. 36: "Possumus nempe typos mysticos in his rebus allegoricae commentari."

(*serpentes*) and that the pages of books from that place can be used as antivenin: "almost everything on that island acts against poison, but also the pages of books from that same place, if they should be scraped and given as a drink, expel the poison."[199] In the passage that follows, he explains the underlying moral meaning:

When it is said that neither snake nor venomous animal can live here, this means that neither a devil nor any destructive man is in communion with the Church. . . . Further, that the pages of the books and all things, which are on that island are resistant to poison shows that all divine speech carried everywhere from there wards off sins sent by the devil, drives them out and instills salvation.[200]

Ermenric's allegorical interpretation is straightforward, but this passage has another layer of meaning.[201] The verb *radare* (to scrape) is used for erasing writing from a manuscript by scraping its surface. Thus, we can also read the description as saying that, if they are erased, the pages expel the poison (their written contents). The astute reader will notice that venomous creatures, as a symbol of evil men, recur throughout the letter and that Ermenric earlier refers to an Irish enemy.[202] Ermenric is making a pun – the pages of the Irishman's books can be rendered innocuous and consumed, if the venomous writing is scraped from them.

WRITING EPIC LIVES

So, the *calx epistolae* does not consist of excerpts drawn from an epic life, but shows the components of such a life being used and generated in the

---

[199] c. 36: "omnia pene quae in eadem insula sunt contra venenum valent, sed et folia codicum ex eadem si radantur et potui dantur, venenum excuciunt."

[200] c. 36: "Quod vero ibi nec serpens nec animal venenatum dicitur vivere posse, significat nec diabolum nec ullum hominem pestiferum in ecclesia communionem habere. ... Quid autem folia codicum et omnia quae in eadem insula sunt venenis resistendo significant nisi quod omnis sermo divinus inde ubique perlatus vitia a diabolo inmissa arcet et excutit et salutem incutit."

[201] The insular custom of using book scrapings in this manner is attested by Bede, who recounts how Irish manuscripts were made into an antivenin: "we have seen how, in the case of people suffering from snake-bite, the leaves of manuscripts from Ireland were scraped and the scrapings put in water and given to the sufferer to drink. These scrapings at once absorbed the whole violence of the spreading poison and assuaged the swelling" (vidimus, quibusdam a serpente percussis, rasa folia codicum qui de Hibernia fuerant, et ipsam rasuram aquae inmissam ac potui datam talibus protinus totam vim veneni grassantis, totum inflati corporis absumsisse ac sedasse tumorem; translation by Colgrave and Mynors). Bede, *Bede's Ecclesiastical History of the English People*, ed. and trans. by Bertram Colgrace and R.A.B. Mynors (Oxford, 1969), I, 1, 20–21.

[202] Ermenric, c. 29; Goullet, pp. 228–230.

classroom. Ermenric provides prose passages and models their transformation through the exercise of *conversio* (or, in one instance, *enarratio*, then *conversio*). We see Ermenric creating parts of a verse life from prose passages. His versification is not an end in itself, but provides the model for the students to undertake their own verse compositions. He goads them:

> Reader, who happens to seize our songs,
> If they should displease you, take up better ones, following,
> And strive to write these pious verses for yourself in the end section,
> Whoever always has good faith.[203]

The *calx*, in which the reader should endeavor to compose his or her own verses, is not just the end of the poem but also the end of the reader's abbreviated educational program. Having learned the intermediate lessons conveyed in the earlier part of the letter, now at the end (*in calce*) of his or her education the reader is ready to compose verse.

The teacher Haimin, in a contemporary letter, similarly tells of using verse – in this case his student Milo's metric *Vita Amandi* – to provoke others into writing.[204] Haimin writes,

> not without particular caution afterwards I showed the brothers, who are with me, how this whole stream should be navigated. . . . I urge the brothers, who do not shrink from such studies, that they freely take up this work and I beseech them so that they might rather wish to be goaded to a similar study [or zeal], rather than burned up with the torches of jealousy.[205]

So Haimin tells Milo that he led the brothers through the *vita* and encouraged them to emulate it.[206] In this way, a teacher could use an epic life to inspire others to compose verse. The advanced readers, the students Ermenric addresses in the appendix, are the prospective writers of epic lives. In Ermenric's final chapters, then, we see not only how epic *vitae* could be used in the classroom but also how they could be generated.

The *progymnasmata* provided a student with the skills for writing an epic life. Several scholars have noted that a student (a monk, or less often a nun or canon) might compose such a work as a kind of "qualifying

---

[203] Ermenric, c. 32: "Hinc, lector, carpis forsan qui carmina nostra / Si haec tibi displiceant sume beata sequens, / Hosque *in calce* pios studeas tibi scribere versus, / Quis valeas rectam semper habere fidem."(My emphasis.)

[204] Haimin, *Rescriptum*, printed with *VA* in MGH Poetae 3, pp. 566–567.

[205] Ibid: "non sine cautela deinceps totum id flumen fratribus, qui mecum sunt, quomodo sit navigandum ostendi. . . . hortor fratres nostros, qui in talibus studiis non abhorrent, munus hoc libenter suscipere et obsecro, ut satius velint ad simile studium provocari quam invidiae facibus concremari."

[206] Ibid., p. 566.

examination" at the end of his or her education.[207] This explains why the epic lives, more than their prose counterparts, employ techniques of composition, which were taught in the classroom including *amplificatio*, *abbreviatio*, and long speeches. The lives reflect the liberal arts curriculum in their content and reflect the *progymnasmata* in form – they are not simply metrical redactions of the prose, but also amplified, digressive, rhetorically adorned versions of the saint's life.[208]

Some students wrote epic saints' lives, encapsulating their education, around the end of their schooling.[209] Hraban Maur instructed the student Candid to write a pair of *vitae* in verse and prose.[210] When Heiric had just completed his studies, he began an epic life at the request of his adolescent student, the prince Lothar.[211] The author of the ninth- or tenth-century *Passio Mauritii* echoes Heiric's claim that he was compelled to write a metric work, despite his youth, "when as a student I should barely come to the first songs."[212] Milo dedicated his *Vita Amandi* to his teacher and called it a *praeexercitamen*, a classroom exercise.[213] The monk known only as "W" dedicated his metric *Vita Gisleni* to his teacher, again suggesting a classroom milieu.[214] In the following century, Walter of Speyer recounts the cathedral school in which he and his fellow student Hazecha, a nun, composed metric passions of Saint Christopher.[215] (As Dolbeau laments, the loss of Hazecha's student *passio* deprives us of information about the education of women and their composition of epic *vitae*).[216] Ekkehard IV describes a nonsaintly epic Ekkehard I had

[207] Lapidge, "Tenth-century Anglo-Latin Verse Hagiography," *MJ* 24–25 (1989/1990): 260. Also, Leclercq, *Love of Learning*, p. 161; de Gaiffier, "Hagiographe," p. 135; Dolbeau, "Domaine négligé," p. 129.

[208] Dolbeau, "Domaine négligé," p. 137.

[209] De Gaiffier, "Hagiographe," p. 135; Dolbeau, "Domaine negligé," p. 129.

[210] Candid, *Vita Aeigili*, MGH Poetae 2, p. 94.

[211] *VG*, p. 431: "I had recently emerged from my studies" (Recens scolis emerseram).

[212] *Passio Mauritii* (BHL 5751) in MGH Poetae 5/1, p. 101: "vix ad primas gradiar scolasticus odas." Strecker, the MGH editor, notes two eleventh-century manuscripts: Wiener Hs. 952 (ol. Salisburgiensis), fol. 113ff., and Münchener Hs. 18628 from Tegernsee, Teg. 628, fol. 109v, which contains the first 44 verses.

[213] Milo, *Epistula ad Haiminum* (printed with Milo's *Vita Amandi* in MGH Poetae 3), p. 566.

[214] *Vita Gisleni* (BHL 3558) in *Novem vitae*, p. 148.

[215] Walter, *Passio Christophori* (BHL 1776) in MGH Poetae 5/1, p. 65. He says that Hazecha's epic poem had been lost.

[216] Dolbeau, "Domaine négligé," pp. 129–130. We have tenth-century metric passions by the nun Hrotsvita, including her passions of Gengulfus (BHL 3329), Pelagius (BHL 6618), Dionysius (BHL 2186), and Agnes (BHL 163), ed. Paul von Winterfield, *Hrotsvithae Opera*, MGH SS rer. Germ. 34. On nuns' education and literary activity, see David

composed in similar circumstances in the tenth century at Saint-Gall: "he wrote for his teacher in school a metrical version of the life of Waltharius the strong handed, of course in a rough form, because although mature he was still a young boy in his disposition. We corrected this as best we knew how and could at the behest of Archbishop Aribo while we were in Mainz."[217] Haimin's use of Milo's *Vita Amandi* shows that poems produced in this milieu could be reincorporated into the curriculum and given to other readers.[218] Epic lives were not the only texts to be recycled in this manner, but they were particularly appropriate.[219] Because the authors used them to showcase their learning, they (like Ermenric's letter) cover a broad swath of the curriculum.

<h2 style="text-align:center">PRAXIS</h2>

Ermenric provides a dynamic picture of a teacher at work, training intermediate and advanced students. We can put this evidence together with other sources to develop a fuller picture of classroom practice. Ermenric's presentation of himself teaching is, of course, not an actual transcription, but is a highly contrived literary piece, no doubt idealized to show the scope of learning and his cleverness. He also represents a specific educational context. The school of a royal abbey, like Saint-Gall, staffed by some of the generation's leading scholars and directed toward educating monastic oblates and the sons of nobility, would have different standards and aims than the local parish schools.[220] Students' native languages also affected how a *magister* taught Latin grammar and vocabulary.

N. Bell, *What Nuns Read: Books and Libraries in Medieval English Nunneries* (Kalamazoo, 1995); Rosamond McKitterick, "Nuns' Scriptoria in England and France in the Eighth Century," *Francia* 19 (1992): 1–35; Alison I. Beach, *Women as Scribes: Book Production and Monastic Reform in Twelfth-century Bavaria* (Cambridge, 2004).

[217] Ekkehard IV, *St. Galler Klostergeschichten (Casus Sancti Galli)*, c. 80, ed. Hans F. Haefele (Darmstadt, 1980), p. 168, cited and translated by Grotans, *Reading*, p. 126. "Scripsit et in scolis metrice magistro – vacillanter quidem, quia in affectione, non in habitu puer – vitam Waltherii manufortis. Quam Magontiae positi Aribone archiepiscopo iubente pro posse et nosse nostro correximus."

[218] Haimin, *Rescriptum*, in MGH Poetae 3, pp. 566–567.

[219] Ekkehard IV notes a teacher's collection of shorter student poems intended for classroom use. Ekkehard IV, *Der Liber Benedictionum Ekkeharts IV: nebst den kleineren Dichtungen aus dem codex Sangallensis 393*, ed. Johannes Egli (Saint-Gall, 1901), p. 279; cited in Grotans, *Reading*, p. 78.

[220] Luitpold Wallach, "Charlemagne's *De litteris colendis* and Alcuin: A diplomatic-historical study," *Speculum* 26 (1951): 289. On the question of external schools that were attached to monasteries, but catered to students who were not monastic oblates, see

Nonetheless, Ermenric's letter affords us a different perspective on the Carolingian classroom than other sources. Reformers emphasized the results they wanted, rather than the means educators should use to achieve them.[221] Schoolbooks, personal notebooks, *scholia*, medieval library catalogues, letters, and treatises show the texts *magistri* taught and their emphases, yet it is difficult to reconstruct actual practice from them.[222] Interlinear and marginal glosses or separately copied commentaries are static and abbreviated. Earlier and contemporary works show interactions of teachers and students, but none is as sustained or as ambitious as Ermenric's depiction.[223]

Ermenric's picture of the classroom complements these other sources. As we have seen, in the first section of his work, he depicts a teacher instructing the *parvi* (and the readers), honing their knowledge, until they are ready for the *progymnasmata*. In doing so, he intermingles theology, grammar, and other liberal arts. He returns to topics and themes, teaching through repetition. He does not, however, simply restate his previous point, but draws on the earlier discussion. Thus, the readers experience the efficacy of Ermenric's teaching, because they are able to deploy what they learned earlier. The teacher proceeds, as we have seen, often via tangent and the requirements of the material being glossed rather than according to an overarching structure. He draws on the works of others, both excerpting (*enucleatim*) and quoting directly. He gives several examples to support points, piling up (*conglobare*) examples from Christian and Classical sources. He raises questions, and only sometimes answers them. Like Aldhelm and Alcuin, he employs a humorous and informal tone.[224]

Ermenric conveys knowledge *and* skills. As well as communicating factual information (such as points of prosody and orthography), he teaches the student to apply methods of allusive and allegorical reading. In the last chapters of the letter (the *calx*), advanced students draw on what they have learned about meter and allegorical reading to undertake the

---

M.M. Hildebrandt, *The External School in Carolingian Society*, Education and Society in the Middle Ages and Renaissance (Leiden, 1992).

[221] Contreni, "Irish Contribution," pp. 81, 88.

[222] Ibid., p. 85.

[223] In *De metris*, a *discipulus* pesters Aldhelm with constant questions (in MGH AA 15, pp. 82ff.). Alcuin also depicts himself in didactic dialogues. Alcuin, *Disputatio Pippini cum Albino* in Migne, PL 101, cols. 978–979 and *Disputatio de rhetorica et de virtutibus* in W.S. Howell, *The Rhetoric of Alcuin and Charlemagne* (New York, 1965); also, see Ælfric, *Ælfric's Colloquy*, ed. G.M. Garmonsway, 2nd ed. (Exeter, 1978).

[224] Ruff, "Desipere in loco," pp. 91–103.

exercises of the *progymnasmata*. He thus requires increasingly active participation of readers, asking them to recognize allusion, to engage in allegorical interpretation, and, eventually, to compose verse.

AN IMAGINARY LIFE

As we have seen, Ermenric shows himself teaching from some version of his metric *Vita Galli*, in the latter chapters (c. 30a–36) and possibly in the earlier ones as well. There is no evidence, however, that Ermenric ever completed his epic *vita*. He probably was a slow poet, as he claims, because the standard of his verse shows a limited aptitude, despite his knowledge of prosody. The caliber of his Latin composition does not match the originality of his conceit.

There is evidence that Ermenric only intended to produce a small amount of epic verse. Although he locates himself in the epic tradition, he adopts the lyric poets' criticisms of epic and applies them to his rival. Augustan lyric poets (following their Hellenistic forebears) use the metaphor of gushing rivers to compare the torrent of epic unfavorably to the small streams of their own succinct verse. The satire in which Horace criticizes the voluminous outpourings of a rival is one source for Ermenric's use of the trope.[225] It seems strange for the would-be epic poet to adopt the minimalist rhetoric of lyric poets. Ermenric, however, as he tells us, writes slowly. He does not produce a vast flood of verse, but only the short selection appended to Grimald's letter. His "joking" muse expresses herself "in brief form."[226] Perhaps Ermenric, knowing where his strengths lay, never intended to compose an entire epic *Vita Galli* but rather wrote this letter in its place. He refers to another unwritten work, a collection for the king, from which he claims to draw one example (c. 8), and early medieval writers often cite nonexistent works.[227]

As noted previously, some students wrote epic lives at the end of their education or soon after and sent them to their teachers.[228] These writers

---

[225] Horace *Satire* 1.10, lines 35–36: "While slow Alpinus strangles Memnon and while he muddies the Rhine's source, I compose these things" (Turgidus Alpinus iugulat dum Memnona dumque / Diffingit Rheni luteum caput, haec ego ludo). Ermenric also refers to the River Rhine.

[226] c. 30a: *musa … sub brevitate iocans*.

[227] Citations of fictional works are found in earlier and contemporary texts (Pseudo-Dionysius, for instance, is rife with references to works he probably never wrote). I discuss this topic in my next book, *A History of the Imaginary Book*.

[228] Lapidge, "Tenth-Century Anglo-Latin," p. 260.

often became teachers themselves, and so it seems that the composition of such a work – which had its genesis in the *progymnasmata* and that demonstrated the poet's eloquence and range of erudition – may have been one way that a monk could exhibit his credentials as a teacher. (The writer would then be well placed to teach his own epic *vita* in the class-room, because he would be familiar with the allusions, rhetorical devices, meter, and prosody.) If promotion was Ermenric's goal, it would have been more usual to compose an actual epic life. Instead, he depicts himself using an essentially nonexistent epic *Vita Galli*. In this case, Ermenric's letter, as a depiction of him teaching intermediate and advanced students and using an epic *vita*, could stand in place of 2,000 lines or more of Latin verse. The letter, a gloss on the absent epic *vita*, substitutes for the *vita* itself. The extensive front matter of the verse lives – the prefatory letters and poems – has in this instance taken over the function of the epic *vita* and supplanted it almost completely. Here we see Ermenric at work in a ninth-century literary tradition characterized by humor, creativity, obscurity, allusion, and in-jokes.[229] In Carolingian trickster mode, he offers Grimald a text that is largely imaginary.

Ermenric's letter is a novel kind of schoolbook – one that imitates the actual classroom and engages the reader in an active educational process while demonstrating the teacher's abilities. The epic *vita* was not periph-eral but was key to this undertaking, tying together Ermenric's stated aims of educating students and acquiring patronage. The epic life (or, in this case, the idea of one) was so useful for different pursuits – glossing, teaching composition, showing one's erudition, and impressing a patron – because it could encompass many aspects of a liberal education and place them in service of Christian ends. In doing so, it shows the integration of Classical and Christian literary traditions in monastic education. It is to these that I turn in the following chapter.

---

[229] The innovation continued at Saint-Gall, with the prosimetric *Vita Galli* (BHL 3256), attributed to Notker I, written as a dialogue between Notker and Hartmann. The dialogue, which survives in fragmentary form, comprises various meters and prose. Notker, *Vita Galli* in MGH Poetae 4/3, pp. 1094–1108. The preface (BHL 3255t) locates the work in the tradition of Walafrid's *Vita Galli* and the text refers to him by name (e.g., pp. 1100 and 1102). See Walter Berschin, "Notkers Metrum de vita S. Galli," in *Florilegium Sangallense, Festschrift für Johannes Duft zum 65. Geburtstag*, ed. Otto P. Clavadetscher, Helmut Maurer, and Stefan Sonderegger (Saint-Gall-Sigmaringen, 1980), pp. 17–121.

3

Classical Nightmares: Christian Poets and the Pagan Past

The monk Ermenric tells of a terrifying apparition, which visited him when he finished reading Virgil and laid his head down on the book:

Then, in the first sleep, which is usually the sweetest after work, a certain shadowy monster immediately appeared. He was terrible in all aspects and was sometimes wielding a book, sometimes a stylus around his ears, as if about to write something. He would laugh at me because I was reading his words or mock me. But, since I was awake, I would cross myself and throw his book far away from me, and then I gave my limbs over to rest. But his specter did not stop terrifying me. He carried a trident in his hands – I don't know whether it belonged to Pluto or one of his familiars or someone else – and in his dark face, only his bright white teeth gleamed.[1]

This vision of a demonic Virgil draws on a tradition of nightmares inspired by the pagan Classics going back to Saint Jerome's famous dream in which

---

[1] Ermenric, c. 24: "in primo sopore, qui post laborem solet esse dulcissimus, statim affuit monstrum quoddam fuscum, et per omnia horribile, interdum gestabat codicem, interdum calamum ad aures, veluti scripturus aliquid, ridebat ad me, vel, quia dicta eius legebam, irridebat me. Ast ego evigilans signabam me signaculo crucis, librum eius longeque proiciens iterum membra dedi quieti. Sed nec sic cessavit fantasma ipsius terrens me, ferens tridentem, nescio utrum Plutonis domestici eius, an alicuius alterius pre manibus, facie furva solos dentes candidos ostendit." Goullet, p. 213, interprets "gestabat ... calamum ad aures" as meaning that he carries a pen behind each ear, because scribes are sometimes depicted in this manner. *Ridere* is ambiguous and can mean smile or laugh at (in a derisive sense). In Classical usage, *ridere* takes an accusative to mean "laugh at." Regardless of which translation is preferred here, the following *irridere* makes clear that it is not a pleasant smile. See R.D. Williams, "Virgil Eclogues 4.60–63," *Classical Philology* 71 (1976): 119–121. On *ridere* and *risus* and the Virgilian allusion, see Chapter 2.

Christ berated him for being a Ciceronian rather than a Christian.[2] Surprisingly, however, Ermenric's vision did not serve as a warning to the monk to avoid the Classics but rather as a sign of their integration into his own learning, teaching, and poetic composition. The confrontation between the pagan literary heritage and the Christian context was a creative tension that underlay the reading and writing of epic verse lives.

At the very end of his letter to Grimald, Ermenric tells of a second demonic visitation, in which the pagan god Orcus appeared to his rival, another poet who claimed to compose an epic life of Gall. These supernatural incursions are key to understanding the composition and use of an epic life and the role of Classics in education. Ermenric's treatment of these visions is part of his strategy for proving his poetic preeminence. The apparitions and the responses to them provide new perspectives on the role of the Classical heritage in Christian culture. We find that the hostility expressed toward the Classics is far more complicated and ambivalent than a superficial reading would suggest. The previous chapter explored Ermenric's letter as evidence for the place of epic lives in the classroom. This chapter, which examines another aspect of the same text, looks at how the integration of the Classical tradition was key to writing and using epic lives in the monastery.

Ermenric's approach to the Classics is embedded in the bitter monastic politics at Saint-Gall, in which epic *vitae* were used as a currency of self-promotion. The composition of the epic *Vita Galli*, at the heart of a contested poetic legacy, was a means of attaining status within the cloister and beyond. At Saint-Gall, around 850, Ermenric was embroiled in a competition for patronage; his letter, a bid to attain Grimald's support, seethes with sarcastic compliments and barely concealed hostility.

As discussed in the previous chapter, Walafrid Strabo, one of the most esteemed writers of his age, had written a *Vita Galli*, around late 833 or 834. Walafrid was the third to write a prose life of the saint, since, in the early ninth century, his teacher, Wettin of Reichenau had redacted the oldest anonymous version.[3] During the following century, monks of Saint-Gall would compose three other Latin works on Gall: a mid-ninth-century epic

---

[2] Werner Suerbaum, "Ein heidnischer Klassiker als "Dünger" christlicher Bildung: Quellen und Bedeutung des Vergil-Bildes bei Ermenrich von Ellwangen (um 850)," in *Panchaia: Festschrift für Klaus Thraede*, ed. M. Wacht, Jahrbuch für Antike, and Christentum supp. vol. 22 (Münster, 1995), pp. 238–250, at pp. 239–240.

[3] The anonymous prose *Vita Galli* (BHL 3245), Wettin's *vita* (BHL 3246), and Walafrid's (BHL 3246t-3251d) are all ed. by B. Krusch in MGH SRM 4, pp. 229–237.

life, a prosimetric dialogue-form life attributed to Notker I, and, around the first half of the tenth century, a short rhythmic Latin life.[4]

In the letter dedicating his *Vita Galli* to the elder Gozbert (abbot of Saint-Gall, 816–837), Walafrid had promised to versify it: "if God is willing, I will later spice up this rustic little dish with meter."[5] Walafrid had died without writing such a life, and, according to Ermenric, some monks at Saint-Gall had asked him to complete the task:

> But he [Walafrid] himself wished to adorn the deeds of blessed Gall with a lofty poetic style, but prevented by death, he finished his life in life. For this reason I was called upon by certain brothers and especially by most devoted Gozbert (don't call him bald, but bare of hairs of his head all the way to his ears, and nonetheless full of holy benevolence), nephew of the most blessed [former] abbot Gozbert, and I was compelled by a certain force to complete what the pious master did not finish, following humbly in his footsteps.[6]

So, according to Ermenric, he was nominated as the heir to Walafrid's poetic undertaking.[7] He assumed the duty, "plucking the little flowers of his [Gall's] virtues and weaving them together in metric songs like a flowery garland."[8]

When, however, Ermenric proved slow, the impatient Gozbert looked to other poets. One was Rihbert, a monk of Saint-Gall, an "Alpine Apollo"

---

[4] The anonymous epic *vita* (BHL 3253) is ed. MGH Poetae 2, pp. 428–473. For the prosimetric dialogue *vita* attributed to Notker I (BHL 3255t-3256), see Walter Berschin, "Notkers Metrum de vita S. Galli," in *Florilegium Sangallense, Festschrift für Johannes Duft zum 65. Geburtstag*, ed. Otto Clavadetscher, Helmut Maurer, and Stefan Sonderegger (Saint-Gall-Sigmaringen, 1980), pp. 17–121. The eighty-five-line rhythmic Latin life (BHL 3254), translated (according to a manuscript note) by Ekkehard IV from a German version by Ratpert, is ed. J. Grimm and A. Schmeller, *Lateinische Gedichte des X. und XI. Jh.* (Göttingen, 1838), pp. xxxi–xxxiii.

[5] Walafrid, *Vita Galli*, prologue in MGH SRM 4, p. 282: "Si Dominus permiserit, huius operis agreste pulmentum postmodum aliquibus metrorum condimentis infundam." For evidence of the date of Walafrid's *Vita Galli*, see the discussion of the anonymous epic *Vita Galli* at the end of this chapter.

[6] c. 28: "voluit vero ille poætico coturno gesta beatissimi Galli comere, sed morte praeventus vitam in vita finivit. Unde ego rogatus sum a quibusdam fratribus, et praecipue a devotissimo Gozperto, ne dicas calvo sed pilis zephali aure tenus nudo, omni tamen sancta benivolentia, felicissimi abbatis Gozperte nepote cum quadam vi inpulsus sum, ut quod magister devotus non implevit, ego cliens adsecla compleam illum secutus." *Zephalus*, a variant form of *cephalus*. Goullet prints *auretenus*. I take it as two words, *aure tenus* (*tenus*, preposition "as far as" with the ablative *aure*, "ear").

[7] The elder Gozbert was abbot, 816–837.

[8] c. 28: "virtutum eius quosdam floscellos decerpere, et metricis melodiis ceu floreum diadema ... conponere." In c. 33, Ermenric again refers to his own verses about Gall as *floscelli*: "It is now my task to pluck some little flowers of the mind regarding Gall" (Est mihi nunc mentis floscellos carpere quosdam de Galli).

who composed in lyric verse (*lyrico . . . sono*). Ermenric's nemesis was not Rihbert, but a poet he sarcastically calls "some New Homer":

parched, he [Gozbert] thought that a single source could not sate his thirst for these things. He ran to the sea, that is to say, he summoned for this purpose some new Homer – I don't know who – on this side of the Rhine, one who does not run in verse in the manner of Flaccus [Horace, a lyric poet], but gushes.[9]

The extant epic *Vita Galli* is almost certainly the work of this unknown individual.[10] Because Gozbert and others at Saint-Gall were now hostile, Ermenric sought the patronage of the abbot and courtier Grimald. In doing so, he placed himself in a lineage of teachers, students, and dedicatees. He repeatedly calls Grimald his *magister*. Although it is unclear if he ever actually taught Ermenric, it was strategically useful to address Grimald this way. Grimald had taught Walafrid, and Walafrid had taught Ermenric, so by emphasizing the association with Grimald, Ermenric also strengthened his connection to the deceased poet:

Therefore, my aforementioned teacher wrote a life of that same confessor and man of Christ [Gall]. Blessed Walafrid, well known to you, a man who lived the simplest of lives and behaved righteously in all things, whom you yourself, a skillful teacher, raised as a skilled orator. . . . But alas, for sorrow, bitter death, which knows no mercy, suddenly took him from us, but nothing conquered his soul, which Christ raised to himself.[11]

By dedicating the letter and prospective epic *vita* to Grimald, Ermenric underlined his association with the late poet, because Walafrid had dedicated one of his poems, the *Visio Wettini*, to Grimald. This implicit parallel between the *Visio Wettini* and Ermenric's work further implicated Ermenric in the chain of teachers and students around Saint-Gall and Reichenau. Walafrid had composed the *Visio* based on the prose text in which *his* teacher Heito recounted the vision of yet another of

---

[9] c. 29: "Ad haec etiam de uno fonte non putavit sitibundus sitim suam posse sedari, ad mare cucurrit, scilicet Homerum nescio quem novum pro hac revocans cis Hrenum, qui in morem Flacci non currit in poemate sed fluit." Ermenric alludes to (and identifies himself with) the Classical lyric poet Horace who compares his own shorter verses to the epic poets' gushing torrents. This was a major topos of the Hellenistic and Roman lyric poets, for example, Horace, *Satire* 1.10.

[10] Printed in MGH Poetae 2, pp. 428–473. See discussion at the end of this chapter.

[11] c. 28: "Scripsit itaque eiusdem confessoris Christi vitam supradictus preceptor meus, vir simplicissimae vitae et per omnia recte, beatus Walahfredus tibi notissimus, quem etiam tu ipse ut peritus cathegeta peritum sophistam enutristi, et . . . Sed, heu pro dolor, mors acerba, quae nulli parcere novit, subito eum nobis tulit, nec tamen sibi animam illam vindicavit, quam Christus assumpsit."

Walafrid's teachers, Wettin. Further, as noted earlier, Wettin was the author of a prose *Vita Galli*, and, like Walafrid's life of that saint, Wettin's *vita* was dedicated to the elder Gozbert. Walafrid's prose life of Gall, based on Wettin's version, was a redaction of a teacher's work, as Ermenric's would be.[12] Like other writers of epic lives, such as Heiric and Milo, Ermenric cast himself as his teacher's literary heir. By emphasizing his role as Walafrid's student and asserting his right to continue his teacher's work, Ermenric vied for inclusion in the lineage of the era's preeminent poets.

HAUNTINGS

As well as locating himself in an immediate lineage of teachers and students, Ermenric situated himself as heir to the long literary heritage of Classical epic while showing that his rival was unfit to continue the tradition. He staked his claim through a strangely inverted literary anecdote and through two dream-visions – his own haunting and that of the enemy poet.[13]

After recounting his confrontation with the Virgilian shade and flying through a list of Classical myths (*fabulae*), Ermenric defends the utility of pagan literature by telling a chronologically impossible story in which the early Latin epic poet Ennius (d. BCE 169) likens finding merit in Virgil (d. BCE 19) to finding gold in excrement.[14] The original version of the story, as told in Donatus's *Vita Vergilii* and Cassiodorus's *Institutiones*,

---

[12] Wettin, *Vita Galli*, ed. in MGH SRM 4, pp. 256–280.

[13] On dreams and visions (which were fluid categories in the ancient and medieval world), see Louis Napithali, *Dreams and Portents in Antiquity* (Wauconda, IL, 1996); Steven F. Kruger, *Dreaming in the Middle Ages* (Cambridge, 1992). See also John Contreni, "The Carolingian Renaissance: Education and Literary Culture," in *The New Cambridge Medieval History*, ed. R. McKitterick (Cambridge, 2005), p. 728. Cf. *Vita Alcuini* (BHL 242), ed. W. Arndt, MGH SS 15.1, p. 185.

[14] *Vita Vergilii* in C. *Suetoni Tranquilli Praeter Caesarum Libros Reliquiae*, ed. Augustus Reifferscheid (Leipzig, 1860), p. 67. Donatus, *Vita Vergilii*, 46. The literature on the Classical tradition in the Middle Ages is vast. A recent summation is Winthrop Wetherbee, "The Study of Classical Authors: From Late Antiquity until the Twelfth Century," in *The Cambridge History of Literary Criticism*, vol. 2: *The Middle Ages*, ed. Alastair Minnis and Ian Johnson (Cambridge, 2005), pp. 99–143. Particularly relevant works include Birger Munk Olsen, "La réutilisation des classiques dans les écoles," *Settimane di studio del centro italiano di studi sull'Alto Medioevo* 46 (1999): 227–25; Birger Munk Olsen, "L'espirit critique à l'égard de la littérature païenne au Moyen Age, jusqu'au XIIe siècle," *La Méthode critique au Moyen Age*, ed. Mireille Chazan and Gilbert Dahan. Bibliothèque d'Histoire culturelle du Moyen Age, 3 (Turnhout, 2006) pp. 27–45;

has Virgil make this remark of his forebear, Ennius: "Virgil, while he was reading Ennius, was asked by a certain man what he was doing and he answered 'I'm looking for gold in dung.'"[15] Perhaps Ermenric inadvertently confused the two poets, but given his Carolingian predilection for inversion and hidden meaning, it is likely that he chose to reverse Virgil and Ennius.[16] Andrew Laird observes that "Ermenrich's perverse manipulation of this literary anecdote and his utter disregard for chronology is extraordinary to modern eyes – but it could well have been deliberate."[17] Other writers also reversed the order of poets, and Fulgentius has his apparition of Virgil quote poets from later centuries.[18] The habit of poets and courtiers of nicknaming themselves and others after great literary figures of the past, such as Homer and Virgil, suggests a kind of metaphorical poetic reincarnation and therefore a chronological fluidity.[19] Further, because Virgil was "the chief representative of the Classical pagan tradition," his texts stood for the literature as a whole.[20] Thus, in

Michael McCormick, *Five Hundred Unknown Glosses from the Palatine Virgil: The Vatican Library, MS. Pal. lat. 1631.* Studi e Testi 343 (Vatican, 1992); P.G. Walsh, "Virgil and Medieval Epic," in *Virgil in a Cultural Tradition: Essays to Celebrate the Bimillenium,* ed. Richard A. Cardwell and Janet Hamilton. University of Nottingham Monographs in the Humanities 4 (Nottingham, 1986), pp. 52–64; Claudio Leonardi and Birger Munk Olsen, eds., *The Classical Tradition in the Middle Ages and the Renaissance: Proceedings of the First European Science Foundation Workshop on The Reception of Classical Texts, Florence, Certosa del Galluzzo, 26–27 June 1992* (Spoleto, 1995).

[15] Cassiodorus, *Institutiones,* 1.1, ed. R.A.B. Mynor (Oxford, 1937): "Vergilius, dum Ennium legeret, a quodam quid faceret inquisitus respondit, 'Aurum in stercore quaero.'" In a reversal of the usual practice of using quotations from the fathers to support the reading of the Classics, Cassiodorus brings up this example to justify reading a Christian heretical author, Origen. On the application of this trope to Virgil, see G. Folliet, "La fortune du dit de Virgile 'Aurum colligere de stercore dans la littérature chrétienne,'" *Sacris Erudiri,* 41 (2002): 31–53.

[16] Suerbaum, "Ein heidnischer Klassiker," pp. 238–250; Andrew Laird, "The Poetics and Afterlife of Virgil's Descent to the Underworld: Servius, Dante, Fulgentius and the Culex," *Proceedings of the Virgil Society* 24 (2001): 52. See Goullet, p. 219, for other inversions of source and successor.

[17] Laird, "Poetics and Afterlife," p. 52.

[18] Fulgentius, *Expositio Virgilianae continentiae secundum philosophos moralis,* ed. Rudolf Helm, *Fabii Planciadis Fulgentii Opera* (Leipzig, 1898), pp. 83–107; Laird, "Poetics and Afterlife," p. 59. I discuss Fulgentius's Virgil later.

[19] For example, Homer for Angilbert and Grimald, Virgil for the grammarian and one of Alcuin's students, and Flaccus (Horace) for Alcuin. Louis Holtz, "Alcuin et la réception de Virgile du temps de Charlemagne," in *Einhard: Studien zu Leben und Werk,* ed. Hermann Schefers (Darmstadt, 1997), pp. 67–80; Goullet, p. 205, cites Walafrid Strabo (as well as Ermenric, c. 13) for Grimald as Homer. Walafrid Strabo, *De imag. Tet.,* in MGH Poetae 2, p. 377, line 228.

[20] Laird, "Poetics and Afterlife," p. 52.

Ermenric's letter, Ennius's statement about Virgil provided a model for reading pagan literature in general, whereas the original anecdote, in which Virgil read Ennius, did not. Virgil's symbolic function mattered more than chronology.[21]

Through the story of Ennius reading Virgil, Ermenric also underscored the place of Virgil, his personal apparition, in the succession of the epic poets Homer, Ennius, and Lucretius.[22] By allusion, intertext, and vision narratives, he further emphasized the connections among the Classical poets and demonstrated his place in their literary lineage. In describing the Virgilian apparition, Ermenric drew on a visitation recounted by the epic poet, Lucretius (early first-century BCE).[23] Near the beginning of his *De rerum natura*, Lucretius established the legitimacy of his novel project (writing natural history in epic verse) by invoking Ennius and, through him, Homer.[24] Lucretius cites "our Ennius," the first Latin epic poet to employ dactylic hexameter, as his source on the soul and says that Ennius in turn derived his knowledge from the shade of Homer:

> For they do not know the nature of the soul,
> Whether it is born or is implanted at birth,
> And at the same time if it perishes when death dissolves us
> Or if it attends the shades of Orcus and the vast empty spaces
> Or if it divinely implants itself in other flocks,
> As our Ennius sings, who first bore the crown,
> With the immortal wreath from pleasant Helicon,
> Which is renowned through the Italian tribes,
> Nonetheless, even he said that hereafter were the temples of Acheron.
> Ennius set forth in everlasting verse, relating
> That neither would our souls nor bodies endure,
> But a certain pale likeness, in strange manner,
> Whence, he recalled, a likeness of always flowering Homer
> Appeared to him and burst into salty tears
> To lay out in words the nature of things[25]

---

[21] Goullet, p. 219.

[22] On Lucretius establishing himself in a poetic lineage, see Monica R. Gale, "Etymological Wordplay and Poetic Succession in Lucretius," *Classical Philology* 96 (2001): 168–172.

[23] On Lucretius, see David Ganz, "Lucretius in the Carolingian Age: The Leiden Manuscripts and their Carolingian Readers," *Medieval Manuscripts of the Latin Classics: Production and Use. Proceedings of the Seminar in the History of the Book to 1500, Leiden, 1993*, ed. Claudine A. Chavannes-Mazel and Margaret M. Smith (Los Altos Hills, CA, 1996), pp. 91–102.

[24] Peter Aicher, "Ennius' Dream of Homer," *American Journal of Philology* 110. 2 (1989): 227. The interpretation of these fragments is contested.

[25] Lucretius 1.112–125: "ignoratur enim quae sit natura animae, / nata sit an contra nascentibus insinuetur/et simul intereat nobiscum morte dirempta / an tenebras Orci visat

By alluding to this passage, Ermenric tied himself to Lucretius and cast his own experience as parallel to Ennius's encounter with Homer, linking these three epic poets into his literary genealogy; Lucretius's Ennius learned about the soul from Homer, and Ermenric quotes Lucretius in turn.[26]

Ermenric probably knew that other versions of the poetic succession of Homer and Ennius posited a much stronger connection between the two by presenting Ennius as Homer reincarnated.[27] Early in his *Annals*, Ennius recounts a dream in which Homer appeared to him and announced that his soul had returned in Ennius. A gloss on the poet Persius summarizes the story: "Ennius . . . in the beginning of his *Annals* says that he saw Homer in his dreams, telling him that he had previously been a peacock and that from this form his soul was transferred into him [Ennius], according to the beliefs of Pythagorean philosophy."[28] Horace also alludes to the idea of Ennius as Homer.[29]

vastasque lacunas / an pecudes alias divinitus insinuet se, / Ennius ut noster cecinit, qui primus amoeno / detulit ex Helicone perenni fronde coronam, / per gentis Italas hominum quae clara clueret; / etsi praeterea tamen esse Acherusia temple / Ennius aeternis exponit versibus edens, / quo neque permaneant animae neque corpora nostra, / sed quaedam simulacra modis pallentia miris; / unde sibi exortam semper florentis Homeri / commemorat speciem lacrimas effundere salas / coepisse et rerum naturam expandere dictis."

[26] Ermenric earlier, in c. 17, quotes five lines from the next passage of Lucretius (1.150–155).

[27] Horace, *Epistulae* II, 1, 50; C.O. Brink, "Ennius and the Hellenistic Worship of Homer," *American Journal of Philology* 93.4 (1972): 547–567.

[28] "Ennius . . . in Annalium suorum principio . . . dicit se vidisse in somnis Homerum dicentem fuisse quondam pavonem et ex eo translatam in se animam esse secundum Pythagorae philosophi definitionem." J.P. Elder, "A Medieval Cornutus on Persius," *Speculum* 22 (1947): 240. Persius 6.9: "'Lunai portum, est operare, cognoscite, cives.' / Cor iubet hoc Enni, postquam desertuit esse / Maeonides, Quintus pavone ex Pythagoreo." Ermenric probably encountered the idea in the earlier-ninth-century glosses because Persius was a popular school author. (In the tenth century, Saint-Gall certainly owned a copy of Persius and may well have possessed one in Ermenric's day.) Three extant ninth-century manuscripts transmit the Persius commentary. See Wendell Clausen, "Codex Vat. Reginensis 1560 of Persius," *TAPA* 80 (1949): 238; Elder, "Medieval Cornutus on Persius," p. 245. Elder attributes the commentary to Heiric of Auxerre, author of the verse *Vita Germani*. Dorothy M. Robathan, "Two Unreported Persius Manuscripts," *Classical Philology* 26.3 (1931): 288. A manuscript, which Robathan dates to the late tenth or early eleventh century on the basis of the Carolingian minuscule was copied at Saint-Gall. A late-tenth-century book list from Saint-Gall notes that the monastery possessed a copy of Persius (Vatican, BAV, MS Reg. lat. 1562, which includes a copy of Persius, is probably from Saint-Gall). For the Saint-Gall booklist, Robathan cites P. Lehmann, *Mittelalterliche Bibliothekskataloge Deutschlands und der Schweiz*, vol. 1 (Munich, 1918), p. 111.

[29] Horace, *Epistulae* II, 1, 50–53: "Ennius, wise and strong and another Homer, according to the critics, seems to have little concern of his promises and Pythagorean dreams falling" (Ennius, et sapiens et fortis et alter Homerus, / Ut critici dicunt, leviter curare videtur / Quo promissa cadant et somnia Pythagorea). Also Cicero, *Somnium Scipionis* 1: "fit enim fere, ut cogitationes sermonesque nostri patiant aliquid in somno tale, quale de Homero scribit Ennius, de quo videlicet saepissime vigilans solebat cogitate et loqui." Cited by

For other Classical writers, Virgil, not Ennius, was the new Homer. Donatus's *Vita Vergilii* quotes Propertius on the *Aeneid*: "Give way Roman writers, yield Greeks, something greater than the *Iliad* – I do not know what – is born."[30] Jerome calls Virgil "our second Homer."[31] Macrobius discusses Virgil's emulation of Homer at length and describes the *Aeneid* as a "mirror of Homer's work."[32]

The ties among the four poets Ermenric invokes – Homer, Ennius, Virgil, and Lucretius – are complicated. Later traditions trace Virgil's poetic descent from Lucretius as well as Homer. According to Donatus, Virgil received the toga that marked his transition to adulthood on the day Lucretius died (*Vita Vergilii*, c. 6). Another life of Virgil, used by Ermenric, recounts the story that Lucretius was Virgil's maternal uncle.[33]

Ermenric alludes to another Classical poetic tradition, that of Horace *Satires* 1.10, in his vision narratives.[34] In his programmatic poem on satire, Horace recounts an important figure from the past appearing in a dream as a result of his literary pursuits. Quirinus (the deified Roman founder Romulus) instructed Horace to abandon Greek verse:

And when I was making little Greek verses (even though I was born this side of the sea), Quirinus appeared after midnight when dreams are true and admonished me with words like this:

"you take a twig to the forest like a crazy person
if you would rather fill up the vast ranks of the Greeks."[35]

J.H. Waszink, "The Proem of the 'Annales' of Ennius," *Mnemosyne* 4th ser. 3 (1950): 215–240 at p. 224. The Pythagorean doctrine of metempsychosis – the idea that souls were reborn in new bodies – was also familiar to Ermenric from book 6 of the *Aeneid* (6.749; pp. 102–103), in which Aeneas visits the underworld, and from Fulgentius's *Continentia*.

[30] Donatus c. 30; Propertius, *Carmina* 2.34.65: "cedite, Romani scriptores, cedite Grai: / nescio quid maius nascitur Iliade."

[31] Jerome Ep. 121, 10, 5: "alter Homerus apud nos." Cf. *Comm. In Mich.* 2, 7, 5–7, noted in Brink, "Ennius," p. 567.

[32] Macrobius, *Les Saturnales*, ed. and trans. Henri Bornecque and François Rochard (Paris, 1937), vol. 2, pp. 46–52; 5.22.13, cited by Irvine, *Textual Culture*, p. 146.

[33] This *vita* was transmitted in a ninth-century schoolbook from Reichenau, Saint Paul in Lavanttal MS Samblasianus, 86, fols. 1r–1v. Ermenric drew his list of Virgil's friends (c. 25) from this work. See Goullet, p. 147, n. 180. Hollis Ritchie Upson, "Medieval Lives of Virgil," *Classical Philology* 38 (1943): 104; Suerbaum, "Ein heidnischer Klassiker," pp. 238–250; Jan M. Ziolkowski and Michael C. J. Putnam, *The Virgilian Tradition: The First Fifteen Hundred Years* (New Haven, 2008), p. 103 (life translated on pp. 278–280).

[34] Ermenric also alludes to Horace, *Sat.* 1.10 in c. 36; see the following discussion.

[35] 1.10, lines 31–34: "Atque ego cum graecos facerem, natus mare citra, / Versiculos, vetuit me tali voce Quirinus / Post mediam noctem visus, cum somnia vera: / 'In silvam non ligna feras insanius ac si / Magnas Graecorum malis inplere catervas.'"

Quirinus as the quintessential Roman authorized Horace's composition of short verse in Latin, a tradition to which Ermenric also refers.[36] So, Ermenric, through his vision of Virgil and his misquotation of the "gold from manure" anecdote, places himself in the tradition that links Homer, Ennius, Virgil, Lucretius, and others through ideas of poetic succession, emulation, and rebirth.

THE EQUIVOCAL MUSE

Ermenric also draws on the sixth-century writer Fulgentius.[37] In his *Continentia Virgiliana*, Fulgentius, a Christian, invokes the muses and uses them in turn to summon the revenant (persona, *imago*) of Virgil: "Give to me now the persona of the Mantuan prophet!"[38] He performs this act of literary necromancy to place his allegorical reading of the *Aeneid* in the mouth of the poet himself. Virgil condescendingly agrees to teach Fulgentius: "raising an eyebrow and wrinkling up his face, he said 'I was thinking, little man, that you despise anything obscure. I would put my heavy baggage in your vehicle, but you are denser than a clod of earth and would belch up anything rich."[39] Virgil adopts the gestures of an orator, similar to those described by Quintilian, "in the mode of speaking with two fingers raised in an iota and the third pressing his thumb," and proceeds to lecture Fulgentius.[40]

Virgil, in Ermenric's letter, also functions as a kind of muse. Ermenric asks Grimald, "at least let me see Maro's [Virgil's] muses, or the poet himself."[41] Like other muses, Virgil appears to the poet before the epic

[36] Classical poets of satire contrast their genre's own modest scope to the gushing of epic, as Ermenric characterizes his own verse in comparison with that of New Homer. Ermenric c. 29, cf., for example, Horace *Satire* 1.10, lines 35–36.

[37] Fulgentius, *Expositio Virgilianae continentiae secundum philosophos moralis*, *Fabii Planciadis Fulgentii Opera*, ed. Rudolf Helm (Leipzig, 1898), pp. 83–107.

[38] Ibid., p. 8: "Cede mihi nunc personam Mantuani vatis."

[39] Ibid., p. 142: "Tum ille contracto rugis multiplicibus supercilio: 'Putabam,' inquit, 'vel te, homuncule, creperum aliquid desipere, in cuius cordis vecturam meas onerosiores exposuissem sarcinulas; at tu telluris glabro solidior adipatum quidpiam ructuas [ruptuas].'" Laird prefers the alternate manuscript reading "ructuas," which he translates "snore." Laird, "Poetics and Afterlife," p. 61." "Adipatum" could refer to something rich or greasy, possibly a pastry.

[40] Fulgentius, *Continentia*, p. 86: "Compositus in dicendi modum erectis in iotam duobus digitis tertium pollicem comprimens." Cf. Qunitilian, *Institutio Oratoria*, ed. Charles Halm, (Leipzig, 1868), 11.3.

[41] Ermenric, c. 24: "saltim vel Maronis musas cernere, vel ipsum licentiam da." Ermenric borrows the Virgilian muses from Fulgentius, *Continentia*, p. 85.

proper begins (Ermenric's *Vita Galli*, here approximated by the *calx* appended to the letter). Similarly, in Ennius's *Annals* and Lucretius's *De rerum natura*, a dead poet appears or is invoked by his successor near the beginning of a text to locate it within the epic tradition.[42] Both Ennius and Lucretius attempted unprecedented kinds of epic (Latin dactylic hexameter and natural history, respectively), and the magisterial predecessor implicitly sanctions their work and asserts its place in the epic tradition.[43]

Ermenric's implication that Virgil is his literary ancestor and muse, on one hand, and his portrayal of the demonically grinning dead poet, on the other, underscore the complicated responses that medieval Christians often expressed toward the Classics. Ermenric introduces the entire episode in a way that stresses ambivalence toward Virgil, asking to see him and then changing his mind: "I don't want to see him, he whom I believe resides in the very worst place, also because a vision of him terrifies me."[44] Despite his fear, he frames his haunting in the peaceful Virgilian language of sleep. Virgil appears to him "in the first sleep, which is usually sweetest after work" and a second time, when "I again gave my limbs over to rest."[45]

Ermenric's response to the Virgilian apparition is also ambivalent. He throws his book far away, suggesting a rejection of the poet, but immediately launches into his excursus on Virgilian *fabulae*. Drawing on a similar passage in Gregory of Tours, Ermenric demonstrates his great familiarity

[42] Peter Aicher, "Ennius' Dream of Homer," *American Journal of Philology* 110.2 (1989): 227.

[43] Fulgentius also does something unusual in his (prose) *Continentia*, in producing the first complete Christian allegorization of the *Aeneid*. He places almost the entire text in the poet's mouth. In epic *vitae*, Virgil's "Musa, mihi causas memora" (*Aen.* 1.8) is customarily replaced with addresses to God (in one or all persons of the Trinity) and the saint (for example, Ermenric's appeal to Gall in c. 33). These appeals, although stating the poet's Christian affiliation, do not bind him to the Classical tradition.

[44] Ermenric, c. 24: "nolo tamen ipsum videre, quem credo in pessimo loco manere, et quia terret me visus eius."

[45] Ibid.: "in primo sopore, qui post laborem solet esse dulcissimus ... iterum membra dedi quieti." Virgilian reminiscences cited by Laird, "Poetics and Afterlife," p. 78, n. 6. Also used in *Culex*, lines 158 ("mitem concepit proiectus membra soporem") and 205 ("vadit et in fessos requiem dare comparat artus"). Each time Ermenric falls asleep, he alludes to a passage in the *Aeneid* in which the hero's slumber is soon interrupted by a supernatural *visus* (the lacerated Hector and the god Tiberinus, respectively; *Aen.* 2.268ff., 8.30). Ermenric's language perhaps also echoes a Benedictine prayer for protection from demonic attack during sleep. The Gelasian sacramentary of Gellone contains the prayer: "Benedic domine hoc famulorum tuorum dormiturio, qui non dormis neque dormitas, qui custodis israel, famulos tuos huic domui *quiescentes post laborem* custodi ab inlusionibus fantasmice satane." Antoine Dumas, ed., *Liber Sacramentorum Gellonensis*, CCSL 159 (Turnhout, 1981), #468 (2862), p. 453.

with Virgilian material.[46] Ermenric thus undercuts his derision of pagan literature by parading his knowledge of mythology and by couching his vitriol toward it in Classical allusion, with an irony that other educated individuals would have recognized.[47] His grudging acceptance of the utility of these works accords with the knowledge he demonstrates rather than the superficial message of condemnation.

HOMER AND ORCUS

At the very end of the letter, Ermenric recounts another vision inspired by Virgil. This encounter, he says, was experienced by his rival:

> He consumed, once, some wheat, as he depicted landscapes,
> But he was struck – alas! – by a sudden pain in his stomach,
> While he heads for Inarime, sending his own words to Virgil,
> Orcus appeared to him with a trident and holding a louse.
> And observed him with a laugh. Learned Homer,[48]
> Immediately, turning himself away, makes a sign with a finger on his mouth,
> And first casts all the things about Troy away from himself,
> And at the same time orders all the monsters to leave.[49]

Orcus's appearance echoes Ermenric's own visitation and Lucretius's "shades of Orcus" noted previously.[50] This haunting is a partial inversion

[46] Gregory of Tours, *De gloria martyrum*, preface. Migne, PL 71, 714ff. ("Iunonis iram"); Virgil, *Aen.* 1.4 ("Iunonis ob iram").

[47] Laird, "Poetics and Afterlife," p. 51.

[48] I have punctuated the text differently from Goullet, because having Orcus laugh, rather than New Homer, introduces another parallel (like the trident) between this apparition and his Virgilian counterpart from c. 24. It also makes more sense in this context for Orcus to be laughing. *Risus* is an allusion to the end of Virgil's *Eclogue* 4, to which Ermenric refers in the tale of his own haunting (c. 24). "Begin little boy, to recognize your mother with a smile . . . he upon whom parents did not smile, neither a god judged worthy of his table, nor a goddessof her bedroom" (Incipe, parve puer, risu cognoscere matrem. . . . Cui non risere parentes / nec deus hunc mensa, dea nec dignata cubili est; *Ecl.* 4, lines 60, 62–63). Servius, in his commentary, paraphrases line 60: "For just as parents recognize each other by speech, thus infants show that they know their parents with laughter [or a smile]" (sicut enim maiores se sermone cognoscunt, ita infantes parentes risu se indicant agnoscere. ergo hoc dicit – incipe parentibus arridere). Servius, *Comm. in Ecl.* in *Servii grammatici qui feruntur in Vergilii carmina comentarii*, ed. George Thilo and Hermann Hagen, vol. 3.1 (Lepizig, 1887), p. 53.

[49] Ermenric, c. 36: "ille momordit ador quondam, dum climata pinxit, / sed – pudor, ah! – ventris subito dolore relisus / dum petit Inarimen mittens sua dicta Maroni, / olli occurrit habens Orcus tridente peduclum, / perspicit ut talem, cum risu. Doctus Homerus / protinus avertens digito se signat in ore, / et primum Ilaiacas varias res abicit a se / monstraque cuncta simul discedere iussit."

[50] Lucretius, *De rerum natura*, 1.115: "tenebrae Orci."

of Ermenric's own experience and features many verbal reminiscences of it,[1] bringing the previous incident to the reader's mind as he or she encounters the text's second infernal apparition. New Homer, says Ermenric, seeks Inarime, identified as Ischia, an island near Virgil's burial place, Naples. (Inarime, according to Ovid, is also the home of the raucously squawking and mendacious Cercopes, whom Jupiter transformed into apes.)[51] Unlike Ermenric, New Homer actively sought out Virgil "sending words to him," but what appeared to him was not the poet, but Orcus, a pagan god brought on by a stomach ache. In the earlier passage, summarizing Virgilian *fabulae*, Ermenric conflates Orcus with Vulcan (an appropriate figure to encounter near the volcanic island of Ischia) and gives a jumbled version of his birth:[52]

Juno gave birth from her thigh to Vulcan, whom she named Orcus.[53] And seeing that he was misshapen, she angrily cast him away from herself. Falling, he broke his hip and became lame. Because of this he made himself the smith of the infernal gods. Not much after that, when all the gods had been invited to a dinner, he saw his mother Juno, sitting on a throne he had made, enjoying herself and smiling at his craft. Let my soul not attend this banquet, nor let it be in the number of such phantoms.[54]

A reader familiar with the story of that banquet, related in Servius's commentary on Virgil's famous "Messianic" fourth *Eclogue*, would know that Vulcan's gift was untrustworthy and that Juno's throne was a

---

[51] *Inarime* is a Virgilian usage, *Aen.* 9.715–716: "durumque cubile / Inarime Iovis imperiis imposta Typhoeo," a reference to the place where Jupiter buried the giant Typhoeus. Servius's commentary on this line of the *Aeneid* explains the etymology as deriving from the Etruscan word for apes. Ovid, *Metamorphoses*, 14.89–100, describes the Cercopes, the inhabitants of Inarime, as liars whom Jupiter transformed into apes as punishment (making them both similar and dissimilar to humans) and divested of speech: "he took away the use of words and in terrible perjury of their inborn language, he left them only able to protest with raucous screeching" (abstulit usum / verborum et natae dira in periuria linguae: / posse queri tantum rauco stridore reliquit). Ovid, *Metamorphoses*, ed. Hugo Magnus (Gotha, 1892), 14.98–100; and Martianus Capella, *De Nuptiis Philologiae et Mercurii*, in *Les noces de Philologie et de Mercure. Tome VI. Livre VI. La géométrie*, ed. Barbara Ferré (Paris, 2007), 6.644. On Virgil's connection with Naples, Marbury B. Ogle, "The Later Tradition of Vergil," *Classical Journal* 26 (1930): 72.

[52] Servius, *Comm. in Aen.* 8.454; Isidore, *Orig.* 8.11.40.

[53] For Vulcan's birth from Juno's thigh, Isidore, *Orig.* 8.11.40.

[54] Ermenric, c. 24. "Iuno genuisse ex femore suo Vulcanum, quem Orcum nominavit. Vidensque eum deformem irata proiecit a se. Qui cadens fractus est coxa et catax efficitur. Quamobrem posuit eum fabrum diis infernalibus. Nec post multum ille diis omnibus ad caenam suam invitatis, Iunonem in sella, quam ipse fabricavit, gaudentem ac ridentem pro ipsius fabrica matrem agnovit. Ad eius convivium non veniat anima mea, nec sit in numero talium fantasmatum."

trap.[55] Vulcan, spurned by the gods, used the throne to force his mother to acknowledge him and admit him to the divine company.[56] Ermenric alludes to this gloss and the fourth *Eclogue* when he says that his soul does not want to be admitted to this feast. As with the reference to Inarime, the association of New Homer with Orcus/Vulcan hints at deception. Further, the Fourth *Eclogue*'s last lines, to which he here alludes ("he upon whom parents did not smile"), echo Ermenric's depiction of the laughing (*ridere*) and mocking (*irridere*) Virgil and presage the laughter (*risus*) of the Orcus episode.[57]

Orcus is not usually conflated with Vulcan, but with Pluto (Hades), god of the underworld (Ermenric's Orcus retains Pluto's attribute of the trident).[58] Orcus may have been a particularly apposite pagan god, because evidence from a penitential suggests that people were celebrating him in Francia, or at least that churchmen feared that they were.[59] Richard Bernheimer sees an etymological association between Orcus and the European wild men revered in the Christian Middle Ages.[60] Thus, the vision of Orcus may have implied a more real threat of heathenism than did the *fabulosae* Ermenric lists or the apparition of Virgil. Medieval traditions also cast Orcus, conflated with the devil, as the lord of *stercus*, a term Ermenric uses to refer to Virgil and pagan literature generally.[61] Despite this possible association with Virgil, Orcus, as a god of the dead, could hardly be less like the deathless muses who provided poetic

---

[55] Servius, *Comm. in Ecl.* 4.62–63, explaining "cui non risere parentes / nec deus hunc mensa, dea nec dignata cubili est."

[56] Virgil, *Ecl.* 4.62: "cui non risere parentes." The Bern Scholia on the Eclogues, ed. George Thilo and Hermann Hagen *Servii Grammatici qui feruntvr in Vergilii carmina commentarii. Appendix Serviana ceteros praeter Servium et scholia bernensia Vergilii commentatores continens*, vol. 3.2 (Leipzig, 1902).

[57] Classicists argue about the reading of this line, usually emending it from "cui non risere parentes," to "qui non risere parenti." See, for example, R.D. Williams, "Virgil Eclogues 4. 60–63," *Classical Philology* 71 (1976): 119–121.

[58] Virgil, *Georgics* 4, line 502; Isidore, *Orig.* 8.11. 42.

[59] *Poenitentiale Vigilanum*, c. 84, from Biblioth. d Escurial (Ff. 148, Scr. 976), ed. F. W. H. Wasserschleben, *Bussordnungen der abendländischen Kirche* (Halle, 1851), p. 533 (see also p. 71). Noted by Richard Bernheimer, *Wild Men in the Middle Ages: A Study in Art, Sentiment and Demonology* (Cambridge, MA, 1952), p. 43. The Spanish penitential, thought to be based on a Frankish source, prescribes a year's penance for those "who wear women's clothing in the dance and monstrously outfit themselves as Maia, Orcus, and Pela" (Qui in saltatione femineum habitum gestiunt et monstruose se fingunt et maias et orcum et pelam).

[60] Bernheimer, *Wild Men*, pp. 42–43.

[61] c. 25; Emily Allen Hope, "The Influence of Superstition on Vocabulary: Two Related Examples," *PMLA* 50.4 (1935): 1043.

inspiration. It is Orcus who takes the epic heroes from life and the muses' role to recall them for the poet.[62]

Ermenric's Orcus is an enigmatic figure. Like the ghostly Virgil, he carries a borrowed trident, but whereas Virgil also holds a book and a pen, he wields his trident with an incongruous louse (*peduclum*).[63] Ermenric's sources provide clues to this strange image. In Paul the Deacon's short eighth-century poem *De pulice et podagra* (*On the Flea and Gout*) and in Alcuin's riddle to Pippin, lice or fleas signify poverty.[64] In the *Dialogue of Alcuin and Pippin* (a text presented as a discussion between teacher and student), Alcuin tests the prince's ability at answering riddles:

ALCUIN: I was hunting with others – if we captured anything there, we carried nothing with us, but what we were unable to catch, we carried home with us.
PIPPIN: This is the peasants' hunt.[65]

As is often the case with his riddles, the solution requires further decoding.[66] Thus, Pippin responds only obliquely to the riddle, the simple answer to which is "lice."[67] Ermenric's reference to the *peduclus* may also allude to the Pseudo-Virgilian *Culex* (a near homophone for *pulex*, "flea"), a miniature epic poem in which the eponymous martyred mosquito appears to its killer in a dream and tells him about the

---

[62] *Ilias Latina*, lines 1–3: The poet calls on the muse to lay out the story including "the brave souls of heroes it sent to Orcus" (atque animas fortes heroum tradidit Orco).

[63] Goullet, pp. 239–240, makes a convincing case for *peduclum* as "flea," rather than "net." Either way, Orcus is ridiculous. If he carries a net and trident, he is equipped as a *retiarius*, a kind of gladiator depicted as effeminate by Juvenal (Juvenal 2 and 8, Oxford fragment of Juvenal 6) and is outfitted for a different kind of *ludus* (a gladiatorial game) than those Ermenric plays. See Steven M. Cerutti and L. Richardson, "The Retiarius Tunicatus of Suetonius, Juvenal and Petronius," *American Journal of Philology* 110 (1989): 589–594.

[64] Paul the Deacon, *De pulice et podagra* from the manuscript St. Gallen, Stiftsbibliothek, MS 889, in Jan M. Ziolkowski, *Talking Animals: Medieval Latin Beast Poetry, 750–1150* (Philadelphia, 1993), p. 290.

[65] Alcuin, *Disputatio Pippini cum Albino* in Migne, PL 101, cols. 978–979: "Albinus: ... Fui in venatione cum aliis, in qua si quid cepimus, nihil nobiscum portavimus; quem non potuimus capere, domum portavimus nobiscum. Pippin: Rusticorum est haec venatio."

[66] Dieter Bitterli, *Say What I Am Called: The Old English Riddles of the Exeter Book and the Anglo-Latin Riddle Tradition* (Toronto, 2009), p. 110; Frederick Tupper, Jr., "The Comparative Study of Riddles," *Modern Language Notes* 18.1 (1903): 3.

[67] Goullet points out that this riddle is a variant of the one that, according to Plutarch's *Vita*, caused Homer's death, and so the *peduclum* could be another link to the epic tradition, although there is no evidence that the story was known in the ninth-century West. Goullet, p. 240.

underworld.[68] The parasitic insect might hint at the tradition, attested in later centuries, of likening pagan authors to flea-ridden dogs.[69]

Etymology and folklore suggest an old association of Orcus and lice. The name Orcus became associated with demons generally and is glossed with the Old English *thurse* (giant, demon), a term that is in turn associated with lice, especially the thurse-louse (woodlouse).[70] The association of insects with the demonic (particularly as familiar spirits) existed in several European folklore traditions, and a ninth-century Saint-Gall glossary defines "Belzebub" (a common name for the Devil) as "the man of flies."[71]

Finally, Orcus's *peduclum*, literally "little foot," is a pun on the metrical foot (*pes*) to which poets allude when making genre statements. The Orcus passage echoes the outset of Ovid's *Amores*, in which the poet says Cupid, also armed, laughed at him (*ridere*) and stole a foot of his verse in order to transform epic dactylic hexameter into the elegiac couplets suitable for

---

[68] Both Ermenric, c. 24 and the *Culex* poet draw on some of the same passages of *Aeneid*, book 6, which was the locus classicus for underworld descriptions and the most revered book of the *Aeneid*. Many other echoes show Ermenric's familiarity with the *Culex*, including chirping crickets, branches, wandering paths through forests, the repeated use of *ludus/ludere* and the reference to the "Ascrean" poet (Hesiod). The pseudo-Ovidian *De pediculo*, "On the Flea," which Lenz interprets as a parody of a bad teacher, and William of Blois's *Pulicis et musce iurgia* (*Conflict of the Flea and the Fly*) seem to postdate Ermenric by several centuries. The earliest manuscripts containing *De Pediculo* are twelfth-century and it is not mentioned in medieval biographies of Ovid. Frederick Walter Lenz, "[P. Ovidii Nasonis] *De Pediculo Libellus,*" *Eranos* 53 (1955): 61–74. Fausto Ghisalberti, "Medieval Biographies of Ovid," *Journal of the Warburg and Courtauld Institutes* 9 (1946): 37, n. 2.

[69] A Cluniac monk could silently request a pagan book by impersonating a dog scratching its ear. Scott G. Bruce, "Monastic Sign Language in the Cluniac Customaries," in *From Dead of Night to End of Day: The Medieval Customs of Cluny*, ed. Susan Boynton and Isabelle Cochelin. Disciplina Monastica: Studies on Medieval Monastic Life (Turnhout, 2005), p. 284.

[70] Charles P.G. Scott, "The Devil and His Imps: An Etymological Inquisition," *TAPA* 26 (1895): 79–146 at 127, 135–140. Eighth-century English glosses link the word with orc and Orcus. See Nicolas K. Kiessling, "Grendel: A New Aspect," *Modern Philology* 65 (1968): 191–201, 200–201; Hope E. Allen, "The Influence of Superstition on Vocabulary: Robin Goodfellow and His Louse," *PMLA* 51 (1936): 904–920 at 904. The earliest mention of the bronze apotropaic fly of Naples, allegedly made by Virgil, dates to the twelfth century; see J.W. Spargo, *Virgil the Necromancer: Studies in Virgilian Legends* (Cambridge, MA, 1934), pp. 69ff.

[71] On demonic insects generally, see Allen, "The Influence of Superstition," *PMLA* 50 (1935): 1033–1046, and *PMLA* 51 (1936): 904–920. Beelzebub is defined as the "man of flies" (*vir muscarum*) in the ninth-century glossary printed in Minton Warren, "On Latin Glossaries, with Especial Reference to the Codex Sangallensis 912," *TAPA* 15 (1884): 10.

lighter subjects.[72] A "little foot," would be a trochee or an iamb of short verse (such as the hendecasyllables of Catullus or the iambs of Ambrosian hymns), as opposed to the longer dactyl of epic hexameter. Cupid usurped the prerogative of the muses by dictating Ovid's meter and therefore subject matter, stopping him from composing in dactylic hexameter, the meter of epic.[73] As Cupid acted as Ovid's muse, Orcus has usurped the role for New Homer. Orcus appeared with "a little foot" for New Homer, signaling that he should write "small songs."

Ermenric chooses Orcus as New Homer's apparition based on the tradition of Orpheus as the paradigmatic poet. As discussed in Chapter 1, Hilduin alludes to the figure of Orpheus in his depiction of Dionysius and as a literary ancestor for himself. Medieval tradition drew on the Classical narratives in which Orpheus's song brought trees and rocks to hear him, and moved even the lords of the underworld.[74] It is a story about poetry's power to overcome even death. Thus, the monk Abbo of Saint-Germain-des-Prés, in the preface to his epic verse account of the Viking raids on Paris, writes, in his humility topos, that the *figmenta* of the highest poets (*summi ... poetae*) would not be found in his verses. He has not "in the manner of Silenus" rounded up the fauns and wild beasts for a ritual dance, "nor," he continues, drawing on Ovid, "have I compelled the hard oaks to shake the mountain tops, nor did the forests and birds ever follow in our footsteps due to the sweetness of the song; nor by any melody from have I rescued souls from Orcus or other hands in the Tartarean gloom through the rite of Orpheus."[75] Abbo's ostensible self-effacement allows him to emphasize the power of poetry. Orpheus's encounter with Orcus, alluded to in Abbo and other medieval writers, underpins

---

[72] Ovid, *Amores* 1.1.1–7 and 24–30: "arma gravi numero violentaque bella parabam / edere, materia conveniente modis / par erat inferior versus; risisse Cupido / dicitur atque unum surripuisse pedem. / "Quis tibi, saeve puer, dedit hoc in carmina iuris? / Pieridum vates, non tua turba sumus. / quid, si praeripiat flavae Venus arma Minervae.... "quod" que "canas, vates, accipe" dixit "opus!" / me miserum! Certas habuit puer ille sagittas. / uror, et in vacuo pectore regnat Amor. / sex mihi surgat opus numeris, in quinque residat: / ferrea cum vestris bella valete modis! / cingere litorea flaventia tempora myrto, / Musa per undenos emodulanda pedes!"

[73] Ovid, *Amores* 1.1.27.

[74] Virgil, *Georgics* 4.454–527; Ovid, *Metamorphoses* 10.11–144, 11.1–2.

[75] Abbo, *Praefatio* to *De bellis Parisiacae urbis*, ed. G.H. Pertz in MGH SS 2, p. 778: "neu rigidas motare cacumina quercus coaegerim, tum vero silvae avesque menia quoque nunquam nostris sunt comitata [corr. comitatae] vestigiis prae dulcedine cantionis; nec quovis modulamine Orco aliisve manibus animas tartarea aeripuerim caligine ritu Orphei." Cf. Ovid, *Met.* 11.1–2: "Carmine dum tali silvas animosque ferarum / Threicius vates et saxa sequentia ducit."

Ermenric's account.[76] New Homer wanted to meet Virgil, a denizen of the underworld, but instead encountered Orcus. Whereas Orpheus's song persuaded Orcus to release his wife, Eurydice, New Homer has no such power over the lord of the dead, who merely laughs at him. New Homer is a failed Orpheus.

New Homer's response to Orcus underlines his shortcomings. Ermenric reacts to his apparition by crossing himself, but New Homer puts his finger to his lips (*digito se signat in ore*) in a hushing gesture.[77] Following this symbolic silencing, New Homer threw his books away from himself (*abicit a se*), just as Juno cast Vulcan/Orcus away from her in Ermenric's mythological account (*proiecit a se*, c. 24). Ermenric threw only Virgil's own book, but New Homer spurned a larger class of the classics (*Ilaiacae variae res*) and their *figmenta*. Whereas Ermenric follows his recollection of the haunting by immediately launching into his mythological digression, undercutting his apparent contempt of Virgil, New Homer abandoned mythological topics:

> First, he throws away from himself the various things related to Troy,
> And at once orders all the monsters to depart[78]
> He does not sing of Eurydice nor compose songs of mourning for Orpheus,
> He cares for neither the apples of the Hesperides not the gifts of Dis
> He is enraged at the Nymphs and casts the Furies from his heart,

[76] The eleventh-century poem "Quid suum virtutis," line 989, also invokes Orcus in the description of Orpheus in the underworld: "miratur flecti frendens furor ipsius Orci," cited by Jaeger, "Orpheus in the Eleventh Century," *MJ* 27 (1992): 152. *Quid suum virtutis*, ed. A. Paravicini, *Eine Lehrdichtung des 11. Jahrhunderts*, Editiones Heidelbergenses 21 (Heidelberg, 1980).

[77] Ermenric draws on Alcuin's riddle to depict this gesture. Before posing the riddle, Alcuin says, "Place a finger over your mouth, so that boys don't hear what it is" (Sed pone digitum super os, ne pueri hoc audiant, quid sit). Alcuin, *Disputatio Pippini cum Albino* in Migne, PL 101, cols. 978–979. In later, more sophisticated monastic sign systems, devised to preserve silence within Cluniac abbeys, touching the mouth or lips could indicate not knowing, or could signify one who spoke a foreign language as well as conveying the meaning familiar to us of hushing another. Scott G. Bruce, *Silence and Sign Language in Medieval Monasticism: The Cluniac Tradition c. 900–1200* (Cambridge, 2007), pp. 107, 181. According to Quintilian's *Institutia oratoria*, which was still being read in the ninth century and that is the source of Virgil's oratorical gesture in Fulgentius's *Continentia*, a similar gesture denotes fear: "the movement of the fingers, with their tops converging, toward the mouth. For we do this when we are slightly surprised and at times also employ it to express fear or entreaty when we are seized with sudden indignation" (digitos, cum summi coierunt, ad os referre, cur quibusdam displicuerit, nescio. Nam id et leviter admirantes et interim subita indignatione velut pasvescentes et deprecantes facimus). Quintilian, *The Institutio Oratoria of Quintilian*, ed. and trans. Harold Edgeworth Butler (Cambridge, MA, 1922), 11.3.103. This is Butler's translation.

[78] An allusion to Gregory of Tours, *De gloria martyrum*, pref., PL 71, 714ff.

He rejects Dido's grief on the shore;
And he does not wish to tell us of Aeneas and his people,
Nor the stones hurled, once upon a time, nor the reign of Saturn,
He does not wish to speak of the birds of the Caucuses or Tityos.
He plays with these things briefly and leaves the gifts of the Myrmidons,
And he leaves also Dolopes of Pyrrhus and the arrogant Hellenes
And the Dardanian scions and the unvanquished race of the Greeks
He does not care to say that Troy and Priam have fallen.[79]

Ermenric uses New Homer's rejection of pagan literature as another opportunity to show his own Classical learning. The passage echoes the earlier mythological passage (c. 24–25), from which we recognize several figures: Eurydice, Orpheus, the Furies, Aeneas, and Priam. The list in chapter 36 is a rewriting of a passage of Virgil's sixth *Eclogue*, in which the hungover satyr Silenus, finally forced to sing, tells many of these stories.[80] As Ermenric couches his own (supposed) disdain for the Classics in classicizing language and allusion, he now presents his rival's repudiation by invoking the very material New Homer rejected. Further, by alluding to this *Eclogue*, he implicitly likens the other poet to Silenus, a fat old satyr who is a particularly comic exemplar of that notoriously drunken and lecherous species. The allusion also contains a hidden joke for the educated reader, because one of Silenus's topics in the sixth *Eclogue* is Cornelius Gallus, a poet and friend of Virgil (whom Ermenric mentions in c. 25) and a homonym for the saint, who is now to be New Homer's only subject. Echoing Virgil's tenth *Eclogue* (which is about Cornelius Gallus), Ermenric says of his rival: "Let him turn himself entirely to sing of Gall, / Blessed Gall I say, holy in God and filled with kind piety / Out of love for whom we indeed want to write something."[81]

---

[79] c. 36. "Et primum Ilaiacas varias res abicit a se / Monstraque cuncta simul discedere iussit / Nec canit Eurydicen nec Orphea threnora pangit, / Nec poma Hesperidum curat nec munera Ditis; / Iratus Nymphis, Furias ex corde refutans, / Didonis spernit in litore luctus; / Aeneanque sua cum gente edicere non vult, / Nec lapides iactos quondam et saturnia regna, / Caucaseas Volucres, Titiones dicere mavult. / Sed breviter his ludit Myrmida dona relinquens, / Et Dolopos Pyrrhi linquit Danaosque superbos / Daedanidasque proles invictae gentis Achivae / Dicere non curat Troiam Priamumque subactum."

[80] Goullet, p. 240, notes the Virgilian allusion. Ermenric omits Virgil's fairly long description of Pasiphae's love for the bull.

[81] Ibid.; Ermenric, c. 36. "Totum se versat Gallum cantare – beatum / Gallum inquam, Domini sanctum et pietate benignum, / Cuius amore quidem cupimus nos scribere quae- dam." Cf. Virgil, *Ecl.* 6: "Then he sings of Gallus wandering to the rivers of Permessus, how one of the sisters [muses] led him into the Aonian mountains" (Tum canit, errantem Permessi ad flumina Gallum / Aonas in montis ut duxerit una sororum . . .); Donatus, in

As we have seen, Ermenric invokes the Classical rhetoric of poets who abandon one mode of poetry and take up another at a god's insistence. Usually, in this tradition, the poet rejects epic and its subjects in favor of shorter pastoral or lyric compositions. (For example, in this tradition, in *Amores* 1.1, Ovid blames Cupid – yet another supernatural interloper – for making him write love poetry.)[82] Subject, meter, and genre are all related in Classical poetry, and thus changing one of these means changing the others. Therefore, New Homer's rejection of Classical mythological topics signifies a wider rejection of Classical forms. At the beginning of this passage, Ermenric presents New Homer as being armed, which is appropriate since epic was the proper form for military topics. Echoing an earlier passage, in which he likens Grimald's virtues to pieces of armor,[83] Ermenric addresses the Rhine: "in what capacity do you gird New Homer with grammar for his melodious duty?"[84] Whereas, as the reader would know, Aeneas put on armor crafted by the god Vulcan, the personified Rhine – a gushing river symbolic of poetic excess – outfitted the rival poet, who was then scared off by Vulcan (assimilated to Orcus). Having *somehow* been armed for verse by a gushing river ("in what capacity" could the Rhine arm someone?), the poet fled the traditional armorer of epic, signifying his unfitness for the task. Ermenric's heavy reliance on Virgil's sixth *Eclogue*, which lurks just beneath the surface of chapter 36, reinforces the sentiment. The *Eclogue* begins with the shepherd-poet Tityrus rejecting (again at divine insistence) war, the subject matter of epic, in favor of small song (*deductum carmen*) on pastoral topics (lines 1–10). New Homer, like Tityrus of *Eclogue* 6, is turned from epic, to other themes. The subjects Tityrus turns to in the sixth *Eclogue*, however, are exactly those that New Homer rejects.

Unlike his rival, Ermenric did *not* take his infernal visitation as a sign that he should reject pagan literature. Ermenric's use of *saepe* (often) and the imperfect tense show that his Virgilian haunting was a recurring affliction (c. 24). He failed to exorcise the phantom, who returned and

---

Vita Virgilii c. 25, says that Augustus killed Cornelius Gallus on suspicion of conspiracy (making him the victim of a pagan Roman emperor, like a Christian martyr). Cf. Virgil, *Ecl.* 10.1–2: "Now I must sing a few songs for my Gallus: who would deny songs for Gallus?" (pauca meo Gallo ... / carmina sunt dicenda: neget quis carmina Gallo?).

[82] In *Amores* 1.1, Ovid complains that Cupid has stolen a foot of his meter transforming the epic meter, dactylic hexameter, into elegiac couplets – alternating lines of dactylic hexameter and pentameter – appropriate to more modest themes. Also, cf. Ovid, *Amores* 2.9.23.

[83] Ermenric, c. 6. Virgil names the River Eurotas as the audience at the end of *Ecl.* 6. Ermenric addresses the Rhine in his final chapter.

[84] Ibid., c. 36: "Sed qua parte novum cingas cum grammate Homerum / Arguto offitio."

continued terrifying him (*terret me visus eius*). Ermenric tells us that despite his fear, he responded to the specter with apparent scorn "as *if* I previously judged his work laughable and valueless,"[85] but clearly he did not truly consider it so, because he follows the anecdote with a series of myths and explains the necessity of pagan literature. Instead of rejecting the tradition, Ermenric employed an apotropaic response to fear by laughing back at Virgil's work as if it were a "game" (*ludus*). This seems to fly in the face of reason. New Homer's response to Orcus seems both more pragmatic and more Christian. How was Ermenric correct to fundamentally ignore a demonic vision while New Homer heeded the message? The divergent responses to the apparitions are explained by antique and early medieval ideas about dreams.

READING DREAMS

Ancient and medieval accounts do not necessarily distinguish between dreams and visions, and it is often unclear whether the recipient was awake or asleep.[86] In the early Middle Ages, dream-vision narratives were used to convey political points, moral lessons, and divine messages. They could demonstrate an individual's sanctity or impiety; they warned, admonished, satirized, and entertained.[87] They could reveal special knowledge, but were slippery and unreliable.

Ermenric draws together three dream-vision traditions: the Christian nightmare of being punished for devotion to pagan literature, the Classical topos of poetic inspiration, and the descent to the underworld (*katabasis*), which occurs in both Classical and Christian texts. As noted, the trope of

---

[85] Ibid., c. 24: "veluti ludum eius ante risibilem pro nihilo habui."

[86] From the large literature on medieval dreams, see in particular, Lisa Bitel, "'In Visu Noctis': Dreams in European Hagiography and Histories, 450–900," *History of Religions* 31 (1991): 39–59; Paul Dutton, *The Politics of Dreaming in the Carolingian Empire* (Lincoln, 1994); Isabel Moreira, *Dreams, Visions, and Spiritual Authority in Merovingian Gaul* (Ithaca, 2000); Isabel Moreira, "Dreams and Divination in Early Medieval Canonical and Narrative Sources: The Question of Clerical Control," *Catholic Historical Review* 89 (2003): 621–642; Jacques Le Goff, "Dreams in the Culture and Collective Psychology of the Medieval West," in Jacques Le Goff, *Time, Work and Culture in the Middle Ages*, trans. Arthur Goldhammer (Chicago, 1980), pp. 201–204. See Kruger, *Dreaming in the Middle Ages*, p. 7 for Scriptural examples. Macrobius, *Ciceronis Somnium Scipionis cum Commentariis Macrobii* in *Opera quae supersunt*, vol. 1, ed. Ludwig von Jan (Quedlinberg, 1848).

[87] On the first of these, see Dutton, *Politics of Dreaming*, pp. 30–31. An example of a vision parody is Walafrid Strabo's poem *De quodam somnio ad Erluinum*, in MGH Poetae 2, pp. 364–365. Discussed in Kruger, *Dreaming in the Middle Ages*, p. 127.

the nightmare about the Classics derives from Jerome's famous dream.[88] As the most-read pagan author and the tradition's representative, Virgil was often the focus of the expressions of anxiety about the Classics and, therefore, a recurring figure in Classical nightmares.[89] The second tradition, in which a vision figure provides divine poetic inspiration, reaches back to the Greek poets Hesiod and Callimachus. Ermenric would have encountered it in works by Latin writers including Horace, Lucretius, Ovid, Boethius, and Fulgentius.[90] The third tradition, the *katabasis*, is common in both Classical and Christian literature (the latter also features heavenly ascents). Its *locus classicus* is *Aeneid*, book 6, which draws on Homer's *Odyssey*, as medieval readers knew from Servius's commentary.[91] Christian examples include the prose and verse *Visiones Wettini*, by Heito and Walafrid Strabo, respectively.[92] Ermenric's account also draws on parodies of these vision literatures, including the Pseudo-Virgilian *Culex* (a mock epic account of a mosquito's *katabasis*) and Fulgentius's *Continentia Virgiliana* with its unpleasant and sarcastic ghost Virgil.[93]

Despite variant taxonomies, Classical and early medieval authorities on the subject agree that it is difficult to glean the source, meaning, and veracity of a dream. In epic tradition, true dreams are sent from the underworld through the gate of horn and false ones through the gate of ivory. Dream theorists from late antiquity complicate this notion by writing that dreams could be inspired by the dreamer's physical or emotional state or by external powers, benevolent or divine.[94] The problem for medieval dreamers was determining the source of their experiences in

---

[88] Jerome, *Ep.* 22.30 *Ad Eustochium*.

[89] Laird, "Poetics and Afterlife," p. 52; Comparetti, *Vergil in the Middle Ages*, pp. 92–93; Ziolkowski and Putnam, *Virgilian Tradition*, pp. 893ff., for more examples.

[90] Horace, *Sat.* 1.10. On Lucretius, see discussion in the following. See Bede on Caedmon, for an entirely Christian example of this trope. Bede, *Historia ecclesiastica gentis Anglorum*, book 4, c. 24, in *Bede's Ecclesiastical History of the English People*, ed. B. Colgrave and R.A.B. Mynors (Oxford, 1969). Fulgentius, *Mitologia*, Book 1, prologue, ed. Rudolf Helm, *Fabii Planciadis Fulgentii Opera* (Leipzig, 1898), p. 8.

[91] "Indeed all of Virgil is full of wisdom and this book most of all, of which the greater part derives from Homer" (Totus quidem Vergilius scientia plenus est, in qua hic liber possidet principatum, cuius ex Homero pars maior est). Maurus Servius Honoratus, *In Vergilii carmina commentarii. Servii Grammatici qui feruntur in Vergilii carmina commentarii*, ed. George Thilo and Hermann Hagen (Leipzig, 1881), pref. to book 6.

[92] Laird, "Poetics and Afterlife," p. 72, on the *Visio Pauli*. Other examples include Pseudo-Dionysius's *Visio Carpi* (see chapter 1). On the *Visio Wettini*, see Dutton, *Politics of Dreaming*, pp. 63–67.

[93] Laird, "Poetics and Afterlife," pp. 67–71, on what Laird calls the "gnatabasis" (p. 71).

[94] On the causes of dreams, see Manfred Weidhorn, "The Anxiety Dream in Literature from Homer to Milton," *Studies in Philology* 64 (1967): 65–82.

order to act on them correctly. According to Macrobius, dreams can be divided into five categories of which three (*oraculum, visio,* and *somnium*) convey truth while the others (*insomnium* and *visum*) give false information.[95] In the first category, an *oraculum* features an authority figure who imparts information, whereas a *somnium* conveys the truth in hidden form.[96] Calcidius, another popular authority on dreams from late antiquity, employs the terms differently, but expresses similar ideas.[97] He writes that dreams can originate from mundane sources, such as the sleeper's concerns, anxieties, emotions, and physical state, or they can be imposed by an external force as a warning or punishment.[98] The writers agree that dreams need to be understood according to their origins and type. Some should be dismissed as meaningless or deceptive. Among meaningful dreams, some can be easily comprehended and yet others (those Macrobius calls *somnia*) require interpretation and can only be understood allegorically (*allegorice*). The language Macrobius and Calcidius use for dream classification and interpretation is extremely similar to the terminology Christian writers use for poetry (*mendacia, inania, fantasmata, ficta*), another realm in which truth could hide under the guise of *figmenta*.[99] Cicero, in his refutation of divination, likens dreams, which are obscure and difficult to interpret, to poetry and philosophy.[100] Dreams, like literature (both pagan writings and Scripture), need to be read for their underlying meanings rather than on a merely superficial level. So, as Bitel summarizes it,

sleepers find it particularly difficult to distinguish between false and true dreams because they dream in symbols and allegory.... Thus, only virtuous men understand dreams, while foolish dreamers mistake illusions for the real thing. Clearly, only the righteous recognize true dreams.[101]

---

[95] Kruger, *Dreaming*, p. 21.

[96] Macrobius, *Commentarius in somnium Scipionis*, 1.3.8, 1.3.10; Kruger, *Dreaming*, pp. 22–23.

[97] Calcidius, *Commentarius*, c. 249–56, ed. J. H. Waszink, *Timaeus a Calcidio translatus commentarioque instructus* (Leiden, 1962), discussed in Kruger, *Dreaming*, pp. 24–32.

[98] Calcidius, *Commentary on the Timaeus*, c. 250.

[99] Kruger, *Dreaming*, p. 35. The examples are taken from Strabo, *Visio Wettini*, pp. 53–54, cited by Kruger, p. 127. On truth and poetry, see Chapter 1 of the present book.

[100] Cicero, *De Divinatione*, 2.64. Cicero quotes Chryssipus as saying divination is "the power to discern and explain what is signified by gods to men in sleep" (esse vim cernentem et explanantem quae a dis hominibus significentur in somnis). Cicero the skeptic asks, "Wouldn't this require wisdom and outstanding intellect and complete learning?" (prudentia an et ingenio praestanti et eruditione perfecta). Thus, the skills and qualities of the dream interpreter would need to parallel those of the philosopher.

[101] Bitel, "In Visu Noctis," p. 46.

Ermenric does not explicitly state what kind of dream-vision he experienced, but he gives a context and implies a cause for his vision – he was reading Virgil and fell asleep with his head on the book. Sleeping with books under one's head was a literal *in-cubation* affecting sleep, and dream theorists since Aristotle were aware that the thoughts and concerns of waking life could cause dreams.[102] Ermenric implies that his dream was brought on by his reading rather than the result of a demonic visitation. He is more straightforward about the etiology of New Homer's vision: his rival was suffering from indigestion. According to Gregory the Great's much-read *Dialogues*, this is one of the causes of dreams.[103] (Cicero says that the Pythagoreans prohibited the eating of beans for this reason.)[104] Clearly, New Homer did not consider this possibility when he responded to Orcus. In Macrobius's terms, he mistook a *visum* (in which the dreamer, half-asleep, sees illusory figures, including incubi and specters) for an *oraculum* sent to warn or punish and responded accordingly.[105] Ermenric, by contrast, followed the advice given in Prudentius's hymn before sleep (to which he alludes):

> Be sure, when sleep calls
> And you seek your chaste cell,
> To sign your forehead and the place of your heart
> In the form of a cross.
> The cross repels every crime.
> Shades flee from the cross:
> Marked with such a sign,
> The mind cannot be restless.
> Go away, away, omens of

[102] Dutton gives a Greek example from Plutarch of Alexander the Great sleeping with a poem and a dagger under his pillow. Dutton, *Politics of Dreaming*, p. 4. Hildebert of Lavardin's early-twelfth-century prose *vita* of Hugo, abbot of Cluny, echoes Ermenric's encounter, because his bad dream is inspired by having a book of Virgil under his pillow. See *Vita Sancti Hugonis* 18 (PL 159, 872A–B), printed and trans. in Ziolkowski and Putnam, *Virgilian Tradition*, pp. 893–894. On waking life as the cause of dreams, see Manfred Weidhorn, "The Anxiety Dream in Literature from Homer to Milton," *Studies in Philology* 64 (1967): 72. Weidhorn cites Latin sources for this idea including Cicero, *De Divinatione* 2.62, 67–68; Lucretius 4.962ff.; Petronius, fragment 31; Claudian's *Panegyric* to Honorius.

[103] Walafrid Strabo, *Ad Erluinum*; Kruger, *Dreaming*, pp. 45, 128. Gregory, *Dialogues* IV, 40.2, a discussion that Kruger notes is repeated almost identically in Gregory's *Moralia in Job* I. See also, Cicero, *De Divinatione* 2.58, on indigestion as a cause of dreams: "iam Pythagoras et Plato, locupletissimi auctores, quo in somnis certiora videamus, praeparatos quodam cultu atque victu proficisci ad dormiendum iubent; faba quidem Pythagorei utique abstinere, quasi vero eo cibo mens, non venter infletur."

[104] Cicero, *De Div.* 2.58.

[105] Macrobius, *Commentarius*, 1.3.7.

> Wandering dreams.
> With this steadfast gesture,
> Deceiver, be far away,
> Twisting snake,
> You who stir up quiet hearts
> With a thousand convoluted ways
> And twisting lies,
> Depart! Christ is here.
> Here is Christ – melt away.
> You know the sign that
> Condemns your crowd.[106]

Both Ermenric and New Homer responded to the visions with fear, but only the former employed the religious gesture Prudentius recommended as the response to the ambiguity of dreams. Since the sign of the cross did not expel the Virgilian shade, he clearly was not a demon, according to Prudentius's criteria. By contrast, New Homer took his vision of Orcus at face value and therefore misunderstood it. The lesson of the Virgilian vision was, surprisingly, not that the Classics are a danger to be shunned, but rather that they were useful in the service of Christian learning. The spectral forms of Virgil and Orcus, then, functioned, like other Christian nightmares about the Classics, to test (and perhaps rebuke) the dreamer's loyalties. The shades acted (as monsters so often do) as the trial in a rite of passage. Both Ermenric and New Homer faced the test, but only Ermenric responded correctly by not taking Virgil's works too seriously (treating them *as if* they were laughable) and simultaneously recognizing their value. New Homer read the dream, as he read his Classics, literally. By rejecting the Classics entirely, the rival poet misinterpreted the meaning of his encounter with Orcus.

Faced with a threatening pagan writer, Ermenric came to the conclusion, conventional since Tertullian, Jerome, and Augustine, that the Classics are useful and should be read: "the words of the pagan poets, although foul because false, provide much assistance in understanding Scripture."[107] Christian *auctores* profess hostility toward pagan literature

---

[106] Prudentius, *Cath.* 6, line 129ff.: "fac, cum vocante somno / castum petis cubile, / frontem locumque cordis / crucis figura signet. / crux pellit omne crimen, / fugiunt crucem tenebrae: / tali dicata signo/ mens fluctuare nescit. / procul, o procul vagantum / portenta somniorum, / procul esto pervicaci / praestigiator actu. / o tortuose serpens, / qui mille per meandros / fraudesque flexuosas / agitas quieta corda, / discede, Christus hic est, / hic Christus est, liquesce. / signum quod ipse nosti / damnat tuam catervam...."

[107] Ermenric, c. 25: "dicta paganorum poetarum licet foeda sint, quia non sunt vera, multum tamen adiuvant ad percipiendum divinum eloquium." Cf. Tertullian, *De Praescr.* 7 and *De Idol.* 10; Jerome's dream: Jerome, *Ep.* 22.30.

and, like Ermenric, insult and abjure it, but also grudgingly allow its educational utility. Tertullian, who asks what Rome had to do with Jerusalem, nonetheless acknowledges profane learning as a tool for gaining divine knowledge.[108]

Repudiating one's Classical learning was not only undesirable but also practically impossible, because it was bound up in the writer's fundamental education. Even if Christian writers wanted to rid themselves of its influence, as they sometimes claimed, they seemed unable to do so. Jerome's writing, after his Classical nightmare, still retains a Classical flavor, and well after despairing of his youthful zeal for Virgil, Augustine continued to draw on him heavily.[109]

As Horace and Sedulius agree, verses that were read repeatedly and imbibed in youth were imprinted in the mind.[110] In an unusually positive statement about the poet, an annotation in a ninth-century schoolbook from Reichenau states that "the very small ones definitely should read Virgil, because he is certainly the best and most renowned poet of all, and the best thing lapped up by tender souls is not easily erased. As Horace says: 'The pot that is doused when new will preserve the scent for a long time.'"[111] The author of this sentiment draws on Augustine but implicitly

---

[108] J.E. Sandys, *A History of Classical Scholarship*, vol. 1 (Cambridge, 1903), p. 615, citing Tertullian *De Praescr.* 7 and *De Idol.* 10. The *auctores* justify their use of the pagan sources using Scriptural metaphors. Jerome likens pagan *sapientia* to the prescriptions on converting and marrying a captive gentile woman in Deuteronomy 21.10–14 (*Ep.* 22; *Ep.* 70.2, 5), and Hraban Maur follows him (*De clericorum institutione* III, 18, PL107, 396). Augustine also uses an image from the Old Testament to justify the Christian appropriation of the Classics, likening it to the theft of the pharaoh's gold in Exodus (*De Doctrina Christiana*, 2.40). Cassiodorus takes Moses as a precedent for using Classical sources (*Div. Lect.* C. 28).

[109] Jerome's *Ep.* 22 was written in 384 and *Ep.* 70 in 397. Sabine MacCormack, *The Shadows of Poetry: Vergil in the Mind of Augustine* (Berkeley, 1998). Augustine recounts his own youthful devotion to pagan texts in harsh terms: "flebam Didonem extinctam ferroque extrema secutam, sequens ipse extrema condita tua relicto te, et terra iens in terram" (*Confessiones*, 1.13), but concedes their utility: "Sicut enim Aegyptii non solum idola habebant et onera gravia, quae populus Israel detestaretur et fugeret, sed etiam vasa atque ornamenta de auro et argento, et vestem, quae ille populus exiens de Aegypto sibi potius tamquam ad usum meliorem clanculo vindicavit" (*De Doctrina Christiana*, 2.40, drawing on Exodus 12.33–36).

[110] Sedulius, *Ep. to Macedonius*, discussed in the Introduction to this book, printed in Springer, "Sedulius," p. 10.

[111] "Virgilium nempe propterea parvuli legunt, ut videlicet poeta magnus omnium praeclarissimus atque optimus teneris ebibitus animis non facile oblivione posit aboleri, secundum illud Hoartii: 'Quo semel est imbuta recens, servabit odorem testa diu.'" Printed and translated in Ziolkowski and Putnam, eds., *The Virgilian Tradition* (New Haven, 2008), pp. 280–281. The quotation within this passage is to Horace, *Epistles* 1.2.69–70. *Vita*

reverses the church father's negative valuation.[112] This education, which imbued students with Classical learning at an impressionable age, would leave the language and imagery imprinted in their minds, even if they ceased to read it in later in life.[113]

Some modern scholars, taking medieval pronouncements on the Classics at face value, have posited a contradiction between the ethics and practices of Christian writers, who both repudiate and employ pagan sources.[114] The condemnation of the Classics, however, is a literary trope, which, like the humility topos, should not often be read literally. Framing the rejection of pagan literature in Classical allusions and form is common in early medieval literature.[115] The topos represents a rhetoric of rejection, which their learned allusions simultaneously expressed and subverted. The professed repudiation gave the writer opportunity for parading his or her learning. For example, Gregory of Tours, in his preface to the *Libri miraculorum*, starts with Jerome's dream and then employs the Classical trope of *praeteritio*, and by enumerating precisely what he claims to bypass exhibits the knowledge he manifestly condemns.[116] So, Alcuin uses a Virgilian quote to admonish a friend for reading Ovid.[117]

These repudiations, then, were not in earnest. As Ermenric's response to Virgil – treating his *ludus* as laughable – shows, the threat of the Classical tradition was the object of literary play. The hostility of Christianity to the

---

Noricensis II, cited by Goullet, p. 219; Hollis Ritchie Upson, "Medieval Lives of Virgil," *Classical Philology* 38 (1943): 104; Sankt Paul im Lavanttal MS Samblasianus d. 86.

[112] Augustine, *De civitate Dei*, 1.3, ed. B. Dombart and A. Kalb, CCSL 47 (Turnholt, 1955).

[113] Leclercq, *Love of Learning*, p. 156.

[114] This idea is pronounced, for example, in the scholarship of C.H. Haskins. *The Renaissance of the Twelfth Century* (Cambridge, MA, 1933). Sandys, *History of Classical Scholarship*, vol. 1; Leclercq, *Love of Learning*.

[115] Bede's metric *carmen* of Queen Etheldrida, on pp. 122–123 of the Ermenric manuscript provides a similar example; Bede, lines 3–7: "Let Maro [Virgil] sing about wars, we sing of the gifts of peace, let Maro sing about the wars. / My songs are chaste, not the rape of Helen / Opulence will be for the shallow people, my songs are chaste. Let me speak of heavenly gifts, not the battles of wretched Troy ..." (Bella Maro resonet, nos pacis dona canamus / Munera nos Christi, bella Maro resonet. / Carmina casta mihi, fedae non raptus Helenae; / Luxus erit lubricis, carmina casta mihi. / Dona superna loquar, miserae non proelia Troiae). Gneuss and Lapidge note that Bede recycles this hymn in his *Historia Ecclesia* IV.18. Helmut Gneuss and Michael Lapidge, "The Earliest Manuscript of Bede's Metrical *Vita S. Cudbercti*," *ASE* 32 (2003): 53.

[116] P.J. Archambault, "Gregory of Tours and the Classical Tradition," in *The Classics in the Middle Ages*, ed. A.S. Bernardo and S.L. Levin (Binghamton, NY, 1990), pp. 25–34, at p. 29.

[117] Alcuin *Ep.* 13, ed. E. Dümmler, MGH Ep. 4, p. 39, cited in Leclercq, *Love of Learning*, p. 140.

Classics was, in fact, a creative tension.[118] For example, Fulgentius approaches the problem by having Virgil appear from beyond the grave to allegorize his own work. Instead of ignoring the conflict between Virgil's paganism and his Christian interpretation of the *Aeneid*, Fulgentius has Virgil say, in a meta-textual exchange, that he will not address the issue because he did not sign up for that when he agreed to be the narrator.[119]

By the mid-ninth century, there was a corpus of Christian epic verse, including epic *vitae*, which incorporated many features of its pagan forebears, including learned allusion, mythology, and rhetorical tropes. Because it was thoroughly embedded in the Classical tradition, Christian writing could not supplant pagan literature without losing much of its own resonance.[120] Many features that made these works erudite and scholarly by Carolingian standards – including the window allusions to melded Classical and Christian sources and the subverted repudiation trope itself – would be rendered moot were their Classical sources suppressed or removed from the canon. Christian literature did not replace but complemented the Classical tradition. The further Christian writing moved from its Classical heritage, the less it would appeal to learned readers, and the less appropriate it would be for education, which sought to impress eloquence and erudition on its students. Classicism and culture remained intertwined. Classical literature, particularly Virgil, not only taught eloquence and textual interpretation but also provided the source that writers, especially poets, mined for allusion to illustrate their subtlety and skill. The late antique Christian epic poets and the more recent epic saints' lives could complement but not supplant the Classical heritage.[121]

SMALL SONGS FOR THE SMALL ONES

New Homer's failure to grasp the function and correct use of the Classics has, according to Ermenric, three intertwined consequences. First, as we have seen, it will prevent him from composing epic. Ermenric's myriad allusions to Classical texts in which the poet is converted from one genre

[118] As Allen characterizes Andreas Capellanus's response to Ovid. See P.L. Allen. *The Art of Love: Amatory Fiction from Ovid to the* Romance of the Rose (Philadelphia, 1992), pp. 59–60.

[119] Fulgentius, *Continentia*, p. 103.

[120] Irvine, *Textual Culture*, p. 153.

[121] On the late antique Christian epic poets in the curriculum, see Günter Glauche, *Schullektüre im Mittelalter*, Münchener Beiträge zur Mediävistik und Renaissance-Forschung 5 (Munich, 1970).

(usually epic) to another (a shorter form) underline this.[122] Following New Homer's rejection of the Classics, Ermenric counsels him: "yield the great things to great teachers, / And give our little odes of song to the little ones."[123] Second, instead of composing great songs, New Homer is to teach "our small odes of song" (*paruae nostrae carminis odae*) to the small (*parui*). He should not be one of the "magni magistri," but a teacher of the young.

The *parvi* were students like those Ermenric addresses in the first part of his letter (c. 1–29).[124] As we saw in the previous chapter, they were not beginning students – they had already mastered the basics of literacy and were now at an intermediate level at which they began to learn scansion and interpretation. The first complex (and explicitly pagan) text these students met and the core of their curriculum was the *Aeneid*.[125] Virgil's readers are referred to as *parvi* and *parvuli*: a schoolbook from Reichenau says that the *parvi* should read Virgil, and, according to his *vita*, Alcuin was excessively devoted to Virgil when he was *parvulus*.[126]

Young students did not initially read Virgil allegorically, but literally, to learn grammar and *Latinitas*. Allegorical interpretation was a more sophisticated skill that they learned as they became more adept. Read literally, Virgil's subject matter and eloquence presented a dangerous temptation. The Classical nightmare trope expresses the dangers of youthful enthusiasm for the Classics at the expense of Scripture and Christian learning. The solution, as we have seen, was not utter rejection of this literature. Rather, the *infantes* needed to learn how to integrate the Classics into their Christian learning.

---

[122] In addition to those noted already, in c. 29 (a particularly obscure passage, apparently about his rival), he alludes to *Ecl.* 10 (lines 59–60), a poem Virgil addressed to *his* Gallus in which hunting symbolizes the rustic poetry the heartbroken Gallus undertakes in place of love elegy.

[123] Ermenric, c. 36. "Quin etiam magnas magnis concede magistris, / At parvas parvis nostras da carminis odas."

[124] Ermenric uses terms such as *parvi*, *parvuli*, and *infantes* for the beneficiaries of his teachings.

[125] Paul A. Olson, *The Journey to Wisdom: Self-Education in Patristic and Medieval Literature* (Lincoln, NE, 1995), p. 88.

[126] Annotation in the Reichenau schoolbook printed and translated in Ziolkowski and Putnam, *The Virgilian Tradition*, pp. 280–281. *Vita Noricensis* II, cited by Goullet, p. 219; Hollis Ritchie Upson, "Medieval Lives of Virgil," *Classical Philology* 38 (1943): 104; *Vita Alcuini*, ed. W. Arndt, in MGH SS 15.1, pp. 185–186. This is probably the context, also, of Ermenric's haunting, which occurred, he says, "when I was reading him [Virgil]," that is, when he was a student.

Before launching into the anecdote of the Virgilian haunting and the excursus on pagan mythology, Ermenric explains that he does so because "not all the young ones are the kind who know these things. Because of this, I lay out, if not everything, then at least a taste of the essentials for those who are ignorant or who are slow readers."[127] The context shows that "these things" (*haec*) of which some of the young are ignorant are the matters he has just been discussing, namely, the comprehension of the mystical pronouncements of the prophets "whose words are full of hidden meaning."[128] In order to understand their meaning (*intellectus*), the *infantes* must read Ermenric's disquisition on Virgil and Classical mythology that follows. The *infantes* had to learn how to incorporate Virgil, standing for Classical literature, into the Christian schema before they could employ the eloquence and the methods of reading for Christian ends (here represented by the verse composition and allegorical reading performed in Ermenric's *calx*). Like Ennius in Ermenric's anecdote, they had to learn how to get the *aurum* from the *stercus* of Virgil's literature.

Following Fulgentius and Servius, medieval readers interpreted book 6 of the *Aeneid*, one of Ermenric's sources for his vision passages, as an allegory for education.[129] As Aeneas descended into Hades and encountered his father's shade to learn of Rome's future, the students (like the young Ermenric) must endure the trial of the ghosts of the pagan past in order to achieve wisdom. Rather than rejecting this wisdom, or falling prey to its charms, they must learn how to use it in order to interpret Scripture and write eloquent Christian literature. In the arc of learning that Ermenric traces in his letter (discussed in the previous chapter), he only teaches *progymnasmata* – advanced composition exercises – after he has shown the *infantes* and *legentes*, by way of his vision and subsequent discussion, that the Classics should be integrated into Christian education.

Rumination and digestion are common metaphors for reading comprehension, and thus, New Homer's indigestion, which precipitates his vision,

---

[127] Ermenric, c. 24: "scito vero quod omnes infantes tales non sunt, qui haec ita sciant. Quapropter et si non omnia, tamen gustum ex aliquantis necessariis porrigo illis, qui nesciunt, vel qui ad legendum tardi sunt."

[128] Ibid.: "whose words are full of mystical meaning, which are established by none other than the pronouncements of the Holy Spirit, and revealed and made manifest through the mouth of the holy prophets.... I know most certainly, that all these things are little concealed from your infinite wisdom" (Quorum dicta eo sunt mystico intellectu plena quo constant non ab alio, sed ex Spiritu sancto dictata, et per os sanctorum prophetarum prolata ac propalata.... scio certissime, quod hęc omnia sapientiam tuam inexhaustam minime latent).

[129] Fulgentius, *Continentia*, p. 95; Olsen, *Path to Wisdom*, chapter 6.

signifies a failure to absorb the material.[130] Ermenric also expresses the teacher's role in alimentary metaphors; he is to excerpt, summarize, and explain the material for the students, giving them "a taste" (*gustum*) appropriate to their capacities.[131] A teacher could not perform these functions if he himself were unable to digest the curriculum's core works. He certainly could not guide the more advanced students in allegorical readings. He could not produce his own *sapientia* from the readings he had gathered and therefore could neither compose an epic *vita* nor instruct the *progymnasmata*, both of which required the digestion and transformation of reading. New Homer, who failed to digest Classical literature, cannot teach higher levels of students. In rejecting the Classics, New Homer has failed an educational rite of passage. Unlike Ermenric, he did not understand their use in the monastic curriculum. He was therefore equipped neither to teach these techniques of Scriptural (allegorical) interpretation nor to write in the classicizing genre of epic, but only to sing little songs. An epic life was an advanced text, and, as a classicizing highly allusive work, it could not be composed, or taught without a grounding in the Classics. His youthful devotion to Virgil – like Augustine's and Alcuin's – was excessive, but so was his reaction against it. Thus, like Silenus, in Virgil's sixth *Eclogue*, New Homer must sing for the *pueri*.[132]

THE BEST BREAD

The third consequence of New Homer's failure would be in relation to his patron. Because he could not interpret the meaning of dreams or Classical literature, he would not be properly prepared to read Scripture. Ultimately, liberal arts education prepared the student to understand Scripture, and therefore, it was salvific. New Homer, unfit for teaching any except the *parvi*, will be similarly unhelpful to a patron because, as Ermenric implies, he would be unable to explain the mysteries of religion. He offers a challenge: "if he doesn't cease abusing my words with his gossip, / I say, let him explain this riddle to you."[133] Posing and answering a riddle

---

[130] See Chapter 4 for alimentary metaphors for reading and writing. Also, John Scattergood, "Eating the Book: *Riddle 47* and Memory," in John Scattergood, *Manuscripts and Ghosts: Essays on the Transmission of Medieval and Early Renaissance Literature* (Dublin, 2006), pp. 83–94.

[131] Ermenric, c. 24.

[132] Virgil, *Ecl.* 6.14, 24.

[133] Ermenric, c. 30a: "si non cesset lacerans mea dicta susurro, / hoc ipse exponat posco problema tibi."

(*problema*) was a way of demonstrating intellectual stature (as Theodulf shows when he mocks Alcuin for asking riddles that everyone could answer), and they were used in the classroom.[134] Riddles are a feature of Virgil's third *Eclogue*, much to the commentator Servius's distress.[135] Ermenric then sets forth the *problema* in five lines of verse, which alternate Latin and transliterated Greek glossed in Latin. He again invokes the alimentary metaphor:

> Drink old wine, honey, milk, oil,
> And don't be surprised that you know sweet things.
> Look I speak a new word, I place the best bread before you –
> You, who will be able to eat, you and your poet.
> The wise guardian, who is dead, infuses us with zeal.[136]

The *problema* here is a riddle, but it is also, more broadly, the mystery of the incarnation. The paradoxical figure of the dead guardian who breathes life into his followers, who offers the bread, is of course Christ.[137] Presumably, New Homer would not be able to explain the riddle or the mystery of the Eucharist because he could not read Greek and would not recognize the allusions. Because a Classical education was necessary for understanding Scripture, New Homer would be unable to assist his patron's salvation. Isidore, following earlier sources, defines *aenigma* as allegory of a particularly veiled (*obscurus*) kind, shadowed and perceived through images (*per quasdam imagines adumbratus*).[138] New Homer's inability to answer the riddle would be part of his demonstrated wider inability at allegorical interpretation. Christ's cross was fertile and

---

[134] Theodulf, *Carmen* 25 in MGH Poetae 1, pp. 483–489; and Godman, *Poetry*, pp. 150ff. See also Martha Bayless, "Alcuin's *Disputatio Pippini* and the Early Medieval Riddle Tradition," in *Humour, History and Politics in Late Antiquity and the Early Middle Ages*, ed. Guy Halsall (Cambridge, 2002), pp. 157–178.

[135] Virgil, *Ecl.* 3, lines 104–107; Servius's commentary on *Ecl.* 3: "sciendum aenigmata haec sicuti pleraque carere aperta solutione." D.E.W. Wormell, "The Riddles in Virgil's Third Eclogue," *Classical Quarterly* 10 (1960): 29–32. The obscurity of medieval riddles in general is attested by the vast number of articles generating variant solutions. Randall Munroe of xkcd observes that "there's no reason to think that people throughout history didn't have just as many inside jokes and catchphrases as any modern group of high-schoolers."

[136] "*Oenon paleon pimelin gallan eleon* / Et non miraris dulcia nosse tua / *Neon ide lalo rema sison ripho ariston* / Vescere quis poteris tuque poeta tuus. / *Phrontistes phronimos phisa philoponia nechros*." Italics indicate lines in transliterated Greek. The last line is glossed with the Latin "curator sapiens sufflat studium mortuus," with the verb *sufflare* perhaps indicating a reference to the insufflation of the Holy Spirit in baptismal rites.

[137] John 6:35: "dixit autem eis Iesus 'ego sum panis vitae qui veniet ad me non esuriet et qui credit in me non sitiet umquam.'"

[138] Irvine, *Textual Culture*, p. 231, citing Isidore, *Etymologiae*, 1.37.22.26.

produced the crop (eternal life). From this crop, Ermenric can offer the "bread of life," which allows others to share in the blessing.[139] New Homer, by contrast, just gets indigestion.

Ermenric uses the familiar trope of sweet things and other foodstuffs as the support that patrons provide poets and the sustenance that teachers provide students.[140] Wine, butter, milk, and oil are all recurring Biblical images, although all four never occur in the same passage.[141] Goullet notes that Walafrid's *Vita Galli* includes a similar list of foodstuffs,[142] and so the poet offers his patron something Gall's disciple gives the saint. The references to honey and eating also tie Ermenric's *problema* to Samson's famous Scriptural riddle of the lion.[143]

Ermenric uses metaphors of eating and drinking for intellectual and spiritual nourishment throughout his letter (most frequently in the trope of drinking wisdom through the ears). Ultimately, the good poet/teacher was the interpreter for both the patron and the student and led them to the understanding necessary for salvation. The "new speech" (again, presumably Greek) and the "best bread" will nourish both patron and poet ("vescere … tuque poeta tuus"), both Grimald and Ermenric. The poet will be able to eat because his patron feeds him, and they will both eat the bread of salvation, understanding the mystery of the resurrection. Although it is impossible to praise Christ enough, says Ermenric,

> Nonetheless, take a taste of this with praise of his triumph.
> Examine the last things in the noted verses attached,
> And remember to support me with holy prayer,
> So that the Muse can play, by carrying the pears (*pyres*).

---

[139] Among the copious Scriptural references: Matthew 4:4; Luke 22:19; John 6:33, 35, 41, 48–52, 59; 13:18; 1 Corinthians 5:8, 10, 16–17; 11:23, 26–28.

[140] Godman, *Poets*, c. 1 discusses alimentary imagery for patronage.

[141] These four substances appear together in the apocryphal Apocalypse of Paul and as the four rivers surrounding the city of Christ and in Pseudo-Jerome, associated with the four evangelists. See Jennifer O'Reilly, "Patristic and Insular Traditions of the Evangelists: Exegesis and Iconography of the Four-Symbols," n.p., http://www.ucc.ie/latinbible/oreilly.htm#_edn38 (accessed August 9, 2010).

[142] Walafrid, *Vita Galli*, c. 17; Goullet, p. 233. Walafrid's *Vita Galli* contains slightly different foodstuffs: "in accordance with custom, John the deacon brought him unleavened bread, a small flask of wine, oil and butter, and honey in a small container, with roast fish" (Joannes diaconus, secundum consuetudinem obtulit ei panes azymos et lagunculam vini, oleum et butyrum, et mel in vasculis cum piscibus assis).

[143] Having eaten (*comedere*) the honeycomb (*favus mellis*) that he found in the mouth of the slain lion, Samson challenged the Philistines, asking the *problema* of what "food came from the devourer and sweetness from the strong" (de comedente exivit cibus et de forte est egressa dulcedo; Judges 14:8–14).

These are better than cakes and Syrian pears.[144]
In these things we ask for God's help.
The Muses will not weave soft songs with fine thread,
With my shining garment of the lord.[145]

The soul needs sustenance as much as the body, but Ermenric implies that
Gozbert derived no spiritual food from his protégé: "such a bald man will
never be saved."[146] Ermenric draws together the themes of the student
deriving sustenance from the teacher (expressed in the image of drinking
from the river) and the salvific power of the host to imply that New Homer,
unlike Ermenric, could provide his patron with no spiritual benefit.

IF THE SHOE FITS

The previous chapter explored how Ermenric depicts himself instructing
intermediate and advanced students in order to show his qualifications for
being a teacher. He makes the same point through his claims to poetic
succession. He places himself not only in the epic tradition of Homer,
Ennius, Lucretius, and Virgil but more immediately sets himself up as
heir to the teachers Grimald and Walafrid also.

Ermenric expresses the transmission of magisterial and poetic authority
using the symbol of the *coturnus*. The *coturnus*, a kind of boot worn in
Classical comedy, becomes a medieval metaphor for poetry as a whole.[147]
Ermenric associates three individuals with the *coturnus*. Initially, Grimald
wears the boot as well as the garment of the seven liberal arts (a Boethian
allusion): "you are supremely clever in poetry as in all the ancestral arts, so
much so that you go forth wondrously, sometimes wearing the comic boot,
at other times a seven-fold garment that Wisdom herself had woven for
you."[148] Later, Ermenric associates the *coturnus* with Walafrid, who

---

[144] Ermenric puns on *pyra* (for *pira*) and Pyerides (*muses*). In keeping with the theme of life in
death, he uses *suprema* (also meaning funeral rites) and *pyra* (pyres). On the Virgilian
Syrian pears, see Goullet, pp. 227–228.

[145] "Sume tamen gustum hic huius cum laude triumphi, / Versibus innixis cerne suprema notis /
Et sancta prece sic me sustentare memento, / Ludere quo possit Musa ferendo pyra. /
Crustumiis Syriisque pyris sunt haec potiora / In quibus auxilium poscimus ad
Dominum. / Mollia Pyerides subtili carmina filio/ Non nebunt, Domini veste nitente mihi."

[146] Ermenric, c. 29: "talis calvus numquam erit salvus." On the soul requiring sustenance as
the body does, Ermenric, c. 6.

[147] Goullet, p. 192.

[148] c. 1: "te tam in poemate quam in omni arte priorum adprime catum, intantum, ut
interdum comico coturno, aliquando vero veste septemplici, quam Sophia sibi suis
manibus texuerat, indutus mirifice procedi."

"truly wished to adorn the deeds of most blessed Gall with poetic style."[149] Finally, when he embarks on the verse that is the culmination of the letter, he claims the *coturnus* for himself. He prays:

> that I might sing in playful poetic style (*ludente coturno*) the life of Gall,
> Which Walafrid had once composed without meter –
> O would that he had lived, joyous in our time –
> So that he could have completed the work in song with his own muse.[150]

Ermenric takes possession of the *ludens coturnus* in which Walafrid would have composed, had he lived. It is thus passed, during the letter, from poet to poet and from teacher to student, from Grimald to Walafrid to Ermenric. *Ludere* means "to mock," "to play," and "to compose verse," and the noun *ludus* means "game" or "school."[151] It is also the term that Ermenric uses for his response to the demonic Virgil, whose works he treated "as if a game" (c. 24). Goullet notes that *ludus* with its double meaning, of joke and school, is a good description of Ermenric's letter.[152] The *ludens coturnus* is not only playful but also scholarly, both a literary game and schoolwork, appropriate to Ermenric's joking muse (*musa ... iocans*).[153]

Ermenric asserts his position not only as Walafrid's poetic heir, but as Grimald's successor as *magister* and offers himself as the solution to the scarcity of teachers. He uses the novel format of the teaching letter, with verse and prose mélange appended, to demonstrate that he has the appropriate erudition and understanding of the value of the Classics to write an epic saint's life and the requisite pedagogical skills to teach one, leading students through the curriculum to the composition exercises of the *progymnasmata*.

THE REAL EPIC *VITA GALLI*

Although Ermenric probably did not complete an epic *vita*, his rival did. Allusions in the anonymous epic *Vita Galli*, dedicated to the younger

---

[149] c. 28: "voluit vero ille poǽtico coturno gesta beatissimi Galli comere."

[150] c. 33: "Rite canam ut vitam Galli ludente coturno / Quam Walafredus aplos compserat absque pede / O utinam vixisset nunc in tempore laetus, / Quo compleret opus carmine musa sua."

[151] Goullet, p. 199; Virgil, *Ecl.* 1.1, "ludere versu"; and Horace, *Satire* 1.10, line 36, "haec ego ludo"; Jerome, *Ep.* 22, "metro ludere."

[152] Goullet, p. 199.

[153] Ermenric's jokey muse (c. 30a) is an allusion to Ovid's "musa iocosa mea" (*Tristia* 2, line 354), also employed by Ermoldus, *Ep.* 2, line 24, discussed in Godman, *Poets*, p. 126.

Gozbert, show that it is almost certainly his. In the preface, the poet alludes to both Walafrid's unfulfilled intention of composing a verse counterpart to his prose and Ermenric's attempt:[154]

Now, remember my promise, dear Gozbert –
That which I once swore, I wish now to fulfill.
That rustic little dish, which at that time the cauldron had served up in prose,
It will spice up with metric flavors.
I do not miss the fact that certain people blame me for delays,
Although late, nonetheless, I repay the debt.
Since nephews know that they deserved the things promised to the fathers,
And that after many days, the seeds that were sown are reaped.
Now, if I am not deceived, sixteen times have crops returned,
Since we wrote the deeds of excellent Gall.
Then King Louis had been stripped of honor
Now another of the same name is his heir.
I begin, now, living in the wilderness [Saint-Gall],[155] a laborer in this place,
Which father Gall inhabited and loved, nourishing it.
Making verses from certain things previously written
I will tread with new steps the stony track of the well-worn way.
I will use the loftier things more than the briefer ones,
joining many crossroads in the places where they meet.[156]

The poet seems to speak in the voice of Walafrid, finally fulfilling his promise of a metric life, and being chastised for his sixteen-year delay.[157] He alludes to his source ("certain things previously written")[158] and shows that it is Walafrid by echoing that writer's statement that he would spice his "rustic little dish" (*agreste pulmentum*) of the prose *Vita Galli* with meter (*aliquibus metrorum condimentis*).[159] The anonymous

---

[154] Goullet, p. 223.

[155] *Eremus* is a name for Saint-Gall.

[156] *Vita Galli* (metric) (BHL 3253) in MGH Poetae 2, pp. 428–473, preface, lines 1–18. "Promissi memor ecce mei, Gotzberte, quod olim / Devovi ad praesens solvere, care, volo. / Pulmentum, quod agreste lebes pro tempore prosae / Apposuit, metricis condiet en salibus. / Non ignoro aliquos memet culpare morarum, / Qui quamvis sero debita solvo tamen, / Cum promisssa sciant patribus meruisse nepotes / Post multosqie dies semina iacta meti. / Iam, ni fallor, enim messes rediere bis octo / Ex quo actus Galli scripsimus egregii / Tunc Caesar Hludowicus erat nudatus honore: / Nunc heres eius nominis alter adest. / Ordior ergo heremo degens, operator in ipsa, / Quam pater incoluit Gallus amatque fovens. / Scripturae faciens epigrammata certa prioris / Tritae calle viae gressibus ibo novis / Quoque magis celsis tanto brevioribus utar / Iungens contiguis compita multa locis."

[157] A comparison of this metric *Vita Galli* with Walafrid's extensive and securely attributed verse and his prose shows that he did not write it.

[158] *Vita Galli* (metric), line 15: "Scripturae faciens epigrammata certa prioris."

[159] Walafrid, prologue to *Vita Galli* in MGH SRM 4, p. 282.

poet places Walafrid's composition at the time when "King Louis had been stripped of honor," a reference to Louis the Pious's deposition, his forced confession, and his humiliation from late 833 until his restoration in Spring 834. He locates the present work "sixteen growing seasons later" during the reign of another of the same name, that is, Louis the German. If the anonymous poet's dating is precise (the exigencies of poetry and meter may trump accuracy), then he is placing the poem in 849–850. The time frame he implies for the work would allow it to have been written by Walafrid at the very end of his life, or by a successor immediately after his death in August 849.

The anonymous epic *Vita Galli* alludes to Ermenric's letter, which suggests that Ermenric published his letter before the poet completed his epic *vita*[160] or that the poet was familiar with Ermenric's rhetoric of complaint. Ermenric describes Gozbert becoming impatient: "he was so eager in his enthusiasm, that he wished that in one and the same hour I milk the cow and make the cheese, although Rome was not built in a day and grain is not harvested on the day it is sown."[161] The anonymous author echoes Ermenric in stating that his work, although late, is reaped not one but many days after it was sown.[162] Throughout the preface, the poet draws on Ermenric's tropes and in doing so obliquely responds to his allegations. "I will tread with new steps on the stony track of the well-worn way / I will use the loftier things so much more than the briefer ones, joining many crossroads in the places where they meet."[163] He casts himself as a poet who innovates within the traditional format, taking new steps on the old path (rather than subverting the tradition completely, like Ermenric) and who connects many sources, bringing them together

---

[160] Dümmeler, the editor, gives 833 or 834 as the date implied for Walafrid's composition. Louis was not ritually reinstated until 835 by the recoronation at Metz. Louis's humiliation took place after the harvest of 833, meaning that the next harvest was 834, though it is unclear whether the verse author would place strict chronological accuracy over metric concerns and poetic expression ("bis octo," and occasion for another reference to crops and harvests, which are the metaphors he borrows from Ermenric), so we cannot be too pedantic in assigning a strict date.

[161] Ermenric, c. 28: "Est enim tam ferventis studii, ut in una eademque hora et lac velit mulgere et caseum praemere, cum nec Roma una die sit condita, sed neque triticum eo die metitur, quo seminatur."

[162] *Vita Galli* (metric), pref., line 8. See also, line 1604: "Ad calcem iam nunc propero sub calle citato," which also echoes Ermenric.

[163] Ibid., lines 16–18: "Tritae calle viae gressibus ibo novis / Quoque magis celsis tanto brevioribus utar, / Iungens contiguis compita multa locis." Dümmeler notes an allusion to Ovid, *Amores* 3.1.18, and possibly to *Ars Amatoria*. I, 52.

where they overlap, in order to produce, in best Carolingian poetic style, a densely layered allusive text.

The anonymous author, like Ermenric, practices emulation rather than imitation, although his method is different; he almost obsessively avoids verbal echoes of his prose source while speaking as if in his voice. This poet asserts his place as Walafrid's heir, on one hand, by erasing almost all trace of his predecessor's literary text and, on the other, by actually merging identities with him. Contrary to Ermenric's story, New Homer was not scared of the Classics and was capable of writing epic, as his nickname befits. The epic *Vita Galli* is heavily Ovidian, drawing frequently on the *Metamorphoses, Fasti, Ars Amatoria, Amores*, and *Tristia*, as well as on Scripture, Virgil, and Christian poets. Even if he had suffered the haunting Ermenric imagines, such an experience would not have turned him from the Classics, any more than it did Jerome, Augustine, and Alcuin.

*

Ermenric's apparitions draw together the themes of poetic inspiration and the use of pagan literature. His own paired visions of the mocking Virgil and the comforting saint provide the perfect muses for an epic *vita*, a text that exemplifies the integration of Classical and Christian traditions. Ermenric asserts his place as a teacher and a poet by placing himself in the dual lineages of Frankish Christian poets, particularly Walafrid Strabo, and pagan epic poets. He does so by employing a strikingly original form, a kind of literary *problema* or *ludus* to demonstrate his abilities.

As discussed in the previous chapter, Ermenric implies that he was a junior *magister* at Saint-Gall, who prepared the *infantuli* for more advanced studies with senior *magistri*.[164] I have suggested that he depicted himself at work in the classroom as a bid for promotion in order to become a master who taught the more advanced students. His epic *Vita Galli*, as a work encapsulating its writer's erudition and a teaching text, was central to Ermenric's claims, but, as discussed in the previous chapter, it probably never existed. He asserted his place in the epic tradition, without actually writing an epic poem. The letter, thus, served in place of the epic, proving both his erudition and his having properly assimilated the Classics. Ermenric showed both the extent of his Classical learning – and through the novelty of his conceit – his ability to subordinate it to his own ends.

---

[164] Ermenric, c. 16.

Again, the study of the composition and exchange of epic *vitae* offers new perspectives on the culture of the Central Middle Ages. Examining attitudes toward the Classics from this angle provides insight into how Christians understood the role of the Classics in the intertwined areas of education, patronage, and epic verse composition. Like the Classics themselves, the trope of their rejection should not be read at face value. Far from being repudiated, they were recognized as necessary in learning how to interpret Scripture and one's own experience. New Homer's inappropriate response to them (personified by Orcus) revealed his supposed incapacity as an epic poet, as a teacher, and as an *amicus* who could assist his patron in understanding Scripture. Unlike Ermenric, who combined these roles in his letter (which was a pedagogical work, a theological discussion for Grimald, and a substitute epic poem), New Homer would be unable to teach advanced students, write epic, or help his patron attain salvation. He approached everything too literally, even his own dreams.

4

Bishops, Monks, and Mother Bees: An Epic *Vita* at the Millennium

Around the year 1000, Johannes of Saint-Amand composed an epic *vita* of Amand's disciple, Rictrude. Writing a century and a half after his abbey's preeminent poet Milo composed the epic *Vita Amandi*, Johannes sent his work out into a very different world. Territorial fragmentation, dynastic change, and cultural developments had rendered Saint-Amand, once a school of the Carolingian princes, peripheral to networks of power and patronage. At the turn of the millennium, the abbey was on the borders: in Capetian France, close to the boundary with Ottonian Lotharingia, in the territory of Flanders. The abbey was also subject to competing local authorities, including bishops and reformers. Further, Saint-Amand was no longer a royal abbey. Whereas the Carolingians had been its major bene-factors in the eighth and ninth centuries, the tenth-century Carolingian and Capetian kings were not great patrons of learning, and the counts of Flanders directed their munificence to other abbeys.[1] Meanwhile, the rise of courtier bishops in the mid-tenth century challenged monasticism's cultural centrality. These men, educated at cathedral schools rather than monasteries, formed networks of power and patronage from which regular clergy were increasingly excluded.

Faced with his abbey's diminished wealth and influence, Johannes framed the forms of cultural capital available to him – Saint-Amand's patron saint and its past prestige – in an epic *vita* that demonstrated his place in spiritual and intellectual communities beyond the cloister. He did so by writing "like a mother bee," as his reader Rainer describes it, crafting an epic that

---

[1] McKitterick, *Frankish Kingdoms*, pp. 278–279.

appealed to the common educational traditions of monks and bishops.[2] The bee image is a leitmotif in this chapter, representing a way of reading and writing that characterized both Johannes and Rainer and demonstrated their membership in the educated elite. Their "textual community," constituted by the literary canon and interpretive methods acquired in cloister and cathedral schools, valued the composition of poetry as the preeminent sign of education and culture.

Johannes's subject Rictrude was the saint of Marchiennes, a lesser abbey on the River Scarpe, but, by featuring Amand prominently, he made her epic life a monument to his own house's patron. By drawing heavily on the works of his abbey's two most famous literary figures, Milo and Hucbald, Johannes invoked Saint-Amand's ninth-century apogee and the set of relations created and embodied by the exchange of epic *vitae* in that period. By dedicating the epic *vita* to Erluin of Cambrai, he sought to ingratiate himself with a bishop whose network included the cathedral schools of Liège and Rheims and the imperial court of Otto III and, after 1002, Henry II.[3] Johannes also sent the life to Rainer and Stephan, two monks of another of Amand's foundations, Saint-Pierre-au-Mont-Blandin in Ghent (Blandin) to associate himself with this prosperous and prestigious branch of the saint's spiritual family.

After briefly describing Johannes's text, I explore its contexts – the regional politics of Saint-Amand and the rise of courtier bishops and cathedral schools – in order to understand why he wrote a saint's life in epic verse. To see how Johannes appealed to the cultural heritage he shared with bishop Erluin and the monks of Blandin, I examine how the cathedral and monastic schools perpetuated interpretive methods, characterized by reading and writing "like a bee." Some scholarship has posited a radical break between the Carolingian monastic schools and the later tenth- and eleventh-century cathedral schools, but I argue that there was considerable commonality among the institutions and that Johannes was able to draw on this shared heritage. Poetry continued to be the apex of education, the highest of literary gifts for patrons, and a vehicle for rivalries. I then turn to Johannes's composition to explore how this epic *vita* reflects the intellectual continuities between cathedral and cloister. Finally, I consider

---

[2] *Epistola Raineri* (printed with Johannes's VR in MGH Poetae 5/3), p. 595.

[3] Until its division in 1094, the diocese of Arras-Cambrai (usually referred to as Cambrai) traversed French and German territories. Arras, on the west bank of the Scheldt was in Flanders, in the Capetian kingdom, and Cambrai, on the east bank, was in German Lotharingia. Diane J. Reilly, *The Art of Reform in Eleventh-Century Flanders: Gerard of Cambrai, Richard of Saint-Vanne and the Saint-Vaast Bible* (Leiden, 2006), p. 9.

Rainer's short and densely allusive reply to Johannes. His unusual inter-pretation of the bee metaphor demonstrates the competitive nature and vitality of the intellectual culture in which epic lives were transmitted, as well as its considerable creativity.

JOHANNES'S EPIC LIFE

Johannes wrote his epic *Vita Rictrudis* between 995 and 1012, when Erluin was bishop of Cambrai. Johannes says he wrote at the behest of Erluin and unnamed others.[4] He mentions additional audiences for his work: monks of Blandin (including Stephan and Rainer) and, in a condescending and dismissive manner, the *clerici* of Saint Rictrude's house, Marchiennes.[5]

His *Vita Rictrudis* is found in two medieval manuscripts, both from Marchiennes. In each, it is prefaced by three affiliated texts (Johannes's six-teen-line acrostic poem of dedication to Erluin, Johannes's letter to Stephan, and Stephan's reply) and followed by the correspondence between Johannes and the monk Rainer.[6] The eleventh-century manuscript Douai, BM, MS 849 includes works on saints associated with Marchiennes (see Appendix B).[7] The second manuscript, Douai, BM, MS 836, from the later twelfth century, depends on Douai, BM, MS 849 for Johannes's *Vita Rictrudis*. It is a large lectionary largely comprising saints' *vitae* and *passiones* in prose.[8]

In more than 1,000 lines of epic dactylic hexameter, Johannes tells of Marchiennes's first abbess, Rictrude.[9] He borrows language from Milo's epic *Vita Amandi*, and bases his version of events almost entirely on the prose *Vita Rictrudis*, which Milo's student Hucbald wrote in 907.[10] As his

---

[4] Writers often deny their own abilities and claim that they wrote because compelled. Heiric says Prince Lothar begged him to write the epic *VG* (see Introduction); Ermenric says Gozbert and others asked him to compose the verse *Vita Galli* (see Chapters 2 and 3).

[5] In a variation on the humility topos, Johannes ascribes his epic's (supposed) simplicity to the limitations of the Marchiennes readership. *Epistola*, p. 566.

[6] According to the BHL, Johannes's *VR* is also in Vatican, BAV, MS. Barb. lat. 3385, fols. 201r–203v (xvii). Poncelet, "Catalogus," p. 405; Dehaisnes, *Catalogue*, pp. 595–596.

[7] Douai, BM, MS 849, fols. 93v–125v (xi$^{2/4}$). Douai's Bibliothèque municipale has been renamed the Bibliothèque Marceline Desbordes-Valmore, but for ease of reference, I give manuscript shelfmarks their conventional designation (Douai, BM) in the text. The acros-tic, BHL 7248a, is published in Poncelet, "Catalogus," p. 405.

[8] Douai, BM, MS 836, fols. 83v–92r (xii^2). Dehaisnes, *Catalogue*, pp. 567–572; Poncelet, "Catalogus," p. 382. This 233-folio codex, written in two columns, measures 450 mm × 300 mm.

[9] Julia M.H. Smith, "The Hagiography of Hucbald of Saint-Amand," *Studi medievali*, ser. 3, 35 (1994): 520.

[10] Ibid.

reader Stephan says, Johannes "gave feet to Hucbald."[11] According to Johannes's narrative, Rictrude, noble in family and character, married Adalbald (also a saint) and had four holy children, Eusebia, Clotsend, Adalsend, and Mauront.[12] After Adalbald was murdered, the king tried to force Rictrude to remarry.[13] However, with Bishop Amand's help, Rictrude tricked the king into allowing her to take the veil. Amand installed her as abbess of the double house of Marchiennes, which he had founded and entrusted to his male disciple Jonat.[14] Johannes, like Hucbald, focuses on Rictrude's role as a mother, who mourned her daughter Adalsend's death[15] and worried about her son Mauront's religious path and her daughter Eusebia's soul. This last concern led to a brutal conflict in which Rictrude ordered Mauront to beat his sister with a cane, which (according to Johannes, but not Hucbald) miraculously burst into leaf.[16] After recounting this struggle, Johannes tells of Rictrude's death, funeral, and posthumous miracles.[17]

In addition to the fairly skeletal biography of Rictrude, Johannes narrates her family's encounters with missionary bishops, particularly Amand, Richarius, and Amat.[18] Johannes also relates these bishops' interactions with royal authority, even when the meetings do not concern Rictrude. His emphasis is not on Rictrude, so much as the holy men, notably Amand, Marchiennes's original founder. For Johannes and most of his monastic and episcopal readers, Rictrude was of less interest than were the saintly bishops.

We know little of Johannes or the monastic recipients of his *vita* and only the broad outlines of Erluin's career, but we can establish the general social and political context of the work's composition and reception.[19] A short survey of the history of the abbey, the territory of Flanders, and Erluin's diocese through the early eleventh century reveals a situation marked by fragmentation of authority, violence, and changing patterns of patronage.

---

[11] Stephan, *Rescriptio Stephani*, ed. in MGH Poetae 5/3, p. 567. "Hucbaldi ... pedes dedisti."

[12] Johannes, *VR* 1.355ff.; 1.398–409.

[13] Ibid., 1.441ff.; 2.44ff.

[14] Ibid., 2.57–133.

[15] Ibid., 2.166–190.

[16] Ibid., 2.372ff.

[17] Ibid., 2.467–527.

[18] Ibid. 1.207ff.; 2.24ff.; 2.114ff.; 2.203ff.; 2.300ff.

[19] A later hand in Douai, BM, MS 849 (fol. 96r) attributes the *VR* to "Johannes of Marchiennes," but accompanying letters contradict this information. Ugé conjectures that Johannes could have been transferred there later or this could simply be a case of wishful thinking by the monks of Marchiennes. See, Ugé, *Monastic Past*, p. 128.

SAINT-AMAND

Foundation to Tenth Century

Saint-Amand-les-Eaux, also known as Elnon, was founded by the epony-mous bishop before 640 at the confluence of the Escaut (Scheldt) and Scarpe rivers in southeastern Flanders.[20] According to much later Saint-Amand sources with a vested interest in claiming royal origins, the Merovingian Dagobert (r. 629–639) donated the land.[21] Its neighbors on the Scarpe were the abbeys Marchiennes, Hamage, and Saint-Vaast. Like contemporary foundations, it contained multiple oratories.[22] Initially, its two churches were dedicated to Saint Peter and Saint Andrew, respectively. Amand was originally interred in Saint-Pierre, but by the Carolingian era, a third church had been built for his relics.[23] Alcuin's poems for the restoration of Amand's crypt in the late eighth century show that Mary, Martin, Lawrence, and Stephen were also revered, probably each at a separate altar within the third

[20] Henri Platelle has written extensively on Saint-Amand: Platelle, *Temporel*; "Les relations entre Saint-Amand et Saint-Servais de Maastricht au Moyen Âge," *Revue du Nord: Histoire & archéologie, nord de la France, Belgique, Pays-Bas* 63, no. 248 (1981): 7–13; "La ville et l'abbaye de Saint-Amand au Moyen Âge," in *Terre et ciel aux anciens Pays-Bas. Recueil d'articles de M. le Chanoine Platelle publié à l'occasion de son élection à l'Académie royale de Belgique*, Mélanges de science religieuse, numéro spécial (Lille, 1991), pp. 55–68; "Les moines dans une ville d'abbaye: le cas de Saint-Amand," in *Les moines dans la ville, actes du colloque de Lille 31 Mars et 1er Avril 1995*, Histoire médiévale et archéologie, vol. 7 (Lille, 1996), pp. 125–138; "Le premier cartulaire de l'abbaye de Saint-Amand," *Le Moyen Age* 62 (1956): 301–329; "Les relations entre l'abbaye de Saint-Amand de Rouen et l'abbaye de Saint-Amand d'Elnone," in *La Normandie bénédictine au temps de Guillaume le Conquérant* (xie siècle), ed. L. Gaillard and J. Daoust (Lille, 1967), pp. 83–106; "L'abbaye de Saint-Amand au ixe siècle," in *La Cantilène de sainte Eulalie*, Actes du Colloque de Valenciennes, 21 mars 1989, ed. Marie-Pierre Dion (Lille, 1990), pp. 18–34.

[21] Milo of Saint-Amand (d. 872), *Suppletio* (BHL 339), ed. B. Krusch in MGH SRM 5, p. 471.

[22] Platelle, *Temporel*, p. 50.

[23] P. Héliot, "Textes relatifs à l'architecture du haut Moyen Âge dans le nord de la France," *BEC* 114 (1957): 10. Milo places the construction of the third church in 677, whereas Alcuin, in his verses for Saint-Amand, says that abbot Gislebert (769–782) constructed the church of Saint-Amand. According to Milo, Eligius dedicated the church sixteen years after Amand's death on the same day that the relics were transferred to it. Platelle questions Milo's chronology, because Eligius supposedly died the year before Amand. This church is referred to as Saint-Étienne (in earlier sources) and Saint-Amand (later), perhaps, as Héliot suggests, over time becoming identified with the abbey's patron, whose relics it contained. Milo, *Suppletio* (BHL 339), ed. B. Krusch in MGH SRM 5, pp. 472–475; Alcuin, *Carmen* 88, *Inscriptiones Elnonensis monasterii*, in MGH Poetae 1, p. 305: "Hic Gislebertus praesul requiescit humatus / ... Hic pius ecclesiam sancti construxit Amandi / Cunctaque iam renovans claustra monasterii." For discussion, see Platelle, *Temporel*, pp. 50–52.

church.[24] In the early ninth century, Amand's body was exhumed and placed in a new sarcophagus.

The Carolingian kings controlled the abbacy, often granting it to their followers.[25] That a number of the abbots, from the late eighth century on, went on to become bishops attests to the abbey's importance.[26] In the imperial partition of 843, Saint-Amand fell into the eastern part of Charles the Bald's West Frankish kingdom. Five diplomas attest to his generosity to Saint-Amand.[27] His sons Pepin and Drogo were sent there in the 860s, and another, Carloman, was its abbot until his rebellion of 870.[28] Gozlin, son of the count of Mans, succeeded Carloman. He was concurrently the abbot of several houses (including Saint-Denis and Saint-Germain-des-Prés in Paris) and Charles's archchancellor.[29] As important figures with many other responsibilities, the abbots were often absent and were not necessarily invested in the abbey's well-being. Lay abbacies allowed secular magnates to exploit its resources. Saint-Amand suffered Viking attacks around 883, and Amand's relics were taken to Saint-Germain for safekeeping.[30] The raids seem to have had little long-term impact; the monks returned fairly soon, and its continued book acquisition and luxury manuscript production suggest little interruption of its prosperity or intellectual life.[31]

In first half of the tenth century, powerful laymen governed the house; Robert, brother of King Odo of Western Francia (r. 888–898) and himself king (922–923), is named abbot in documents of 906 and 921.[32] He was followed by Roger I (d. 926), count of Laon, and his son Roger II (d. 942).[33] A Count Otger is attested as the abbot in charters of 950 and 952.[34]

At this time, Saint-Amand came under the jurisdiction of Arnulf I (the Great), Count of Flanders.[35] The counts had been expanding their power for almost a century, and from the mid-tenth century, they became the

[24] Alcuin, MGH Poetae I, pp. 305–308; Héliot, "Textes relatifs," p. 11.

[25] Platelle, *Temporel*, p. 53.

[26] Ibid.

[27] For a list of Charles the Bald's diplomas in Saint-Amand's favor see Platelle, *Temporel*, p. 58, n. 28.

[28] Platelle, *Temporel*, pp. 58–59. Epitaphs for Pepin and Drogo suggest that they died at Saint-Amand. See MGH Poetae I, pp. 677–678.

[29] Platelle, *Temporel*, p. 59.

[30] Abou-El-Haj, *Medieval Cult*, p. 62.

[31] Platelle, *Temporel*, p. 69.

[32] Platelle, *Justice seigneuriale*, p. 52. Platelle notes the charters attesting to their abbacies.

[33] Ibid.

[34] Count Otger is attested in a diploma printed in Ch. Duvivier, *Actes et documents intéressant la Belgique*, vol. I, p. 22.

[35] Platelle, *Temporel*, p. 111; David Nicholas, *Medieval Flanders* (London, 1992), p. 39.

most important political figures and patrons in the region of Saint-
Amand.[36] These counts, unlike the Carolingians and Ottonians, were
not great supporters of learning and culture. They strategically cultivated
monastic houses with long-standing connections to their family, especially
Saint-Bertin in Saint-Omer to the west and Blandin in Ghent to the north.
(Baldwin I and his successors were their lay abbots, and Blandin became
the family's mausoleum.)[37] Through the counts' *translationes*, these two
abbeys became the great relic centers in Flanders.[38] Arnulf I was fanatical
about relic acquisition.[39] He needed, explains Felice Lifshitz, "a relic base,
which could serve both as a source of miraculous *virtus* and as a symbol of
identity for political community."[40] He acquired them with help from the

[36] The counts traced Carolingian royal lineage to Judith, daughter of Charles the Bald, who
had eloped with Baldwin I, Arnulf's grandfather and the first known count of Flanders.
They eloped in 861, when he was probably already the count of Ghent in northeastern
Flanders (see MGH Ep. 8, no. 155–156, p. 120, and *Annales Bertiniani* for 862).
Reconciled to his father-in-law, he received from him the countship of Flanders (the
pagus Flandrensis, the area around Bruges). Although Baldwin acted as the king's agent
in Flanders, his descendants ruled the territory virtually autonomously as a hereditary
possession and his son with Judith, Baldwin II (r. 879–918), cemented the family's prestige
by marrying Elftrude, daughter of king Alfred the Great. In the wake of Viking invasions,
Baldwin II expanded his territories and fortified the coast. Count Arnulf I "the Great" of
Flanders (r. 918–964), continuing the southward expansion, incorporated Arras, Artois,
Montreuil, and Ponthieu in the south and Ostrevant in the southeast, including Saint-
Amand. See Nicholas, *Medieval Flanders*, pp. 16–17, and François-L. Ganshof, *La Flandre
sous les premiers comtes*, 3rd ed. (Brussels, 1949), pp. 15–16.

[37] Nicholas, *Medieval Flanders*, p. 41. The *Annals of Saint-Vedast* claim that Baldwin I was
interred at Saint-Bertin (Sithiu), whereas the *Annals of Saint-Pierre-au-Mount-Blandin*
(unsurprisingly) claim he was buried at their own house. A marginal addition to Folcuin's
Gesta abbatum S. Bertini Sithiensium say that Baldwin I was buried at Saint-Bertin, but his
"cor ... et intestina" were taken to Blandin (MGH SS 13, p. 623). Cf. *Ann. Vedast et
Bland.* for 879.

[38] Edina Bozóky, "La politique des reliques des premiers comtes de Flandre (fin du IXe–fin
du XIe siècle)," in *Les reliques. Objets, cultes, symboles*, Actes du colloque international de
l' Université du Littoral-Côte d'Opale, Boulogne-sur-Mer, 4–6 septembre 1997, ed.
Edina Bozóky and Anne-Marie Helvétius (Turnhout, 1999), pp. 277–279. Arnulf seized
relics from newly acquired territories and deposited them at Saint-Bertin. He took Walric
from Leuconay in Ponthieu, Richarius from Centula, and Silvin from Auchy. Folcuin
relates Arnulf's translation of Omer's relics in 954 in *Gesta abbatum S. Bertini*, c. 109,
MGH SS 13, pp. 630–631; *Relatio Sancti Walerici*, ed. O. Holder-Egger in MGH SS 15/2,
pp. 693–698. For Arnulf's translations, see also Felice Lifshitz, "The Migration of
Neustrian Relics in the Viking Age: The Myth of Voluntary Exodus, the Reality of
Coercion and Theft," *EME* 4 (1995): 185–186.

[39] Folcuin (d. 990) describes him as "zealous about holy relics" (sanctarum reliquiarum
avidus). Folcuin, *Gesta abbatum S. Bertini*, MGH SS 13, p. 630.

[40] Lifshitz, "Migration," p. 185.

reformer and "major thief of Norman relics" Gerard of Brogne and even claimed descent from one of the stolen saints.[41]

Arnulf I also promoted monastic reform.[42] In 952, at a convention of regional bishops and abbots, he appointed Leudric, a monk from a wealthy and powerful local family, to reform Saint-Amand.[43] Arnulf also "restored all the possessions of this abbey and contributed many of his own to it in addition."[44] These reforms did not diminish the counts' influence at the abbeys.[45] The spiritual dimensions of Saint-Amand's reform are unknown, but its material effects were fleeting, as Leudric's successor, Genulf (956–968), had to disperse much of its property due to taxation.[46]

In 962, after the death of his son, Baldwin III, Arnulf negotiated with the French king Lothar; in return for receiving territory in southern Flanders on Arnulf's death, the king would support the succession of his young grandson, Arnulf II.[47] Accordingly, in 965, when the count died, Lothar reclaimed Artois and Ostrevant, which included the abbey of Saint-Amand.[48]

---

[41] Ibid., p. 183, n. 28. Arnulf forcibly obtained the relics of Wandrille and Ansbert from Thérouanne in 944 and, within a decade, was claiming the former among his ancestors. Van Werveke, "Saint-Wandrille et Saint-Pierre de Gand (IXe et Xe siècles)," in *Miscellanea mediaevalia in memoriam Jan Frederik Niermeyer*, ed. D.P. Blok et al. (Groningen, 1967), pp. 79–92.

[42] Arnulf I appointed Gerard of Brogne abbot of Blandin (where he imposed the Benedictine Rule on the reluctant canons in 941), Saint-Bertin (around 945), and other abbeys. He reformed Saint-Bavo and Saint-Vaast in 953. Nicholas, *Medieval Flanders*, p. 41; Platelle, *Temporel*, p. 114.

[43] Platelle, *Justice seigneuriale*, p. 51, and *Temporel*, p. 114. Saint-Amand's *Annals* date the reform to 952. *Annales Elnonenses*, ed. Ph. Grierson, in *Les annales de Saint-Pierre de Gand et de Saint Amand*, Recueil de textes pour servir à l'étude de l'histoire de Belgique 4 (Brussels, 1937), p. 151.

[44] Platelle, *Temporel*, p. 113; *Annales Elnonenses*, for 952: "omnes possessiones ipsius abbatie ipsi restuit et insuper de suo multa contulit." Echoed in the twelfth-century *Breve chronicon* and the thirteenth-century *Chronica brevis*. The *Chronica brevis* is edited as "Catalogus abbatum S. Amandi Elnonensis uberior" by G. Waitz in MGH SS 13, pp. 386–388. Platelle edits the *Breve Chronicon* in *Revue du Nord* 37 (1955): 217–227.

[45] For example, after its reform, Arnulf remained the "comes et abbas" of Saint-Bertin and oversaw its property, whereas a regular abbot supervised the monks' spiritual life. Platelle, *Temporel*, p. 117.

[46] Platelle, *Temporel*, pp. 115–116. *Breve chronicon*, cited by Platelle: "Genulf, for the *servitium*, which he owed the king or the count, gave more than 20 villas and ill-advisedly dispersed many other things" (Genulfus pro servitio quod debebat regi aut comiti plus quam XX villas dedit multaque alia male distraxit).

[47] Jean Dunbabin, "The Reign of Arnulf II, Count of Flanders, and its Aftermath," *Francia* 16 (1989): 56.

[48] Platelle, *Temporel*, p. 116. *Gesta Ep. Cam.* I. 100: "Sub huius autem tempore, Arnulfo sene Flandrensium comite mortuo, mox irruens Lotharius rex, possessiones illius, abbatias videlicet sancti Amandi, sanctique Vedasti cum castello, Duvaicum quoque, sed et omnia usque ad fluvium Lis cum omni occupatione invasit." Lothar's conquest would have

Under Lothar, lay authority over the abbey continued unabated.[49] After Genulf, Lothar apparently tried to sell the abbacy (according to Folcuin, he sold it to Verona's intermittent bishop Rather, who remained in the post one night).[50] Guerric (abbot 968–996) tried to recover Genulf's losses.[51] Saint-Amand was incorporated back into the Flemish territory by the early 990s, during the reign of Arnulf II or his son, Baldwin IV.[52]

This overview shows the increasing challenges Saint-Amand faced. By the later tenth century, its wealth and prestige were diminished from its ninth-century golden age. Nonetheless, it possessed the potent relics of its patron, the region's premier saint. As the counts' *translationes* attest, relics retained their cache. In fact, the use of relics expanded in the tenth and eleventh centuries.[53] As we shall see, Johannes drew on this saintly capital to compose his epic *vita* of Amand's protégé Rictrude.

included Marchiennes and Hamage as well. It is not surprising that the *Gesta Ep. Cam.* does not mention them specifically, because the diocese had more than eighty religious houses, and these two were not among the most important (in fact, he only mentions them in the context of Bishop Gerard's reforms in 2.26–27). The *Annals* of Saint-Amand for 966: "Lotharius rex Atrebatum, Duacum, abbatiam Sancti Amandi et omnem terram usque Lis invasit."

[49] Platelle, *Temporel*, p. 117.

[50] Folcuin, *Gesta abbatum Lobbiensium*, c. 28 ed. G. Pertz MGH SS 4, p. 69: "he [Rather] bought from king Lothar the abbacy of Saint-Amand, which he barely held for one night, since he was an amazingly inconstant man" (a Lothario rege mercatus est sancti Amandi abbatiam; qua vix una nocte potitus ut erat mirae levitatis vir). The thirteenth-century *Chronica brevis* says he left because the monks expelled him: "he was barely able to hold the abbacy of Elnon for one night and on the next day the monks threw him out" (abbatia nostri Elnonis vix una nocte enim potitus, in crastino a monachis est eiectus; ed. in MGH SS 13, p. 387). Rather, spectacularly unsuccessful at holding an episcopal post, was appointed bishop of Verona on three occasions (the longest lasting seven years) and bishop of Liege for one short term.

[51] Platelle, *Temporel*, p. 118; *Chronica brevis*, MGH SS 13, p. 387.

[52] Dunbabin, "Reign of Arnulf II," pp. 60–61; D.C. Van Meter, "Count Baldwin IV, Richard of Saint-Vanne, and the Inception of Monastic Reform in Eleventh-Century Flanders," *RB* 107 (1997): 131. According to Dudo of Saint-Quentin's partisan early-eleventh-century account, which is incredibly hostile to the elder Arnulf, Lothar occupied Arras because of Arnulf II's refusal to provide military service and relinquished it due to the benevolent (and highly improbable) intervention of Duke Richard of Normandy. See Lair's note on page 294 for the probable date (978) of Lothar's siege of Arras (mentioned in *Gesta Ep. Cam.* 1.100–101). Dudo, *De moribus et actis primorum Normanniae Ducum*, ed. J. Lair (Caen, 1865), p. 294.

[53] Tenth- and eleventh-century *miracula* attest the continued importance of relics in attracting pilgrims, controlling local lords, bringing prosperity, protecting the town, and promoting a unified identity among a region's inhabitants. They were used to affirm secular power and lend it celestial authority. Bozóky argues that with the collapse of Carolingian power, relics were assigned previously royal functions of promoting peace and justice. Counts and bishops assembled them for oaths of peace and for church

Saint-Amand at the Millennium: Count Baldwin IV and Bishop Erluin

The immediate context for Johannes's work was the reign of Baldwin IV of Flanders (r. 988–1035). During this period we see the continued dominance of the abbey by outsiders and unrest engendered by competing regional sources of authority.

The involvement of Saint-Amand with Rozala-Susanna, daughter of King Berengar II of Italy, widow of Arnulf II of Flanders and mother of Baldwin IV, implies a complicated relationship with secular powers.[54] Around 990, Rozala married Robert the Pious, son of Hugh Capet, and took the name Susanna.[55] Robert soon repudiated her, and she went to live at Saint-Amand, where the abbot built her a palatial dwelling.[56] Saint-Amand's return to the counts may have been part of the marriage agreement or a result of the hostilities after its dissolution in 991 or 992.[57] Given that Saint-Bertin had refused to allow even a dead woman in its abbey, Saint-Amand's accommodation of Susanna is anomalous.[58] Perhaps Saint-Amand lacked the power to refuse her. Despite her interest in relics, there is

---

dedications. Monks took them on fund-raising tours. Vanderputten has shown that relics were used in conjunction with new documentary modes for transacting public business. See Bozóky, "Politique," pp. 272, 289; Edina Bozóky, "Voyage de reliques et démonstration du pouvoir aux temps féodaux," in *Voyages et voyageurs au Moyen Âge*, XXVIᵉ Congrès de la S.H.M.E.S. (Paris, 1996), pp. 272–273; Patrick Geary, "Humiliation of Saints," in *Saints and their Cults*, ed. Stephen Wilson (Cambridge, 1983), pp. 123–140; Steven Vanderputten, "Monastic Literate Practices in Eleventh- and Twelfth-Century Northern France," *JMH* 32 (2006): 101–126; P. Charruadas, "Principauté territoriale, reliques et Paix de Dieu. Le comté de Flandre et l'abbaye de Lobbes à travers les *Miracula s. Ursmari in itinere per Flandriam facta* (vers 1060)," *Revue du Nord* 89:372 (2007): 703–728.

[54] Platelle, *Temporel*, p. 118.

[55] *Vita Bertulfi Reticensis*, c. 33, ed. O. Holder-Egger MGH SS 15/2, p. 638.

[56] *Chronica brevis*, MGH SS 13, p. 387.

[57] Platelle, *Temporel*, p. 119, n. 37, interprets a note written in the *Breve Chronicon* between 1119–1121: "iam enim (1018–1065) ipsa Mauritania cum appenditiis suis de iure Sancti Amandi in manum comitis Flandrie transierat, quia loca illa Susanna regina manens ante monasterium antea, permissu abbatis Werrici, in vita sua tenuerat." Dunbabin, drawing on Dudo of Saint-Quentin, argues that it was returned before Arnulf II's death as part of the peace brokered by Richard, Duke of Normandy between King Lothar and Arnulf II. (See Dunbabin, "Reign of Arnulf II," pp. 60–61.) Dudo claims that, at an unspecified date, Lothar returned the territories as part of a peace negotiation brokered by Richard, duke of the Normans. It is, however, highly unlikely that Richard acted in the interests of his Flemish rival. As Dunbabin acknowledges, Dudo is an unreliable source, and we do not have adequate evidence for the date of Saint-Amand's return to the Flemish counts.

[58] Nicholas, *Medieval Flanders*, p. 20. In 918, Elftrude had her husband Baldwin II buried at Blandin in Ghent instead of Saint-Bertin because the latter house would not allow her to be interred there.

no suggestion she had entered religious life, nor does her dwelling sound like the appropriate home for a recluse.[59] Susanna's relationship to Saint-Amand is unclear. She was not a good patron, since she divested it of property.[60] When she died in 1003, she was interred at Blandin, her family's mausoleum.[61]

Like his mother, Baldwin IV involved himself in the ecclesiastical sphere.[62] Seeking to expand his power, he interfered in diocesan politics. When Rotard, bishop of Cambrai, died in 995, Baldwin tried to secure the position for his uncle Azelin.[63] Because Cambrai was in Ottonian Lotharingia, both Azelin and his rival Erluin sought the appointment from German emperor, Otto III. According to the *Gesta* of the bishops of Cambrai (written from 1024 at the behest of Erluin's successor Gerard I), both aspirants enlisted the help of the emperor's female kin:

Bishop Notker [of Liège] of revered memory warned him [Erluin] to hasten to Matilda, to whom Erluin was known [*familiaris*], the daughter of old emperor Otto [I], abbess of the church of Quedlinburg, so that he might attain the rank of bishop through her support [*suffragium*]. A certain man by the name of Azelin, from the villa Truncinis, son of Baldwin, count of Flanders, from a concubine, and later bishop of Paris, approached Sophia, sister of the young emperor, with money in order to attain by deceit the elevated ecclesiastical office. Thus, the emperor was assailed on both sides, but in accordance with divine will, he was persuaded by the

[59] On Suzanne overseeing the translation of relics, see Bozóky, "Politique," p. 279; *Vita Bertulfi Reticensis*, c. 34, p. 639.

[60] Platelle, *Temporel*, pp. 118–19.

[61] *Chronica brevis*, MGH SS 13, p. 387. Susanna's epitaph from Ghent is printed in MGH Poetae 5/1–2, p. 299.

[62] Van Meter, "Count Baldwin IV," p. 131.

[63] *Gesta Ep. Cam.* 1.110. The *Gesta*, our main source for Erluin, was written by a canon of Cambrai. The first book traces the episcopal history of the diocese before Gerard, the second describes its religious houses, and the third focuses on Gerard's deeds. Books 1, 2, and 3 up to chapter 50, were written in 1024–1025 and updated around 1036 to include events from the intervening years. In 1049, under Gerard's successor Lietbert, another writer added a *Vita Lietberti* and rewrote the later sections of book 3. The *Gesta*'s central themes are peace (represented by the bishop) and violence (represented primarily by the castellan); see Georges Duby, *Three Orders*, p. 23. It is a justification of the bishop's power, as he stands at the head of a well-ordered and just Christian society, and is, therefore, exceptionally hostile toward enemies of episcopal power. See Robert M. Stein, *Reality Fictions: Romance, History, and Governmental Authority, 1025–1180*, chapter 1; and Georges Duby, *The Three Orders: Feudal Society Imagined*, trans. Arthur Goldhammer (Chicago, 1980), pp. 19–21; Georges Duby, "Gérard de Cambrai, la paix et les trois fonctions sociales. 1024," *Compte rendus de séances de l'Académie des Inscriptions et Belles-Lettres* 1976, pp. 136–146. On the dates of composition, see Erik Van Mingroot, "Kritisch onderzoek omtrent de datering van de Gesta episcoporum Cameracensium," *RBPH* 53 (1975), 281–332; and David C. Van Meter, "The Peace of Amiens-Corbie and Gerard of Cambrai's Oration on the Three Functional Orders: The Date, the Context, the Rhetoric," *RBPH* 74 (1996): 633–657.

other's petition. For, without his sister Sophia knowing, he had agreed with his aunt Matilda, and, on the holy feast day of Dionysius, he had entrusted the pastoral duty to Erluin.[64]

Whereas Erluin's machinations were based on personal ties of patronage (he was *familiaris* with Otto's aunt Matilda), and thus shown as legitimate, the pro-episcopal *Gesta* unsurprisingly present Azelin's maneuverings as illegitimate, and based on bribery (akin to simony, which the author denounces).[65]

Erluin became bishop in 995 and accompanied the emperor to Rome, where Pope Gregory, consecrated him.[66] Even with imperial and papal endorsement, Erluin had difficulty asserting his rights. He returned to Cambrai to find "the castellan Walter and others who should have been soldiers of the Church ... laying waste to the possessions of his predecessor Rotard."[67] The castellan of Cambrai, first noted in 972, was nominally the bishop's vassal, but his fortified garrison meant that he rivaled his power within the city.[68] Fuldrad, abbot of Saint-Vaast, allied with Baldwin against Erluin. Armed with his own *milites* and a forged charter of episcopal exemption, Fuldrad resisted the bishop until 1004 when Baldwin (after a change of heart), Erluin, and the brothers of Saint-Vaast replaced him with

---

[64] "Hunc Nocherus bonae memoriae episcopus ad Mathildem, cui ipse Erluinus familiaris erat, filiam videlicet Ottonis senis imperatoris, abbatissam aecclesiae Quitinaborch, monuit ire festinanter, ut suo suffragio ad episcopii dignitatem adtingeret. Quidam quoque Azelinus nomine, de Truncinis villa, Balduini Flandrensium comitis de concubina filius, postea tamen Parisiorum episcopus, Sophiam sororem iuvenis imperatoris pecunia adorsus est, ut eius obtentu pontificii culmen sortiretur. Ab utraque igitur parte imperator pulsatur, sed tamen, Deo disponente, magis alterius rogationi inflectitur. Nam sorore Sophia nesciente Mathildi amitae consenserat, atque Erluino in die solemni sancti Dionisu regimen pastorale commiserat" (*Gesta Ep. Cam.* 1.110).

[65] For example, *Gesta Ep. Cam.*, 1.101. The *Gesta* charges Azelin with a similar strategy in his second attempt on the episcopate in 1012 (1.122).

[66] Erluin refused to have Gerbert (future Pope Sylvester II), archbishop of Rheims, consecrate him because he considered Gerbert an interloper. *Gesta Ep. Cam.* 1.110–111; 3.1. Hugh Capet had appointed Gerbert to replace Archbishop Arnulf, the nephew and supporter of his Carolingian rival. See Jason Glenn, *Politics and History in the Tenth Century: The Work and World of Richer of Reims* (Cambridge, 2004), p. 3.

[67] *Gesta Ep. Cam.* 1.110: "bona antecessoris sui Rothardi a Waltero et ab aliis, qui milites aecclesiae esse deberent, vastata."

[68] Stein, *Reality Fictions*, p. 15; for mention of the castellan in 972, see *Gesta Ep. Cam.* 1.93; Van Meter, "Count Baldwin IV," p. 132. On the castellan, see Duby, *The Three Orders*, pp. 22–24; J. Dhondt, "Note sur les châtelains de Flandre," in *Études historiques dédiées à la mémoire de M. Roger Rodière*, Commission départementale des Monuments historiques du Pas-de-Calais, Mémoires t. 5, fasc. 2 (Arras, 1947), pp. 40–51.

the monk Heribert.[69] Baldwin and Walter cooperated with Erluin only intermittently during his reign. With the count's support, Walter II, the new castellan, hounded Erluin on his deathbed and tried to prevent his burial in 1012.[70]

Baldwin's territorial ambitions in Ottonian Lotharingia further added to the unrest. In 1006, Baldwin occupied the imperial city of Valenciennes and threatened Cambrai. Erluin appealed to Henry II, who responded by invading Flanders and capturing Ghent, the counts' ancestral base.[71] Meanwhile, the French king Robert the Pious gathered his forces in September 1006. Robert's men marched through Arras toward Valenciennes, looting as they went.[72] Baldwin retreated from Valenciennes and made peace with Henry. In 1007, Henry granted comitial power over the Cambrésis to the bishop to secure the latter's position (the bishop already held this power within the city of Cambrai).[73] The tumultuous regional politics would certainly have affected Saint-Amand.

Saint-Amand would also have been affected by Baldwin IV's concerted efforts at monastic reform,[74] since abbeys often resented and resisted these reforms, which imposed a stricter interpretation of the Benedictine Rule.[75] Unlike contemporary Cluniac reforms, those in Flanders did not undermine episcopal authority and were often carried out with cooperation from bishops.[76] In 1008, Baldwin replaced Heribert, abbot of Saint-Vaast, with

---

[69] *Gesta Ep. Cam.* 1.107; Van Meter, "Count Baldwin IV," pp. 132–133. The *Gesta*'s portrayal of Fuldrad's debauchery must be read in light of the work's agenda.

[70] Late in 1011, with Erluin ailing, Baldwin again tried to make Azelin bishop. The *Gesta*'s allegations of secret dealings are problematic given its hostility toward enemies of episcopal power, especially the castellans; the *Gesta* claims that Baldwin also plotted with the castellan Walter to support his son (Walter II) as heir to his position. The younger Walter, succeeding his father, immediately started harassing the dying bishop (who threatened him with excommunication) (*Gesta Ep. Cam.* 1.117). Erluin's death reported in *Annales Quedlinburgensis*, A. 1012, ed. G. Pertz in MGH SS 3, p. 80.

[71] Van Meter, "Count Baldwin IV," p. 135.

[72] Ibid., pp. 135–136.

[73] Stein, *Reality Fictions*, p. 15.

[74] Baldwin's interest in reform came from both strategic and pious motivations. See Van Meter, "Count Baldwin IV," p. 134.

[75] The monks of Saint-Vaast attempted to resist Richard of Saint-Vanne. Richard used a divine message and the threat of eternal damnation against Baldwin to try to gain a foothold in Saint-Bertin. Van Meter, "Count Baldwin IV," pp. 138, 141; David C. Van Meter, "Apocalyptic Moments and the Eschatological Rhetoric of Reform in the Early Eleventh Century: The Case of the Visionary of St. Vaast," in *The Apocalyptic Year 1000: Religious Expectation and Social Change, 950–1050*, ed. Richard Landes, Andrew Gow, and David C. Van Meter (Oxford, 2003), pp. 311–325.

[76] Van Meter, "Count Baldwin IV," p. 138; *Gesta Ep. Cam.* 3.6.

the reformer Richard of Saint-Vanne.[77] Richard's success there led Baldwin to assign him and his protégés other abbeys.[78] Baldwin's usual modus operandi was to appoint a reformer on the death of an incumbent abbot.[79] Accordingly, when Abbot Ratbod of Saint-Amand died in 1013, he appointed Richard (r. 1013–1018).[80] So, by Johannes's time, Saint-Amand was diminished in importance and subject to external influences and the chaos engendered by competing sources of local and regional authority. In addition to the local politics, Johannes's context was informed by a broader cultural change associated with the Ottonians, namely, the ascendency of the courtier bishops, whose wealth, power, and influence challenged that of the monasteries.

COURTIER BISHOPS

Until the mid-tenth century, palace courtiers, diplomats, and leading churchmen were largely drawn from men educated in the foremost monastery schools.[81] They included the writers and readers of epic lives – such

[77] *Gesta Ep. Cam.* 1.116; Hugh of Flavigny, *Chronicon*, book 2, chap. 10, erroneously says that Bishop Gerard of Cambrai appointed Richard. Van Meter, "Count Baldwin IV," p. 136. Van Meter argues that Baldwin cooperated due to coercion from Erluin and other magnates. The *Gesta Ep. Cam.* presents Baldwin as a willing participant in the reform, suggests Van Meter, because by the time of composition (1024–1025), Bishop Gerard and Baldwin were allies and Gerard would not have wanted to alienate him.

[78] Van Meter, "Count Baldwin IV," p. 130. Writing about a century later, Hugh of Flavigny lists a large number of abbeys he reformed, including Saint-Bertin (1021) and Blandin (1029). "Balduinus vero Flandrensis abbatias ei quamplures tradidit, abbatiam scilicet sancti Petri Gandensis, abbatiam sancti Amandi, abbatiam sancti Bertini, abbatiam sancti Richarii et abbatiam sancti Iudoci. Rexit et alia quamplurima cenobia, Bretuliensem, Humulariensem, sancti Quintini de Monte, sancti Wandregisili, sancti Huberti, sancti Remacli, Malmundariensem, Waltiodorensem, Belliloci, sancti Urbani, sancti Vincentii Mettensis insulae, et alia perplura quae non occurrunt memoriae, quas omnes in meliorem reparavit statum, et melioratis abbates de suis quos elegit instituit. Cenobium vero Belliloci, sancti Petri Catalaunensis, sancti Urbani a ipse in vita sua rexit." Hugh of Flavigny, *Chronicon*, book 2, chap. 10–11, ed. G. Pertz, MGH SS 8, p. 377; E. Sabbé, "Notes sur la réforme de Richard de Saint-Vanne dans les Pays-Bas," *RBPH* 7 (1928): 551–570. The date for Blandin's reform comes from *Annales Blandinienses* for 1029, ed. Philip Grierson, *Les Annales de Saint-Pierre de Gand et de Saint-Amand, Annales Blandinienses, Annales Elmarenses, Annales Formoselenses, Annales Elnonenses* (Brussels, 1937), p. 24. Richard's protégées included Leduin and Roderic, both of Saint-Vaast, and Poppo of Stavelot.

[79] Van Meter, "Count Baldwin IV," p. 137.

[80] *Annales Elnonenses* for 1013 (ed. Grierson, p. 153): "Obiit Ratbodus abbas, succedit Richardus." Platelle, *Temporel*, p. 117; a list of abbots of Saint-Amand is ed. MGH SS 13, p. 386.

[81] C. Stephen Jaeger, "The Courtier Bishop in *Vitae* from the Tenth to the Twelfth Century," *Speculum* 58 (1983): 300.

as Hilduin, Grimald, Hraban Maur, Hincmar of Rheims, Ermenric, Walafrid Strabo, and Lupus of Ferrières – who became chaplains, chancellors, tutors at court, and royal advisors, as well as monastery teachers, abbots, and bishops. These men advanced through *amicitia*, promoting and maintaining ties to their teachers and fellow students and fostering connections with courtiers, nobles, and the royal household. As we have seen, the dedication of literature (including epic lives) was one means of creating and sustaining associations. From the mid-tenth century, cathedral-trained clerics, rather than monks, increasingly garnered such patronage and rose to important positions, particularly the episcopate.[82]

The rise and transformation of the episcopate, beginning under Emperor Otto I's brother Bruno, archbishop of Cologne (953–965) and Duke of Lotharingia, had profound implications for the influence of monks and monastic schools. Bruno appointed his own students to episcopal sees throughout the German kingdom, especially in Lotharingia, creating "a subtle but pervasive web of ecclesiastical/royal administrators."[83] These bishops were deeply involved in imperial affairs. C. Stephen Jaeger observes that "Otto [I] built the episcopal office into an important political instrument, a buffer against the opposition of the feudal nobility. Loyal bishops could become powerful secular lords while holding episcopal office."[84] Otto's successors followed his policy of recruiting clerics for the imperial episcopate.

Jaeger outlines the typical (or idealized) career of such a cleric.[85] From a noble background, he began his education at a cathedral school where the bishop perceived his exceptional talent and promoted him to service in his

---

[82] Thangmar, *Vita Bernwardi*, ed. Hatto Kallfelz in *Lebensbeschreibungen einiger Bischöfe des 10.–12. Jahrhunderts*, Ausgewählte Quellen zur deutschen Geschichte des Mittelalters (Darmstadt, 1973), pp. 272–361, c. 2: "Ut domnum regem fidei illius literis imbuendum moribusque instituendum consensu cunctorum procerum commendaret." For example, as empress, Judith had brought Walafrid Strabo to court to tutor her son Charles (later Charles the Bald), and Empress Theophanu assigned her son, Otto III to Bernward (d. 1022), bishop of Hildesheim. See Thangmar, *Vita Bernwardi*, c. 13, p. 264.

[83] James Forse, "Bruno of Cologne and the Networking of the Episcopate in Tenth-Century Germany," *German History* 9 (1991): 267; Forse states that of forty-seven bishops and archbishops whose pontificates fell within Bruno's court career (939–965), forty-five were linked to him.

[84] Jaeger, "Courtier Bishop," pp. 291–292. For another perspective, see Johnson, *Secular Activities*, p. 39.

[85] Jaeger, "Courtier Bishop," p. 294. Jaeger distinguishes the tenth- to twelfth-century (prose) *vitae* of courtier bishops from "hagiographical legends and saints' lives," designating the former "biography." I am not convinced of the absolute distinction since some pre–tenth-century saints' *vitae* are quite similar to those of courtier bishops. These bishops' *vitae* were often written soon after their deaths by people who knew them (e.g., Ruodbert's life of his teacher Bruno of Cologne), but many older lives were also written by people who

court. A secular noble, recognizing the usefulness of such men, might also employ him. The emperor would then recruit him to be a chaplain at his court. Sometimes the upwardly mobile cleric taught at a cathedral school on his way to an abbacy or episcopate.

These men, who included scholars and poets and who formed the heart of the court, came from similar backgrounds and were shaped by similar education and experiences.[86] James Forse notes that "after their appointments to ecclesiastical posts, these clerics maintained contacts among themselves through frequent synods and frequent appearance at court."[87] Although the relations of bishops to royal authority differed in the Capetian and Ottonian realms, the patronage networks they formed crossed territorial boundaries, creating an episcopal culture that spanned France and Germany.[88] These bishops were recognized as the paragons of culture in their sees and, as such, were obvious dedicatees for literature.[89]

Erluin and his patron Notker were examples of courtier bishops. Notker was an influential Ottonian courtier, student and friend of Bruno of Cologne, and mentor to Otto II and Otto III.[90] He served at the chancellery for many years before becoming bishop of Liège (972–1008) and was renowned for his learning and for his impact on education in that city.[91] Notker's patronage of students included taking them on official business to gain experience and make contacts.[92] He was behind the appointment of his students as bishops; Rotard and Erluin became bishops of Cambrai, and Adalbold, bishop of Utrecht.[93] As a respected scholar and powerful patron, Notker was both the recipient and subject of epic *vitae*.[94] Erluin, a

---

knew their subjects and contexts, for example, Baudemund's prose *Vita Amandi* (BHL 332) and Candid's early-ninth-century verse and prose *vitae* of abbot Eigil (BHL 2440 and 2441). Although the courtier bishops' *vitae* differ from those of thaumaturgic Merovingian missionary bishops, they are still idealizing representations that include tropes familiar from earlier lives (for example, the young man reading like a bee, discussed later). Further, they are written for overlapping purposes, including promoting veneration.

[86] Jaeger, "Courtier Bishop," p. 293.

[87] Forse, "Bruno of Cologne," p. 272.

[88] Jaeger, "Courtier Bishop," p. 297.

[89] Duby, *The Three Orders*, p. 15.

[90] On Notker, see Godefroid Kurth, *Notger de Liège et la civilisation au Xe siècle* 1 (Paris, 1905); Anselm of Liège, *Gesta Episcoporum Leodiensium*, c. 25–30. R. Koepke in MGH SS 7, pp. 203–206; Aegidius Aureaevallensis, *Gesta Episcoporum Leodiensium*, c. 50–58, ed. I. Heller in MGH SS 25, pp. 57–63; Forse, "Bruno of Cologne," p. 270.

[91] On Notker as a teacher, see Anselm, *Gesta Ep. Leod.*, c. 28.

[92] Anselm, *Gesta Ep. Leod.*, c. 28; Jaeger, *Envy*, p. 203.

[93] Forse, "Bruno of Cologne," p. 268.

[94] Fragments of an epic *vita* of Notker of Liège are preserved in the thirteenth-century *Gesta Ep. Leod.* by Aegidius Aureaevallensis. (They are printed together in MGH Poetae 5/1, pp. 491–493.) The monk Richarius of Gembloux sent his epic life of Erluin (d. 986), his

less prominent figure, came from a family with strong ties to the church in Liège, where he became a student and archdeacon.[95] He was related to the first and third abbots of Gembloux, who shared his name.[96] The *Deeds of the Bishops of Cambrai* describe him as a man learned in ecclesiastic and secular affairs and a frequent presence at royal courts.[97]

Modern scholars have claimed that, from the later tenth century, a cathedral school education and, in Germany, service in the imperial chapel were practically requisite for high ecclesiastical office.[98] This is an overstatement because cathedrals and monasteries were not mutually exclusive systems, and there was exchange among monastic and courtly circles. Some monks and students of monastic schools still became royal advisors and bishops.[99] This was the case for students from schools such as Saint-Gall and Reichenau, which had imperial patronage and, in the former, a long tradition of educating clerics as well as monks.[100] Conversely, a cathedral school education could lead to a monastic career, as in the example of

house's first abbot, to Notker, according to Sigebert of Gembloux, *Gesta abbatum Gemblacenisum*, c. 1, ed. Pertz MGH SS 8, p. 523. The life was lost by Sigebert's time.

[95] *Gesta Ep. Cam.* 1.110.

[96] He was related to Erluin, the first abbot of Gembloux (d. 986), and was the uncle of its third abbot, Erluin II (d. 1008). Sigebert, *Gesta abb. Gemb.*, c. 24.

[97] *Gesta Ep. Cam.* 1.110.

[98] Jaeger, *Envy*, p. 47. Klewitz presents service in the chapel as necessary training for the imperial episcopate. Hans-Walter Klewitz, "Königtum, Hofkapelle und Domkapitel im 10. und 11. Jahrhundert," *Archiv für Urkundenforschung* 16 (1939): 107. The standard work on the chapel is Fleckenstein, *Hofkapelle*.

[99] In the second half of the tenth century, a number of bishops were drawn from monasteries including Folcmar of Paderborn (r. 961–983) from Corvey, Anno of Worms (r. 950–979) from Saint Maximin of Trier, and Ingram of Cambrai (r. 963–971) from Corvey. See Forse, "Bruno of Cologne," pp. 275–277. Lanfranc of Bec is an English parallel. See Priscilla D. Watkins, "Lanfranc at Caen: Teaching by Example," in *Teaching and Learning in Northern Europe*, ed. Sally N. Vaughn and Jay Rubenstein (Turnhout, 2006), pp. 71–97.

[100] In the tenth and early eleventh centuries, monks of Saint-Gall moved in court and cathedral circles. Clerics and lay students attended the school, ensuring ties that traversed the division between regular and secular clergy. Ekkehard II was a tutor to Otto II. Several Saint-Gall students became bishops. Grotans, *Reading*, p. 50, provides these examples: Salomo became bishop of Constance; Robert became bishop of Metz in 916; Ulrich became bishop of Augsburg in 923. Ekkehard IV mentions three bishops among his Saint-Gall alumni. See *Vita Ouadalrichi episcopi Augustani* (BHL 8359), c. 1, ed. D. G. Waitz, MGH SS 4, p. 386; Ekkehard IV, *Casus sancti Galli*, c. 66, in *St. Galler Klostergeschichten*, ed. Hans F. Haefele (Darmstadt, 1980), pp. 140–142. Otto III and Henry II had *familiares* among monastic circles. Otto III appointed Abbot Alawich II of Reichenau bishop of Strasbourg in 1000. Henry II, educated at Saint-Emmeram in Regensburg, knew several monks of Reichenau. As Mayr-Harting notes, itinerant kingship led to connections beyond the court, and Otto I stayed at Reichenau at least twice (965, 972). See Henry Mayr-Harting, "Artists and Patrons," in *The New Cambridge Medieval History*, vol. 3, c. 900–c. 1024, ed. Timothy Reuter (Cambridge, 1999), p. 227.

Richard of Saint-Vanne.[101] Nonetheless, a monastic background could be presented as a disadvantage.[102] The opponents of Wazo of Liège (r. 1042–1048) seized on his monastic education and lack of experience in the royal court as a shortcoming. Disregarding his long service at Liège – he had been master of the cathedral school, ca. 1005–1030 – Wazo's enemies presented his background as an impediment: shaped by his cloistered monastic life (*informatus subiectione claustralis oboedientiae*), he had not learned to rule.[103] So, it seemed, to Wazo's contemporaries, that the cathedral and the monastery prepared men for separate paths; the cathedral schools educated a man for public administration and leadership rather than for a life of pastoral care or spiritual devotion.[104] The avenues of power increasingly bypassed second-tier monasteries like Saint-Amand, which were outside the sphere of imperial or royal patronage. Students at such monastery schools, however gifted, would be unlikely to attract attention from bishops or important patrons. Although there was an undeniable shift in ecclesiastical power to men from cathedral schools, as we shall see, the rise of these institutions did not render traditional monastic education obsolete. In practice the situation was more complex.

CATHEDRAL AND MONASTIC SCHOOLS

Jaeger has underscored the innovations of tenth- and eleventh-century cathedral schools, but there was also a considerable commonality between

---

[101] Richard of Saint-Vanne, as a boy, was educated at the cathedral of Notre Dame at Rheims. See *Vita Richardi Abb. S. Vitoni Virdunensis*, ed. W. Wattenbach in MGH SS 11, pp. 280–290, c. 2, at p. 281; *Gesta Episcoporum Virdunensium continuatio*, c. 6 and 8, ed. G. Waitz in MGH SS 4, pp. 47–48. According to a necrology (in Rheims, BM, MS 15, fol. 14v), one Richerus, who trained as a canon at Rheims, became a monk at nearby Saint-Remigius (this may be the same Richer of Saint-Remigius who wrote the *Historia* in the 990s; see Glenn, *Politics and History*, p. 21). Wibald of Stablo, educated at the cathedral school of Liège, became an abbot and a statesman (see Jaeger, *Envy*, p. 80). Gebhard, bishop of Augsburg (996–1001), educated at the cathedral school of Augsburg, was a monk at Saint-Emmeram and abbot of Tergernsee and Ellwangen, before becoming a bishop. See David A. Warner, "Saints and Politics in Ottonian Germany," in *Medieval Germany: Associations and Delineations*, ed. Nancy van Deusen (Ottawa, 2000), p. 20.

[102] Jaeger, *Envy*, p. 47.

[103] Anselm, *Gesta Ep. Leod.*, c. 50; Jaeger, *Envy*, pp. 207–209; Anselm, writing in the mid-eleventh century admittedly has a point to make about the moral decline, which had resulted in laxity at the cathedral school in Liège since Notker's day, in educational practices generally, and at the imperial court (see, for example, *Gesta*, c. 28). That Wazo's critics would attack him on the grounds of his monastic way of life exemplifies, for Anselm, their perverse values.

[104] Jaeger, *Envy*, p. 48.

older and newer modes of education and the practices of cathedral and monastery in teaching the language arts of the trivium. Further, the distinction posited between old and new pedagogy does not map neatly onto the division between cathedral and cloister schools. This emphasis on the differences between cathedral and cloister is only one way of describing the varied pedagogical ideals and practices around the millennium. Although the subject requires far more specialized research, we could also distinguish large prosperous intellectual centers (including the abbeys of Reichenau, Saint-Gall, and Saint-Germain of Auxerre as well as cathedral schools) from smaller monastic institutions, or could focus on the significant variations perpetuated at individual schools by dominant personalities (such as Gerbert, discussed later) and local intellectual traditions. In what follows, I refer to cathedral and monastic schools in general terms, but the division was far from absolute. The considerable overlap between the older, largely monastic education, which Johannes had received, and the newer forms promoted at the cathedral schools allowed Johannes to compose an epic *Vita Rictrudis* that could speak to both bishops and monks.

The institutions shared an intellectual heritage because students from leading ninth- and tenth-century monasteries shaped the most important cathedral schools. Hilduin's student Hincmar (who was also associated with Saint-Amand) became archbishop of Rheims (r. 845–882), home to one of the most influential of the cathedral schools.[105] In 893, Hincmar's successor, Fulk (r. 882–898) employed the teachers Hucbald of Saint-Amand and Remigius of Auxerre.[106] Michael E. Moore explains that "to revive the cathedral school of Rheims ... Fulk had called upon ... the foremost intellectual centres of the late Carolingian world."[107] These preeminent Carolingian royal abbeys – Saint-Denis, Saint-Amand, and Saint-Germain of Auxerre – were, not coincidentally, places that produced epic *vitae*. Further, the teachers of Hincmar, Hucbald, and Remigius – Hilduin, Milo, and Heiric, respectively – were the authors of epic *vitae*. The tradition of Classical scholarship, poetic composition, and hagiography that

---

[105] Michael E. Moore, "Prologue: Teaching and Learning History in the School of Rheims, c. 800–950," in *Teaching and Learning in Northern Europe*, ed. Sally N. Vaughn and Jay Rubenstein (Turnhout, 2006), p. 25. Hincmar's family origins were from Northern Francia. On Hincmar and Saint-Amand, see Helmut Reimitz, "Ein karolingisches Geschichtsbuch aus Saint-Amand: Der Codex Vindobonensis palat. 473," in *Text – Schrift – Codex: Quellenkundliche Arbeiten aus dem Institut für Österreichische Geschichtsforschung*, ed. Christoph Egger and Herwig Weigl (Vienna, 2000), especially pp. 62–76.

[106] Moore, "Prologue," pp. 36–39.

[107] Ibid. p. 39.

these scholars conveyed to Rheims is evident in the work of Flodoard, canon of Rheims (d. 966), who wrote an epic 20,000-line poem, *De triumphis Christi*, celebrating numerous martyrs and confessors.[108]

The movement of scholars and students between monastic and cathedral schools throughout the tenth century resulted in an ongoing exchange of ideas, methodologies, and texts. The monastery school of Saint-Gall, which experienced its own renaissance in the late tenth and early eleventh centuries,[109] educated Balderic, who was bishop of Speyer (970–986) and master of its cathedral school.[110] Balderic, in turn, taught Walter (perhaps the same Walter who was bishop of Speyer, 1004–1027), who composed an epic *Passio Christophori* in 984 when he was a student.[111] The resemblance of Walter's epic to Ermenric's letter (discussed in Chapters 2 and 3) in range of sources and showy obscurantism is not coincidental. Ermenric's letter, used as a school text at Saint-Gall, directly or indirectly influenced Walter's epic *vita*. Other teachers from Saint-Gall also taught at cathedral schools.[112] Some leading scholars were educated at both monastery and cathedral school. Gerbert, *magister* of Rheims (971–989), learned *grammatica* at the monastery of Saint-Gerald in Aurillac and mathematics from Archbishop Hatto of Vich.[113] Due to their continued interaction, tenth-century educational changes affected both kinds of institutions.

Given the monastic teachers' influence, it is unsurprising that many pedagogical innovations of tenth-century cathedral schools descended from practices of the earlier institutions. As Margaret Gibson notes,

---

[108] Flodoard, *De triumphis Christi*, printed in PL 135, cols. 491A–886C. Peter Christian Jacobsen is editing the poem. On Flodoard, see Michel Sot, *Un historien et son église au Xe siècle: Flodoard de Rheims* (Paris, 1993), pp. 87–101; Peter Christian Jacobsen, *Flodoard von Reims: sein Leben und seine Dichtung 'De triumphis Christi'* (Leiden, 1978).

[109] During 978–1022 under Abbots Immo and Burckhardt. McKitterick, *Frankish Kingdoms* p. 297.

[110] Franz Anton Specht, *Geschichte des Unterrichtswesens in Deutschland von den ältesten Zeiten bis zur Mitte des dreizehnten Jahrhunderts* (Stuttgart, 1885), p. 334. Balderic describes his education at Saint-Gall in the prologue addressed to his teacher Notker (Notker Piperisgranum, d. 975) in his *Vita Sancti Fridolini* (BHL 3170), ed. Mechthild Pörnbacher (Sigmaringen, 1997), p. 218.

[111] Walter, *Passio Christophori* (BHL 1776), in MGH Poetae 5/1–2, pp. 11–63; prose *Passio Christophori* (BHL 1777) at pp. 66–79.

[112] Grotans, *Reading*, p. 50. In the second half of the tenth century, the monk Victor taught at the Strasbourg cathedral school. Ekkehard IV was a master at Saint-Gall and later at the cathedral school at Mainz (1022–1031).

[113] Richer, *Historia*, 3, c. 43, MGH SS 38, pp. 191–192: "he was raised from boyhood in the monastery of the confessor Saint Gerald and taught grammar" (in coenobio sancti confessoris Geroldi a pueri altus, et grammatica edoctus est). See also, Hugh of Flavigny, *Chronicon Virdunense seu Flaviniacense*, ed. G. Pertz, MGH SS 8, p. 367.

"Gerbert and his younger contemporaries did rely on the Carolingians at almost every point."[114] Alcuin and Ermenric had presaged the increasing concern with dialectic.[115] Newly popular texts such as Boethius, Porphyry's *Isagoge*, and the late-fourth-century Pseudo-Aristotelian *De decem categoriis* had been read and taught by ninth-century scholars.[116] Similarly, in that century, teachers such as Ermenric and Heiric had foreshadowed the cathedral schoolmasters by teaching from a wide range of Classical sources. Likewise, the "charismatic teacher" Jaeger describes was neither entirely new nor exclusive to the cathedral school. The Benedictine Rule stipulates that the abbot function as a model for monks, imparting "all that is good and holy more by deeds than by words," and saints had long been put forth as models *ad imitandum*.[117] Ermenric's praise of Grimald as a font of wisdom is similar to tenth- and eleventh-century depictions of charismatic cathedral school teachers.[118]

The institutions' shared features meant that their alumni participated in the same broad "textual community," that is, in Brian Stock's formulation, a community characterized by a common canon and shared interpretive methods.[119] Despite educational changes, monastic oblates and cathedral school clerics around the turn of the millennium read some of the same texts and learned to use them in similar ways.

Canon

The canon used to teach the language arts or trivium at the leading schools was transformed. Although we should not assume too standardized a set of

---

[114] Margaret Gibson, "The Continuity of Learning, ca. 850–1050," *Viator* 6 (1975): 1.

[115] Grotans, *Reading*, pp. 79–81.

[116] Leonardi, "Intellectual Life," pp. 187–88; Grotans, *Reading*, pp. 79–82.

[117] *RB* 2.11–12: "omnia bona et sancta factis amplius quam verbis ostendat . . ." Watkins shows how the monk, teacher, abbot and eventually archbishop, Lanfranc of Bec, embodied this tradition. See Watkins, "Lanfranc at Caen"; Peter Brown, "The Saint as Exemplar in Late Antiquity," in *Saints and Their Cults*, ed. Stephen Wilson (Cambridge, 1983), pp. 183–194.

[118] Ermenric emphasizes Grimald's character – his *caritas*, his possession of the four virtues – far more than he does any other features, and he even uses one of the same tropes – drinking from the teacher's font of wisdom – employed by cathedral school students, for example, the master in the Würzburg poem, lines 29–30: "The living river of teaching flows from his chest. The river gives the eternal spirit of his speeches" (Doctrine rivus fluit eius pectore vivus, / Eternum numen sermonum dat sibi flumen . . .). Ed. Walther Bulst, MGH Die Briefe der deutschen Kaiserzeit (Briefe d. dt. Kaiserzeit) 3: Die ältere Wormser Briefsammlung, p. 120.

[119] Stock, *Implications*, pp. 90–91; Brian Stock, *Listening for the Text: On the Uses of the Past* (Baltimore, 1990), pp. 22–23; Irvine, *Textual Culture*, p. 1.

curriculum authors, we can observe a general shift toward a more diverse pagan curriculum and away from the late antique Christian epics that had dominated Carolingian monastic schools.[120] Alcuin and Theodulf, poets of Charlemagne's court, had named far more Christians than pagans in their lists of poets.[121] By contrast, most of the authors Walter claims he read at Speyer's cathedral school were pagan: Virgil, Homer (i.e., the *Ilias Latina*), Horace, Persius, Juvenal, Boethius, Statius, Terence, Lucan, and Martianus Capella.[122] He does not mention the Christian authors Prudentius and Sedulius, although verbal reminiscences show his familiarity with them. Gerbert, according to Richer, who was probably his student, used a similar set of Classical poets to prepare students for rhetoric

because without the ways of speaking, which are learned from the poets, one could not attain the art of oratory. Accordingly, he employed the poets whom he judged the students should be familiar with. Therefore, he read and taught the poets Virgil, Statius, and Terence and the satirists Juvenal, Persius, and Horace and also the historian Lucan [the epic verse *Pharsalia*].[123]

Persius, who appeared only occasionally in the ninth-century schools, attained a more prominent role, as did Terence and Horace.[124] Richer's own writing reflects this entirely pagan poetic curriculum; he shows little knowledge of any Christian poets except Prudentius.[125] None of the lists represents something as simple as the required reading, but they do

---

[120] On the dangers of assuming too standard a curriculum, see M.L.W. Laistner, "Review of Curtius, *Europäische Literatur und lateinisches Mittelalter*," *Speculum* 24 (1949): 260.

[121] Alcuin, *York Poem*, lines 1551–1554. Alcuin lists books belonging to the scholar Aelberht. When it comes to poets, he notes nine Christians (Sedulius, Juvencus, Avitus, Prudentius, Prosper, Paulinus, Arator, Fortunatus, and Lactantius) and three Classical authors (Virgil, Statius, and Lucan). Theodulf, in discussing the books he had read, presents a similar picture. Of the poets he names, seven are Christian (Sedulius, Paulinus, Arator, Avitus, Fortunatus, Juvencus, and Prudentius) and only two are Classical (Virgil and Ovid). Theodulf, *Carm.* 45, lines 13–18 in MGH Poetae 1, p. 543.

[122] On Walter, see Martin Armgart, "Walter von Speyer," in *Biographisch-bibliographisches Kirchenlexikon* (BBKL), vol. 13 (Herzberg, 1998), pp. 236–239; and Günter Glauche, *Schullektüre im Mittelalter. Entstehung und Wandlungen des Lektürekanons bis 1200 nach den Quellen dargestellt* (Munich, 1970), pp. 75–83.

[123] Richer, *Historiae*, Book 3, c. 47, MGH SS 38, p. 194: "quod sine locutionum modis, qui in poetis discendi sunt, ad oratoriam artem ante perveniri non queat. Poetas igitur adhibuit, quibus assuescendos arbitrabatur. Legit itaque ac docuit Maronem et Statium Terentiumque poetas, Iuvenalem quoque ac Persium Horatiumque satiricos, Lucanum etiam historiographum."

[124] Heiric alludes to Persius (*VG* 1.73, 1.81, 3. 483f., 3.492) and mentions him in the teaching glosses, for example, 1. 273, *Praefatio* to book 2, line 9. Ermenric quotes Persius (c. 15).

[125] Hoffman in his edition of Richer identifies one allusion to Arator and none to other canonical biblical epic poets (MGH SS 38, pp. 316–325).

demonstrate the use of a wide range of Classical sources and the prosimetric works of Boethius and Martianus Capella, all of which had been used sparingly in the ninth century.[126]

The shift toward pagan Classics was a development rather than an innovation and does not represent a radical break from monastic education. Verse and particularly Virgil, the touchstones of grammar education since antiquity, would remain central for centuries.[127] Certain monastic schools (such as Saint-Germain of Auxerre) had long taught many pagan poets and monastic scriptoria, including Echternach, Freising, Tegernsee, and Saint-Maximin of Trèves, copied a wide range of Classical texts in the tenth and eleventh centuries.[128] Further illustrating the continuity in practices, cathedral-trained writers adopted monasticism's ambiguous rhetoric toward pagan sources, using overt criticism as an opportunity for parading Classical learning.[129]

The late antique Christian poets did not disappear. Several tenth-century epic saints' *vitae* draw on them heavily, and they were included in eleventh-

---

[126] As always, the author's purpose shapes the perspective. Thus, prose *vitae* of tenth- and eleventh-century bishops usually give cursory descriptions of education to show the protagonist's youthful talent, his erudition, and his abilities as a teacher. When a writer (such as Richer) speaks of his own teacher, he will probably represent him particularly favorably, because he is vaunting his own education. Other sources seek to glorify the intellectual caliber of an institution, perhaps at the expense of another (e.g., the Würzburg poem, discussed in the following). Nonetheless, we can glean ideals regarding texts, subjects, pedagogical practices, and emphases.

[127] Curtius, *European Literature*, p. 49. For a list of classroom texts given in the manuscript Cambridge, Gonville and Caius College, MS 385, pp. 47–56, see Charles Homer Haskins, "A List of Text-Books from the Close of the Twelfth Century," *Harvard Studies in Classical Philology* 20 (1909): 75–94, esp. pp. 90–91. There is an extensive bibliography of the Classics in education for the twelfth century and later Middle Ages. Charles Homer Haskins, *The Renaissance of the Twelfth Century* (Cambridge, MA, 1927), especially c. 4. An example of poetry's continued importance is the Würzburg cathedral students' praise of their *magister* Pernolf in 1029: "he illuminates the beauty of all kinds of poets" (Ipse poetarum fulget decus omnigenarum). Würzburg Poem, line 24, MGH Briefe d. dt. Kaiserzeit 3, p. 120: Jaeger, *Envy*, pp. 67–68.

[128] Birger Munk Olsen, "La réutilisation des classiques dans les écoles," *Ideologie e practiche del reimpiego nell' alto Medioevo* (Spoleto, 1999), p. 247. Notable examples include the highly annotated illuminated eleventh-century copy of Lucan's *Pharsalia* from the abbey at Anchin (Douai, BM, MS 761) and the annotated eleventh-century Horace from Marchiennes (Douai, BM, MS 760).

[129] In a passage reminiscent of Ermenric (see Chapter 3), the Würzburg students decry their opponents' dedication to the pagans and simultaneously parade their own Classical learning through mythological allusion (to Hercules, Orpheus, Argus, and Arethusa). Jaeger, *Envy*, pp. 67–69. Würzburg Poem, lines 206–225, MGH Briefe d. dt. Kaiserzeit 3, pp. 125–126.

century schoolbooks.[130] The vitality of the manuscript tradition of Sedulius, the most popular of the Christian epic poets, attests to his continued currency into the High Middle Ages.[131] Nonetheless, they were far less visible in the cathedral setting. Walter's failure to mention his acquaintance with Sedulius and Prudentius suggests that although Christian poets still formed part of his received cultural heritage, the prestige belonged to the pagans.[132]

This shift in the value ascribed to the Christian and pagan poets disadvantaged students of schools like Saint-Amand that had never embraced a broad Classical tradition. As the rise of the courtier bishops diminished monasticism's political influence, the rise of the Classics reduced the cultural authority of the poets taught at these schools. Johannes's sources reflect a conservative monastic curriculum, similar to the one Milo would have taught, rather than that of a ninth-century innovator like Heiric or Ermenric, or a tenth-century cathedral schoolmaster.[133] His *Vita Rictrudis* shows limited knowledge of pagan authors except Virgil. His canon only partially overlapped with that of the courtier bishops. A textual community, however, is based not only on common texts, but also their interpretation.

---

[130] On late antique Christian poets in the eleventh century, see Michael Lapidge, "Versifying the Bible in the Middle Ages," in *The Text in the Community: Essays on Medieval Works, Manuscripts, Authors, and Readers*, ed. Jill Mann and Maura Nolan (Notre Dame, 2006), p. 30. Conrad of Hirsau, in the first half of the twelfth century included the Christian writers (Sedulius, Juvencus, Prosper, Arator, and Prudentius) along with the pagans (Lucan, Horace, Ovid, Juvenal, Homer, Persius, Statius, and Virgil). Curtius, *European Literature*, p. 49. Conrad's *Dialogus super auctores* is ed. R.B.C. Huygens in *Accessus ad auctores, Bernard d'Utrecht, Conrad d'Hirsau: Dialogus super auctores* (Leiden, 1970). Adalbero draws most heavily on Virgil, Prudentius, and Persius. Adalbéron de Laon, *Carmen ad Rotbertum regem*, ed. and trans. Claude Carozzi, *Poème au roi Robert*, Les classiques de l'histoire de France au Moyen Âge 32 (Paris, 1979), p. xl.

[131] Springer, "Sedulius," p. 6; Max Manitius, *Handschriften antiker Autoren in mittelalterlichen Bibliothekskatalogen* (Leipzig, 1935), pp. 268ff.

[132] The twelfth-century poet Sextus Amarcius shows the diminished prestige of the Christian poets: "Alcimus [Avitus], Arator, Sedulius and Juvencus place royal meals in badly turned pots, I admire them and dare not criticize" (Alchimus, Arator, Sedulius atque Juvencus / non bene tornatis appontunt regia vasis / Fercula: miror eos non audeo vituperare). *Sermones* 3.220–222, ed. Karl Manitius, MGH, Quellen zur Geistesgeschichte des Mittelalters 6, p. 136; discussed in Lapidge, "Versifying the Bible," p. 29.

[133] Dudo of Saint-Quentin quotes Classical and Christian authors, including Virgil, Prudentius, Sedulius, and Fortunatus. Many of his Classical reminiscences derive from intermediate sources, rather than from knowledge of the original. Shopkow takes this as evidence that he was not educated at Gerbert's cathedral school. Shopkow, "The Carolingian World of Dudo of Saint-Quentin," *JMH* 15 (1989): 23; Manitius, *Geschichte*, vol. 2, pp. 257–265.

Interpretive Methods at Cathedral and Monastic Schools

Although Johannes's sources did not reflect the new curriculum, his allusive mode of poetic composition embodied ways of reading and writing current in both monastic and cathedral schools. In order to see how Johannes used an interpretative method common to cathedral and cloister, I briefly examine how cathedral masters modeled methods of interpretation, which in turn informed how their students would read and write throughout their lives. Cathedral school teachers, like their ninth-century monastic forbears, explicated a text for students of different levels. Like Ermenric, the eleventh-century master Pernolf of Würzburg, according to his students' idealized picture, adapted his teaching according to their needs, creating a unified community among them.[134] Going through the text, the teacher would point out rhetorical devices and tropes and resolve difficult passages. Describing Gerbert teaching, Richer employs a similar vocabulary of explanation to Ermenric: *enodare, explanare, enucleare.*[135] Richer describes the master "running through dialectic in the order of the books, he made it clear with the lucid words of his thoughts."[136]

Like Carolingian monastic teachers, tenth- and eleventh-century cathedral masters taught students to glean the deeper meanings of the text.[137] Pernolf, according to his students, "lays open (*pandere*) the hidden things (*abdita*) of the poets."[138] The example of Wolfgang, who would become bishop of Regensburg (r. 972–994), suggests that similar methods of exegesis pertained at monastic and cathedral schools. Wolfgang was a student first at Reichenau, then at the cathedral of Würzburg. At his new school, learned (*edoctus*) Wolfgang explicated textual difficulties on Martianus Capella when the teacher could not.[139] He did not read on a carnal or superficial

---

[134] *Würzburg Poem*, lines 45–46, MGH Briefe d. dt. Kaiserzeit 3, p. 120: "He strengthens the wise, while chastising the foolish. We are all joined together by one will" (Firmat prudentes, dum corripit insipientes; Omnes communi voto sibi iungimur uno).

[135] Richer, *Historia*, 3, c. 46, p. 193.

[136] Ibid.: "dialecticam ergo ordine librorum percurrens, dilucidis sententiarum verbis enodavit."

[137] Guibert of Nogent, writing in the twelfth century, also describes his teacher having him read texts on four levels – literal, allegorical, moral, and anagogical (1.17), discussed by Vaughn, "Anselm of Bec," in *Teaching and Learning in Northern Europe*, p. 118.

[138] Line 21: "qui pandunt abdita vatum." *Würzburg Poem*, MGH Briefe d. dt. Kaiserzeit 3, p. 120. For a twelfth-century example, cf. Bernard of Chartres' teaching described by John of Salisbury, *Metalogicon* 1.24, ed. J.B. Hall, CCCM 98 (Turnhout, 1991), pp. 52–54.

[139] Otloh of Saint-Emmeram, *Vita Wolfkangi episcopi*, c. 5, ed. D. G. Waitz, MGH SS 4, p. 528: "iuvenes, ut soliti fuerunt, ad perspicacioris sensus virum Dei Wolfkangum venerunt, et ut numeri difficultatem explicaret, unanimiter postulaverunt. At ille, sicut

level, but was able to extract the hidden things (*penetralia*): "from that time ... he understood the innermost matters of the writings according to nothing of the flesh."[140] To Otloh, a monk of Regensburg writing in the 1030s, it was plausible that the training Wolfgang received at Reichenau (described as the leading scholarly center of the day) was also esteemed at the cathedral school. Thangmar, teacher at the cathedral school of Hildesheim, describes his student Bernward delving into hidden meanings in a similar way: "by a subtle contemplation, he was probing the inner matters (*interiora*) of divine wisdom with continual zeal."[141]

Reading Like a Bee

Teachers in both monastic and cathedral classrooms also continued to use and impart learning based on critical selection and memorization. We saw in Chapter 2 that Ermenric excerpted and digested his sources and then offered them in a form appropriate for the beginning or intermediate student. Students also learned to read in this manner, choosing the best parts of their sources, which they stored in their memory to reuse. The common metaphor for this kind of reading was the bee gathering nectar from flowers, storing it in the honeycomb, and producing honey, that is, the image Rainer uses to represent Johannes.[142]

The bee trope was used in monastery and cathedral settings, demonstrating that teachers and students continued thinking about reading and writing in the same terms. The popular medieval image, adapted from Classical sources and drawing on the notion of bees as virtuous and chaste, plays on

---

erat benignus et edoctus, non solum quod rogaverant, verum etiam omnem huius sententiae scrupulositatem aperiens insinuavit." See also Jaeger, *Envy*, p. 65.

[140] Otloh of Saint-Emmeram, *Vita Wolfkangi episcopi*, c. 5: "ex illo itaque tempore ... de nullo carnali demonstratore scripturarum apprehendit penetralia."

[141] Thangmar, *Vita Bernhardi*, c. 1: "subtili meditatione interiora divini sophismatis iugi studio rimabatur"; Cora E. Lutz, *Schoolmasters of the Tenth Century* (Hamden, CT, 1977), p. 119.

[142] G. Penco, "Il simbolismo animalesco nella letteratura monastica," *Studia Monastica* 6 (1964): 31–34. For a fuller discussion with earlier medieval examples, see my article "Just like a Mother Bee: Reading and Writing *Vitae Metricae* around the Year 1000," *Viator* 36 (2005): 119–148. Carruthers discusses the bee as an image for the relationship of memory to composition and creativity. Mary J. Carruthers, *The Book of Memory: A Study of Memory in Medieval Culture* (Cambridge, 1990), pp. 35–39. Also Thomas M. Greene, *The Light in Troy: Imitation and Discovery in Renaissance Poetry* (New Haven, 1982), pp. 73–74, 84, 98–99.

the double meaning of *legere*, to pick or to read.[143] The Christian *prudens apis* (wise bee) critically selects the best flowers from diverse fields and then carefully arranges them in the memory or "beehive of the heart."[144]

The image was used of the student, storing away the flowers of learning. For example, in his early-ninth-century epic *Vita Aeigili* (BHL 2441), Candid represents the young saint's education in these terms:

> And as a hungry bee when, in the first days of spring,
> Shining, flies through the grasses with balanced wings
> And struggles to pluck the flowers sprung from the field,
> Then flying higher on humming wings,
> Now with its mouth it picks (*legere*) the gray willow,
> Now the fiery plane-tree blooming with flowers.
> From here it buzzes about the honey-drenched lime-tree,
> With renewed vigor, to set it aside in its secret lair.
> No differently does this youth first ... graze on the poetry of books,
> Accomplished in age and with acute wisdom,
> He deserved to feed upon the draught of shaded nectar.[145]

This passage is a concatenation of Virgilian and Ovidian allusions, suggesting that Eigil was reading the Classics. Eigil, in his role of teacher (and then abbot), would have drawn on these stored sources. The bee image is also used to show the teacher or preacher imparting the best of his knowledge to his audience.[146]

[143] Mary Carruthers and Jan M. Ziolkowski, *The Medieval Craft of Memory: An Anthology of Texts and Pictures* (Philadelphia, 2002), p. 5. Horace (*Odes* 4.2.27–32) drew on a Greek poet-as-bee tradition to depict himself buzzing about the banks of the Tiber gathering nectar for his songs, and Seneca parlayed the image into advice on the selection and digestion of sources. Horace, *Odes* 4.2.27–32; Seneca, *Ep.* 84: 3–4, ed. L.D. Reynolds, *Epistulae morales ad Lucilium* (Oxford, 1965). For Classical Greek examples, see Ernest Leslie Highbarger, "The Pindaric Style of Horace," *TAPA* 66 (1935): 224–225.

[144] Athanasius describes Antony as *sophe melissa*. Athanase d'Alexandrie, *Vie d'Antoine*, ed. G.J.M. Bartelink, Sources Chrétiennes (Paris, 1994), 3.4. Robert A. Boehler brought this example to my attention. Athanasius's vita was known in the West in two Latin translations, one by Evagrius who intensified the adjective (*apis prudentissima*, PG 26, cols. 843–844, *Versio Evagrii*). Iohannes Cassian, *De institutis coenobiorum*, ed. Michael Petschenig, CSEL 17 (Prague, 1888), 5.4.

[145] Candid, *Vita Aeigili*, book 2 (BHL 2441), c. 2, lines 20–31 in MGH Poetae 2, p. 98: "Utque apis esuriens primo cum tempore veris / Enitens paribus volitat per gramina pennis, / Campigenosque sibi certat dercerpere flores, / Altius inde volans glaucas stridentibus alis / Nunc salices, nunc namque pyrum platanumque nitentem / Floribus ore legit, tiliam fervore recenti hinc / Mellifluam satagit caeco sub condere tecto: / Haud secus hic iuvenis librorum carmine primum / ... pascitur ... / Proficiens aetate simul sensuque sagaci / Pasci promeruit umbrati nectaris haustu."

[146] For example, Rainer, *Miracula Gisleni*, c. 9 (ca. 1000), ed. O. Holder-Egger in MGH SS 15/2, p. 583.

Writers continued using the bee trope to describe students learning in both monastic and cathedral school settings in the tenth, eleventh, and twelfth centuries. A cleric, ca. 990, asking to be taken into Archbishop Aethelgar's service, represented himself "like an obedient bee" (*veluti apis obediens*), who would bring the flowers he had gathered as a student at the cathedral school of Liège with him to the archbishop's beehive.[147] Several future bishops are depicted learning like bees in their youth. In each case, the image emphasizes the collection and subsequent dissemination of learning. Felix Manlius's prose *vita* of Gebhard (bishop of Constance 979–995) describes the boy's reading in typical terms: "as the wisest bee gathers honey from many kinds of flowers, thus through diverse pages of holy Scripture, he was storing up the sweet-sounding words of wisdom in the beehive of his heart, with which he would later sweeten the mouths of the people."[148] In a twelfth-century prose *vita*, the young Conrad (bishop of Constance, 934–975) is also depicted as an *apis prudentissima*.[149] Engaged in liberal studies, "he was piling these things up in his youth, so that having been imbued with these things, he would not lack them in old age."[150] Thangmar's prose life of Bernward, future bishop of

[147] Letter 21, ed. William Stubbs, *Memorials of St Dunstan, Archbishop of Canterbury* (London, 1874), p. 385: "if to some extent I shall have stored up anything in my soul from the sweet fragrant flower of salvific teaching, willingly, just like an obedient bee, I will carry it with my swift flight and store it in your paternal beehive" (si qua sanae doctrinae flore odorifluo dulci anima adgregavero libens in vestrum paternitatis alverarium, veluti apis obediens, praepeti volatu revehere et condere curabo).

[148] Felix Manlius, *Vita Gebhardi* (BHL 3292), book 1, c. 1 in AASS August, vol. 6, col. 116D. "ceu prudentissima apis per multigenos flores mella, ita ille per diversas sacrae Scripturae paginas in alveario cordis dulcisonas congerebat sententias, quibus postmodum populorum dulcificaret fauces." Similarly, Anno II, archbishop of Cologne (d. 1075) at his studies at the cathedral school of Bamberg is likened to the "apes prudentissima" storing up his learning in the "beehive of his heart" (*alveolo cordis*). *Vita Annonis archiepiscopi Coloniensis* (BHL 507), ed. R. Koepke in MGH SS 11, pp. 462–518, at p. 468. "Quicquid ad exercendum ingenium, quicquid ad nobili tandos mores competens et iocundum auribus vel oculis se offerebat, statim, ut apes prudentissima, ingeniose perlustrans, alveolo cordis intulit." There are two short metric lives of Saint Anno (BHL 510 and 511), ed. Aegidius Müller, *Anno II. der Heilige, Erzbischof von Köln und dreimaliger Reichsverweser von Deutschland 1056–1075. Sein Leben, sein Wirken und seine Zeit, nach den Quellen bearbeitet* (Leipzig, 1858), pp. 188–196 and 196–200.

[149] Adriaan Breukelaar "Konrad von Konstanz," in BBKL, vol. 4, cols. 416–417.

[150] *Vita altera Conradi episcopi Constantiensis* (BHL 1918), c. 3, ed. G. Pertz in MGH SS 4, p. 437: "Like the most prudent bee, he was producing honey from many kinds of flowers of wisdom. At another time he was using these things to soothe the throats of many by preaching" (Ut apis prudentissima ex multigenis sentenciarum floribus mella conficeret, quibus quandoque multorum fauces praedicando demulcet). Conrad's first school is not specified, but he was subsequently sent to Constance Cathedral.

Hildesheim (d. 1022), similarly uses the bee as a trope for the gathering and subsequent dissemination of learning. Eavesdropping on lessons,

after questions had been posed, he was winnowing any difficulties in his heart. In the manner of the wisest bee, sitting in a more distant place, by listening intently, he would seize each of the readings, which I was explicating in lessons on diverse books. Afterwards, sitting with the boys, he would teach these things he had acquired perfectly from his happy theft and he would impress on them his knowledge of these things.[151]

The image encapsulates not just a selective (and in this case furtive) gathering of *lectiones*, but also their subsequent teaching to others. The survival of the trope indicates the continuity of interpretative method and therefore a textual community; the cathedral schools also trained students to read and write like bees.

The bee is a dynamic image for gathering and producing wisdom. The result of learning "like a bee" in either the cathedral school or the monastery was that the student stored up the best sources (the *flores*), digested them, and produced the metaphorical honey, which could be, as in these examples, teaching or preaching. Another way that the "bee" drew on the stored flowers of learning was by writing. Poetry, because it was densely allusive, was suited to composition that simultaneously synthesized and displayed its sources. Both Milo and Rainer use the bee metaphor to describe the composition of an epic *vita*.[152] Because poetry remained central to the school curriculum, the student used it to demonstrate that he had, like a bee, read, selected, and synthesized the best parts of his education.

As was the case at the monastic schools, the apex of the cathedral school curriculum was verse composition.[153] Teachers continued to have their students practice writing verse and prose in imitation of what they had read.[154] In 1031, the students of Worms described a poem they had written

---

[151] Thangmar, *Vita Bernhardi* (BHL 1253), c. 1: "propositis quaestionibus scrupulosa quaeque ad medullam eventilabat. More prudentissimae apis singulas lectiones, quas in scolis in diversis libris exponebam remotiori loco sedens intento auditu captabat, quas tamen postea pueris considens felici furto perfecte docebat et illorum scientiae inprimebat." Ed. George Pertz, MGH SS 4, p. 758.

[152] Milo, *VA*, 1.280–281: "In the manner of the bee, plucking the flowers of Scripture from the seed, I leave out many things, passing over them in my zeal for brevity" (more apis excerpens scripturae germine flores, / Plurima praeteriens studio brevitatis omitto). Johannes borrows Milo's line 1.281.

[153] Jaeger, *Envy*, p. 140.

[154] John of Salisbury, *Metalogicon* 1.24 on Bernard of Chartres (ca. 1149), cited by Jaeger, *Envy*, pp. 129–130: "he would also explain the poets and orators who were to serve as models for the boys in their introductory exercises in imitating prose and poetry," and he had them "compose prose and poetry every day" (trans. Jaeger).

as a "classroom exercise" (*exercitium*).[155] The anonymous *De nuptiis Mercuriae et Philologiae* (based on Martianus Capella's work of the same name), written around 1080, shows verse composition (represented by the poet-priest Orpheus) as the pinnacle and culmination of the liberal education.[156] This opinion persisted into the twelfth century, with Ulrich of Bamberg proclaiming (around 1125), in verse: "I confess that no one will be perfect in my sight, who knows how to compose nothing worth hearing; what is more, I say, of a sign / or an argument, what is a surer proof (*documentum*) / of a rich mind ... than if / a speaker should pleasantly soothe the minds and ears?"[157]

POETRY, PATRONAGE, AND RIVALRY

In the world beyond the classroom, as the pinnacle of education, poetry remained an appropriate vehicle for expressing bonds of *amicitia* and for bestowing status on the recipient. Like their ninth-century predecessors, poets dedicated works, including epic *vitae*, to kings, bishops, dukes, and other important figures.[158] Dudo of Saint-Quentin shows how literature could be the currency of *amicitia*, offered to a patron in return for status, positions at court, and other rewards.[159] Dedicating his *De moribus* to another patron, Adalbero, bishop of Laon, Dudo described Richard I of Normandy inveigling him on the basis of their shared affection to write of "the customs and deeds of the Norman land." Drawing on Virgil and epic *vitae*, Dudo completed his assignment in an eclectic prosimetric form for

---

[155] Jaeger, *Envy*, pp. 66–67; *Ep.* 15 in MGH Briefe d. dt. Kaiserzeit 3, p. 32.

[156] Jaeger, *Envy*, p. 140.

[157] Ulrich of Bamberg, *Ars dictaminis*, lines 31ff., in "Eine Bamberger Ars Dictaminis," ed. Franz Bittner, *Bericht des historischen Vereins für die Pflege der Geschichte des ehemaligen Fürstbistums Bamberg* 100 (1964): 145–171, at p. 156, quoted in Jaeger, *Envy*, pp. 142, 418: "Fateor me iudice nemo ... / Nec perfectus erit, qui nil componere novit / Auditu dignum; quod maius dic rogo signum / Aut argumentum quod certius est documentum / Divitis ingenii ... quam si / Dictator mentes et grate mulceat aures?"

[158] Flodoard dedicated his massive poetic undertaking *De triumphis Christi* to the pope (printed in PL 135, 491A–886C). Wipo sent several kinds of poems to the Ottonian court. Warner dedicated his *Moriuht* to Robert, archbishop of Rouen, in Warner of Rouen, *Moriuht: A Norman Latin Poem from the Early Eleventh Century*, ed. Christopher McDonough (Toronto, 1997), p. 44. Hrotsvita dedicated her metric saints' *historiae* and *Gesta Ottonis* to Gerberga, her abbess at Gandersheim and niece of Otto 1. Ed. in MGH SRG 34, ed. Paul Winterfield, pp. 4, 77, 201. Other epic *vitae* dedicated to patrons include Richarius's *Vita Erluini* sent to Bishop Notker and Walter's *Passio Christophori* dedicated to his bishop (both discussed earlier).

[159] Leah Shopkow, "The Carolingian World of Dudo of Saint-Quentin," *JMH* 15 (1989): 19–37.

Richard II around 1015.[160] The Norman dukes' desire for the work seems surprising, given that they lacked the Latinity to appreciate the recondite, allusive, and metrically diverse work.[161] Rather, Richard commissioned it "to show he was cultivated enough himself to play the role of patron; he wanted his Normans to be commemorated in a form that would be a recognized sign of achievement inside or outside Normandy."[162] This work was intended not for the dukes' enjoyment, but as a "literary monument" for posterity in emulation of Carolingian royal practice.[163]

As the preeminent language of elite culture, poetry also remained a competitive endeavor capable of expressing rivalries. Around 1030, the students of Würzburg responded to the abusive verse of their counterparts at Worms, by sending a poem to the chancellor Bruno at the imperial court.[164] Bruno, who was from Worms (and who would later become the bishop of Würzburg), clearly had regional and imperial influence, and impressing him with their poetry may have been their best entry point into the learned court culture. According to the Würzburg poem, the Worms students' failure to write grammatically correct verse demonstrated their ignorance and rusticity.[165] As had been the case in the ninth century, poetry was a way of proving the culture of an individual and the caliber of the school.

Another earlier eleventh-century poem, Warner's *Moriuht*, likewise shows verse used as a vehicle for both *amicitia* and enmity. Moriuht, says Warner, failed to gain the bishop's patronage through poetry, because he wrote so terribly.[166] (In another example of failure, Moriuht

---

[160] Dudo, *Praefatio* to *De moribus et actis primorum Normannie ducum*, ed. Jules Lair (Caen, 1865), p. 119. For Adalberon's poem, see Adalbéron de Laon, *Carmen ad Rotbertum regem*, ed. and trans. Claude Carozzi in *Poème au roi Robert*, Les classiques de l'histoire de France au Moyen Âge 32 (Paris, 1979); Duby, *Three Orders*, pp. 44–46; G.-A. Hückel, "Les poèmes satiriques d'Adalbéron," in *Mélanges d'histoire du Moyen Âge*, ed. Achille Luchaire (Paris, 1901), pp. 139–167.

[161] Shopkow, "Dudo of Saint-Quentin," p. 31. Adémar of Chabonnes says Richard gave up his own language for Latin. Adémar, *Chronicon*, book 3, c. 27, ed. Jules Chavanon, *Chronique: publiée d'apres les manuscrits* (Paris, 1897), p. 148. Searle, however, sees the assimilation of the Norman dukes as a slow process. See E. Searle, "Fact and Pattern in Heroic History: Dudo of Saint-Quentin," *Viator* 15 (1984): 212.

[162] Shopkow, "Dudo of Saint-Quentin," p. 31.

[163] Ibid., p. 19.

[164] C. Stephen Jaeger, "Friendship and Conflict at the Early Cathedral Schools: The Dispute between Worms and Würzburg," *Medieval Germany: Associations and Delineations*, ed. Nancy Van Deusen, Claremont Cultural Studies (Ottawa, 2000), pp. 49–62.

[165] *Würzburg Poem*, lines 143–148, Jaeger, p. 69; cf. Haimin's comment to Milo, that he had given the epic *VA* to students after he had judged it theologically and metrically sound (MGH Poetae 3, p. 566).

[166] Warner, *Moriuht*, line 338, p. 94, and passim.

provided sexual rather than poetic service to his *domina*.)[167] Warner dedicated his work, which slandered Moriuht's character and poetry to demonstrate his own erudition, to Robert, whom he describes as "always brilliant
towards learned protégés," the archbishop of Rouen and brother to Duke
Richard II of Normandy.[168] Warner's invective could hardly be further
from epic *vitae* in subject, but like those poets, he demonstrated his
skill by drawing on *auctores* in sophisticated ways learned in the classroom,
and presupposed an audience who would appreciate his use of literary
tradition.[169]

From this discussion of the interpretation and composition perpetuated
in cathedral and monastic circles, we can see that Johannes, taught to read
and write like a bee, could draw on this shared tradition to frame his other
major resource, his abbey's patron saint Amand, mentor of his nominal
subject, Rictrude. As noted previously, saints, like poetry, retained their
power in the late tenth and eleventh centuries. When we turn from
Johannes's context to the text itself, we see how he combined the power of
the saints with the prestige of poetic form and his abbey's celebrated literary
heritage.

"THE FLOWERS OF PARADISE": JOHANNES AND HIS SOURCES

Johannes manipulated his sources, "the flowers of paradise" in Rainer's
metaphor, and wrote "like a bee" to show his erudition, to emphasize
Saint-Amand's prestige, and to strengthen his connections with the bishop
and with monks at Blandin. Thus, he sought to prove his place in wider
textual and spiritual communities while presenting a version of the saint's
life. An examination of Johannes's borrowings from earlier saints' *vitae*
and other works, such as Virgil's *Aeneid*, shows how the author of a verse
life could draw on his predecessors to create a poem that was simultaneously original and firmly grounded in the shared literary traditions.

---

[167] Ibid., lines 181–188.
[168] Ibid., line 1: "Rotberto doctis fulgenti semper alumnis."
[169] On Warner's sophisticated metareferential allusions, see McDonough, "Introduction" to
Moriuht, p. 11. Warner (line 433) employs a half-line of the *Aeneid* (6.164) in describing
the anecdote (from Donatus' *Life of Virgil*) of Virgil's extemporaneous completion of
unfinished verses. McDonough explains: "With this the poet not only mimicked Virgil's
happy ability to complete half-finished verses extemporaneously, but, in addition, by
skillfully constructing the couplet (433–434), he used Virgil's own words to laud his
unique status among Roman poets."

Johannes uses various sources. In addition to Scripture, especially the Psalms, he alludes to the familiar monastic educational texts: Virgil, Prudentius, Juvencus, and the *Disticha Catonis*. Johannes takes phrases, lines, and even whole passages from Milo's *Vita Amandi*. He draws, though less frequently, on the same poet's *De sobrietate*.[170] He also derives one incident from the anonymous prose *vita* of Rictrude's daughter Eusebia, but it is unclear whether he knew the epic version of Eusebia's life.[171] Johannes also seems familiar with the anonymous epic *Vita Lamberti*.[172]

On the surface, Johannes follows Hucbald's *Vita Rictrudis*, retaining its order of events and even its metaphors.[173] A closer reading, however, reveals that Johannes adapts Hucbald's material and supplements it with Milo's *Vita Amandi*.

Some of Johannes's alterations can be attributed to the demands of meter and the conventions of epic lives. For example, he employs epic diction, replacing Hucbald's prosaic *equus* and *serpentina* with the evocative Virgilian *sonipes* and *chelidrus*.[174] Similarly, he frames the narrative in wider theological terms, by locating it in the scheme of salvation history, and he includes more prayers and invocations to the saints.[175] Many of the verse *vita*'s transformations are based on classroom exercises, such as the composition of speeches for literary characters and the *amplificatio* and *abbreviatio* of source material.[176] Johannes introduces several new speeches into the narrative. For example, Hucbald reports in thirteen words that King Dagobert begged Amand to be his son's teacher in divine law.[177] Johannes expands the king's request into ten lines of direct speech.[178]

Johannes also amplifies and abbreviates Hucbald's narrative to suit his own purposes. For example, he augments the passage in which the bishops Audoenus (Dado) and Eligius persuade their friend Amand to return to Gaul and tutor Dagobert's son.[179] At other points, Johannes compresses

---

[170] Milo, *De sobrietate*, ed. in MGH Poetae 3, pp. 613–675.

[171] See Figure 12 in Chapter 5, for the relationship of these texts.

[172] BHL 4682, ed. in MGH Poetae 4/1, pp. 141–157.

[173] For example, compare the young Rictrude growing up among pagans to a rose among thorns. Hucbald, *VR*, c. 5; Johannes, *VR*, 1.142. On the image, see Rachel Fulton, "The Virgin in the Garden, or Why Flowers Make Better Prayers," *Spiritus* 4 (2004): 1.

[174] Hucbald, *VR*, c. 22, 25; Johannes, *VR*, 2.217, 2.378.

[175] On typical epic adaptions of prose, see Tilliette, "Modèles," pp. 394–395. Johannes, *Pref.* to *VR*, and 1.1–58; 1.270–288; 2.322–341.

[176] Dolbeau, "Domaine négligé," p. 137; Michael Roberts, *Biblical Epic and Rhetorical Paraphrase in Late Antiquity* (Liverpool, 1985), passim.

[177] Hucbald, *VR*, c. 8.

[178] Johannes, *VR*, 1.249–258.

[179] Ibid., 1.294–306.

the story, sometimes informing the reader that he is doing so. Omitting Hucbald's defense of Rictrude, Mauront, and Eusebia, Johannes states, "Passing over many things in my zeal for brevity, I return duly to the exceptional acts of that holy woman."[180] Johannes also bypasses Hucbald's lengthy appeals to scriptural authority.[181] We shall see that these omissions are significant.

By supplementing Hucbald's narrative with quotations from Milo's *Vita Amandi*, he pays homage to the two great teachers and writers of Saint-Amand and underlines his abbey's heritage.[182] The passage in which Dagobert begs Amand to teach his son provides an example.[183] Fourteen lines are repeated almost verbatim from Milo's account of the incident.[184] Yet into this citation of Milo, Johannes introduces one line that is characteristic of his own style, which he borrows from Hucbald's poetic compositions. Hucbald tends to string verbs together and Johannes takes this characteristic even further.[185] In one line, Dagobert begs Amand with seven verbs: "oro, precor supplexque rogo, expeto, postulo, posco."[186] Dagobert's speech, with its line of beseeching verbs, allows Johannes to emphasize the king's utter abjection before the saintly power.

Johannes's borrowing is heavy, but not mindless. As seen in the example of Dagobert's plea, Johannes marks the material with his own style. He also rejects one of Milo's distinctive flourishes, drawn from Fortunatus, the entirely alliterative line.[187] So, he changes Milo's "praecelsi proceres Petrus Paulusque priores" to "praecelsi proceres praeclara luce nitentes," using the ending of a different line from the *Vita Amandi*.[188] He also modifies a block quotation with additional historical narrative. In the

---

[180] Ibid., 2.465–466: "plurima preteriens studio brevitatis, ad actus / eximios sanctae mulieris rite recurro."

[181] Hucbald, *VR*, c. 9. When Rictrude marries, Hucbald has a lengthy passage of scriptural justification, which, as noted earlier, Johannes omits; Hucbald, *VR*, c. 28–30.

[182] For example, Johannes, *VR*, 1.294–305; Hucbald, *VR*, c. 8. Johannes takes lines 1.294–305 verbatim from Milo, *VA*, 3.302–314, omitting line 308.

[183] Johannes, *VR*, 1.249–266.

[184] *VA*, 3.264–280.

[185] For example, in recounting Adalbald's choice of Rictrude, Johannes adapts Hucbald's words ("videtur, diligitur, atque eligitur"; c. 9) to produce the even more tautologous "cernitur, eligitur, blanditur, diligiturque" (1.358).

[186] Johannes, *VR*, 1.252: "I beg, I pray and as a suppliant I ask, I seek, I request, I demand."

[187] Fortunatus, *Vita Martini* (BHL 5624), also includes some highly alliterative lines (e.g., 1.506, ed. F. Leo in MGH AA 4/1, p. 312). Milo's student Hucbald takes this tendency to a new level, a poem composed entirely of words beginning with the letter C. See Hucbald, *Ecloga de calvis* in MGH Poetae 4/1, pp. 267–271.

[188] Milo, *VA*, 1.51: "Peter and Paul, previous, preeminent princes"; Johannes, *VR*, 1.61: "Preeminent princes shining with a bright light." Milo, *VA*, 2.49.

passage preceding Dagobert's request, Johannes replicates twenty-three entire lines of Milo but inserts three of his own lines, repeating a point made by Hucbald, but not Milo, that Dagobert had been educated by a holy bishop, Arnulf.[189] Johannes here includes information relevant to his own interest in the relationships of bishops to kings.

Johannes manipulates his sources with ingenuity, as his transformation of Hucbald's Virgilian quotation shows.[190] In this scene, Rictrude, who had been at odds with the king over her refusal to remarry, has invited him to a banquet, ostensibly to celebrate their reconciliation. After the feasting, under the guise of proposing a toast, she asks him for leave to do as she wishes and, when the king agrees, she puts on a veil blessed by Amand, signifying her commitment to monastic life. In Hucbald's version, two lines of Virgilian verse (one from the *Aeneid*, the second closely adapted from the *Eclogues*) precede Rictrude's request to the king.[191] Johannes uses the same first line, but substitutes another line from the *Aeneid* for the second. Johannes's chosen line of verse, like that it replaces, refers to wine at a banquet, and the substitution does not alter the passage in a superficial reading.[192] Comparison with its Virgilian context, however, reveals it as a careful choice. Hucbald's line borrowed from the *Eclogues* features shepherds banqueting and offering libations to Bacchus. The line from the *Aeneid* Johannes substitutes features Queen Dido of Carthage in a situation analogous to Rictrude's. The queen, who like the saint has been widowed through the violence of her family and has sworn not to remarry, is feasting in her own home in the company of a prince (in this case, Aeneas). Dido, like Rictrude, stands for a toast. At this junction, their fates dramatically diverge. Dido immediately abandons her commitment to celibacy by beginning to fall in love with Aeneas. Rictrude, however, does not actually give a toast but affirms her commitment to a monastic life. Dido's choice leads to death; Rictrude's, to eternal life. Johannes "relies on context-specific meaning" in choosing his Virgilian quotations.[193] Given the central place of the *Aeneid*

---

[189] Johannes, *VR*, 1.223–228, 1.232–247; Milo, *VA*, 3.241–246, 3.247–262.

[190] Hucbald, *VR*, c.14; Johannes, *VR*, 2.69–70.

[191] Virgil, *Aeneid*, 8.184, *Eclogues* 5.69. The first line, used by both Hucbald and Johannes, reads "After hunger had been satisfied and love of eating curbed . . ." (Postquam exempta [Johannes substitutes the participle *victa* for *exempta*] fames et amor compressus edendi).

[192] Virgil, *Aeneid*, 1.724: "They set up great wine bowls and garland the wine" (Crateras magnas statuunt et vina coronant). For a similar substitution of Virgilian references in a saint's life, see David C. Van Meter, "St. Adelard and the Return of the *Saturnia regna*. A Note on the Transformation of a Hagiographical Tradition," *AB* 113 (1995): 297–316.

[193] Irvine employs this phrase to describe Bede's similar use of Virgilian quotation. Irvine, *Textual Culture*, p. 279.

in medieval education, Johannes's readers would have recognized this quotation and would have appreciated the artistry of Johannes's characterization of Rictrude as the anti-Dido. His transformation of Hucbald's citation shows how subtly a poet could rework his sources. His sophisticated borrowings demonstrate his participation in a tradition of verse and prose *vitae* and show his familiarity with the core curriculum text, the *Aeneid*.

"THE FLOWER AND THE GLORY": THE DEDICATION TO ERLUIN

Johannes composed an epic *vita* that would appeal to the aesthetic tastes and interpretive habits of educated clerics as well as monks and dedicated it to Erluin of Cambrai. He probably chose this bishop, not simply because Rictrude's abbey Marchiennes was in his diocese, but because of Erluin's place in imperial and ecclesiastical networks.[194] The diocese of Cambrai traversed Ottonian and Capetian realms, and the bishop was an imperial appointment, although it was a suffragan of the archdiocese of Rheims, in France. As noted earlier, Erluin was well connected, having been a chaplain at the imperial court and a protégé of Notker of Liège. Johannes's dedicatory acrostic flattered Erluin while further likening his *vita* to Milo's epic. Hucbald had dedicated Milo's *Vita Amandi*'s to Charles the Bald in dedicatory acrostics, and so Johannes, by imitating their form, implied that his patron was an equally deserving recipient. Johannes's dedication of the *vita* to Erluin may also have echoed a roughly contemporary dedication of an epic *vita* of Erluin, first abbot of Gembloux, to Bishop Notker.[195] Given that the protagonist of Richarius's epic *vita* was Erluin's relative and namesake, Johannes's dedication of an epic *vita* to Notker's protégé seems a flattering echo.

---

[194] On Erluin, see also Chapter 5.

[195] Sigebert of Gembloux, *Gesta abbatum Gemblacensis*, c. 1, MGH SS 8, p. 523. The monk Richarius must have sent his epic *Vita Erluini* to Notker before the latter's death in 1008. Was Johannes familiar with this *vita*? Given that only a small fragment remains, it is impossible to know if Johannes alluded to it.

Johannes also compliments Erluin by addressing him as "the people's flower and glory."[196] This usage recalls the familiar bee trope, invoking a tradition in which holy men (saints and bishops), rather than texts, are the *flores* on which the bees (here the devotees, the populace) feed. The trope derives from Athanasius's *Life of Anthony*, and Milo also uses it to characterize Amand as a "flower shining in winter, growing in summer."[197]

The holy-man-as-flower motif was current in Johannes's milieu. Rainer uses it to describe the saint in his prose *Vita Gisleni*.[198] Slightly later sources depict Erluin's contemporaries in this way. Hugh of Flavigny (who had been a novice at Saint-Vanne) alludes to it in his laudatory account of Richard of Saint-Vanne, written in the earlier twelfth century. He likens the abbess Adelberga to the "wisest bee" in seeking out the great men Richard and Odilo of Cluny.[199] The *Deeds of the Bishops of Liège* compare Erluin's patron Notker to a flower around whom the bees (people) swarm.[200] Although these works are later, they suggest that the imagery of the holy man as flower, a source of wisdom and a model of piety to whom the people swarmed, remained relevant. Through his dedication, Johannes placed Erluin in the company of effective and powerful religious men, both historical and contemporary.

MONASTIC RIVALRY: THE MOTHER BEE

Johannes also sought to strengthen his ties to two monks of a more powerful abbey, Blandin, which in the tenth century had become a prosperous and important center. Blandin's rise was recent, and, by emphasizing Amand as the founder of Marchiennes, Johannes reminds his recipients that his own abbey's patron had also established their house. In this way, Johannes asserts the primacy of Saint-Amand over Blandin. As noted previously, Johannes also celebrates the literary history of Saint-Amand by invoking Milo and Hucbald. Milo was particularly important at

---

[196] Johannes, *Ad Erluinum*, l. 5: "tu flos et gloria plebi."

[197] *VA*, 3.128: "Conspicuo flori hieme atque aestate virenti." Athanasius likens the young Antony to a wise bee seeking out good men from whom he can gather diverse virtues; ed. G.J.M. Bartelink, in Athanase d'Alexandrie, *Vie d'Antoine*, Sources Chrétiennes (Paris, 1994), 3.4. Cassian similarly says the monk in search of spiritual honey (*mella*) should be like a *prudens* bee, picking (*deflorare*) the exemplars of virtues from each person and storing them away in his heart (*De inst.* 5.4).

[198] Rainer describes people returning from the saint's oratory to their own abbeys like bees bearing nectar back to the hive (*Vita Gisleni*, c. 18).

[199] Hugh, *Chronicon*, book 2, c. 16, ed. G. Pertz in MGH SS 8, p. 391.

[200] Anselm, *Gesta Ep. Leod.*, c. 40.

Blandin because he provided the justification for the monks' claim that Amand had founded their house, giving them priority over their neighbors and rivals at Saint-Bavo.[201]

Rainer replied to Johannes's implicit claims of superiority in kind by demonstrating his own skill at learned and allusive composition. Once again, we see poetry and the response to it as a competitive endeavor. Rainer uses the familiar image of the bee, discussed earlier, as both a metaphor for Johannes's method of composition and as an example of his own work as a reader and writer. While Johannes writes an entire epic life and Rainer a short letter, the latter's dense allusion shows that he can also read and write *veluti mater apis*. By unpacking Rainer's reply, we see Rainer's participation in the interpretive community, an example of poetry as a token of literary rivalry:

In short, because, just like the mother bee, who has feasted on the flowers of paradise, you bring eternal life to those hungering, you bear the basket overflowing with the sweetness of honey and filled with the light of faith and honestly and brightly adorned with the teaching art, we gratefully receive this just as a heavenly treasure and we desire to entrust it to eternal memory throughout every age.[202]

The bee as a trope for reading and writing was a favorite of Rainer's.[203] Seneca's letter to Lucilius (*Ep.* 84), the *locus classicus* for the image, is not only Rainer's most obvious source in his letter to Johannes, but is also the key to his compositional method.[204] In this letter, Seneca discusses the proper use of sources. He advises his correspondent to synthesize the works he has read into his own original writing:

---

[201] Milo, *Suppletio* (BHL 339, a copy of which was at Blandin) refers to Amand's foundation at Ghent as "monasterium Blandinium" (i.e., Saint-Pierre au Mont-Blandin), supporting the monks' contention that their house, not their rival Saint-Bavo, was the original foundation at Ghent. Milo, *Suppletio*, ed. B. Krusch, MGH SRM 5, pp. 450–485 at p. 450. Christoph Maier, "Saints, Traditions and Monastic Identity: The Ghent Relics, 850–1100," *RBPH* 85 (2007): 237. A collection on Amand, Ghent CBR MS 224, includes the *Suppletio* on fols. 19r–26v.

[202] *Epistula Raineri* (printed with Johannes's *VR* in Silagi's ed.), MGH Poetae 5/3.595. My punctuation. "Denique quia aeternam vitam esurientibus, veluti mater apes paradysi depasta flores, offertis canistrum dulcedine mellis refertum ac lumine fidei plenum satisque honeste ac lucide arte magistra decoratum, gratanter illud suscipimus sicut caelestem thesaurum aeternaeque memoriae commendare desideramus per omne aevum."

[203] For example, Rainer, *Sermo Super Miracula Gisleni*, c. 6: "velut apes paradisi depasta flores alveraria fratrum revisens, totus mellifluus omnes hortabatur nec mortale sonans, ut gustaret quam suavis est Dominus."

[204] Many copies survive, including several from ninth- and tenth-century Francia. See L.D. Reynolds, *The Medieval Tradition of Seneca's Letters* (Oxford, 1965), p. 17.

As they say, we should imitate the bees, which wander around and pluck the flowers that are suitable for making honey, then arrange whatever they have gathered and distribute it through the honeycombs and, as our Virgil says, "pack in the flowing honey and stretch the cells with sweet nectar." ... Certain men believe that the sorts of things, which the bees plucked from the youngest of the flourishing and flowering plants, are transformed by preserving and arranging them, into this substance [honey] not without a certain, if I may say so, fermentation, by which the diverse materials are melded into one.[205]

Here, Seneca demonstrates the method as he discusses it, incorporating the literary flowers of his sources, Virgil and Pliny.[206] He continues with the organic imagery, likening writers incorporating the sources they have read to the body digesting its food. Seneca advises his reader to excerpt the best pieces of his sources and combine them into a new whole. In his short letter to Johannes, Rainer does exactly that, simultaneously employing the bee as an image and an example of this method of reading and writing. Like Seneca's letter, to which he alludes, Rainer simultaneously describes the bee trope and demonstrates its application by excerpting elements from his sources and distilling them into his own text. In this short letter, Rainer shows that he can excerpt far more broadly and succinctly than Johannes, by drawing in a range of Classical, biblical, and patristic allusions, and even alluding to his own work.[207] Like Johannes, Rainer relies on a reader's recognition of his allusion and his knowledge of the original context to create levels of meaning beneath the text's surface. Thus, his reference to Sedulius implicitly characterizes Johannes's epic in a less than flattering manner.[208]

---

[205] Seneca, *Ep.* 84, 3–4: "apes, ut aiunt, debemus imitari, quae vagantur et flores ad mel faciendum idoneos carpunt, deinde quicquid attulere, disponunt ac per favos digerunt et, ut Vergilius noster ait, 'liquentia mella / Stipant et dulci distendunt nectare cellas.' [Virgil, *Aeneid*, 1.432ff.] ... Quidam existimant conditura et dispositione in hanc qualitatem verti, quae ex tenerrimis virentium florentiumque decerpserint, non sine quodam, ut ita dicam, fermento, quo in unum diversa coalescunt."

[206] I have omitted this section from my excerpt of Seneca. Pliny the Elder, *Naturalis Historia*, ed. Karl Friedrich Theodor Mayhoff (Leipzig, 1906), 11.4–23, discusses bees and bee-keeping in some detail.

[207] These include "arte magistra" from Virgil, *Aeneid*, 8.442. For a full discussion of his allusions, see my article, "Just like a Mother Bee."

[208] Sedulius (drawing on Classical satire's culinary metaphor for literary genres) characterizes his own work as a humble meal in comparison to the overblown rhetoric of other writers (implicitly epic), which is likened to overly ornate dishes and honeycomb in golden baskets. In likening Johannes's work to a honey-filled basket (*canistrum dulcedine mellis refertum*), Rainer identifies it with the excessive grandiose epic criticized by Sedulius. Sedulius, *Opus paschale*, *pref.* in Sedulii *Opera Omnia*, ed. Iohannes Huemer, CSEL 10 (Vienna, 1885), pp. 175–176: "even in these dishes, overly adorned with a precious variety of gems, their honey grows golden with sweet wax [*cerea* can also mean wax-covered writing tablet], and the honeycomb placed in the golden basket shines with the

One aspect of Rainer's expression is unusual: although the bee trope has a long pagan and Christian tradition, few sources refer to the *mother* bee.[209] Writers used maternal imagery to characterize churchmen nurturing and protecting their flocks,[210] but the maternal and bee images are combined infrequently.[211] The term *mother bee* does not gender Johannes feminine, but equates him with the liturgical bee that provides the sacrifice

metal's color" (in ipsis etiam ferculis pretiosa nimis varietate gemmatis flavescunt nectareis sua mella cum ceris, et aureis adpositus in canistris colore metallo favus adludit).

[209] The term *apis mater* is also used by Rupert of Deutz (ca. 1070–1129/1130) in his *Liber de diuinis officiis*, in a passage that relies heavily on the blessing of the paschal candle. Baldric, in his *vita* of Robert Arbrissel (BHL 7259), applies the term *mater apis* to Robert, whom he usually describes as a *magister* (*Vita* 3, AASS Feb. 3, p. 612). *De vocalibus animalium*, a text contained in the thirteenth-century codex, Admont Stiftsbibliothek MS 759, also uses the term.

[210] Caroline Walker Bynum, *Jesus as Mother: Studies in the Spirituality of the High Middle Ages* (Berkeley, 1982), pp. 110–169; Anselm describes himself like a mother hen in his concern for the monks at his former abbey of Bec. He writes to the new abbot that even though he is absent from his "nest" (*nidum*), he carries it in his heart with all his "chicks" (*pulli*). Anselm, *Ep.* 205, in Anselm, *Opera Omnia*, ed. Franciscus Salesius Schmitt, v. 4 (Edinburgh, 1956), p. 98. Discussed by Sally N. Vaughn, "Anselm of Bec: The Pattern of his Teaching," in *Teaching and Learning in Northern Europe*, ed. Sally N. Vaughn and Jay Rubenstein (Turnhout, 2006), p. 100. In addition, the Church (*mater ecclesia*), the philosophy, a city, or a monastery could be characterized as the nurturing mother. Goswin's letter (ca. 1065) to his former student Walcher, now also a teacher, likens the city of Liège (*mater Legia*) to a mother hen "just like a mother hen gathers her chicks, thus she (Liège) warms her sons under her wings, nourishes, instructs, and teaches them" (sicut gallina pullos suos, ita haec filios suos sub alas colligit fovet et nutrit et … informat et instruit). Discussed by Jaeger, *Envy*, p. 222. *Apologiae Duae: Gozechini epistola ad Walcherum; Burchardi, ut videtur, Abbatis Bellevallis Apologia de barbis*, ed. R.B.C. Huygens, CCCM 62 (Turnholt, 1985), pp. 11–43, at p. 14, c. 6, 14.98–100. Cicero uses the term *mater artium* for philosophy (Cicero, *Tusculan Disputations*, 1.26.64), which Ruotger borrows for his *Vita Brunonis*, c. 20, ed. G. Pertz in MGH SS 4, p. 261. In Purchard's metric *Gesta Witigowo*, written at Reichenau in the eleventh century, the monastery, *Augia*, is personified female and addressed as *mater* by the poet whom she calls *filius* (MGH Poetae 5/1–2, pp. 260–279).

[211] The prudent bee is juxtaposed with maternal activity in the prose *vita* of the Merovingian bishop Betharius of Chartres, which describes his activities in these terms: "he began to flourish in holy zeal and just like the most prudent bee, he was constantly governing and nourishing his subject people with his maternal womb" (Coepit namque florere in studiis sanctissimis et quasi prudentissima apis populum sibi subiectum quasi ex maternali utero gubernare ac pascere non cessabat). *Vita Betharii episcopi Carnoteni* (BHL 1318), ed. Dümmeler in MGH SRM 3, c. 6, p. 616. Walafrid's teacher Wettin (d. 824) uses the term "mother bee" to describe people who had been converted by the "honeyed words" (*melliflua verba*) Saint Gall had poured into their hearts. Wettin, *Vita Galli* (BHL 3246), c. 6, ed. Bruno Krusch, in MGH SRM 4, p. 260. "And there, that outstanding athlete of Christ remained for three years, with his dependents and disciples, who, in the manner of the smallest mother bee were cultivating their minds (*ingenium*) in different arts" (Ibique egregius athleta Christi cum clientibus sibi alumnis mansit triennio. Qui in morem parvissimae matris apis ingenium exercebant in artibus diversis).

of wax for the paschal candle. Although the term *mater apis* occurs in a few other sources, Rainer and Johannes would have been most familiar with it from the blessing of the Easter candle in the Gregorian sacramentary. This passage celebrates the virtues of bees:

> Holy Father, receive the evening sacrifice of this incense, which for you, in the solemn offering of wax through the hands of your ministers, from the works of the bees, the holy Church returns.... It is nourished by the flowing wax, which the mother bee brought forth as the substance of this precious light. The bee precedes other animals, which are subject to man. Although she is very small in her little body, she turns a great mind in her narrow chest. She is weak in strength but strong in character.[212]

After describing the bees' industrious activities, including picking flowers (*legere flosculos*) and carrying them home, the benediction continues:

> and here [at their home] some, with remarkable skill, build little cells with sticky gum, others compress the flowing honey, some turn flowers into wax, others form the offspring in their mouth [a reference to bees' supposedly parthenogenic reproduction], some store up the nectar collected from plants. O truly blessed and marvelous bee, whose sex males do not violate, whose chastity offspring do not shake nor children tear apart! Just like the holy virgin Mary, conceived as a virgin, she gave birth and remained a virgin.[213]

In this blessing, the bees are, as usual, industrious, well organized, and virginal. Only beeswax is appropriate for the paschal candle because, as the blessing makes clear, the wax, like Jesus, is produced by a virgin mother, the *mater apis*.[214] The bee's product – here, the candle – likewise produces

[212] *Gregorian Sacramentary*, 1022b, *The Blessing of the Easter Candle* in *Le sacramentaire grégorien: Ses principales formes d'après les plus anciens manuscrits*, vol. 1, ed. Jean Deshusses (Fribourg, 1971), pp. 361–362: "suscipe, sancte pater, incensi huius sacrificium vespertinum, quod tibi in hac caerei oblatione sollemni per ministrorum manus de operibus apum, sacrosancta reddit ecclesia. ... Alitur liquentibus ceris quam in substantiam praetiosae huius lampadis apis mater eduxit. Apis ceteris quae subiecta sunt homini animantibus antecellit. Cum sit minima corporis parvitate, ingentes animos angusto versat in pectore. Viribus inbecillis, sed fortis ingenio."

[213] *Gregorian Sacramentary*, 1022b: "ibique aliae inaestimabili arte, cellulas tenaci glutino instruunt, aliae liquentia mella stipant, aliae vertunt flores in caeram, aliae ore natos fingunt, aliae collectis e foliis nectar includunt. O uere beata et mirabilis apis, cuius nec sexum masculi violant, foetus non quassant, nec filii distruunt castitatem. Sicut sancta concepit virgo Maria, virgo peperit, et virgo permansit."

[214] D. Germain Morin, "Pour l'authenticité de la letter de S. Jerôme à Présidius," *Bulletin d'ancienne littérature* 3 (1913): 58. For an early association of the imitation of the bee with the candle, see the letter to Praesidius attributed to Jerome and cited by Morin: "Learn this from the waxen song: embellish that light for yourself from diverse flowers. And you yourself be a bee" (Id de cerei carmine disce: illud tibi de variis floribus lumen exorna. Esto et ipse apes).

light. If Johannes is also a *mater apis*, then the illuminating product of his labor is not a candle but an epic *vita*.

Rainer's use of the term from the sacramentary shows how thoroughly the monks imbibed the language of liturgy and stored it away in their memories. This blessing of the paschal candle in turn reflects how the authors of liturgy had gathered the flowers of their Classical education.[215] The expression "she turns a great mind in her narrow chest" is from Virgil's *Georgics*, and Virgil writes "aliae liquantia mella stipant" in the *Aeneid*.[216] The latter is one of the lines cited by Priscian and, as seen earlier, it is quoted by Seneca in his advice on composition.[217] So, Rainer combines two images of the bee (the bee as a writer and the mother bee) drawn from two sources, one Classical and one Christian, that quote exactly the same line of Virgil. This blessing made on the night "on which heavenly things are joined to earthly" shows how thorough was his synthesis of Christian and Classical in monastic culture.[218]

The bee is more than just a way of talking about reading and writing. As an image with a complex history, it is itself a way of alluding to a literary tradition. By deploying the metaphor of the bee, the readers and writers invoke a chain of references, stretching back to Scripture, the Classical Latin *auctores*, the church fathers, and earlier hagiographers. At its most sophisticated, the bee metaphor operates like the complex, multilayered allusions of Classical Latin verse, demonstrating the writer's familiarity with a whole series of previous authors.[219] So, by characterizing Johannes as a bee and by alluding to numerous sources, Rainer demonstrates his *own* erudition. Rainer shows that he too reads and writes like a bee. The allusive bee is a meta-referential image, one that simultaneously talks about *and* demonstrates how a writer draws on his reading.

Like the mother bee as a figure for the incarnation in the blessing of the paschal candle, the bee is a small image that illuminates something of much larger significance. It is a metaphor for methods of reading, learning, and

---

[215] I am indebted to Alison Frazier for this point.

[216] Virgil, *Georgics*, 4.83: "ingentes animos angusto versat in pectore"; and 4.163–64: "aliae purissima mella / stipant et liquido distendunt nectare cellas"; *Aeneid*, 1.432–433: "aut cum liquentia mella / stipant et dulci distendunt nectare cellas."

[217] Rust, "Art of Beekeeping," p. 366; Priscian, *Institutiones*, 479.11–12.

[218] Gregorian Sacramentary 1022b: "in qua terrenis caelestia iunguntur."

[219] For discussions of allusion in Classical Latin writing, see Richard F. Thomas, *Reading Virgil and his Texts: Studies in Intertextuality* (Ann Arbor, 1999); and Stephen Hinds, *Allusion and Intertext: Dynamics of Appropriation in Roman Poetry* (New York, 1998). Irvine discusses Statius's composition of silver Latin epic in similar terms. See Irvine, *Textual Culture*, pp. 83–84.

composition that drew selectively on the best sources and used them to create a new work. The bee trope underlines a fundamental continuity in engaging with and responding to the past, both as a source of *auctoritas* and a tradition to be emulated. In his monograph on Renaissance poetry, Greene takes Petrarch's use of the bee metaphor as an image for the era's poetic originality, its competitive *aemulatio* of tradition, as opposed to the stale *imitatio* of medieval composition.[220] Rainer's subtle and complicated use of the same image, however, undermines this view of medieval imitation. He illuminates how writers used and emulated their literary predecessors exhibiting a kind of creativity that can be masked for us by their heavy (often verbatim) reliance on their sources.

The *Vita Rictrudis* was a consciously nostalgic work, hearkening to a glorious Carolingian past. Nonetheless, its highly allusive form of composition and the genre of the epic life were still relevant at the turn of the millennium, illustrating the strong continuity between the monastic and cathedral school cultures. Epic *vitae*, written and read by both regular and secular clergy, remained a vital part of the intellectual tradition. Although his abbey had been marginalized by political and cultural transformations, Johannes could draw on the textual culture that he shared with his contemporaries and writers from his house's past to compose a new work glorifying both Saint-Amand and its patron. Sent to the bishop and to other monks, the epic *Vita Rictrudis* demonstrates the persistence of a textual community, despite cultural and political upheavals, and the continued efficacy of combining saintly and poetic capital into an epic *vita*. The composition, dedication, and reception of the epic *Vita Rictrudis* shows that the exchange of poetry continued to be a means of creating and expressing ties. As was the case with earlier epic lives, Johannes's *Vita Rictrudis* was an attempt to create bonds of patronage beyond the cloister by impressing readers with the poet's erudition, his abbey's culture, and the saint's *virtus*. The reader Rainer replied with a competitive response, showing that rivalry as much as *amicitia* continued to inform the production and reception of epic lives.

Poetry continued to be the preeminent language of elite *amicitia* and also a competitive arena. The epic *vita* reflects the persistence of ways of reading and writing that coexisted with the much-vaunted tenth-century transformations in education and literate modes. Johannes's work, like

---

[220] Greene, *Light in Troy*, pp. 98–99. Petrarch, *Familiares*, I.8 and 23.19, in Francesco Petrarca, *Le familiari*, ed. Vittorio Rossi (Florence, 1997), pp. 40–42, 202–203.

other epic *vitae*, provides new perspectives on its historical context. Some sources for the millennium reveal radical transformation in the uses of literacy, including the innovations of the cathedral schools.[221] The epic *vita*, by contrast, emphasizes connections with the Carolingian past and the commonalities between monastic and cathedral education and culture.

---

[221] Jaeger, *Envy*; M.T. Clanchy, *From Memory to Written Record: England 1066–1307* (Cambridge, MA, 1979); Stock, *Implications*; Glenn, *Politics and History*, p. 10, n. 43. On the narrative of decline, McKitterick, *Frankish Kingdoms*, p. 278.

5

Mothers and Daughters: Affiliation and Conflict in the Lives of Rictrude and Eusebia

Rictrude, abbess of Marchiennes, and her twelve-year-old daughter Eusebia were embroiled in a fierce conflict. Eusebia had succeeded her paternal great-grandmother Gertrude as abbess of Hamage. Rictrude, fearing that the young girl would be corrupted, had forced her and the other nuns to leave Hamage for Marchiennes. Undeterred by her mother's repeated injunctions, Eusebia would creep out at night to perform the office at the abandoned abbey. Therefore, Rictrude ordered her son Mauront to beat the girl, who was grievously injured: "blood flowed from her mouth, very often mixed with spit, and she is said to have endured these torments until the end of her life."[1]

This, at least, is the story according to *vitae* written around the tenth and early eleventh centuries for Marchiennes and Hamage. Like Marchiennes, the neighboring abbey of Hamage produced or commissioned *vitae* in prose and epic verse of its patron saint. The *vitae* of Rictrude and Eusebia depict a familial conflict played out between mother and daughter saints. Although the *vitae* tell the story of the houses through their female founding figures, and Marchiennes still housed both male and female residents when these works were composed, the gender of the saints does not clearly map onto that of the readers or recipients. Rather, the familial relationship of mother and daughter is symbolic of the relations between the two houses whose association supposedly stretched back to their seventh-century origins. In the fraught and violent years of the tenth

---

[1] VE (metric), fol. 55r: "cruor emanabat ab ore / Eius persaepe sputo permixtum et usque / Extremum vitae haec fertur tormenta tulisse."

and early eleventh centuries, the relationship between Marchiennes and Hamage was characterized by conflict.

Like other rivals with affiliated patron saints, Marchiennes and Hamage engaged in competitive hagiography. Hamage transformed the story of Rictrude to exalt its own patron in prose and then epic form. Johannes's allusive, recondite verse life of Marchiennes's patron Rictrude, discussed in the previous chapter, was matched by the epic *Vita Eusebiae*, which was also ornamented with classicizing details and miracles. The epic *vita* combined the *virtus* and compelling narrative of the fiercely independent Eusebia with the prestige of poetry. For a small embattled house to produce or commission an epic life of its patron saint as Hamage did is itself an act of defiance akin to Eusebia's rebellion against her mother. Offered to an educated patron such as the bishop and used within a community, the epic *Vita Eusebiae* would have provided a prestigious narrative of origin and, because divine intervention assured Eusebia's ultimate victory, a justification for Hamage's autonomy from Marchiennes.

We again see an epic *vita* employed in monastic rivalry, but in this case, I argue, an abbey's very survival was at stake. Understood in its context, the epic *Vita Eusebiae* represents a lost voice from Hamage, the attempt of the small house to maintain autonomy from its larger neighbor during the monastic reforms of the earlier eleventh century. Because the prose and epic *vitae* of Eusebia represent the perspective of independent Hamage, their inclusion in a manuscript of Marchiennes is puzzling. Their transmission illustrates the polyvocal nature of a manuscript, whose compiler sought to subordinate Rictrude's unruly daughter. The manuscript represents Marchiennes's reappropriation from Hamage of their shared past.

Summarizing the work of recent decades on history and memory, McKitterick states that "it has become a commonplace that ideas about the past could define societies and that the present plays a crucial role in molding understanding of the past."[2] Medieval historians have explored this relationship of (reimagined) past and present by examining how narratives about saints reflect and seek to shape local political agendas, by providing role models for correct behavior, by establishing precedents for contemporary relations, and by warning of incurring the saint's wrath. These studies rarely consider epic *vitae*, which scholars often dismiss as redactions.[3] Karine Ugé, in her discussion of the legends of Saint Rictrude and her family, devotes only one paragraph to the epic *vita* of Rictrude and

---

[2] McKitterick, *History and Memory*, p. 1.
[3] Tilliette, "Poésie metrique," pp. 381–82.

even less to that of her daughter Eusebia: "as far as the transformations of Rictrude's legend are concerned, the *VR metrica* is of little interest because [the author] John faithfully stuck to his model."[4] The paucity of editions reflects this lack of interest; the epic *Vita Eusebiae* has never been edited or even fully published.

Epic lives were not interchangeable with other works employed in local competitions for power and resources. Though they told similar narratives to their prose counterparts (and were commonly transmitted with them), they often made important additions, omissions, and alterations. Even small changes could transform a work's emphasis.[5] Further, even in rare cases when the narratives were virtually identical, their functions were not. The use of verse – difficult, time-consuming, and intended for a specific audience – required a calculated investment of resources.

Epic *vitae* offer new perspectives for historians interested in iterations of institutional history. In this case, an epic *vita* gives evidence for a voice that often goes unheard – that of those threatened and cast out – as opposed to the triumphalist narratives of the reformers, which make up most of the surviving evidence. Further, challenging common assumptions about medieval culture, we again see that poems intended for elite audiences emphasize the miraculous more than the prose lives.

To understand the epic *Vita Eusebiae*, we must consider its historical context and piece together the sparse evidence for Hamage and its relations with Marchiennes. Turning to the texts, the four lives of the Rictrude-Eusebia cycle (Rictrude's prose and verse lives by Hucbald and Johannes, and the anonymous prose and epic lives of Eusebia), we see how contrasting depictions of the saints represented the abbeys' conflict.[6]

A further context, the codicological, provides evidence for the transformations of the tradition. The earliest copy of the texts of the Rictrude-Eusebia cycle reveals how prose and epic *vitae* could be incorporated into a manuscript context that changed their meanings without necessarily altering

---

[4] Ugé, *Monastic Past*, pp. 127, 129. In her article, Ugé mentions Johannes's *VR* in passing and the prose *VE* twice (pp. 294, 296), but does not even note the existence of the epic *VE*. Karine Ugé, "The Legend of Saint Rictrude: Formation and Transformations (Tenth–Twelfth Century)," *Anglo-Norman Studies* 23 (2000): 281–297. Although she mentions both epic *vitae* in the book, she does not note certain divergences from the prose tradition relevant to her argument, such as Adalbald's cephalophory in the epic *VE*.

[5] McKitterick, *History and Memory*, p. 9.

[6] McKitterick notes (ibid., p. 58) that we must consider the groupings of texts, which informed their meanings for readers. Accordingly, I do not read the epic *VE* in isolation, but also consider the prose *VE*, with which it was transmitted and both lives of Rictrude, which are part of its literary and historical context.

their text. Finally, the evolving traditions of Eusebia show how the saint changed after Hamage was thoroughly incorporated into Marchiennes.

CRISIS AND REFORM

The prose and epic *vitae* of Eusebia were written during a time of upheaval in Flanders in the late tenth and early eleventh centuries. The monasteries on the Scarpe River were on the border between Capetian and Ottonian realms and were subject to the counts of Flanders and the French crown. As discussed in the previous chapter, it was a time of diminished patronage. Additionally, the reform movement supported by Count Baldwin IV threatened monasteries not only with unwanted regulation, but with extinction in the case of moral or financial insolvency. In 1012, Bishop Erluin of Cambrai died and was succeeded by Gerard I (d. 1051), who battled heretics, the ever-troublesome castellans of Cambrai, and his fellow bishops. He also aggrandized his see, through church building and the use of relics and by commissioning the *Gesta* of the bishops of Cambrai with its supporting evidence.[7] Like Erluin, Gerard had been educated at a cathedral school, and they moved in similar circles.[8]

If the situation was challenging for Saint-Amand, it was worse for more marginal abbeys like Hamage. The previous chapter considered Johannes's *Vita Rictrudis* in the context of the *amicitia* and competition among highly educated men; this chapter examines a near-contemporary epic *vita* in a much more humble setting. To understand why the clerics of Hamage used recondite epic poetry to promote Eusebia at the expense of her mother, we need first to consider the abbey's history.

[7] On Gerard, see Theodor Schieffer, "Ein deutscher Bischof des 11. Jahrhunderts: Gerhard I. von Cambrai (1012–1051)," *Deutsches Archiv für Geschichte des Mittelalters* 1 (1937): 323–360; Heinrich Sproemberg, "Gerhard I. Bischof von Cambrai," in *Mittelalter und demokratische Geschichtsschreibung* (Berlin, 1971), pp. 103–18; Georges Duby, *The Three Orders: Feudal Society Imagined*, trans. Arthur Goldhammer (Chicago, 1980); Georges Duby, "Gérard de Cambrai, la paix et trois fonctions sociales, 1024," *Compte rendus des séances de l'Académie des inscriptions et belles lettres* (Paris, 1976), pp. 136–146; Theo Riches, "Bishop Gerard I of Cambrai-Arras, the Three Orders, and the Problem of Human Weakness," in *The Bishop Reformed: Studies of Episcopal Power and Culture in the Central Middle Ages*, ed. John S. Ott and Anna Trumbore Jones, Church, Faith and Culture in the Medieval West (Aldershot, 2007), pp. 122–136; Robert M. Stein, *Reality Fictions: Romance, History, and Governmental Authority, 1025–1180* (Notre Dame, 2006), chapter 1.

[8] *Gesta Ep. Cam.* 3.1. Erluin had studied with Notker at Liège, and Gerard was taught by one of Notker's fellow students, Adalbero (archbishop of Rheims 969–989). On the school at Rheims, see Jaeger, *Envy*, pp. 56–62. Other bishops educated at Rheims included Lietry of Sens, Gerard of Crépy-en-Valois, and Fulbert of Chartres. See Joel T. Rosenthal, "The Education of the Early Capetians," *Traditio* 25 (1969): 371.

HAMAGE: FORGOTTEN HISTORY

Sources

There are no comprehensive secondary works on Hamage or detailed accounts of how it came to be absorbed into Marchiennes.[9] The most sustained investigation is Étienne Louis's series of excavation reports.[10] The scholarly neglect reflects the state of the primary evidence, which is sparse and contains only scattered mentions of the abbey. Little survives from or about the eighth, ninth, and tenth centuries. Hucbald of Saint-Amand claims that he reconstructed his information (for the *Vita Rictrudis*, written in 907) from oral testimony about a lost text, and the information on Hamage in the other three lives of the cycle is based largely on his evidence. We can nonetheless glean hints from a variety of sources, including charters from Marchiennes and the eleventh-century *Deeds of the Bishops of*

---

[9] It receives brief notices in the *Dictionnaire d'histoire et de géographie ecclésiastiques* and the *Gallia Christiana* and in works on monasticism in northern Gaul or Marchiennes. Henri Platelle, "Hamage," in R. Aubert, ed., *DHGE*, vol. 23 (Paris, 1990), pp. 199–200; *Gallia Christiana*, vol. 3 (Paris, 1739–1880), p. 370; Léon Spriet, *Marchiennes, son abbaye, son histoire* (Paris, 1993 [1898]), p. 4; Michèle Gaillard, "Les origines du monachisme féminin dans le nord et l'est de la Gaule (fin VIe siècle–début VIIIe siècle)," in *Les religieuses dans le cloître et dans le monde des origines à nos jours*, Actes du deuxième colloque international du CERCOR, Poitiers, 29 septembre–2 octobre 1988 (Saint Etienne, 1994), p. 54; B. Delmaire, *Le diocèse d'Arras de 1093 au milieu du XIVe siècle*, vol. 1 (Arras, 1994), pp. 197–198; M. Alex Faidherbe, *Notice historique et critique sur l'abbaye de Marchiennes de 630 à 1024* (Lille, 1856), pp. 38–44; Jean-Pierre Gerzaguet, *Marchiennes une abbaye, un village au Moyen Âge* (Marchiennes, n.d.), p. 5; J. Nazet, "Crises et réformes dans les abbayes hainuyères du ixe au début du xiie siècle," in *Recueil d'études d'histoire Hainuyèreo offertes à Maurice-A. Arnould*, ed. J.-M. Duvosquel (Mons, 1983), pp. 476–478. Ugé briefly discusses Hamage in *Monastic Past*, pp. 98ff.

[10] Louis has been excavating the site since 1991. Étienne Louis, "Aux débuts du monachisme en Gaule du Nord: les fouilles de l'abbaye mérovingienne et carolingienne de Hamage (Nord)," in *Clovis histoire et mémoire: Le baptême de Clovis, son echo à travers l'histoire*, vol. 2, ed. Michel Rouche (Paris, 1997), pp. 843–868; "Sorores ac fratres in Hamatico degentes. Naissance, évolution et disparition d'une abbaye du haut Moyen Age: Hamage (France, Nord)," *Journée d'étude: une abbaye et ses domaines au Haut Moyen Age* (Logne, 26 septembre, 1998), *De la Meuse à l'Ardenne* 28 (1999): 15–47; "Fouilles de l'abbaye mérovingienne puis carolingienne de Hamage," *Handelingen de Maatschappij voor Geschiedenis en Oudheikunde te Gent* (Ghent, 1996), pp. 45–69; "Archéologie des bâtiments monastiques, viie – ixe s. Le cas de Hamage (France dép. du Nord)," in *Papers of the "Medieval Europe Brugge 1997" Conference, Religion and Belief in Medieval Europe*, vol. 4, ed. G. De Boe, F. Verhaeghe (Zellick, 1997), pp. 55–63; "Hamage (Nord) – espaces de bâtiments claustraux d'un monastère mérovingien et carolingien," in *Actes du colloque de Liessies – Maubeuge "practique et sacré dans les espaces monastiques au Moyen Âge et à la époque moderne,"* ed. P. Racinet, Histoire médiévale et Archéologie, 8 (Amiens, 1998), pp. 73–97; *Archéologie en Nord-Pas-de-Calais* (Villeneuve d'Ascq, 2002).

Cambrai. Most of the texts (including the *Poleticum* of Marchiennes, the *Chronicle of Marchiennes,* four *Miracula* of Rictrude, and two *Miracula* of Eusebia) were produced in the twelfth century at Marchiennes, after that house had annexed Hamage.[11] (See Figure 7 for the relationship of these texts.) Several charters mentioning Hamage are preserved at the Archives départmentales du Nord at Lille, either as originals or as copies in cartularies from Marchiennes, which date to the twelfth century or later.[12] At least one of the charters may be a forgery, and those in the cartularies may have been created or altered to serve Marchiennes's interests.

The second book of the *Deeds of the Bishops of Cambrai,* written from 1024, is the earliest narrative source after the saints' prose and verse lives. It contains a short chapter on Hamage and a slightly longer one on Marchiennes. The remaining narrative sources are from the twelfth century. The *Poleticum,* composed ca. 1120 by a monk at Marchiennes, is a short history of Marchiennes and Hamage, followed by a discussion of Marchiennes's holdings. The *Poleticum,* like the cartularies, was produced with the express purpose of defending the abbey's possessions, including Hamage.[13] It provides the most sustained account, but gives little information.[14] The writer, acknowledging a lack of evidence, draws on Hucbald's *Vita Rictrudis,* both lives of Eusebia, the *Deeds of the Bishops of Cambrai,* and oral tradition.[15] The other twelfth-century sources – the two saints' *Miracula* and the *Chronicle* by the monk Andre of Marchiennes (written 1199–1201) – rely almost entirely on the earlier works and add little about Hamage, although they are excellent evidence for the rewriting of its history.[16]

---

[11] Poncelet, "Catalogus," pp. 382, 394–398, 405. The manuscripts from Marchiennes are Douai, BM, MSS 840, 846, and 850.

[12] M. Le Glay, *Mémoire sur les archives de l'abbaye de Marchiennes* (Douai, 1854), p. 13; A. de Loisnes, "Les miniatures du cartulaire de Marchiennes," *Bulletin archéologique du comité des travaux historiques* (1903): 476–489.

[13] Gerzaguet, *Marchiennes une abbaye,* p. 9. *Poleticum,* c. 2, 20, notes advocates threatening Marchiennes.

[14] The *Poleticum* is from Douai, BM, MS 850, fols. 119v–142r (a manuscript that contains Andre's *Chronicle* of Marchiennes and *Miracula* of Eusebia, Rictrude, and Jonat), ed. Delmaire, *Histoire-polyptyque,* pp. 65–79. Delmaire convincingly dates it to the early years of the reign of Abbot Amand of Marchiennes (r. 1116–1136). On the manuscript, see Delmaire, pp. 3–9, and Poncelet, "Catalogus," p. 405. C. 8–14 relate Hamage's history.

[15] *Poleticum,* c. 13–14; Delmaire, *Histoire-polyptyque,* p. 32.

[16] The first *ME* (BHL 2738) must date to 1133–1164, since it notes Eusebia's translation of 1133 but not Rictrude's elevation of 1164. (See Delmaire, *Histoire-polyptyque,* p. 14; AASS Mar., vol. 2, cols. 457D–461E). The BHL lists a single copy in the twelfth-century (Douai, BM, MS 840, fols. 137r–140v). A second *ME* (BHL 2738a, in Douai, BM, MS 846; excerpted in Poncelet, pp. 460–462) was composed after 1164. There are four *MR* (BHL 7249, 7251, 7252, 7252a). The earliest (BHL 7251), composed by the monk

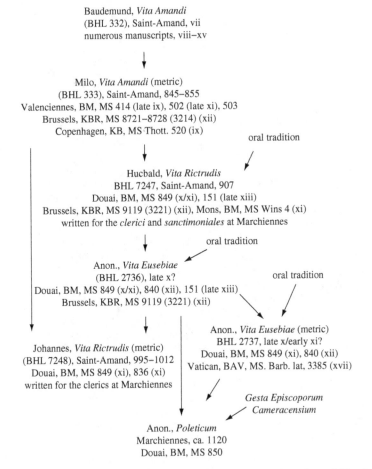

FIGURE 7. The relationship of the texts pertaining to Rictrude and Eusebia[17] (note that the *Miracula* writers were also influenced by the *vitae* of the Rictrude-Eusbia cycle).

Galbert around 1120, was revised in the 1160s when the other three (all anonymous) were written, presumably inspired by Rictrude's elevation. (*MR*, printed in AASS May, vol. 3, cols. 89C–154F; BHL 7252a is printed in Poncelet, "Catalogus," pp. 449–460. BHL 7249 and 7251, transmitted in Douai, BM, MS 850. BHL 7252a transmitted in Douai, BM, MS 846. The BHL does not list mss for BHL 7252.) On Andre's *Chronicle*, see Steven Van Der Putten, "Compilation et réinvention à la fin du douzième siècle. André de Marchiennes le Chronicon marchianense et l'histoire primitive d'une abbaye bénédictine (édition et critique des sources)," *Sacris Erudiri* 42 (2003): 403–436.

[17] This figure is based on the table after p. 436 in Van der Essen, *Étude critique*; information in Delmaire, *Histoire-polyptyque*, pp. 13–16; and Ugé, "Legend of Saint Rictrude," pp. 281–297. The dates of the *Miracula*, *Poleticum* and *Chronicon* come from Delmaire. I have omitted certain sources (such as Milo's *De sobrietate* used by Johannes), which do

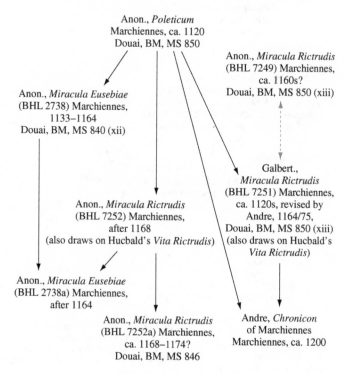

Anon., *Poleticum*
Marchiennes, ca. 1120
Douai, BM, MS 850

Anon., *Miracula Rictrudis*
(BHL 7249) Marchiennes,
ca. 1160s?
Douai, BM, MS 850 (xiii)

Anon., *Miracula Eusebiae*
(BHL 2738) Marchiennes,
1133–1164
Douai, BM, MS 840 (xii)

Galbert.,
Miracula Rictrudis
(BHL 7251) Marchiennes,
ca. 1120s, revised by
Andre, 1164/75,
Douai, BM, MS 850 (xiii)
(also draws on Hucbald's
Vita Rictrudis)

Anon., *Miracula Rictrudis*
(BHL 7252) Marchiennes,
after 1168
(also draws on Hucbald's *Vita Rictrudis*)

Anon., *Miracula Eusebiae*
(BHL 2738a) Marchiennes,
after 1164

Anon., *Miracula Rictrudis*
(BHL 7252a) Marchiennes,
ca. 1168–1174?
Douai, BM, MS 846

Andre, *Chronicon*
of Marchiennes
Marchiennes, ca. 1200

FIGURE 7. (cont.)

Much of the evidence for Hamage and Marchiennes comes from the *vitae* and *miracula* of Eusebia and Rictrude. The accuracy of these sources, often written long after the events they portray, is doubtful. Lifshitz has discussed the problem of a positivist approach to hagiographic sources, in which the historian goes "bobbing for data" and extracts apparent facts (such as founders and dates) from a narrative while dismissing other aspects of the text (particularly miracles) as fanciful.[18] She notes that hagiography is a modern category formulated to divide the saintly from "serious" history and that earlier medieval writers did not make this distinction, often describing their saints' lives as *historia* and sprinkling their histories with miracles; the *Poleticum*'s

not bear directly on the genealogy of the two *Vitae Eusebiae* or the texts about Marchiennes and Hamage. I have indicated oral tradition as a source when the author mentions it. Dotted lines indicate uncertain influence. Roman numerals indicate dates of composition. Roman numerals in parentheses indicate manuscript dates. Double-headed arrows indicate that influence could have flowed in either direction.

[18] On hagiographic sources for positivist history, see Lifshitz, "Beyond Positivism."

historical survey and Andre's *Chronicle* draw on *miracula* and *vitae*. Even modern archaeological evidence is interpreted with data mined from hagiography. For example, Louis uses evidence from the *vitae* and *miracula* to identify the churches of Sainte-Marie and Saint-Pierre from his excavations of Hamage.[19]

600 through 1000

From these sparse and difficult sources, we can reconstruct only a basic outline of Hamage's history. It is set on a marshy piece of flat ground on the right bank of the Scarpe, less than half a mile to the southeast of Marchiennes.[20] According to the hagiographical works, Gertrude, Adalbald's grandmother, founded Hamage, as either a house of nuns or, like Marchiennes, a double house of nuns and clerics.[21] Hucbald says Gertrude died in 649 at age seventy-five or eighty. Based on this vague evidence, Faidherbe places the foundation of Hamage around 595.[22] Louis prefers a date around 630.[23] His excavations show that the earliest habitations were from the seventh century and consisted of separate wooden huts on stone foundations,[24] a layout that suggests an Irish influence.[25] The area, approximately 35 meters by 70 meters, was surrounded by wooden palisades and ditches.[26] Excavations have turned up fibulae, glass objects, and ceramic goblets, including one inscribed with the woman's name Aughilde.[27] A church, which Louis has labeled Saint-Pierre, was built on the river 50 meters north of the cloister.

In the second half of the seventh century communal living quarters replaced the separate *cellulae*.[28] A wooden structure, 10.5 meters by 18.5 meters, consisted of ten to twelve cells, each with a hearth, grouped

---

[19] Louis, "Hamage (Nord)," p. 90; Le Glay, *Mémoire*, Pièces justificatives II, p. 27; Miraeus, c. 106, p. 712.

[20] Louis, "Hamage (Nord)," p. 74; *Poleticum*, c. 8: "Extat praeterea a littore marceniensi spatio stadiorum ferme quatuor Amagiensis sinus locus amoenus ..." (There exists also, at a distance of almost four stades from the bank of Marchiennes, the bay of Hamage, a charming place ...). A stade is 607 ft or 185 m, so four stades are 0.46 of a mile or 0.74 km; Louis, "Bâtiments monastiques," p. 55.

[21] Faidherbe, *Notice historique*, p. 7.

[22] Ibid., p. 9.

[23] Louis, "Bâtiments monastiques," p. 55.

[24] Louis, *Nord-Pas-de-Calais*, [p. 2].

[25] Louis, "Hamage (Nord)," p. 84.

[26] Louis, *Nord-Pas-de-Calais*, [p. 2].

[27] Louis, "Bâtiments monastiques," p. 58.

[28] Ibid., p. 59.

around three communal rooms, as well as an oven and latrines.[29] This period has yielded brooches, needles, glass beads, bowls, platters, and pitchers.[30] From the remains of the work and tools of glassmakers, bronze workers, blacksmiths, carpenters, and other artisans, Louis has inferred that the residents enjoyed a fairly high standard of living.[31]

Between 690 and 710, a second church was built north of the cloister.[32] This church, 22 meters long, was constructed of wood on stone foundations. It housed the nuns' remains and a chapel.[33] Louis interprets it as Sainte-Marie built by Eusebia's successor, the second abbess Gertrude, and identifies the chapel on its side as the home of Eusebia's relics.[34] In Louis's reconstruction, the cloistered nuns frequented Sainte-Marie, while the resident clerics and visiting laity used Saint-Pierre.[35] (Although presumably pilgrims would seek Eusebia's relics.) Both *Vitae Eusebiae* state that Hatta, abbot of Saint-Vaast, oversaw its consecration.[36] The *Poleticum* claims Eusebia had a chapel on the church's south side, where sick people were healed through incubation, but refuses to speculate on her translation to these quarters (c. 13–14).

In the ninth century, the church identified as Sainte-Marie was replaced by a larger (24 m × 8 m) stone structure and new chapel. Remains of limestone and colored glass show the expense of the building.[37] The living quarters were also rebuilt in the ninth century, apparently in the form of an early cloister.[38] Excavated coins of Louis the Pious date the reconstruction and suggest that the building project was associated with his imposition of Benedictine Rule on all the abbeys of his kingdom in 816–817.[39]

Even at its height, Hamage was a modest community.[40] Its cloister was small, and the foundations suggest the churches were not tall.[41] Nonetheless, material remains suggest a level of prosperity, and twelfth-century charters imply that Hamage had once possessed several local properties. The bull of

---

[29] Ibid.

[30] Ibid.

[31] Louis, *Nord-Pas-de-Calais*, [p. 3].

[32] *Poleticum*, c. 9, attributes the building of this church to the first Gertrude.

[33] Since there is no evidence for Eusebia prior to Hucbald's *VR* of 907, Louis's use of the later hagiographic tradition for interpreting the eighth-century archeological evidence is problematic.

[34] *VE* (prose), c. 13; Louis, "Bâtiments monastiques," p. 62.

[35] Louis, "Bâtiments monastiques," p. 59.

[36] *Poleticum*, c. 9; *VE* (metric), fol. 59r, *VE* (prose), c. 13.

[37] Louis, *Nord-Pas-de-Calais*, [p. 4].

[38] Louis, "Bâtiments monastiques," p. 62.

[39] Louis, "Hamage (Nord)," p. 94.

[40] Louis, "Bâtiments monastiques," p. 59.

[41] Louis, "Hamage (Nord)," pp. 92–94.

Calixtus II, from November 1123, refers to Alnes and Wandignies as Hamage's appendices.[42] The diploma of Philip, count of Flanders from 1176, adds Tilloy to the list.[43] The *Poleticum* also preserves evidence of Hamage as an administrative unit. After noting produce owed from the domains of Alnes and Wandegnies, the author states that "the inhabitants of the parish are subject to Hamage."[44] The same text notes that the woods of Givrus (Gievre) and Erleverceis (Hiverchies) and the marsh of Gislodus (Gislautfait) were under Hamage's guardianship (*sub tutela*), as was the small abandoned farm (*praediolum*) of Warlennium.[45] The twelfth-century charters, like the *Poleticum*, were concerned with preserving Marchiennes's possessions, which by that time included Hamage. Because it did not serve the interests of the monks of Marchiennes any better to claim that these properties were part of Hamage's ancient patrimony rather than their own, this detail seems unlikely to be deliberately fabricated (although it could still be incorrect).

The *Gesta* and the twelfth-century sources recount Hamage's decline. One *Miracula Rictrudis* (BHL 7252) places it immediately after the death of its third abbess, Gertrude II.[46] Archaeological evidence shows that major destruction occurred in the ninth century, when the second Sainte-Marie was destroyed, perhaps by Vikings.[47] The first *Miracula Eusebiae*, written in the mid-twelfth century, puts the Viking devastation "in 850

---

[42] Le Glay, *Mémoire*, pièces justificatives II, 27, with my orthographic corrections from the charters, Pièces 1 and 2 of Series 10 H 1 of the ADN, Lille. Max Bruchet, *Archives Départmentales du Nord, Répertoire Numérique, Séries H (Fonds Bénédictins et Cisterciens) 1 H à XXXV H* (Mons-en Barœul, 2003), p. 184.

[43] "The place Hamage with its dependencies Alnes, Tilloit and Wandegnies" (Locum ... Hamaticensem cum appendiciis suis Alno et Tilloit, et Wandegnies); Miraeus, c. 106, p. 712. Le Glay notes that Miraeus transcribes *Alvo* for *Alno* (Le Glay, *Mémoire*, p. 27).

[44] *Poleticum*, c. 22: "Parroechiae Amagiensi incolae subiecti sunt."

[45] *Poleticum*, c. 21, 23.

[46] *Miracula Rictrudis* written after 1168. AASS May, vol. 3, cols. 102B–C. "While the abbess [Gertrude II] was living, religion was not lacking in the monastery, nor, through a certain person's aggression, was the sustenance of the handmaidens of God taken away, nor had they been diminished through the neglect of those to whom they had been entrusted. But when she had been freed from the bonds of the flesh and matters of the monastery were gradually changing for the worse, the disintegration together with the diminishment of religion were hastening the impending doom" (Abbatissa vero vivente nec in monasterio religio defuit, nec ancillarum Dei subsidia per cuiusdam violentiam sublata, vel per incuriam eorum quibus commissa fuerant sunt imminuta. Sed cum carnis vinculis absoluta esset, cum detrimento religionis, rebus monasterii paulatim in deterius mutatis, desolationem futuram dissolutio praecurrebat).

[47] Louis judges that the remains show destruction rather than removal. Louis, "Hamage (Nord)," p. 94.

when the Normans had set alight the cities, the fortresses and the monasteries of the Gauls and had killed the inhabitants. They also demolished this place [Hamage] and Marchiennes and exterminated the inhabitants."[48] Louis, however, suggests Sainte-Marie was destroyed during the attacks that decimated the Scarpe valley in 881 and 883 (the same raids that destroyed Marchiennes's books).[49]

A charter of contested authenticity, ascribed to Charles the Bald in 877, states that there were still male and female residents at Hamage in the later ninth century.[50] The charter states that wine from the villa of Vergny is "to be divided into three parts, one part for the work of the senior, another also for the use of the sisters and brothers residing at Marchiennes, and the third indeed for the work of the sisters and brothers living in Hamage."[51] If we accept its authenticity, the unusual division of the produce suggests that Marchiennes and Hamage were separate but associated entities. Louis infers from the tripartite division of the wine between the two houses and the abbot's *mensa* (as he interprets the *opus senioris*) that they shared an abbot, abbess, or lay abbot.[52] Ugé suggests, from this evidence, that Hamage was already subordinate to Marchiennes, but it was common for abbots (especially lay abbots) to rule more than one house, and a shared abbot need not imply subordination of one house to another.[53]

According to the first *Miracula Eusebiae*, churches of Hamage and Marchiennes were restored during the reign of Charles the Simple (879–929).[54] The next layer of archaeological evidence, however, from the tenth

---

[48] ME (BHL 2738), c. 9, AASS March, vol. 2, col. 459B: "anno autem Domini octingentesimo quinquagesimo, cum Normanni Gallliarum civitates et castelli et monasteria igni tradidissent et habitatores interfecissent; hunc quoque locum [i.e., Hamage] et Marchianensem deletis habitatoribus destruxerunt."

[49] *Annales Bertiniani*, in C. Dehaisnes, *Les annales de Saint-Bertin et de Saint-Vaast* (Paris, 1871), pp. 308–309, and Hucbald, *VR*, c. 1.

[50] The charter survives in a thirteenth-century copy, inserted into the first cartulary of Marchiennes, and it is unclear whether its formulae are consistent with the ninth century. The general agreement between the possessions the charter lists and Marchiennes's twelfth-century possessions raises the suspicion that it is a forgery created to establish the abbey's rights to its property.

[51] *Receuil des Actes de Charles le Chauve*, II, no. 435: "unam partem ad opus Senioris, alteram quoque ad usus Sororum ac Fratrum in MARCIANIS consistentium, tertiam quidem ad opus Sororum et Fratrum in HAMATICO degentium ..." See Ugé, *Monastic Past*, p. 109. Tessier notes inconsistent elements in the charter, but because there are parallels, he does not reject its authenticity.

[52] Louis, "Hamage (Nord)," p. 76.

[53] Ugé, *Monastic Past*, p. 111.

[54] ME (BHL 2738), c. 2, 9 in AASS March, vol. 2, col. 459B.

and eleventh centuries, shows that Sainte-Marie had not been rebuilt, and that the land was divided up into small plots for intensive agriculture.[55] The *Poleticum* also notes the neglect of Hamage in Ciceronian hyperbole (*O tempora! O mores!*):

Alas! Alas! By the evil acts of the worse men, whose infernal wickedness and tyrannical madness and diabolical cruelty crushed the oaths of peace and the comfort in the agreeable air, the wealth in the most fertile pastures, the wealth in the various crops of the fruitful earth, when the cultivator had been removed and the inhabitants had been put to flight ...[56]

Hamage was not completely abandoned. Graves from the period are found within the perimeter of the Carolingian building, implying a preference for burials in sacred ground and a memory of the structure's location.[57] An eleventh-century manuscript of Gregory's *Dialogues*, Douai, BM, MS 312, is labeled "Liber ecclesiae Hamaticensis," suggesting that a church was still in use there, and that it was a separate entity from Marchiennes.[58] The manuscript is written in an irregular, squarish minuscule, quite distinct from contemporary codices copied at Marchiennes or other local abbeys; it may have been copied at Hamage. This utilitarian unornamented codex complements the picture of a modest independent community in the late tenth and early eleventh century.[59]

Reform

The early-eleventh-century reform movement of Richard of Saint-Vanne and the bishops of Cambrai provides a further key to understanding Hamage's history and the accounts of Rictrude and Eusebia. Richard began his reforms during Erluin's episcopate, with the eventual and somewhat grudging cooperation of Count Baldwin IV.[60] Erluin's successor, Gerard (r. 1012–1051), continued them as part of his program of expanded episcopal power, which also included the composition of the

---

[55] Louis, "Hamage (Nord)," pp. 95–96.

[56] *Poleticum*, c. 12: "vae! vae! malignitatibus hominum pessimorum quorum infernalis improbitas et tirannica rabies atque atrocitas diabolica pacis iura comminuit et amoenitatem in iocundo aere, in pascuis uberrimis opulentiam in fertilis terrae frugibus diversis, sublato cultore et fugatis habitatoribus ..."

[57] Louis, "Hamage (Nord)," p. 97.

[58] Douai, BM, MS 312, fol. 1r; Dehaisnes, *Catalogue*, pp. 163–164.

[59] For other codices from Hamage, see ibid., pp. 66–67.

[60] D.C. van Meter, "Count Baldwin IV, Richard of Saint-Vanne and the Inception of Monastic Reform in Eleventh-Century Flanders," *RB* 107 (1997): 130–148.

main source for the reform, the *Gesta of the Bishops of Cambrai*.[61] Its
second book briefly surveys the diocese's religious houses and the reforms,
which included appointing new leaders, expelling unfit communities,
imposing the Benedictine Rule, and implementing stricter standards. The
passage on Hamage is brief: "now having declined, through much secula-
rization, it has barely a few canons."[62] The *Gesta* does not mention any
reform there.

In 1024, Leduin, abbot of Saint-Vaast, reformed Marchiennes, ousting
the nuns and installing monks.[63] The *Gesta* claims that the nun's depravity
(a common allegation) necessitated the action.[64] It makes no mention of
monks or clerics at Marchiennes at any time since its foundation by
Rictrude as a community of *sanctimoniales*. There had, however, been
monks or clerics there recently: a charter of 976 refers to *sorores* and
fratres under Abbess Judith at Marchiennes, and Johannes's preface to
the *Vita Rictrudis* mentions the *clerici*.[65] If there were male residents in
1024, it is unclear whether they were expelled with the nuns or incorporated into the reformed male community.

The first *Miracula Eusebiae*, written more than a century later, associates
Hamage's subordination with the 1024 reform: "when Count Baldwin and
Abbot Leduin of Saint-Vaast threw the nuns out of the abbey of
Marchiennes, that same place [Hamage] passed into the authority of the
monks of Marchiennes."[66] One of Rictrude's *Miracula* dates the incorpo-
ration of Hamage to the earlier period when nuns still ruled Marchiennes.[67]
The *Gesta*, however, a more reliable and contemporary source, contradicts
both these *Miracula* since it contains no suggestions that Hamage was a

---

[61] On the composition and function of the *Gesta Ep. Cam.*, see Robert M. Stein, "Sacred
Authority and Secular Power: The Historical Argument of the *Gesta episcoporum
Cameracensis*," in *Sacred and Secular in Medieval and Early Modern Cultures: New
Essays*, ed. Lawrence Besserman (New York, 2006), pp. 149–165, 216–221.

[62] *Gesta Ep. Cam.* 2. 27: "nunc per saecularitatem multum delapsa, vix paucos canonicos
habet."

[63] Ibid.

[64] Ugé, *Monastic Past*, p. 113.

[65] Johannes, *Ep.*, p. 566; Charter of Lothar, Miraeus, *Diplom. Belg. lib.* I, c. 21, p. 143.

[66] *ME* (BHL 2738, written 1133–1164), c. 9; AASS March, vol. 2, 459B: "eo autem tempore
quo sanctimoniales a monasterio Marchianensi per Balduinum Comitem et Lietduinum
Abbatem S. Vedasti eiectae sunt, in subiectionem monarchorum Marchiensensium idem
locum devenit."

[67] *MR* (BHL 7252), written after 1168, implies that the transfer happened at an early date,
because in its scheme Hamage's decline began after the death of its third abbess. It claims
that Hamage was put into the *cura* of the nuns of Marchiennes, before they were replaced
by monks, so in this version, Hamage was annexed before 1024 (AASS May, vol. 3,
102B–C).

dependent of Marchiennes before 1024 or that it was annexed in that year. Given that monastic reform is the main theme of the *Gesta*'s second book, the author would have recorded any reform of Hamage, which he presents as needing intervention. Rather, these *Miracula* from Marchiennes, written over a century later, projected the current state of affairs in which Hamage belonged to Marchiennes onto a known event in the past.

Count Baldwin V's charter of 1046 confirming Marchiennes's possessions does not list Hamage, but he seems to mention only property within Flanders, and Hamage was probably in Hainault.[68] Although Baldwin does not name Hamage, he mentions the *familiae* of Rictrude and Eusebia, which have a single abbot. The inclusion of the *familia sanctae Eusebiae* in a decree confirming Marchiennes's property and prescribing correct behavior toward it implies that Hamage is dependent on or under the *cura* of Marchiennes. Later documents are unambiguous: by the early twelfth century, Hamage was a dependent of Marchiennes. A charter from 1103 of Bishop Lambert of Arras confirms Hamage among Marchiennes's properties, as do charters of 1122, 1123, and 1176.[69]

Thus, it seems that through the tenth century, Hamage's *pauci canonici* eked out an existence, farming the land, living in whatever structures remained, or building ones too ephemeral to mark the archaeological record, and burying their dead on the sacred ground of the destroyed church of Saint-Marie. Some time after 1024, probably by 1046, Hamage was finally annexed to its larger neighbor, and by the late eleventh century, Eusebia's relics had been translated to Marchiennes.[70] (They are attested there by

---

[68] Original charter: ADN, 10 H 6/41, printed in Delmaire, *L'histoire-polyptyque*, pp. 97ff. In 1046, Hamage was probably within the *comitatus* of Hainault as it was in 1103. Delmaire, *L'histoire-polyptyque*, p. 44.

[69] Lambert's charter, which survives in its original form (ADN 10 H 5 pièce 33), confirms "Hamaticum" in the district of Ostrevannus in Hainault. Le Glay, *Mémoire*, p. 7; Bruchet, *Archives*, p. 185. Charters ADN H 5/34 and ADN H 5/35, printed in Delmaire, *Histoire-polyptyque*, pp. 97ff.

[70] The *ME* (BHL 2738) places Eusebia's translation before the Viking invasions of 850. It is unlikely that Hamage would have permitted the removal of its patron's remains in the ninth century, unless for temporary safety. The author admits his ignorance of events: "de secunda autem translatione S. Eusebiae, quomodo ab Hamatico Marchianas translata sit, quod stylo evidentius prosequendum sit, certum nihil occurrit" (Regarding, however, the second translation of Saint Eusebia [the first had been under Abbess Gertrude II], how she was conveyed from Hamage to Marchiennes, because this should clearly be described in more detail with the pen, nothing certain appears; c. 2). As with the annexation of Hamage, the *ME* probably casts the translation of Eusebia further into the past. Marchiennes probably acquired Eusebia's remains after annexing Hamage.

1089.)[71] Twelfth-century liturgical books from Marchiennes contain a feast for Eusebia's translation from Hamage to Marchiennes, celebrated on November 18.[72]

Despite the problematic and meager sources, the outlines of Hamage's history from the late ninth to the early eleventh centuries seem fairly clear: during this time, Hamage was reduced from a fairly prosperous double house to the home of "a few canons." Hamage and Marchiennes were associated and perhaps even shared an abbot. Marchiennes, although not a grand house, overshadowed its small neighbor and, in an era of monastic reorganization, Hamage's survival seemed unlikely. Some time after Marchiennes's reform of 1024, Hamage was finally incorporated into its more powerful neighbor. The years leading up to Hamage's annexation are the context for the composition of Johannes's verse *Vita Rictrudis* and the two *vitae* of Eusebia.

RICTRUDE AND EUSEBIA

Turning from the historical context to the *vitae* themselves, we can see how Rictrude and Eusebia represent both affiliation and conflict between their abbeys. Although Marchiennes and Hamage had been founded in the seventh century, the earliest extant accounts of their

---

[71] In 1070, relics from regional churches were assembled for the dedication of the church at Hasnon, but the list in the *Auctarium Hasnoniense* does not specify the churches that supplied Rictrude and Eusebia; ed. G. Pertz in MGH SS 6, pp. 441–442; Edina Bozóky, "La politique des reliques des premiers comtes de Flandre," in *Les reliques: Objets, cultes, symbols. Actes du colloque international de l'Université du Littoral-Côte d'Opale (Boulogne-sur-Mer)*, 4–6 *septembre 1997* (Turnhout, 1999), p. 281. In 1089, a diploma records a gift "to the church of Marchiennes in which the bodies of Blessed Rictrude and Eusebia, with relics of many other saints, venerably lie." (Ecclesiae MARCHIENENSI in qua Beatarum Rictrudis et Eusebiae corpora, cum aliorum plurimorum Sanctorum pignoribus, venerabiliter requiescunt.) Ed. by Le Mire, *Donat. Belg. lib.* II, c. 29, p. 517. Galbert, writing in the 1120s, also implies that the remains of Eusebia and Rictrude rest in the same place, but since he refers to an episode in which Eusebia and Rictrude were "outside the churches" (*extra basilicorum*), he does not present definitive evidence that they regularly resided in the same church. Galbert, *MR* (BHL 7251), AASS May, vol. 3, p. 131.

[72] This feast was celebrated on November 18, according to the liturgical books Douai, BM, MSS 888 and 134. The *MR* (BHL 7252), c. 13, gives November 18 (XIV Kal. Decembris) as the date for the consecration of the church of Sainte-Marie in Hamage, which Abbess Gertrude II had built to house Eusebia's remains. The coincidence of dates suggests that the later sources may be confusing or conflating two translations of Eusebia, one within Hamage and one from Hamage to Marchiennes. See Victor Leroquais, *Les bréviaires manuscrits des bibliothèques publiques de France*, vol. 2 (Paris, 1932–1934), p. 43.

saints derive from Hucbald's prose *Vita Rictrudis*. Writing in 907 at the request of the clerics and nuns of Marchiennes, Hucbald lamented the absence of sources.[73] Roughly a century later, the epic *Vita Eusebiae* echoes and amplifies his complaints.[74] The three later texts of the Rictrude-Eusebia cycle – Johannes's *Vita Rictrudis* and the anonymous prose and verse *Vitae Eusebiae* – are based on Hucbald's narrative (for the relationship of the texts, see Figure 7). As discussed in the previous chapter, Johannes follows Hucbald almost entirely, but incorporates an incident from the prose *Vita Eusebiae*. The lives of Eusebia omit or abbreviate episodes and, unsurprisingly, elaborate on the sections concerning Eusebia.

The four lives of the Eusebia-Rictrude cycle agree on a basic narrative of mother and daughter saints. According to the story, Rictrude and her noble-born husband Adalbald had a son, Mauront, and three daughters. All members of the family are described as saints. After Adalbald was murdered by members of Rictrude's family who disapproved of the marriage, Rictrude decided to become a nun, and Saint Amand established her in the abbey he had founded at Marchiennes.[75] She lived there

---

[73] He recounts his difficulties: "because I had seen no reliable written accounts, nor heard any about these matters, I was afraid that I might accept doubtful things as certain ones or false ones in place of true" (nulla certae relationis de his scripta videram vel audieram, veritus ne forte dubia pro certis vel falsa pro veris assererem). Hucbald claimed, in the absence of written evidence, to draw on the recollections of those who had read the lost works. The nuns told him stories that were consistent, and "these same things that they were telling me, had once been handed down in writing, but they were destroyed by the Northmen's depredations" (quod haec quae referebant, eadem olim tradita litteris fuerint; sed insectatione Northmannicae depopulationis deperierint). Hucbald, *VR*, c. 1.

[74] *VE* (metric), 1.109–120: "As regards the speech of antiquity, nothing more remains from that time, / And it is not known why, out of so many things, few are preserved in books . . . / Or if they were written, neglect destroyed them, or because / Disaster took them away, for they say the Gallic land was decimated / By the slaughter, plunder, and destruction of the Northmen. / They say that the villages and castles were destroyed, / And that once the churches' relics were plundered, they were burned. / And their splendid treasures were lost / As were the lives of the saints, whose loss the present age mourns above all" (Sermo vetustatis, nihil amplius inde reliquit/ Et cur nescitur, multorum pauca feruntur / In libris . . . / Aut si sunt scripta, situs haec absumpserit, aut quod / Sustulerit casus, nam fertur gallica tellus / Northmanica cede, populatu, perditione / Olim deleta, vici, castella subacta / Ecclesiae sacris incensae despoliatis / Harum thesaurus sic deperiisse probatur / Ornatus, vitae sanctorum † plurima † quaeque/ Supra quae praesens aetas dolet his caruisse). The final line ("Supra . . . caruisse") is an interlinear addition between two other lines in a paler ink in the manuscript Douai, BM, MS 840.

[75] The earliest reference to Amand founding Marchiennes is in Milo of Saint-Amand's *Suppletio* (BHL 339), ed. B. Krusch and W. Levison in MGH SRM 5, p. 450.

with her son and two of her daughters. Her other daughter, Eusebia, was raised by her paternal great-grandmother Gertrude, abbess of Hamage.[76] When Gertrude died, Eusebia succeeded her. Rictrude, fearing that her twelve-year-old daughter would be corrupted, demanded that she return to Marchiennes. Eusebia, complying only when her mother elicited a royal decree, came to Marchiennes with the relics and residents of Hamage, but she refused to renounce her pious duties at her former house. She repeatedly defied her mother by sneaking out at night – barefoot and impervious to the cold – to perform the offices in the abandoned abbey. Rictrude, discovering Eusebia's disobedience, ordered Mauront to beat his sister.

The prose *Vita Eusebia* adds an incredible event to Hucbald's narrative: the stick that Mauront had been using to beat his sister flew from his hand, planted itself in the ground, and burst into leaf.[77] (Both Johannes's *Vita Rictrudis* and the epic *Vita Eusebiae* adopt this episode from the prose *Vita Eusebiae*.) After her ordeal, Eusebia continued her resistance. Rictrude consulted renowned bishops and monks and reluctantly allowed Eusebia to return to Hamage, where she presided as abbess of Hamage until her death at age twenty-three, after which her relics performed healing miracles. She became a patron of Hamage, while her mother was revered at Marchiennes.

THE LIVES OF EUSEBIA: DATES AND ORIGINS

The authorship and dates of the two lives of Rictrude are secure; the circumstances in which those of Eusebia were produced are obscure. The relationship between the lives of the cycle, however, along with internal textual and codicological evidence, suggests their provenance.

---

[76] Hucbald, *VR*, c. 9; Johannes, *VR*, 1.361–362; *VE* (prose), c. 3; *Poleticum*, c. 13; *VE* (metric), 1.15. On Eusebia, see Mireille De Somer, "Eusebia," in *Bibliotheca Sanctorum* vol. 5 (Rome, 1964), cols. 243–245.

[77] The writer of the prose *VE* claims to be the first to record the incident: "and it is surprising because those who wrote other things deprived future generations of its notice in this way" (et mirum cur qui alia scripsere, hoc eo modo posterorum subtraxerunt notitiae). He says he derives the story from popular belief, based on an old tradition: "indeed it is the opinion of the common people that they ruminate upon this because of an ancient tradition" (Est apud vulgus hoc quidem in opinione, quod ab eo ruminatur ex antiquitatis traditione). *VE* (prose), c. 9. As Smith has shown, Hucbald is not interested in depicting miracles. Julia M.H. Smith, "The Hagiography of Hucbald of Saint-Amand," *Studi medievali*, ser. 3, 35 (1994): 524.

Since Johannes, writing in 1012 at the latest, drew on the prose *Vita Eusebiae*, we have a *terminus ante quem* for its composition.[78] (It is unclear from the verbal echoes whether Johannes had read the work of the epic *Vita Eusebiae* poet or vice versa.)

The prose *Vita Eusebiae* survives in four medieval manuscripts, two of which also contain the epic life of Eusebia.[79] The earliest manuscript of the two *vitae* of Eusebia, and of Johannes's *Vita Rictrudis*, Douai, Bibliothèque Municipale, MS 849, was produced around the second quarter of the eleventh century (see Appendix B). The epic *Vita Eusebiae* not only derives from the prose *Vita Eusebiae*, but also draws directly on Hucbald's prose *Vita Rictrudis*.[80] The epic *Vita Eusebiae*'s elaborate and digressive "hermeneutic" style and the prose *vita's* gratuitous classicizing are both typical of later tenth- or eleventh-century composition.[81]

The lives of Eusebia are transmitted anonymously. The prose life is prefaced by a letter that gives us little information on the writer. We learn, from the gender of a participle, that he was male, and he claims to write out of "fraternal love," perhaps implying that he composed the work

---

[78] The staff miracle is the one significant episode Johannes adds to Hucbald's story, which he otherwise closely follows (on Johannes's use of Hucbald, see Chapter 4). Johannes indicates that it is an addition: "something else is added to this, but that thing is no less true" (Additur huic aliud et verum non minus istud; *VR*, 2.432). Verbal resonances show that he takes the episode from the prose *VE*. Johannes's *VR* and the prose *VE* use many of the same words (*virgula, excussus, flagellum, terra, haerere* or *inhaerere, frondere,* and *succus*), whereas the verse version employs different vocabulary (Johannes uses *virgula*, the diminutive of the term *virga* used in the verse *VE*, and *infixa*, compound of *fixum*, used in the latter).

[79] Douai, BM, MS 849 (xi) contains Hucbald's prose *VR* and the earliest witnesses of the three other texts of the Rictrude-Eusebia cycle. Douai, BM, MS 836 (xii), also from Marchiennes, contains Hucbald's *VR* (fols. 78v–83bis) and Johannes's *VR* (fols. 83bisv–91r). The large (460 mm × 305 mm) lectionary from Marchiennes, Douai, BM, MS 840 (xii) contains both the *VE* and many other lives. Brussels, KBR, MS 9119 (3221) (xii) includes the prose *VE* and Hucbald's *VR* (fols. 98r–100r, 147r–152r). Hucbald's *VR* is contained in Mons, BM, Wins 4, fols. 10r–23v (xi). The prose *VE* is also copied in Douai, BM, MS 151, fols. 146v–48v. On these manuscripts, Poncelet, "Catalogus," pp. 363, 394–98, 405; Paul Faider and Germaine Faider-Feytmans, *Catalogue des manuscrits de la bibliothèque publique de la ville De Mons* (Ghent, 1931).

[80] The author of the verse *VE* draws some elements directly from Hucbald that are not featured in the other works of the Rictrude-Eusebia cycle including the lamentation over the Viking destruction of sources and a masculine wrestling metaphor used to characterize Rictrude's spiritual battles after her enclosure. Hucbald, *VR*, c. 19, and *VE* (metric), 1.266.

[81] Michael Lapidge, "The Hermeneutic Style in Tenth-Century Anglo-Latin Literature," *ASE* 4 (1975): 67–111. Examples of the prose *vita*'s classicizing include allusions to Parnassus (home of the muses) and Pegasus in the prefatory letter. *VE* (prose), c. 1.

for his own religious brothers.[82] We learn similarly little about the author of the epic life. He addresses himself to the saint, as "tuus vates" ("your priest" or "your poet"), which could imply that he was a resident of Eusebia's house, or could simply be an expression of his devotion to her.

Because *vitae* (and particularly epic *vitae*) from the Central Middle Ages were almost always about local patron saints, and because Eusebia lacked a wider currency, we can assume that her lives were produced in the vicinity. Because epic lives were often written at the abbey that housed the relics of the featured saint, Hamage is the most obvious source for the lives, but Hamage, like Marchiennes, might have asked an external writer to compose the work. Johannes implies that the clerics of Marchiennes would have been unable to compose an epic *vita* for themselves because, according to his assessment, they were barely capable of reading one: "although in some places I could have used weightier and more circuitous language," he writes, "I thought that this little work would be better received if, in plain speech, it were accessible to the minds of the clerics who serve the aforementioned saint."[83] (Johannes makes no mention of the *sorores* who were still at Marchiennes when he wrote. Presumably, he did not consider them to be part of his audience.)

If Marchiennes's clerics could barely comprehend (let alone compose) an epic life, it seems the residents of Hamage would have been even less equipped to furnish an author of the necessary erudition. Johannes's condescending assessment of Marchiennes is, however, a variant on the humility topos in which a writer apologizes for the *rusticitas* of his language, so we should not take it at face value.[84] Nothing is known of Hamage's educational standards or the origins of its inhabitants. It is also possible that some of its residents had been "exchange students" at other monasteries with strong literary traditions, such as Saint-Amand or Saint-Vaast.[85]

If Hamage did not have a sufficiently accomplished poet of its own, monks from several other houses of the region could have written the *vita*

---

[82] *VE* (prose), c. 1: "compulsus obsequela fraternae caritatis, posterorum notitiae transmitto scriptis" (compelled by compliance with fraternal love, I commit this [life] in writing to the notice of future generations).

[83] *Epistola Iohannis*, MGH Poetae 5/3, p. 566: "licet aliquibus in locis uti quiverim gravior-ibus verborum ambagibus, hoc tamen opusculum futurum putavi acceptius, si clericorum supradictae sanctae famulantium plano sermone pateret intellectibus."

[84] Johannes attributes his style to the limited abilities of his readers rather than his own limitations. As usual, the poem's lofty tenor belies the humility trope.

[85] Grotans, *Reading*, p. 63.

for it. The region around Cambrai was a hotbed of hagiographic innovation in the ninth and tenth centuries and included a number of abbeys with traditions of epic *vitae*.[86] In addition to lives of Amand and Rictrude from Saint-Amand,[87] we have examples from Saint-Bavo in Ghent, Saint-Bertin and Saint-Omer at Sithiu (the town later named for Saint-Omer), Saint-Quentin in Picardy, Saint-Ghislain near Mons, and Fosses and Lobbes near Liège (see the map in the Introduction, Figure 6). These houses were linked by the exchange of letters, codices, monks, and abbots and, through their founding figures, by a web of saintly associations.

An early-twelfth-century source states that one author wrote both Eusebia's lives.[88] The omission of the supposed author's name suggests that the works' origins had already been forgotten, and it is possible that the later writer assumed common authorship because of the tradition of verse and prose "twinned works."[89] Their similar narratives, vocabulary, and expression only prove that one author drew on the other and that they shared literary traditions.[90]

---

[86] Examples of hagiographic innovation include versified liturgy and the first-known vernacular poem to a saint, the *Cantilène of Eulalia* (at Saint-Amand). The area was also a center of scribal and artistic activity. The Franco-Saxon style of illumination was developed at the houses of this region, including Saint-Amand, Saint-Bertin, and Saint-Vaast. The Bible of Charles the Bald, richly illuminated in this style, probably came from Saint-Amand, as did several impressive sacramentaries. See the collection *La cantilène de sainte Eulalie*, Actes du Colloque de Valenciennes, 21 mars 1989, ed. Marie-Pierre Dion (Lille, 1990). On versified liturgy, see Jonsson, *Historia*, and Björkvall and Haug, "Performing Latin Verse," pp. 278–299. On the region's scriptoria, see Rosamond McKitterick, "Manuscripts and Scriptoria in the Reign of Charles the Bald, 840–877," in *L'organizzazione del sapere in età carolingia*, ed. Claudio Leonardi and Enrico Menestò (Spoleto, 1989), p. 220; André Boutemy, "Le scriptorium et la bibliothèque de Saint-Amand d'après les manuscrits et les anciens catalogues," *Scriptorium* 1 (1946): 6–16; Jacques Guilmain, "The Illuminations of the Second Bible of Charles the Bald," *Speculum* 41 (1966): 246–260.

[87] Gunter's epic *Passio Cyrici et Iulittae* (BHL 1812) was also written at Saint-Amand.

[88] The author of the *Poleticum* of Marchiennes excuses himself from describing the life and deeds of Eusebia "quoniam profundioris scientiae quidam et prosa et metro luculentissime edidit" (since a certain man of deeper knowledge related this most splendidly in prose and in meter; c. 13). The earlier *ME* (BHL 2738), written between 1133 and 1164, which draws heavily on the *Poleticum*, echoes this claim. *ME*, c. 1, sec. 3, in AASS March, vol. 2, p. 435; Van der Essen and Delmaire accept the claim of common authorship (Delmaire, *Histoire-polyptyque*, pp. 14, 74; Léon van der Essen, *Étude critique et littéraire sur les vitae des saints mérovingiens de l'ancienne Belgique* (Louvain, 1907), pp. 267–268.

[89] See Introduction for references to twinned works.

[90] Van der Essen (*Étude critique*, p. 268) notes that both use the expression "capulo gladii, ille forte erat accinctus," express numbers similarly, and employ unusual vocabulary (*anastasis, xenia, faex, alalagma*). Both also deploy a gem motif: *VE* (metric), Prologue to Book 1, 1–10; *VE* (prose), c. 5.

There are also many differences between the *vitae* of Eusebia. Many of the features that differentiate the epic from the prose are typical of the "hermeneutic" style, which reflected the curriculum and practices of the classroom, and can be attributed to genre difference.[91] Classical allusions, direct speech, and interludes on learned subjects were all means by which the authors of epic lives amplified their prose originals and invested them with grandeur and didactic value.

Narrative discrepancies, however, cannot be attributed to the conventional differences between prose and epic. The poet adds to the story, most notably by making Eusebia's father a cephalophore, that is, a head-carrying martyr like Hilduin's Dionysius.[92] The poet's additions – along with certain omissions – are significant and, as we will see, produce a somewhat different overall effect, suggesting that his concerns were not identical to those of the prose writer.

Léon van der Essen and others have incorrectly ascribed one or both of the lives of Eusebia to Johannes of Saint-Amand, but Johannes's interests, choice of material, style, and compositional method all belie this identification.[93] In fact, the epic *Vita Eusebiae* and Johannes's epic *Vita Rictrudis* have limited verbal coincidence, suggesting only that one poet read the other. It is more difficult to compare Johannes's style to that of the prose *Vita Eusebiae*, but there is no evidence that he was its author either, and it presents a different perspective from his *Vita Rictrudis*.

The *Acta Sanctorum* attributes the prose *Vita Eusebiae* to an unnamed monk of Saint-Amand. Like the lives of Rictrude, those of Eusebia give Amand an important role as a spiritual advisor. The prose *Vita Eusebiae* casts him as the founder of Marchiennes and the priest who tonsured Mauront.[94] Saint-Amand is thus a possible source for the lives, although it seems that writers from that house would have increased Amand's

---

[91] Tilliette, "Modèles," p. 395.

[92] Van der Essen, *Étude critique*, p. 268; VE (metric), 1.170ff.

[93] Van der Essen, *Étude critique*, p. 268; AASS March, vol. 2, p. 445. The AASS editor ascribes such a view to Beauschamp and Molanus. Johannes's VR emphasizes the conflict of sacred and secular authority and the lives of Eusebia do not. Johannes and the Eusebia poet also use completely different methods of composition, with only the former employing a "patchwork" method, incorporating large sections of Milo's verse. Johannes's other significant poetic tics, whole lines of verbs and half lines of alliteration, are also absent from the epic VE. His vocabulary also differs substantially when describing the same incidents.

[94] VE (prose), c. 5, 6. Amand features heavily in both *Vitae Rictrudis* as the founder, who originally established Marchiennes as a community of monks under Abbot Jonat. In the two *Vitae Eusebiae*, there is no mention of the abbey's history before Rictrude.

presence and would have mentioned Jonat, whom, according to both *vitae* of Rictrude, Amand had installed as the first abbot of Marchiennes, before turning it over to Rictrude. If the writers of the two *Vitae Eusebiae* were from houses whose patrons were associated with the region's spiritual genealogy, we would expect them, like the lives of Rictrude, to introduce and emphasize their own saints.[95] For this reason, it seems reasonable to conjecture that they were composed at Hamage.

Regardless of the writers' origins, the two lives of Eusebia clearly represent Hamage's point of view. They were not composed at or for Marchiennes. Unlike the lives of Rictrude, they take an obvious side in the mother-daughter conflict, underscoring Eusebia's sanctity and righteousness at her mother's expense.

COMPETING SANCTITY

A comparison of the *vitae* of Rictrude with those of Eusebia reveals how differently each pair represents the saints' relationship. Deug-Su has written about the difficulties the conflict presented: if Rictrude is right, then Eusebia is at fault for contravening the central monastic virtue of obedience.[96] If Eusebia is correct, then Rictrude's violent opposition places her in the familiar role of the saintly child's adversarial parent.[97] Deug-Su shows how Hucbald balances the competing sanctities of mother and daughter. Mauront, as the perpetrator of the violence, was also vulnerable to criticism. Hucbald recognizes the problem, attributing the objections to detractors:

Look at what kind of people they call saints – the mother persecutes her innocent daughter who wanted to fight for God; the daughter despises and flees her own mother like an enemy, the son in agreement with the mother assails his fugitive sister, who had been betrayed by a secret sign, almost killing her with the harshest beatings, as if she were guilty of theft; even though she does not die at once, nonetheless, she is weakened by a long painful suffering. Do these things make the saints pleasing to God? What is saintly about them? What peace is there? What love?[98]

---

[95] The narratives contain episodes irrelevant to Eusebia and her family, so it would have been straightforward to insert other contemporary saints, especially if they were associated with Amand's spiritual family.

[96] I Deug-Su, "La <<Vita Rictrudis>> di Ubaldo di Saint-Amand: un'agiografia intellettuale e i santi imperfetti," *Studi medievali* ser. 3, 31 (1990): 545–582.

[97] Ibid., p. 568.

[98] Hucbald, *VR*, c. 28: "en, quales isti dicuntur esse Sancti, Mater innoxiam insequitur filiam, Deo militare volentem: Filia sicut hostem, sic propriam execratur et refugit matrem: Filius

Hucbald raises these points to refute them. He excuses the behavior of Rictrude and Mauront, which he says was based on good judgment and biblical precedent, as human error based on ignorance of Eusebia's divine inspiration.

Johannes, by contrast, does not address the problem, but frames the conflict to minimize Rictrude's culpability. Like the other writers, he attributes her actions to fear that the enemy (*hostis*, i.e., Satan) would corrupt her daughter.[99] He describes Eusebia's activity briefly. The miracle of the cane, which he adds to Hucbald's plot, has no impact on his narrative. Of the four versions, only Johannes omits the gruesome effects of Eusebia's beating, and he downplays her ongoing suffering.[100] Following this episode, he notes her pious life as abbess and her death. Where Hucbald then notes the deaths of Amand and Mauront, Johannes launches immediately into a catalog of Rictrude's virtues, thus juxtaposing her behavior toward Eusebia with an affirmation of her sanctity.[101] Johannes – unlike Hucbald – never suggests that the actions of Rictrude and Mauront require further explanation or defense. He does not even suggest that they committed a human error. Johannes's *Vita Rictrudis*, typically for an epic life, is more interested in narrative details (including miracles) than in defending the subject's historicity or sanctity. His Eusebia is a subordinate saint. She is not a problem for her mother's sanctity, but simply another testament to it.

The lives of Eusebia, by contrast, unequivocally endorse Eusebia over Rictrude. Praising Rictrude in tepid conventional language, neither explicitly questions her sanctity, but they shape the narrative to lessen her standing.[102] In almost every instance, the epic *vita* goes further than the prose in promoting Eusebia at Rictrude's expense, often by drawing on the specific features of verse lives, such as their penchant for direct speech and their tendency toward amplified description.

The *vitae* of Eusebia also diminish Rictrude by omission. They leave out events not simply because they are irrelevant to Eusebia (these lives routinely feature the deeds of other saints peripheral to the protagonist), but in order to lessen Rictrude's glory. Both ignore the incident in

---

matre consentanea, sororem refugam, asportato clam signo proditam, dirissimis velut furti ream afficit verberibus pene usque ad mortem; quam etsi non statim perimit, longo tamen dolorum cruciatu tabescere facit. Haeccine Sanctos Deoque placitos efficiunt? Quae in istis sanctitas? Quae pax? Quae caritas?"

99 Johannes, *VR*, 2.375.

100 Ibid., 2.430: "infirmum ... corpus."

101 Ibid., 2.2.465ff.

102 The prose calls her "felicissima" and "venerabilis" (c. 5). The verse praises her "simplicitas" (fol. 45v).

which Rictrude piously suppresses her grief at Adalsend's death to avoid disrupting the community's liturgical calendar.[103] Recounting this incident, Hucbald praises Rictrude in gendered terms: "the strength of the manly mind, which resided within her, conquered her womanly emotion."[104] By showing her expressing her *muliebris affectus* at a more appropriate time, Hucbald also presents her as a sympathetic mother, adding a dimension unseen in her interactions with Eusebia. The prose *Vita Eusebiae*, however, barely mentions Adalsend,[105] and the epic elides her almost entirely, saying that only her name remains (and then not even naming her),[106] thereby erasing any hint of Rictrude's fortitude at her death. Mauront, allied with his mother against Eusebia, is similarly diminished in the two *Vitae Eusebiae*.[107]

As these omissions lessen the status of Eusebia's familial adversaries, the epic strengthens her father's milquetoast sanctity with a spectacular addition. Adalbald's virtue was generic and he never chose a religious life. The prose *Vita Eusebiae* emphasizes his social standing rather than Rictrude's and notes a posthumous cult.[108] The epic *vita*, in an example of poets' taste for the supernatural, adds a striking miracle:

Behold, the martyr's corpse stood by his own effort.
He took his head in both hands and
Carried it away in his arms, and no one led the walking martyr.

---

[103] Hucbald, *VR*, c. 20; Johannes, *VR*, 2.166–190

[104] Hucbald, *VR*, c. 20: "virilis tamen, quod ei inerat, animi robur muliebrem superavit affectum."

[105] *VE* (prose), c. 4.

[106] Fol. 46v: "She who was third, only comes down to us in name / In the speech of antiquity – from this time nothing more remains" (Tertia quae fuerit, tantummodo nomine pandit / Sermo vetustatis, nihil amplius inde reliquit).

[107] In Hucbald's *VR* (c. 15) and Johannes's (2.271), Amand recognizes a bee circling Mauront's head as a mark of sanctity and tonsures him. Both lives of Eusebia omit the incident. Philip Harvengius, abbot of Saint-Amand, includes this story in his prose *VA* (BHL 334), c. 24, printed in AASS February, vol. 1, col. 846D. On the symbolism of bees visiting a youth, see Corbinian Gindele, "Bienen-, Waben- und Honigvergleiche in der frühen monastischen Literatur," in *Regulae Benedicti Studia*, Annuarium internationale 6–7 (Hildersheim, 1977–1978), p. 8. Pliny (*Naturalis Historia*, 11.18) reports that a swarm of bees landed on the young Plato's mouth, presaging the sweetness of his eloquence, and a similar story survives about Ambrose. An inversion of the trope occurs in an early-eleventh-century account of a heretic who received his inspiration through a dream in which bees invaded his body through his genitals and left through his mouth, stinging him all the while. See Glaber, *Historiae* 2.11.22, discussed in Stock, *Implications*, pp. 101–103.

[108] Ugé, *Monastic Past*, pp. 127–128.

Only a chorus of angels, singing hymns, escorted him
To the place of his tomb . . .[109]

The miracle supports the otherwise dubious claim that Adalbald, who was
killed by relatives rather than for a religious reason, was a martyr:

The martyr Adalbald deserved the heavenly kingdom.
Divine power knew that Adalbald was a companion among the elect,
Worthily honored with the name martyr.[110]

The cephalophory instantly makes Adalbald memorable and provides
Eusebia with a paternal saint more impressive than her mother.

Other more subtle narrative additions support Eusebia's authority,
sanctity, and power. Both her *vitae* present her as an effective abbess.
The epic employs the trope of the *puella senex*, the precociously wise
child, to claim that the twelve-year-old Eusebia was a suitable leader for
Hamage; her congregation unanimously recognized her authority, even if
her mother did not.[111] After her return to Hamage, both describe her
participation in the abbey's public business (*seculares negotia*), which the
epic *vita* couches in the Classical language of male politics (*publica res*).[112]

Other additions to her *vitae* justify Eusebia's unconventional behavior.
Her nightly absences from Marchiennes contravened the ideal of female
claustration. Hucbald does not depict Eusebia roaming alone, but says she
was accompanied by "others of the faithful."[113] Both lives of Eusebia

---

[109] VE (metric), fol. 48r: "Nisibus erectum propriis stetit ecce cadaver / Martyris, ambabus
manibus caput accipit atque / Ulnis devectat, non praedux ullus euntis, / Angelicus tantum
chorus hymnizans comitatur / Usque locum tumuli . . ." This passage is reminiscent of the
cephalophory and angelic escort in Hilduin's epic PD: "Angelicoque gradum ductu per
plana regente /... Ulnis mobilibus coepit vectare patenter ... Nobile dum manibus caput
effert forte cadaver / ... Donec ad usque locum venit qui corpus obumbrat / ... At chorus
ille sacer caelo directus ab alto / Ymnis dulcisonis modulantius ..." (fol. 33v).

[110] VE (metric), fol. 47v: "Martyr Adalbaldus caelestia regna meretur. / Praescierat propriis
consortem vis Deitatis / Martyrem Adalbaldum merito sub honore vocandum."

[111] Ibid., fol. 53r: "The girl was placed in command, and there was no one / Who opposed the
unanimous voices . . . in her mind, she was wiser than her years, and her skilled conduct
conquered the aged" (Praeficitur virgo, nec erat quis qui foret in hoc / Adversans omnes
uno sub nomine voces . . . maior erat annis prudentia mentis / Vincebatque senes annosos
actio sollers).

[112] VE (prose), c. 11; VE (metric), fol. 56v.

[113] McNamara et al. translate Hucbald, VR, c. 25, "cum sua collectanea, aliisque fidis, ut
putabat, sui secreti sociis" as "with her prayer book and a harp, which she considered the
comrades of her secret ..." Taking *fidis* with *aliis* as ablatives of accompaniment after
cum, I translate this as "with her prayer book and with others of the faithful, as she
thought, the allies of her secret." Cf. Johannes, VR, 2.399–400, who mentions no
attendants.

make Amat (and unspecified others) into Eusebia's entourage, providing an episcopal escort and saintly approval. By including Amat, the two *Vitae Eusebiae* also preempt any suspicion that she was usurping priestly roles.

The very structure of the two *Vitae Eusebiae* emphasizes her sanctity. They are not organized like a confessor's *vita*, which typically follows the life in a roughly chronological fashion with thematic sections on virtues, ascetic practices, and other saintly behavior, but like a martyr's *passio*, which culminates in ordeal and death. Both *vitae* use the term *passio* (c. 9, fol. 58r) and describe its effects as lifelong. Eusebia was injured by the sword hilt of a man who was restraining her: "she was hit so hard by this blow that on this occasion she repeatedly coughed up a thick bloody substance and, as evidence of her forbearance and punishment, she was not free of this *passio* until her death."[114]

The most notable additions that the lives of Eusebia make to Hucbald's core narrative cluster around this ordeal. The prose adds the miracle of the staff: "when she was being assailed by the whip, the little rod (*virgula*) was cast down and stuck into the earth and, without any bit of moisture for growth, it immediately burst into leaf."[115] Although the writer presents the miracle as hearsay (*"ferunt ..."*), he supports its veracity and counters potential skeptics by citing the biblical precedent of Aaron whose rod not only blossomed but also germinated and bore fruit.[116] He thus associates her typologically with Aaron, whose priestly status God signals by causing his staff to bloom (Num. 17.1–10). Johannes, in his *Vita Rictrudis*, borrows the episode and vocabulary from the prose *Vita Eusebiae* but omits the Scriptural parallel.[117] The epic *Vita Eusebiae* provides the most detailed version, in which the miracle followed a speech she addressed to her brother.

When these words had been spoken, she is trusting in the Lord.
And the dry rod, taken up and fixed in the soil – amazing to say –
Bursts forth greenly into brilliant new leaf,

---

[114] *VE* (prose), c. 9: "quae illisio adeo inflicta est gravis ut hac occasione saepissime extussiret quamdam faeculentam commixtionem sanguinis, ac in testimonium patientiae et subiectionis non careret hac passione usque diem suae decessionis." Also, *VE* (metric), fol. 55r.

[115] *VE* (prose), c. 9: "a flagello, dum illa corriperetur, excussam virgulam terrae inhaesisse, et absque ullo succi incremento protinus fronduisse."

[116] Ibid.: "potuit non solum reviviscens florere, verum etiam germinans sui seminis fructum proferre."

[117] Johannes, *VR*, 2.433–436: "While the right hand of the assailant threatens unremitting blows, / The cane breaks, cast down by the lash, it flies, / The cane, sticking fast in the earth, / Bursts into leaf, although unnourished by the strength of sap" (Ictibus assiduis dum dextera percutientis / Instat, disrupit, volat hinc excussa flagello / Virgula, quae terrae haerens infixa repente / Frondescit nulla vi suci suppeditata).

And the rod spreads itself forth to provide plentiful shade,
And this remains through the years as a witness to such a great miracle.[118]

The incident draws on the motif of saints' staffs that burst into life to show God working through them.[119] Staff miracles were usually attributed to men, with the exception of the English saint Etheldred.[120] (The similar language in the accounts of Etheldred and Eusebia suggests a common heritage.)

The epic *Vita Eusebiae* echoes the staff miracles in Heiric's descriptions in his ninth-century *Miracula Germani* (BHL 3462) of the saint planting trees by fixing his staff in the ground. Germanus's trees, like that of Eusebia, were the saint's *memoria*. The first staff "flourished into a hazel of great strength as a witness to his holiness, and up until today the monks revere it with such great care that no one would dare to cut any branch from it or do anything unseemly under or around it."[121] The second, a huge beech next to Germanus's church, gave its name to the place, and, like Eusebia's tree, was noted for the shade it provided.[122] These trees remained as monuments to the saint's power

---

[118] VE (metric), fol. 56r: "His dictis, sumptum, domino confisa, flagellum, / Atque solo fixum dictu mirabile siccum / Protulit in viride folium novitatis honestae / Virgaque porrecta larga distenditur umbra / Et manet haec testis tantae virtutis in annis."

[119] Examples of miraculous staffs include those of Maedoc of Ferns, Sénan, and Patrick. The topos of the blossoming rod is motif number F971.1 in Stith Thompson, *Motif Index of Folk-Literature: A Classification of Narrative Elements in Folk-Tales, Ballads, Myths, Fables, Mediaeval Romances, Exempla, Fabliaux, Jes-Books and Local Legends*, vol. 3 (Bloomington, IN, 1934); Gregory of Nyssa, *Life of St. Gregory Thaumaturgist*, cited in E. Cobham Brewer, *A Dictionary of Miracles: Imitative, Realistic and Dogmatic* (Philadelphia, 1834), p. 466; *Life of Maedoc of Ferns*, ed. and trans. Charles Plummer, in *Bethada Náem Nérenn: Lives of the Irish Saints*, vol. 2 (Oxford, 1922), p. 185; *Life of Sénan* in *Lives of Saints from the Book of Lismore*, ed. and trans. Whitley Stokes (Oxford, 1890), p. 218. For other references, see G.-M. Ollivier Beauregard, "Les lances qui reverdissent," in *Révue des traditions populaires* 9 (1894): 504, and in the same journal, Alfred Harou, "Les lances qui reverdissent," in 13 (1898) and 15 (1900) and René Basset "Le bâton qui reverdit," in 19 (1904): 65–66, 336–337, and 532.

[120] The traveling staff of Etheldred, abbess of Ely, bloomed into an ash tree as she slept. A miniature of Etheldred with a blossoming staff in a Winchester benedictional, ca. 980 (London, BL, Add. MS 49598, fol. 90b), shows this legend was already current. Cora E. Lutz, *Schoolmasters of the Tenth Century* (Hamden, CT, 1977), p. 34. Reproduced in Francis Wormald, *The Benedictional of St Ethelwold* (London, 1959), plate 6; *Vita Etheldredae* (BHL 2634), c. 13, 42 in AASS June, vol. 4, col. 507E; Richard John King, *Handbook of the Cathedrals of England* (London, 1862).

[121] PL 124, col. 1213: "haec in eius testimonium sanctitatis in corylum roboris immensi convaluit, atque usque hodie, ingenti ab monibus cautela veneratur, ne aut ramum quis ex ea decerpere, aut indecens quidpiam sub illa, aut circa illam, audeat perpetrare ..."

[122] Ibid.

and presence. Like the churches and abbeys the saint founded, the trees impressed his or her memory on the landscape and transformed it into a sacred geography.

Both Germanus's tree miracles followed his speech (a prayer and a sermon, respectively), and, similarly, in the epic *Vita Eusebiae*, the saint's words preceded the miracle. The poet utilizes epic lives' propensity for direct speech to invest Eusebia (but not Rictrude or Mauront) with greater power. Her words expressed her spiritual authority. Eusebia admonished her brother for his way of life, since he chose the broad path rather than the narrow. Whereas in both the lives of Rictrude, Amat is a mirror (*speculum*) for Mauront and his abbey, in the lives of Eusebia, she provides the example, following Christ's footsteps (*vestigia signo*).[123] Her speech in the epic leaves her brother dumbstruck (*stupere*). Her chastisement and the miracle, as much as the bishops Amand and Amat, cause his conversion to the holy life.

The two *Vitae Eusebiae* rewrite the subsequent narrative to emphasize the miracle's efficacy, attributing to it Rictrude's decision to consult the bishops and abbots (whereas in the lives of Rictrude, it was Eusebia's persistence that prompted her mother to summon them).[124] Although the churchmen decided in Eusebia's favor, Rictrude remained unwilling (*invita*) to accept her departure.[125] In the prose, but not the epic, Rictrude finally gave her blessing (c. 10).

The lives of Eusebia also stress the relationship of the two religious communities. Despite the conflict of their leaders, they had developed a deep bond of *caritas* and were sad to part:

A great joy arose among them all that they would be allowed to return, but a little sorrow also arose at the rending of their fraternal bond, through which, by the intercession of love, they had, from two, almost become as one congregation. They exchanged many kisses and, alternately, repeatedly entrusted each other to God.[126]

---

[123] *VE* (metric), fol. 55v: "Ipse meum speculum, simul exemplar venerandum."

[124] *VE* (prose), c. 10.

[125] *VE* (metric), fol. 56r.

[126] *VE* (prose), c. 10: "fit ingens gaudium pro concesso reditu omnibus suis: sed et aliquantulus moeror pro separatione fraternae sodalitatis, per quam caritate intercedente ex duabus quasi unius erant congregationis: quod tamen instantia temporis patiebatur. Oscula multiplicantur, alterna commendatio ad Dominum affectuosa imprecatione iteratur: quae omnia extremo vale finiuntur."

The epic *Vita Eusebiae* echoes the sentiment.[127]

The *vitae* of Eusebia add one final detail, noting the deterioration of Hamage in the sisters' absence. The epic implies its decay by stating that the nuns had to restore it. The prose gives more detail: "it was as if they came not to their own monastery, but to a certain house that had become dilapidated by long neglect."[128] Hamage had declined due to Rictrude's unwarranted interference and her attempt to absorb its community within Marchiennes.

The lives of Eusebia do not simply emphasize her virtues; rather, they reshape her, justifying her questionable behavior, emphasizing her righteousness, and making her holier and more impressive while downplaying her mother and her brother. In both these works, the young girl is presented as an almost masculine patron – she performed a miracle reminiscent of male spiritual leaders, she conducted public business, and she overshadowed the roles of two important male saints – Amand and Amat – in her brother's life. In the epic life, she even preached to him. The epic also underlines her masculine role by likening her to an apostle: "she dares to scale the apostolic heights, leading the people before her."[129] The lives of Eusebia face the problem of adversarial saints that Hucbald confronts (and Johannes ignores), but they deliver a different solution. In the *Vitae Rictrudis* by Hucbald and Johannes, Eusebia, like Mauront, is an ornament to her mother's holiness, but in the lives of Eusebia, she is presented as the more powerful and righteous saint.

AFFILIATION AND CONFLICT

The interactions of the two saints reflect the relations of Marchiennes and Hamage. Hamage was tied to Marchiennes by a web of saintly familial associations. Although Hamage (according to the *vitae*) seems to predate Marchiennes, the story of its desertion (at Rictrude's behest) and re-foundation from Marchiennes made it a kind of daughter house, as a

---

[127] *VE* (metric), 2.158–159: "They rejoice together in their souls, since they have received the hope of returning. Nonetheless, their affection suffers for this reason, because they are to be separated" (Congaudent animis accepta spe redeundi / Hinc tamen affectus patitur quod dissocientur).

[128] Ibid.: "veniunt ad suum non iam coenobium, sed diutina solitudine quasi quoddam neglectum domicilium."

[129] *VE* (metric), fol. 58r: "Audet apostolicas arces haec scandere, ductans / Plebeculum prae se."

later diploma calls it.[130] Naturally, neighboring houses would have had frequent contact. In the lives of Eusebia, the abbeys' relations are characterized by *caritas* as well as by oppressiveness and rebellion. The two congregations' sadness at parting may express their enduring bonds and the memory of their intertwined histories.

The dominant theme in the *vitae* of Eusebia, however, is not affiliation but conflict. The imperiled Hamage needed a powerful patron capable of resisting annexation, and the lives of Eusebia present their heroine as a martyr and a thaumaturge. As a young girl elected abbess on her grandmother's death, her situation was similar to that of the influential Matilda of Quedlinburg, daughter of Otto I. The lives elevate her above Rictrude and make an argument for institutional autonomy sanctioned by God and ecclesiastical authority. The prose *Vita Eusebiae* provides this narrative, which the metric version enshrines in epic. By producing or commissioning an epic life, the embattled abbey exploited its cultural capital, proving that, like larger and more powerful houses, it could produce an epic life.

Similar instances of hagiographic warfare, in which neighboring rival abbeys, related through tradition, competed for resources, played out elsewhere in the region.[131] Two houses in Ghent, two kilometers apart, Saint-Pierre-au-Mont-Blandin (Blandin) and Saint-Bavo, claimed Saint Amand as their founder. Saint-Bavo (named for Amand's disciple interred there) suffered especially badly from Viking attacks and local lords.[132] Saint-Bavo had initially been the more prosperous of the two, but it was so completely devastated by the Vikings, who took up residence there in 879–880, that the evicted canons remained in exile from Ghent with their

---

[130] Le Glay, *Mémoire*, Pièces justificatives II, p. 27; Bruchet, *Archives Départmentales du Nord*, p. 184.

[131] A. Giry, "Les châtelains de St-Omer (1042–1386)," *BEC* 35 (1874): 325–355 and 36 (1875): 91–117.

[132] Van der Essen, *Étude critique*, p. 354. On Saint-Pierre and Saint-Bavo, see Christoph T. Maier, "Saints, Traditions and Monastic Identity: The Ghent Relics, 850–1100," *RBPH* 85 (2007): 223–277; Oswald Holder-Egger, "Zu den Heiligengeschichten des Genter St. Bavosklosters," in *Historische Aufsätze dem Andenken an Georg Waitz gewidmet* (Hannover, 1886), pp. 662–665; Georges Declercq, "Heiligen, lekenabten en hervormers: De Gentse abdijen van Sint-Pieters en Sint-Baafs tijdens de Eerste Middeleeuwen (7de–12de eeuw)," in *Ganda en Blandinium: de Gentse abdijen van Sint Pieters en Sint Baafs*, ed. Georges Declercq (Ghent, 1997), pp. 13–40; Adriaan Verhulst, "Saint Bavon et les origines de Gand," in *Revue du Nord* 69 (1986), pp. 455–467; Adriaan Verhulst and Georges Declercq, "Early Medieval Ghent between Two Abbeys and the Count's Castle," in *Ghent: In Defence of a Rebellious City: History, Art, Culture*, ed. J. Decavele (Antwerp, 1989), pp. 37–59.

patron's relics until the 920s or 930s.[133] They finally returned to their restored abbey in 946 and only definitively asserted their independence from Blandin (with whom they shared an abbot from 946–953 and again from 965) in 981.[134] Meanwhile, Blandin, mausoleum of the counts of Flanders, with its rich cache of relics, prospered at its neighbor's expense, receiving gifts from the very count who despoiled Saint-Bavo.[135]

In response, the residents of Saint-Bavo forged documents, invented and translated a new saint, Landoald, and rewrote their history accordingly.[136] Epic lives of Bavo were part of this scheme.[137] The first (BHL 1050), composed before 980, made Landoald Bavo's maternal uncle, effectively creating a family of saints.[138] The second, the *Carmen Bavonis* (BHL 1053), composed at the end of the tenth or the beginning of the eleventh century, reaffirmed the identification.[139]

When the monks of Blandin objected to the new saints, the brothers of Saint-Bavo appealed to bishop Notker of Liège, who, in 980, upheld their *miracula* and *vitae* and ordered new works about them. Both sides appealed to the metropolitan, Adalbero of Rheims, but the residents of Saint-Bavo trumped their rivals by persuading the diocesan, Lindulf of Noyon-Tournai, to attend their relics' elevation in 982.[140] In the 970s and 980s, Saint-Bavo and Blandin received numerous imperial favors.[141] Hagiographic production expressed their continued competition in the following century.[142] In addition to the epic life and the

---

[133] Maier, "Saints, Traditions," p. 232.

[134] Ibid., p. 240.

[135] Van der Essen, *Étude critique*, p. 359.

[136] David J. Defries, "Constructing the Past in Eleventh-Century Flanders: Hagiography at Saint-Winnoc," PhD diss. (Ohio State University, 2004). Defries studies the competitive hagiography at Ghent and at Sithiu. On Landoald, see *Translatio S. Landoaldi sociorumque eius auct. Herigero*, ed. O. Holder-Egger in MGH SS 15.2, pp. 599–607. The rivalry continued through the eleventh century, for example, in the dispute over who held the relics of Amand's disciple, Flobert, for which see *Libellus de loco sepulturae Florberti contra monachos S. Bavoni*, from ca. 1079, ed. O Holder Egger in MGH SS 15.2, pp. 641–644.

[137] Defries, "Constructing the Past," p. 64.

[138] Printed in AASS October, vol. 1, pp. 243–252.

[139] *Carmen Bavonis*, ed. O. Holder-Egger in *Neues archiv* 10 (1885): 369ff.; Van der Essen, *Étude critique*, p. 366. Saint-Bavo also received the body of the enigmatic holy man Macaire when he died in 1012. See the *Vita S. Macharii prior* (written in 1014), c. 5, and *altera* (ca. 1067), ed. O. Holder-Egger in MGH SS 15.2, pp. 614–620. Both *vitae* depict Baldwin IV experiencing his miracles.

[140] Van der Essen, *Étude critique*, p. 367.

[141] Defries, "Constructing the Past," p. 62.

[142] Ibid., pp. 79–80.

carmen, writers at Saint-Bavo also composed the *Versus de S. Bavone Gandensi* (no BHL). Blandin, perhaps having less to prove, wrote only prose.

The houses at Sithiu present another parallel. In the early ninth century, Saint-Bertin revolved around two shrines.[143] In 820, Abbot Fridugis divided the community into a congregation of monks at the church of Saint-Bertin, who received two-thirds of the original community's wealth, and a chapter of canons at the church of Saint-Omer, endowed with the remaining third. One abbot ruled both Saint-Bertin and Saint-Omer until the mid-tenth century when the reformer Gerard of Brogne appointed a provost to the canons, further dividing the communities.[144] The houses were plagued by Viking raids and interfering lords (the counts of Flanders were lay abbots of Saint-Bertin).[145] They wrote competing foundation stories asserting their patron's primacy.[146] The competition in the eleventh century was expressed through rival *inventiones*, compositions, and lavish book illustration.[147] (Saint-Bertin was among the most prestigious early-eleventh-century centers of manuscript illumination.)[148]

Both Saint-Bertin and Saint-Omer produced epic lives. A monk of Saint-Bertin composed a metric *Vita Bertini* (BHL 1292) in the late ninth or early tenth century, celebrating Bertin as the founder of Sithiu.[149] The two metric lives of Saint Omer (*Audomarus* in Latin), from the late tenth to

[143] On Saint-Bertin and Saint-Omer, see Alain Derville, *Histoire de Saint-Omer* (Lille, 1981).

[144] Karine Ugé, "Creating a Usable Past in the Tenth Century: Folcuin's <<Gesta>> and the Crises at Saint-Bertin," *Studi Medievali* 37 (1996): 893.

[145] Ibid., p. 897.

[146] Ibid., pp. 890–892.

[147] Defries counts twenty-eight works. Defries, "Constructing the Past," p. 82; Karine Ugé, "Relics as Tools of Power: The Eleventh-Century *Inventio* of St. Bertin's Relics and the Assertion of Abbot Bovo's Authority," in *Negotiating Secular and Ecclesiastical Power: Western Europe in the Central Middle Ages*, ed. Arnoud-Jan A. Bijsterveld, Henk Teunis, and Andrew Wareham, International Medieval Research: Selected Proceedings of the International Medieval Congress University of Leeds, vol. 6 (Turnhout, 1999), pp. 51–72. The situation at Saint-Bertin was additionally complicated by ongoing territorial disputes between the abbey of Saint-Bertin and the town of Saint-Omer.

[148] Defries, "Constructing the Past," p. 62.

[149] The first metric *Vita Bertini* survives in a manuscript copy from the second half of the tenth century, Boulogne-sur-Mer, BM, MS 107, fols. 3v–28v; printed in *Vita Sancti Bertini metrica Prior ab anonymo auctore conscripta*, ed. François Morand (Paris, 1876). For the date, see Morand, p. 5; K. Strecker, "Studien zu Karolingischen Dichtern," *Neues Archiv der Gesellschaft für ältere deutsche Geschichtskunde zur Beförderung einer Gesammtausgabe der Quellenschriften deutscher Geschichten des Mittelalters* 45 (1924): 23–31.

eleventh century, almost completely exclude Bertin from the narrative.[150] Simon, abbot of Saint-Bertin 1131–1136, composed a second epic life of his abbey's patron.[151]

Blandin, Saint-Bavo, Saint-Bertin, and Saint-Omer belonged to the network of Flemish abbeys, discussed in the previous chapter, that circulated manuscripts, monks, and ideas. The exchange of epic lives within this textual community (as shown by the letters of Johannes of Saint-Amand and Rainer of Blandin concerning the verse *Vita Rictrudis*) ensured that the monks would be familiar with the strategies employed at other houses.[152]

Because the epic *Vita Eusebiae* is transmitted without letters, we do not know its dedicatee or intended function, but we can conjecture that, like other epic lives in this textual community, it was sent to patrons, excerpted in liturgy, or used in the classroom. Sent to a potential patron – such as Count Baldwin IV, who supported the reform movement that threatened the Flemish monasteries, or to Matilda of Quedlinburg – the epic *Vita Eusebiae* could have been a plea against Hamage's absorption.

More probably, like Johannes's *Vita Rictrudis* and the works from Saint-Bavo, it was intended for the bishop, in this case, Erluin of Cambrai or his successor Gerard. Embroiled in conflicts with Baldwin IV and the castellans of Cambrai, the bishops certainly understood the nature of overbearing power. Writings from Saint-Bavo had persuaded Bishop Notker of their contested saintly history; the residents of Hamage could hope that the epic *Vita Eusebiae* would perform a similar function.

The epic *vita* of Eusebia, like that of Rictrude, discussed in the previous chapter, would have appealed to elite, cultured patrons with its classicizing, colorful text. Used within Hamage, in the church or the classroom, the epic life of Eusebia would have affirmed the inhabitants' distinct identity from Marchiennes, their special status as spiritual descendants of Eusebia, and their learning and culture. If it was sent to other monastic houses, as Johannes's *Vita Rictrudis* was, it would have publicized the abbey's plight among the network of readers and writers of epic lives.

---

[150] The first metric *Vita Audomari* (BHL 775) was composed in the late tenth or early eleventh century, the second (BHL 772) in the eleventh. They are preserved in late manuscripts, Saint-Omer, BM, MSS 479 (xvii) and 814 (xviii). For the lost manuscripts, the dates, and an edition of BHL 775, see Joseph Van der Straeten, "Les vies métriques de Saint Omer," *AB* 81 (1963): 59–88.

[151] The second epic *Vita Bertini* (BHL 1294), in leonine hexameters, found in Boulogne-sur-Mer, BM, MS 146A, fols. 1r–12r, is ed. François Morand, *Vita Sancti Bertini metrica Simone Auctore. Vie de Saint Bertin, en vers composeé par Simon* (Paris, 1872).

[152] Saint-Bertin was closely associated with Blandin and had ties with Saint-Amand (Hucbald of Saint-Amand resided at Saint-Bertin in 890). Ugé, "Usable Past," p. 901.

THE MANUSCRIPT

The earliest manuscript containing the epic *Vita Eusebiae* offers another perspective on the life's reception and function: along with the other three works in the Rictrude-Eusebia cycle, it is preserved in an eleventh-century codex from Marchiennes, Douai, BM, MS 849. Printed editions of texts transmit only a portion of the information and codicological context provides a great deal of information about the text's uses.[153] Scholars have often privileged origins, trying to reconstruct the earliest version of a work (the "Ur text") and the circumstances of its composition while neglecting its later copies and their contexts.[154] Helmut Reimitz has challenged that idea, advocating that we examine the individual manuscripts' specific features.[155] Each codex provides a certain vision of the texts it contains.[156] As Rosamond McKitterick has expressed it, "the manuscripts, as much as the texts they contain, therefore, potentially have something to reveal of the textual communities they served as well as of the people whose identity they express."[157]

The codicological context suggests the epic *Vita Eusebiae*'s function in shaping the history and communal identity of postreform Marchiennes. It provides evidence for the abbey's cultural and artistic connections and allows us to conjecture about its readers and uses. By considering how the manuscript's texts and the miniatures work together, we see how the material book could affect the meaning of the texts it contained, and we can gain insight into the puzzle of how the works on Eusebia – whose entire narrative revolved around her assertion of independence from Marchiennes – functioned there.

The modest codex contains the readings for the matins of the Nativity and Resurrection, the prose and epic *vitae* of Eusebia, a homily and

---

[153] McKitterick, *History and Memory*, p. 11.

[154] Helmut Reimitz, "The Art of Truth: Historiography and Identity in the Frankish World," in *Texts and Identities in the Early Middle Ages*, ed. Richard Corradini (Vienna, 2006), p. 88.

[155] Ibid. See also McKitterick, *History and Memory*, p. 24. An in-depth example of this approach, examining how Hincmar of Rheims expressed his vision of the Franks in a history compilation produced around 870 at Saint-Amand, is Helmut Reimitz, "Ein karolingisches Geschichtsbuch aus Saint-Amand: der Codex Vindobonensis palat. 473," in *Text – Schrift – Codex: Quellenkundliche Arbeiten aus dem Institut für Österreichische Geschichtsforschung*, ed. Christoph Egger and Herwig Weigl (Vienna, 2000), pp. 34–90.

[156] McKitterick, *History and Memory*, p. 36.

[157] Ibid., p. 39.

elevatio of Jonat, the lives of Rictrude by Hucbald and Johannes (with respective letters), and a homily for Rictrude adapted from Gregory the Great.[158] Its contents, format, script, and miniatures show that it was produced at Marchiennes around the second quarter of the eleventh century, after the reform of 1024. (See Appendix B for a detailed description of its contents, dating, and codicology.) The script, a late Caroline minuscule in black ink, features several distinctive characteristics of the region's scriptoria.[159] Nine miniatures are executed in ink with red, green, yellow, and blue accents.

The codex's collation suggests it may originally have circulated as two booklets: one comprising the liturgical readings and a second featuring the works on the saints. The uniformity of format, however, which was not simply a "default mode" for Marchiennes's scriptorium, shows that the sections are related and that even if they were not always circulated in current form, they were designed to go together.

The script, decoration, and miniatures demonstrate close ties to regional abbeys, especially Saint-Vaast, whose abbot Leduin reformed Marchiennes. Although its production was cheaper and less skilled than that of manuscripts produced at the region's more elite houses, its lively miniatures reveal considerable vitality and iconographic individuality. The artists were influenced by English and local artistic innovations and simultaneously hearken to the Carolingian era. Like Johannes's *Vita Rictrudis* and the manuscript Valenciennes, BM, MS 502, discussed in the Introduction, the artists of Marchiennes looked to the past even as they absorbed innovations.

A POLYVOCAL MANUSCRIPT

The rationale for copying the texts on Jonat and Rictrude is clear. Jonat, despite being woefully lacking in narrative, had the potential to be an important patron for post-reform Marchiennes.[160] His relics added to

---

[158] On the complications of Jonat's identity, see I. Pagini, "Ionas-Ionatus: a proposito della biografia di Giona di Bobbio," *Studi Medievali* 3rd ser., 29 (1988): 45–85.

[159] Anne-Marie Turcan-Verkerk, "Le scriptorium de Saint-Vanne de Verdun sous l'abbatiat de Richard (1004–1046)," *Scriptorium* 46 (1992): 218.

[160] Jonat ultimately failed to catch anyone's imagination. Vanderputten has edited a *Translatio* of Jonat (BHL 4449), by Galbert of Marchiennes, ca. 1127, which attempted to establish him as a miracle-working protector. See Steven Vanderputten, "A Miracle Of Jonatus in 1127. The *Translatio sancti Jonati in Villa Saliacensi* (BHL 4449) as Political Enterprise and Failed Hagiographical Project," *AB* 126 (2000): 55–92. The *Translatio* is

the abbey's saintly capital, and he presented a useful founding figure for the monks forging an identity for Marchiennes as exclusively male community.[161] According to both *Vitae Rictrudis*, Amand had established his disciple Jonat as the first abbot of Marchiennes because he had "wished to establish a flock of monks there."[162] (Neither life of Eusebia mentions Jonat, who added nothing to her story or that of Hamage.) The *Homily* of Jonat in this codex naturally emphasizes this one known fact about him.[163] His *Elevatio* deals with the later ninth-century history of Marchiennes and Jonat only appears in spectral form. Hucbald and Johannes present Rictrude as the abbey's second leader. Nevertheless, with a *vita* by the esteemed Hucbald, an epic life, recorded miracles, and a memorable story, she remained the house's most important figure.

The reasons for the transmission of the *Vitae Eusebiae* at Marchiennes are less straightforward. Clearly, Eusebia was of interest to the monks; she was their patron's daughter, and they had gained control of her relics when they incorporated Hamage. They would also have acquired that abbey's books, which presumably included both her lives. Nonetheless, the copying of these *vitae* soon after Hamage's absorption seems surprising,

preserved in Douai, BM, 850, fols. 87v–99v, which Vanderputten dates to the third quarter of the twelfth century. Jonat's obsolescence is reflected in a twelfth-century copy of Augustine's *Enarrationes in Psalmos* (Douai, BM, MS 250) produced at Marchiennes, which has as its frontispiece a portrait of Augustine (fol. 2r). The frame surrounding the page features rondels with labeled portraits of Marchiennes's saints, Adalbald, Rictrude, Eusebia, Adalsend, Clotsend, and Mauront. Jonat is absent. On this manuscript, see Dehaisnes, *Catalogue*, p. 130; P. Černý, "Les manuscrits à peinture de l'abbaye de Marchiennes jusqu'a la fin du xiie siècle," *Bulletin de la Commission départementale d'histoire et d'archéologie du Pas-de-Calais* 11 (1981): 60, n. 43. Image reproduced in J. Porcher, *Enluminure française* (Paris, 1959), frontispiece.

[161] The *Elevatio Ionati* omits the era between his abbacy and his *elevatio* – the centuries when Marchiennes was a double house. Unlike later writings from Marchiennes, the *Chronicle* of Andre and one *MR* (BHL 7252), the *Elevatio* evinces no overt hostility toward the nuns. A non-scribal hand has, however, made several corrections and glosses that seem to erase the memory of an abbess ruling both male and female inhabitants. For example, on fol. 66v, in the clause "for then the place was being ruled by nuns" (tunc enim locus per sanctimoniales regebatur), the verb *regebatur* (*regere* – to rule) has been overwritten, perhaps by *habebatur* (*habere* – to hold). Similarly, on fol. 67r, in the clause "Judith who was the ruler of the abbey" (Judith quae rectrix erat coenobii), "coenobii" has been glossed "of the nuns of Marchiennes" (monialium marcianensis) indicating that Judith ruled nuns only, rather than the whole *coenobium*.

[162] Johannes, *VR*, 2.122–123: "Illic namque gregem monachorum sanctus Amand / Constitui voluit."

[163] Van der Essen, *Étude critique*, p. 272. He attributes the homily to Hucbald on the basis of linguistic and stylistic similarities, but its reference to Saint Lanoald places it later in the tenth century.

because they make an argument for its autonomy and promote Eusebia at Rictrude's expense. Whereas Jonat lacked narrative, Eusebia presented the opposite problem. She was troublesome, but her story was vivid, and she reflected glory on Rictrude. Therefore, despite the difficulties she posed, both her *vitae* were included.

To understand this codex, we must consider how manuscript context could shape the texts' meanings. Reimitz observes that "very similar texts and historiographical traditions could be employed in devising, through their varying contextualisations, very different identities."[164] Certain codices, which McKitterick has termed "polyvocal," could include works with disparate aims and messages.[165] The objective of the manuscript "compiler," who organized and oversaw the scribes' and artists' production, was central.[166] By determining how the texts were presented, the compiler could transform their meaning in accordance with his or her purposes and audiences.[167] Through miniatures, the juxtaposition of texts, and other means, the compiler could convey certain messages relevant to the manuscript's intended users.[168] Diverse texts could be manipulated so that they adhered (at least broadly) to an institution's preferred version of its past.

Douai, BM, MS 849 is an example of a polyvocal manuscript. The compiler, a monk of Marchiennes, gathered texts composed with various purposes and perspectives and incorporated them into a book aimed at promoting the glory of Marchiennes, its most important patron, Rictrude, and its first abbot, Jonat. The codex, as it was bound, included works in prose and verse, about saints associated with Marchiennes: Jonat, Rictrude, and Eusebia. These texts contain divergent interpretations of Marchiennes's early history and the relative importance of its saints. This earliest codex includes contradictory stories, which exalt and diminish Marchiennes's primary patron. We have seen the problems Eusebia presented for Rictrude's sanctity and Jonat contradicted her role as a founding figure.

The compiler dealt with both difficult Eusebia and dull Jonat by using miniatures to express their subordination to Rictrude and their place within her family. Miniatures show Eusebia and Jonat in static poses, alone and holding books (fols. 33r, 61v; Figures 8–9). In contrast, Rictrude is depicted in complex compositions that underline her

[164] Reimitz, "Art of Truth," p. 88.
[165] McKitterick, *History and Memory*, passim.
[166] Ibid., p. 22,
[167] Ibid., p. 46.
[168] Ibid., p. 59.

FIGURE 8. Douai, Bibliothèque Marceline Desbordes-Valmore, MS 849, fol. 33r. Saint Eusebia.

leadership. The half-page miniatures on the facing leaves 71v–72r delineate the roles and relative importance of the saints. On the lower half of folio 71v, Jonat and Mauront flank the much larger Rictrude (Figure 10). By depicting both men in the same relation to her, the image mediates the traditions of Jonat and Rictrude as founding saints, symbolically incorporating Jonat into her family (as the epic *Vita Bavonis*, noted earlier, added

FIGURE 9. Douai, Bibliothèque Marceline Desbordes-Valmore, MS 849, fol. 61v. Saint Jonat in portrait initial.

Landoald to Bavo's family). Like the stories of her concern for her children's spiritual health, it conflates her roles as abbess and mother. (The *lectio* for Rictrude in this codex also emphasizes her maternal side.)[169] Rictrude's three daughters, on the lower half of the facing page, are the same height as Mauront and Jonat (Figure 11). Eusebia has a green halo but is otherwise undifferentiated from her yellow-nimbed sisters. She is simply one of Rictrude's children, who (as Hucbald says) redound to their mother's reputation.[170]

The second depiction of Rictrude, which precedes her *lectio*, shows her in action (fol. 126r; Figure 12). The page is divided into two registers, like the nativity scene on folios 1r and 2r. In the lower register, a haloed Rictrude, depicted from the side, addresses four individuals. Two robed unveiled

[169] See Appendix B.
[170] Hucbald, *VR*, c. 19.

FIGURE 10. Douai, Bibliothèque Marceline Desbordes-Valmore, MS 849, fol. 71v (detail). Rictrude flanked by her son Mauront and by Jonat, first abbot of Marchiennes.

FIGURE 11. Douai, Bibliothèque Marceline Desbordes-Valmore, MS 849, fol. 72r (detail). Rictrude's daughters Adalsend, Eusebia, and Clotsend.

FIGURE 12. Douai, Bibliothèque Marceline Desbordes-Valmore, MS 849, fol. 126r. Rictrude and onlookers.

figures seem to be monks.[171] A third male figure wears a shorter tunic, not monastic habit. (The fourth figure is only partly visible.) Rictrude is shown

[171] This depiction, which is in contrast to both her *vitae* (Johannes describes her addressing her *fratres* and *sorores* and Hucbald only mentions her addressing her *sorores*), speaks to Marchiennes after its reform. Johannes, *VR*, 2.191–192; Hucbald, *VR*, c. 21. Dehaisnes interprets the figures as her children, but her daughters would be represented wearing nuns' veils.

speaking to an audience. Despite the importance of speech in Eusebia's narrative, and although both she and Jonat also led religious houses, only Rictrude is shown addressing a group. Rictrude is not presented alone but in a community, underlining her role as abbess. The juxtaposition of this scene with the upper register, which shows Christ (with cruciform halo) preaching to a crowd, typologically likens Rictrude to Christ. This, the last image in the codex, combines the themes of the first miniatures, showing the continuation of Christ's salvific work (represented by his birth and resurrection on fols. 1v–2r and 19v, respectively) in Rictrude's own life.

So, although this manuscript includes narratives that undermine Rictrude's preeminence, the miniatures subordinate the other saints to her. The images, which are more immediately obvious than the narrative inconsistencies, proclaim the relative status of the members of Marchiennes's dysfunctional saintly family. As Johannes drew on Hucbald and the prose *Vita Eusebiae* without ever reconciling the competing viewpoints, the compiler has assembled conflicting sources into a new collection full of inconsistencies. As far as we know, the compiler did not actually rewrite the narratives. Such work would be time-consuming and beyond the Latin competency of many. Besides, for some purposes, such intervention would be unnecessary. In choosing readings for a saint's feast day or elements to incorporate into antiphons of versified liturgy, the monks could simply select unproblematic passages.[172]

The codex's function is not immediately clear. The format, content, and lack of annotations show it was not a classroom book.[173] The inclusion of *lectiones* (on the nativity, the passion, and Rictrude) and the *Homily* of Jonat indicate liturgical use. Marginal Roman numerals divide the prose texts into sections for such reading. (As usual, the epic lives are not divided in this manner.) Perhaps it could have been an altar book, a poorer counterpart to the collection on Amand discussed in the Introduction, kept in the church and consulted for readings. It would also be small enough to take to the refectory for meal-time readings. As it is bound, however, Douai, BM, MS 849 is an illogical monastery book, combining works on the house's patron saints, such as one would find in a *libellus*, with readings for the nativity and resurrection, already represented in the church's liturgical volumes.

---

[172] On the use of verse *vitae* in liturgy, see Jonsson, *Historia*, pp. 77–83 and passim; and Björkvall and Haug, "Performing Latin Verse," pp. 278–299.

[173] This accords with the changing codicological contexts of epic *vitae*, which appear less often in schoolbooks after the tenth century.

The volume might have been compiled for private devotional reading. Individuals, whether monks in their cells or secular patrons, could ruminate on epic lives, prose lives, and liturgical texts. The inclusion of miniatures suggests that the book was made for a patron outside the abbey rather than for private monastic contemplation. If the codex was given to a patron, it must have been returned, perhaps as a bequest.[174] Although it might seem an inadequate gift compared to contemporary luxury codices, this was not necessarily the case.[175] Even "relatively scruffy" volumes were expensive to produce, and books were precious for many reasons. For a pious reader, the contents made a book valuable.

If the book were intended for personal reading outside the cloister, that would explain why the readings from Christ's nativity and resurrection (folios 1–30) were bound with the hagiographical works that make up the rest of the volume. Unlike the monks, a lay reader probably would not have easy access to liturgical books containing these readings. Because they contained the church fathers' reflections on the episodes central to the theology of salvation they would have been interesting to a pious reader. Examining the passages chosen for the "selective" Gospelbooks of Judith, daughter of Count Baldwin IV, McGurk and Rosenthal note that one of them contains "the Christmas and Easter passages in all four gospels."[176] This suggests the lay reader's concern with the nativity and resurrection. Could the compilation of Douai, BM, MS 849 be a complement to a selective gospelbook? The inclusion of texts on local saints could reflect the interests of a patron or the monks' attempt to promote their saints with a local potentate, such as a member of the count's family. The counts of Flanders were involved in the exchange of books among monasteries, and Baldwin IV's daughter Judith was a collector of books.[177] The family may have had a

---

[174] Laypeople left books to monasteries. See Patrick McGurk and Jane Rosenthal, "The Anglo-Saxon Gospelbooks of Judith, Countess of Flanders: Their Text, Make-Up and Function," *ASE* 24 (1995): 251–308.

[175] McGurk and Rosenthal suggest that a non-luxurious Gospel book from the low countries (Stuttgart, Württembergische Landesbibliothek, H.B. II 46) was a gift for Judith of Flanders (daughter of Baldwin IV) despite being "incomplete," "a desultory production," and "relatively scruffy" in comparison to her four famous gospelbooks (New York, Pierpoint Morgan Library, M. 708; New York, Pierpoint Morgan Library, M. 709; Fulda, Hessische Landesbibliothek, Aa. 21; Monte Cassino, Archivio della Badia, 437). McGurk and Rosenthal, "Anglo-Saxon Gospelbooks," pp. 303–307.

[176] Fulda, Hessische Landesbibliothek, Aa. 21, discussed in ibid., p. 270.

[177] Francis Newton, *The Scriptorium and Library at Monte Cassino, 1058–1105* (Cambridge, 1999), p. 302.

connection with Marchiennes. (The abbey's last known abbess was named Judith, which was a family name the Flemish counts had inherited through their royal Carolingian ancestry.)[178]

We can speculate that the codex was intended for a female reader. The images are female centered, even taking into account Marchiennes's predominately female saints.[179] Later in the Middle Ages, at least, women were particularly associated with illustrated devotional manuscripts.[180] McGurk and Rosenthal describe the selection of texts deemed appropriate for a female patron.[181] The book's four lives of female saints would have been fitting, as would the emphasis on motherhood, not only in the lives of Rictrude but also in the *lectio* adapted from Gregory. It is even possible that Judith, as a book collector and a monastic patron who lived in Flanders from 1065 to 1070, was the intended recipient.[182]

Finally, the hypothesis of a secular patron could explain the observation that the book may comprise originally separate but related sections. We can speculate (but not prove) that a *libellus* on the abbey's saints was repurposed as a gift for a patron particularly interested in the incarnation and resurrection. This was achieved through the addition of the readings (fols. 1–30), which were deliberately copied in the same format and then bound together with the *libellus*.

A DOMESTICATED SAINT

The prose and epic *vitae* of Rictrude and Eusebia present elaborate versions of the early history of Marchiennes and Hamage, the subtleties of which were not clear to outsiders. The *Gesta of the Bishops of Cambrai* omits any reference to Jonat or Gertrude and refers to Rictrude and Eusebia as their respective houses' sole founders, suggesting that in the

---

[178] Judith, a family name of the Welfs, Counts of Burgundy, entered the Carolingian royal house through Charles the Bald's mother, whose granddaughter of the same name eloped with Count Baldwin I. David Nicholas, *Medieval Flanders* (London, 1992), p. 16.

[179] For example, the miniature depicting the women at the tomb (fol. 19v) shows the three women and a wingless angel, but not the soldiers often depicted in that scene.

[180] Kathyrn A. Smith, *Art, Identity and Devotion in Fourteenth-Century England: Three Women and Their Books of Hours* (Toronto, 2003), p. 5.

[181] McGurk and Rosenthal suggest passages in a selective gospelbook (Monte Cassino Archivio della Badia, 437) were chosen for Judith since they included "three sections devoted to women, which could be regarded as appropriate for a female patron." McGurk and Rosenthal, "Anglo-Saxon Gospelbooks," p. 273.

[182] Ibid., pp. 252–253.

early eleventh century, their most powerful patrons energetically eclipsed the roles of their lesser-known founding figures.[183]

The adversarial narratives of Eusebia had been produced in response to a specific crisis, and after Marchiennes absorbed Hamage, the stories became simpler. Eusebia's versified office in a twelfth-century Marchiennes breviary presents a watered-down story in snippets of verse.[184] (Versified offices – offices that contain antiphons and responsaries in metric or rhythmic verse – originate in the tenth century and first appear in the dioceses around Flanders.) It recounts her pious disobedience and beating, but omits the staff miracle and the extent of her suffering and casts no aspersions on Rictrude.[185] The office was recopied at Marchiennes in the thirteenth, fifteenth, and sixteenth centuries.[186] The necessarily abbreviated story given in antiphons and responsaries would be complemented by the texts chosen for the readings. This office allowed for a selection that would not diminish Rictrude or Mauront in any way.

In the earlier twelfth century, the memory of Hamage as a separate institution was reflected in the use of and appeal to Eusebia's relics, but there is no mention of past conflict between the institutions or the saints. A charter of 1122 unambiguously declares that Hamage belonged to Marchiennes, but notes that it "had been an abbey in former times."[187] A charter of the following year reduces the complicated foundation stories

---

[183] *Gesta Ep. Cam.* 2.27.

[184] Jonsson identifies the office of Eusebia preserved in Douai, BM, MS 134 as one of the earliest versified offices (along with those of Rictrude and Mauront contained in the same manuscript), meaning that it would be a tenth-century composition. The text, however, echoes Johannes as well as Hucbald, so must date to the turn of the millennium or later. Jonsson attributes these offices to Hucbald. Jonsson, *Historia*, p. 19; these three versified offices are published in Analecta Hymnica Medii Aevi (hereafter, AH), vol. 13, *Historiae Rhythmicae: Liturgische Reimofficien*, ed. Guido Maria Dreves (Leipzig, 1892), pp. 133–135, 200–202, 225–228.

[185] AH 13, pp. 133–135. The office, echoing Hucbald (*VR*, c. 26), states that Eusebia was hurt by the sword hilt, but does not describe any effects of the injury or characterize her as a martyr: "By the sword of a certain soldier, the flank of the tender virgin, through the beatings, by the hilt is injured undeservedly" (Ense cuiusdam militis / Latus tenellae virginis / Per verbera a capulo / Laeditur absque merito). In 2 Nocturno, Antiphon 5, AH 13, p. 134.

[186] AH 13, p. 135 lists the manuscripts: Douai, BM, MSS 134 and 138 (breviaries); and MSS 117 and 118 (antiphoners).

[187] In 1122, Robert, bishop of Arras, confirmed Marchiennes's possessions: "the church of Hamage, which in former [or early] times had been an abbey, we confirm is freely held by the aforementioned church of Marchiennes and is free from every revenue" (ut aecclesiam Hamagiensem, quae priscis temporibus abbatia fuerat, ab omni redditu liberam predictae Marchianensi aecclesiae liberaliter possidendam firmaremus). ADN 10 H 5/34.

of the two houses, as told in the *vitae*, to a simple relationship of mother and daughter house, mirroring the relationship of their patron saints.[188] The contemporaneous *Poleticum* (ca. 1120) records an annual ritual from the recent past that alluded to Hamage's former independence and Eusebia's story:

Those who now remain there, both monks and locals of the place, say only this, that until this age ... they practiced a custom of this kind, namely that in each year, on the day before the feast of the dedication of the Church [Sainte-Marie at Hamage], the saint's body would be carried to that place with relics and crosses, accompanied by brothers from the congregation, and with reverence and awe, they would perform vespers and the night office. What is more, on the next day their lord abbot or deacon would arrive with the rest of the congregation and, similarly, they would joyfully celebrate the day office. Then in the middle of the feast day, when the rites and the sacraments of the heavenly mysteries had been performed, they would return to their own place, with bright minds and cheerful spirits, in a voice of exultation.[189]

The brothers of Marchiennes reenacted Eusebia's night journeys without referring to the conflict they had caused. The monks symbolically became her entourage, going with her to perform the night office at Hamage, before returning with her to her domicile, Marchiennes.

A contemporary text, a *Miracula* of Jonat, written at Marchiennes around 1130, also recalls Eusebia without family conflict.[190] The villagers of Sailly-en-Ostrevent, imperiled following the murder of Count Charles of Bruges, asked the abbot of Marchiennes to send Eusebia's relics to defend them (disappointingly, the monks sent Jonat instead).[191] The village had once

[188] Calixtus II in 1123 granted exemption from interference to "the church of Hamage, just like Marchiennes, whose daughter it is" (ecclesiam quoque Hamagiensem ... , sicut et Marceniensem cuius filia est). Le Glay, *Mémoire*, Pièces justificatives II, 27, with my orthographic corrections from charter 2 of the series ADN 10 H 1. Bruchet, *Archives Départmentales du Nord*, p. 184.

[189] *Poleticum*, c. 14: "tradunt tantummodo qui nunc supersunt et coenobitae et loci incolae quod, seculo adhuc ... usus huiusmodi adoleverit ut per singulos annos in dedicatione ecclesiae pridie ante diem festum illuc transferretur corpus sanctae cum reliquiis et crucibus de contione fratrum quibusdam comitantibus, qui cum reverentia et timore vespertinalem synaxim et nocturnalem consuetudinaliter quirent adimplere. In crastinum autem domnus abbas vel decanus superveniret cum collegii parte residua et sic pariter officii diurni precelebrarent festiva gaudia. Iam vero die festo mediante, celebratis missarum sollempniis et misteriorum caelestium sacramentis, cum alacritate animi et iocunditate spirituali redirent ad sua in voce exultationis." The mid-twelfth-century *ME* (BHL 2738) c. 8 repeats this directly. AASS March, vol. 2, cols. 459A–B.

[190] BHL 4449, ed. and trans. Vanderputten, "Miracle of Jonatus," pp. 73–92.

[191] Ibid., p. 73.

been part of Hamage's holdings, and even a century later the inhabitants remembered Eusebia as their special patron.[192] Perhaps they also wanted her assistance because, unlike Jonat, she had defended the disempowered against superior coercive force.

The story of Hamage's neglect followed by Eusebia's return is replayed symbolically in mid- to late-twelfth-century sources. The *Miracula Eusebiae* (BHL 2738), from the middle third of the century, represents a faction hostile to Fulchard (abbot of Marchiennes, 1103–1115). Accordingly, the author blames him for the precipitous decline of both Marchiennes and Hamage:

Under the rule of Abbot Fulchard, it [Hamage], along with Marchiennes was reduced to the worst poverty. The very location of Hamage was so greatly despised that they gave the monastery's guardianship to a peasant and his wife. The abbot also gave it to a certain relative of his, a soldier who was completely debilitated by leprosy, so he could sustain himself with whatever he could find there.[193]

Abbot Amand of Marchiennes restored the house in 1133, says the *Miracula* writer, installing four or five monks and making it a convalescent home (c. 11). Eusebia's bones, encased in a new gold-and-silver reliquary, were returned to Hamage, where they performed healing miracles. A later *Miracula Rictrudis* (BHL 7249), perhaps from the 1160s, represents a pro-Fulchard tradition in which he is the restorer rather than the destroyer of Hamage (the writer antedates the house's decline to its very early years, blaming the nuns' mismanagement and the attacks of outsiders).[194] In both scenarios, Marchiennes's restoration of Hamage and the retranslation of Eusebia's relics were represented as a return to the correct order, as evidenced by the miracles surrounding the rebuilding and the healings that followed.

Hamage was restored as Marchiennes's priory and comfortably assimilated into its holdings and identity. Therefore, we see a simple version of Eusebia.[195] Although the authors of the various *Miracula* and Andre

---

[192] Ibid., p. 59.

[193] *ME* (BHL 2738), c. 9: "[Hamage] sub regimine Fulchardi Abbatis ad summam paupertatem cum Marchianensi redactus, in tantum idem locus Hamaticensis venit despectum, ut cuidam rustico and uxori eius monasterii custodiam delegarent. Abbas quoque cuidam militi cognato suo debili et leproso totum concessit, quidquid ibi ad sui sustentationem posset accipere."

[194] *MR* (BHL 7249), AASS May, vol. 3, cols. 140D-E, 154A-D.

[195] Several books now in the Bibliothèque municipale at Douai imply that Hamage was a priory of Marchiennes. A breviary "ad usum monasterii Marchianensis" from the twelfth century (Douai, BM, MS 135) and a similar book from the fourteenth (Douai, BM, MS 139), are

(writing toward the end of the twelfth century) had access to the four *vitae*, which were all copied in that century, they suppressed the story of familial strife. No longer was Eusebia a troublesome and defiant daughter.[196] With her domestication complete, she could return home once again. Hamage was no longer a problem – it had long been the property of Marchiennes and, if the "mother" house had previously neglected it, it had now restored the "daughter" priory, as the miracles attested.

The domestication of Eusebia begun in the artistic scheme of Douai, BM, MS 849 was complete. Her miracles, as recounted in the twelfth century, were the usual kinds of posthumous healings. The tame Eusebia did not defy her mother or stupefy her brother. She was neither a quasi-masculine protector nor a martyr, and she did not spit up pus and blood. With Hamage absorbed and their conflict suppressed, Eusebia and Rictrude both became conventional saints and neither was again celebrated in epic verse.

*

By participating in hagiographic one-upmanship, Marchiennes and Hamage were engaging in a normal tenth- and eleventh-century practice. The epic *vitae* of Rictrude and Eusebia are both highly classicizing and erudite, replete with verbal ornamentation, visual imagery, and miraculous additions to their prose counterparts. Again, the epic poets lack the prose writers' concern with defending their narrative or their protagonists. These entertaining, memorable, aesthetically sophisticated works were to appeal to the highest level of culture and to regional ecclesiastical authorities, particularly the bishops who could oppose or support reform.

Both lives of Eusebia are stories about power and autonomy, about the disenfranchised defeating a larger rival through piety and persistence.

inscribed with the name of Florentius Le Pers, prior of Hamage. *Catalogue général*, vol. 2, Douai, pp. 66–67. In both books, the ex libris is accompanied by the epigram "Spernit omnia virtus," which is ascribed to Daniel de Landis in the earlier codex. Despite the restoration and translation, Hamage's role may have remained primarily agricultural. A note on Douai, BM, MS 134, fols. 111–112 (late xii, from Marchiennes), which contains the versified offices of Rictrude, Eusebia, and Mauront, appears to name the farmers of the priory Hamage and list its revenues. See Victor Leroquais, *Les bréviaires manuscrits des bibliothèques publiques de France* (Paris, 1932–1934), vol. 2, pp. 41–45; Dehaisnes, *Catalogue*, pp. 65–66.

[196] Eusebia still liked to travel from home, unlike Rictrude. According to Andre's *MR*, the monks quickly returned Rictrude from a church consecration in 1079, because she disliked her relics being used for fund-raising. By contrast, the monks took Eusebia all the way to England on a disastrous fund-raising mission. Andre, *Miracula Sanctae Rictrudis*, rev. ed., ed. A. Poncelet, *AB* 20 (1901): 456, discussed by Steven Vanderputten, "Itinerant Lordship: Relic Translations and Social Change in Eleventh- and Twelfth-Century Flanders," *French History* 25 (2011): 149–150.

Eusebia's claims to institutional independence were divinely sanctioned through miraculous proof and ultimately vindicated by the region's abbots and bishops. The young saint, as the epic *Vita Eusebiae* told it, once used word and miracle to rescue her community from assimilation into Rictrude's house. Although she was unable to save Hamage a second time, her voice persisted to tell the tale in symbolic form. In the absence of more conventional kinds of power, the inhabitants of Hamage asserted their independent status and identity by writing or acquiring an epic life.

As a survival strategy the *Vitae Eusebiae* failed, but the authors succeeded in preserving another version of the originary myths of Marchiennes and Hamage. The two *Vitae Eusebiae* were valuable to Marchiennes because they featured one of its patron saint's daughters and they were incorporated into a polyvocal codex, Douai, BM, MS 849, that minimized the ideological conflict between the competing versions of the past.

Once Hamage (and therefore Eusebia's mortal remains) were securely in Marchiennes's power, its monks had even more reason to celebrate the virtues and healing power of Eusebia in texts such as the *Miracula Eusebiae* and in the church's liturgical calendar as represented by the massive lectionary, Douai, BM, MS 840. Like Hamage and Eusebia's relics, the *Vitae Eusebiae* were subsumed into Marchiennes and deployed by that house for its own ends. In later versions, Eusebia became a good daughter who did not rebel against her mother. In the twelfth-century *Miracula Eusebiae*, her miracles redounded to her mother's glory and induced pilgrims to visit her relics. By this time, Hamage had become a convalescent home for Marchiennes's monks, and a new, less troublesome Eusebia reflected this reality. In her prose and verse lives, preserved in the manuscripts of Marchiennes, however, the dissonant voice of the rebellious girl saint remained, protesting the oppressive authority of her mother and, symbolically, her mother house. Hamage was annexed, but its voice survived.

Conclusion: "Black Seeds on a White Page"

Epic *vitae* were written and copied to glorify saints, aggrandize abbeys, and appeal to powerful patrons who would be flattered by the dedication of a learned text. In the ninth century, the dedicatees were often Carolingian kings, who were the patrons of royal abbeys, and former teachers. Increasingly, poets also offered the works to bishops and courtiers. With the decentralization of royal authority and the multiplication of forms of power that accompanied the decline of the Carolingians, bishops largely replaced kings as dedicatees. Epic *vitae* were written in both monastic and cathedral schools. As the cathedrals eclipsed the abbeys as the leading intellectual centers of the later tenth century, monks continued to produce epic *vitae*. Despite the cathedral schools' pedagogical innovations and the increasingly ornate and classicizing style of their literature, these institutions remained part of the monastic schools' textual communities, perpetuated by a partially shared canon and a common way of reading and writing. Accordingly, monastic epic *vitae* retained currency even among the courtier bishops of the later tenth century.

Patronage was often tied to education. Students sent epic *vitae* to former teachers who could promote their careers. These *vitae* made appropriate dedications, because they demonstrated the student's grasp of the whole curriculum and were themselves classroom texts. As Ermenric's letter shows, a teacher could use an epic *vita* to teach intermediate and advanced students. The wide-ranging and digressive poems allowed the teacher to introduce a number of topics, including dialectic, philosophy, mythology, astronomy, and theology and to teach skills including allegorical reading and paraphrase. Because the works were often about a monastery's patron, their use in the classroom meant that some students imbibed the founding story of their own houses in the lofty epic form that Virgil used to commemorate the origins of Rome. By telling of the house and the saint, an epic *vita* perpetuated the identity of the local religious community. The symbolic representation of different communities' affiliation and conflict, embodied in the relations of their saints, could be presented to both individuals within those communities and outside patrons.

Like the patterns of patronage and educational prestige, the manuscript contexts of epic *vitae* also shifted, albeit somewhat later, suggesting that the works' functions were changing. In the ninth and tenth century, epic *vitae* were included in schoolbooks and *libelli* on a specific saint. After the eleventh century, we find few epic lives in schoolbooks. A number were still copied in *libelli*, but they were mainly transmitted in large lectionaries, where we find occasional epic *vitae* among the prose works. Like biblical epics, epic *vitae* seem to have faded from the classroom during the intellectual transformations of the twelfth century, replaced by a proliferation of new verse pedagogical texts.

I have examined the social functions of the epic *vitae* in their historical context, looking at their production, copying, exchange, dedication, and reception. Although their uses sometimes overlapped with those of other literary forms, such as prose lives and non-hagiographic verse, they did not duplicate the functions of existing works, but presented a unique grammar of sanctity, which constituted and appealed to an elite community of readers and writers including monks, nuns, kings, and bishops.

We have observed several recurring themes, which complicate ideas about sanctity and hagiographic writing. First, we have seen that writers incorporated themselves into imagined lineages of saints and poets. Through the salvific work of spreading the Word, the poet could liken himself to the saint. The saint effects salvation through speech and miracle, the poet through verse composition. Milo, following in the footsteps of Amand, himself a teacher of princes, applied the same metaphors to the saint's work and his own. Hilduin, in his epic *Passio Dionysii*, imitated and mediated Dionysius by assuming the role of hierarch, and simultaneously invoked a lineage of Classical and Christian poetic forebears. Other poets cast themselves as heirs to the great literary figures of their own houses. Thus, Ermenric positioned himself as the successor to Walafrid Strabo, and Johannes followed in the footsteps of Milo and Hucbald, figures from his abbey's past golden age.

Second, we have seen that these texts were to be read on different levels. As intermediaries – teachers, doubles of the saint – poets led readers through their "rocky" (*scrupulosa*) texts to a profound religious understanding. Hilduin's hierarch drew the initiate through the surfaces to mystical understanding of a deeper truth; Ermenric as teacher guided his intermediate and advanced imaginary students (that is, his readers) in allegorical interpretations of Scripture and passages of an epic *Vita Galli*.

Many of the epic *vitae*, with their challenging language and copious allusions, require the reader to delve below the surface. Poets, trained to extract hidden truths from even the most intractable texts, composed works that required similar interpretive strategies. Like the "mother bee" of Rainer's letter (and the mother bee of the Paschal candle's blessing from which it is drawn), the small image here stands for and illuminates a larger point. The bee metaphor, with its densely packed meaning and thoroughly digested imagery, embodies methods of reading and composition. The expression requires that the reader recognize the original context of the allusions for full understanding. As we saw in Johannes's epic *Vita Rictrudis*, Rainer's response to it, and Hilduin's versification of the *Passio Dionysii* for the *sagax lector*, words operate on different levels depending on the reader's erudition and approach.[1]

The lives' dense allusiveness was key to their purpose and prestige. Along with their lofty language, use of meter, and range of subjects, this allowed the poets to demonstrate their erudition and prove their teaching credentials. Their difficulty made the epic lives appropriately flattering gifts for their dedicatees. The works' subtle and manifold references to their literary traditions and their depth of meaning impressed on the readers the status of the writer, the saint, and the monastery, whether the goal was to inveigle the emperor with a work about his favorite saint or to persuade a local bishop to adopt the cause of an embattled house. The most erudite readers of epic *vitae* understood the compact and difficult references, the generation, comprehension, and redeployment of which constituted their participation in their textual communities.

A third and related theme is the particular kind of creativity shown in the writing and reception of the epic *vitae*. We have seen the inventiveness these epic poets brought to their work, variously embellishing saints' stories, composing a poem that functioned like a saint's shining reliquary, guiding readers in contemplation of the divine, collapsing saintly and authorial identity, and teaching from an epic that did not exist. Close reading of the epic *vitae* undermines the idea that imitation and ingenuity are opposed forces and shows instead a light-fingered creativity, in which

[1] *PD* (metric), fol. 16r.

an author transforms the meaning of copious often verbatim borrowings through subtle adaptation, juxtaposition, and recombination. It disproves the misconception that medieval monastic literary culture was devoid of imagination and individuality.

A fourth recurring theme, which implicitly challenges prior ideas about the readership, is the emphasis on the miraculous. In the epic *Vita Eusebiae*, the protagonist's father is shown as a cephalophore who, in imitation of Hilduin's Dionysius, walks away with his decapitated head. Johannes's epic *Vita Rictrudis* adds the miracle of the flowering branch, which is not in his main prose source. That the epic *vitae*, written for an elite and highly educated readership, contain more miracles and less emphasis on historicity than the prose *vitae*, which would reach a wider audience, complicates assumptions about popular and elite ideas of sanctity that cast the most colorful or implausible stories as a concession to popular taste.

*

So, the epic *vitae* reveal a complicated and dynamic monastic culture from the time of Louis the Pious until the turn of the millennium. They illustrate the continuity that the writers created between themselves and figures of the past (local and otherwise) and the communities they perpetuated within and beyond the cloister. They show the intertwined functions of praising the saint, flattering the patron, and educating the young. The lives created and enhanced bonds of *amicitia* between the writers and recipients and expressed rivalries between monks and monasteries. The poets reimagined their saints as epic heroes adorned with myth and miracle.

Appropriately, when they spoke of their work they did so not in terms we would recognize as literary theory, but through allegory and allusion. Milo, like other authors of epic *vitae*, interrupts his narrative to describe the process of composition. He applies a Scriptural metaphor to his writing: "Spreading the black seeds through the white fields / Worn out by the heavy burden at daylight's end, / Now I cease from scattering and, having reached this end, I rest."[2] Here he distills and synthesizes traditions, Christian and Classical, Scriptural and literary. He takes the trope of the *sator* – the sower of men – from a parable told by Jesus in the Gospels and transforms it into an image for his own work.

---

[2] Milo, *VA*, 1.447–450: "Nigra per albentes diffundens semina campos / Lassus fasce gravi completa luce diei / Spargere iam cesso factoque hic fine repauso."

The image is densely layered, because the biblical passages to which it refers are ones in which Jesus performs an allegorical interpretation of a parable for his disciples, thus providing a Scriptural precedent for reading beneath the surface of the text.[3] The *sator* sprinkling the seeds of the divine Word is a frequent image for the apostles and for their spiritual heirs, the missionary bishops, and Milo uses it to depict his patron saint.[4] By applying the same trope to his writing and Amand's preaching, Milo implicitly conflates their work.[5] His words, like the saint's, are salvific.

In addition to Scriptural parable, Milo's description incorporates a second common literary trope. Classical and early Christian authors imagine writing as plowing and the pages or wax tablets they inscribe as fields.[6]

---

[3] Mark 4:2–32; Matt. 13:3–23; Luke 8:5–15.

[4] Amand's preaching, like seed fallen on good earth, produced "a prolific crop growing from the ground [that] / Returned a hundred-fold yield, virtue from the shoots" (fecunda seges de cespite surgens / Reddit centuplicem virtutem gramine frugem; *VA*, 3.147–48). The image of the sower scattering seeds is also used to characterize God: Prudentius, *Liber Cathemerinon*, hymn 4, verse 7; hymn 10, verse 69; hymn 12, verse 45 and 85; Prudentius, *Liber Apotheosis*, verse 74; Sedulius, *Paschale Opus* 4, c. 20; and (the appropriately named) Arator, *Historia Apostolica*, 2.375, 2.443. Juvencus recounts the parable in his gospel epic, *Evangelia*, 2.739–740. Fortunatus often uses the image, ed. F. Leo, MGH AA 4/1, pp. 136, 194, 195, 248, 250. Aldhelm, *In Sancti Pauli*, ed. Rudolf Ehwald in MGH AA 15, p. 20 and *De virginitate*, p. 257; Alcuin, *Vita Willibrordi* (prose), c. 8, ed. W. Levison in MGH SRM 7, p. 123; Balther, *Vita Fridolini*, c. 6, 8, ed. B. Krusch, MGH SRM 3, pp. 357, 359. Alcuin refers to holy men scattering (*spargere*) the Word. Alcuin, York Poem, lines 655, 1035; *Vita Willibrordi* (metric), c. 1, line 10, c. 7, line 2, in MGH Poetae 1, pp. 209, p. 210; c. 16, lines 1–2, p. 212, and c. 34, line 56, p. 219, and his *Ad aram Sancti Dyonisii sociorum eius* (ibid., p. 309). Similar uses in other writers include the Epigram of Wigbod and Jacob, lines 34–35, in MGH Poetae 1, p. 96; Hymn 17 attributed to Hraban Maur closely parallels Milo's language (MGH Poetae 2, p. 25). Other epic saints' lives draw on the parable to describe preaching: Fortunatus, *Vita Martini*, 3.165, ed. F. Leo in MGH AA 4/1, p. 335; Walafrid Strabo, *De vita et fine Mammae Monachi*, c. 25, lines 17–18, in MGH Poetae 2, p. 294 ("Semina quae lacrimis Mammes infusa serebat, / Messuit hic fructu gaudens"); Anon, *Vita sancti Galli confessoris* (BHL 3253), line 8 in MGH Poetae 2, p. 428; Heiric, VG, 1.33–37, 2.224–225, 4.403; Johannes, VR, 1.204–207, 1.261, 1.297, 2.208–209; Anon., *Carmen de sancto Landberto* (BHL 4682), line 41 in MGH Poetae 4/1, p. 144 (3.185, p. 592, cf. Acts 17:18) and, in an entirely alliterative line, Luke as "the saint sowing the sacred seeds."

[5] Milo uses the image for God, the apostles, and Amand. Milo describes God as the "sower and redeemer" (*sator et redemptor*) of men (4.492, p. 609), Paul as "the sacred man sowing sacred seeds in celestial speech" [1.75, p. 570: "semina sancta serens sanctus sermone superno"]). Milo follows his description of the apostles preaching by placing Amand among their ranks (1.83, p. 571). He depicts Amand, like the apostles, "sowing the divine word," spreading his teachings far and wide. "He scattered the pious words of salvation among the scattered peoples" (2.46: p. 580: "Gentibus et sparsis sparsit pia verba salutis"; cf. 2.38–39). Milo also uses the image of the bee to characterize both Amand and himself.

[6] Curtius, *European Literature*, pp. 313–314. Curtius cites Isidore, *Etymologies* 6,9,2, quoting the ancient Roman poet Atta ("vertamus vomerum / In cera ...") as the metaphor's

Milo's composite metaphor is half-baked; seeds cast on snowy fields (*campi albentes*) are unlikely to grow. But perhaps that is the point. As Jesus explains it, the seeds that he and the apostles (and, by extension, the saints and poets) sow will mostly fall on stony ground or be choked by thorns, and few people will understand their words. Many will hear only the surface meaning. Like the parable of the sower, epic lives functioned on different levels. For some readers, they were simply verse narratives of saints, but for others – the *discipuli* who were not slow (as Ermenric says), the *sagaces lectores* seeking salvation, those who read like bees – they contained hidden meanings. Jesus, explaining the parable, said, "the field is the world."[7] For the composers of epic lives, it was also the vellum and the classroom where the poets fulfilled the saints' work.

source. Other Classical examples are discussed by Julián Santano Moreno, "Il solco e il verso: il luogo della metafora," *Rivista di filolofia cognitiva* 1 (2003), n.p., http://w3.uniroma1.it/cogfil/solco.html (accessed October 25, 2011). Classical uses of plowing words (e.g., *sulcare, proscindere, arare*) for writing include Cicero, *Att.*, 12,1; *Fam.*, 9, 26; Ovid, *Met.* 7.119; 9.563; *Amores*, 1, 11, 7; Pliny, *Ep.* 7, 4, 5; and Statius, *Silvae*, 4, 5, 24. Carolingian verse examples include *Versus Pauli* 12, line 1; Dagulf, *Ad Moulinum*, line 5; Paulinus of Aquileia, *Regula Fidei*, line 128 (all ed. in MGH Poetae 1, pp. 49, 93, 129). On the whiteness of parchment, see Michael Lapidge and James L. Rosier, *Aldhelm: The Poetic Works* (Cambridge, 1985), p. 252. An early Christian example of "white fields" is Juvencus, *Evangelia*, 2.313.

[7] Matt. 13:38: "ager autem est mundus."

APPENDIX A

St. Gallen, Stiftsbibliothek, MS 265

A prose and verse miscellany containing Ermenric's Letter to Grimald, a medical Letter of Pseudo-Hippocrates, Bede's verse *Vita Cuthberti*, and other poems by Bede. s. ix².[1]

Contents

1. pp. 3 (line 1)–91 (line 12): ORDITUR EPISTOLA ERMENRICI AD DOMNUM GRIMOLDUM ABBATEM ET ARCHICAP-PELLANUM. Inc.: DIU SANE MIHI PERTRACTANTI PRAECEPTORUM ... Des.: At parvas parvis nostras da carminis odas.

Ermenric, *Epistola ad Grimaldum*, ed. Monique Goullet, *Ermenrich d'Ellwangen, Lettre à Grimald*, Sources d'histoire médiévale 37 (Paris, 2008).

2. pp. 93 (line 1)–97 (line 10): INCIPIT EPISTOLA IPPOCRATIS AD ANTIOCHUM REGEM. Inc.: IPPOCRATES CHOUS ANTIOCHO REGI SALUTEM. Quo te convenit regum omnium ... Des.: sine auxilio medicorum. FINIT EPISTOLA IPPOCRATIS.

Pseudo-Hippocrates, *Epistola ad Antiochum regem*.[2] Axel Herman Nelson, "Zur pseudohippokratischen Epistula ad Antiochum regem," in *Symbolae philologicae O. A. Danielsson octogenario dicatae* (Upsaliae 1932), p. 216.

---

[1] Bischoff, "Bücher," p. 200.
[2] Walafrid's *vademecum*, St-Gallen, Stiftsbibliothek, MS 878, pp. 328–331, also transmits the *Epistola ad Antiochum regem*. See Wesley M. Stevens, "Walahfrid Strabo – A Student at Fulda," in Wesley M. Stevens, *Cycles of Time and Scientific Learning in Medieval Europe*

3. pp. 98 (line 1)–122 (line 7) INCIPIT PRAEFATIO. Inc. pref.:
Domino in domino dominorum dilectissimo iohanni ... Inc. prohemium (p. 98, line 20): Multa suis dominis fulgescere ... Inc. (p. 99,
line 18): Alma deo cari primo caelestis ad aevo ... Des.: Vita manens
castis lumenque salusque per aevum.

> Bede, *Vita S. Cuthberti* (BHL 2020), ed. Werner Jaager, *Bedas metrische
> Vita Sancti Cuthberti* (Leipzig, 1935).

4. pp. 122 (line 9)–123 (line 13): INCIPIT CARMEN EIUSDEM DE
VIRGINITATE EDILDRUDAE REGINAE. Inc.: Alma deus trinitas
quae secular cuncta gubernas ... Des.: Quam affectu tulerat nullus
ab altithroni.

> Bede, *Carmen de virginitate Edildrudae reginae* (BHL 2633). AASS June,
> vol. 4, 516C–517A.

5. pp. 123 (line 14)–124 (line 14) ITEM CARMEN EIUSDEM
SOLILOQUUM DE PSALMO XLI COMPOSITUM. Inc.: Cervus
ut ad fontes sitiens festinat aquarum ... Des.: Dona canam memori
semper replicandi relatu.

> Bede, *Soliloquum de Psalmo XLI*, ed. Guido Maria Dreves, *Analecta hym-
> nica medii aevi* 50 (Leipzig, 1907), pp. 114–115.[3]

6. p. 124 (line 15–23) ITEM CARMEN EIUSDEM DE PSALMO
XXII. Inc.: Laudate altithronum pueri laudati tonantem ... Des.:
Laetari tribuit natorum germine matrem.

> Bede, *De Psalmo XCII*, ed. Guido Maria Dreves, *Analecta hymnica medii
> aevi* 50 (Leipzig, 1907), p. 116.

Description

Parchment. Arranged hair to hair and flesh to flesh. 210 mm x
191mm (text block 156 mm x 133 mm).[4] 126 pages.[5] (Pages 1–2 and
125–126 are guard pages and are not part of the codex's gatherings.)

(Aldershot, 1995), X, p. 16. See also the medical compilation (ix²), St Gallen,
Stiftsbibliothek, MS 751, pp. 163–165, described by Augusto Beccaria, *I codici di medicina
del periodo presalernitano* (Rome, 1956), pp. 372–381. For the identification of Walafrid's
collection, see Bernhard Bischoff, "Eine Sammelhandschrift Walahfrid Strabos (Cod.
Sangall. 878)," *MAS*, v. 2, pp. 34–51; Anton Bruckner, *Scriptoria medii aevi Helvetica*,
vol. 1 (Geneva, 1935), pp. 93–94.
[3] See Manitius, *Geschichte*, vol. 1, p. 86.
[4] Bischoff, "Bücher," p. 200.
[5] The codex is paginated rather than foliated, as is normal for manuscripts in Swiss libraries.

Ruled in dry point with prickings in the outer margins. A vertical column on the left for initials. Rulings extend to the edge of the page. Margins are wide and lines are well spaced, which would allow for annotation, as we often find in schoolbooks. There appears to be little medieval annotation in this volume, but at least some annotations have severely faded (for example, on p. 60), so there may be others that are no longer readily visible. There are twenty-three lines per page. The text on pages 3 through 98 is copied in a single column, except for p. 82, line 8-end (a poem, *the Oratio Ermenrici metro tetrametro acatalecto*). Beginning with the fifth line of the verse *prohemium* to Bede's *Vita Cuthberti* (pp. 99–124) the text is written in two columns. The text starts above the first ruled line.

Brown ink, with no ornamentation or rubrication. The script is a clear and rounded minuscule featuring *st* and *sti* ligature, clubbed ascenders, an open-bow *g*, *e* caudata, tall and short *a*, and dotted *y*. Capitals used for titles and subsections, and to begin sentences are rustic. The scribes use standard abbreviations (ampersand, *per*, *prae-*, *–us*, *sacra nomina*, *est*, *e* with cedilla). There are interlinear and marginal corrections and additions, some in the main scribal hands. Bruckner identifies three main hands.[6] Bischoff identifies the second of these hands (p. 28, line 13–p. 97) as the scribe who copied the *Vita Karoli* in Vat. MS Reg. lat. 339, fols. 19v–38v.[7]

There are two main parts to the codex: pages 3 through 92, containing Ermenric's letter, and pages 97 through 124, containing the other texts.

A slightly later medieval annotation, at the head of page 3 (the beginning of Ermenric's letter) reads "Grammaticae studium monachos pernoscere fervens potes adhibuisse Hoc lib(r)o (e)gregio / [sinistr]e hunc pentametru(m) legas."[8] A later hand has added EP(ISCOP)I over ERMENRICI to the title on page 3, and ET between the descriptors of Grimald ABBATEM and ARCHICAPELLANUM. There are postmedieval annotations on pages 1–2 and 88. The codex contains a diagram on page 77.[9]

Saint-Gall is the book's origin and provenance.[10]

---

[6] Albert Bruckner, *Scriptoria medii aevi Helvetica*, vol. 3 *Schreibschulen der Diözese Konstanz: St. Gallen* (Geneva, 1938), p. 89; Bischoff, "Bücher," p. 200.

[7] Ibid. Cf. Gustav Scherrer, *Verzeichniss der Handschriften der Stiftsbibliothek von St. Gallen* (Halle, 1875), pp. 99–100.

[8] Cf. Goullet, p. 36, n. 70.

[9] Reproduced by Goullet, p. 261.

[10] Bruckner, *Scriptoria*, vol. 3, p. 89.

Collation[11]: i + I[7] + II-III[8] + IV[6] +V–VIII[8] + i

Although it is not included in the list of Grimald's books,[12] Bischoff has identified it as Grimald's *vademecum* or "commonplace book," a collection of excerpts for teaching and reference, similar to Walafrid's collection (St. Gallen, Stiftsbibliothek, MS 878).[13] Grimald left a large number of books to Saint-Gall's library. The lack of decoration, combined with the wide margins and line spacing, as well as the contents, show it was a schoolbook.[14] Like Walafrid's collection, Grimald's may have been copied over a long period, hence the variations in script. The title on page three describes Grimald as *archicapellanus*, suggesting it was copied after 857, when he is first attested in that role at Louis the German's court.[15] The addition of "episcopi" to Ermenric's name (in lighter ink), was made after 866 when he became bishop of Passau, if the identification of the monk of Saint-Gall with the bishop of Passau is correct.

Ermenric's letter appears to be contained in the first six quires (p. 92, the last page of the sixth, is blank). The Pseudo-Hippocrates letter and the beginning of Bede's epic *Vita Cuthberti* comprise the seventh, and the remainder of the *Vita Cuthberti* and three poems of Bede, the eighth.

Catalogues

Gustav Scherer, *Verzeichniss der Handschriften der Stiftsbibliothek von St. Gallen* (Halle, 1875), pp. 99–100.

Augusto Beccaria, *I codici di medicina del periodo presalernitano* (Rome, 1956), pp. 371–372.

---

[11] I have relied on the facsimiles on e-codices, Virtual manuscript library of Switzerland, http://www.e-codices.unifr.ch/.

[12] Bischoff, "Bücher," p. 200.

[13] Ibid. Cf., also, Heiric's *Collectanea*. Riccardo Quadri, "Aimone de Auxerre alla luce dei Collectanea di Heiric di Auxerre," *Italia medioevale e umanistica* 6 (1963): 1–48.

[14] Bischoff, "Bücher," p. 200.

[15] The earliest extant mention of Grimald as archchaplain is April 21, 857, in MGH, Dipl. regum Germ. 1, no. 80, pp. 116–117, cited by Depreux, *Prosopographie*, p. 222.

APPENDIX B

Douai, Bibliothèque Marceline Desbordes-Valmore, MS 849

Lectiones, vitae and homilies from Marchiennes. s. xi²ᐟ⁴.

Contents

Folios 2v–18v contain readings and homilies for the nativity (#1–7, see following list).[1] (The readings from Isaiah are contained in full, whereas other scriptural readings are abbreviated with "et reliqua.") Folios 20r–30v (#8–11) contain readings and homilies for the Resurrection (*Lectiones ad matutinum in Paschate Resurrectionis*), again featuring abbreviated scriptural readings.[2] Folios 31v–60v feature works on Saint Eusebia (#12–13), folios 61r–68r those on Saint Jonat (#14–15), and folios 68v–129v those on Saint Rictrude (#16–18).

1. Fols. 2v–4v. Readings from Isaiah (9.1–8, 40.1–17, 52.1–10) Inc.: PRIMO TEMPORE alleviata est terra Zabulon ... Des.: fines terrae salutare Dei nostri.

2. Fols. 4v–5v. [No title] Inc.: NATALIS DOMINI DIES EA decausa patribus ... Des.: revocetur quod natus est Christus.

> Isidore of Seville, *De ecclesiasticis officiis* I. 26 (25), ed. Christopher M. Lawson, *Isidori Episcopi Hispalensis Opera*, CCSL 113 (Turnhout, 1989), pp. 29–30.

---

[1] Dehaisnes, *Catalogue*, p. 595, identifies the lessons of the Roman breviary *ad matutinum in Nativitate*. For clarity, I have not assigned separate numbers to the scriptural readings and the homilies that discuss them or to the letters that accompany the *vitae*.

[2] Ibid. Dehaisnes notes that these lessons are not identical to the Roman breviary, although the Gospel passages are.

3. Fols. 5v–7v. SERMO LEONIS BEATI PAPAE. Inc.: SALVATOR
   NOSTER DILECTISSIMI hodie natus ... Des.: qui misericordia te
   redemit Christus Iesus dominus noster.

   Leo the Great, *Tractatus* 21, ed. A. Chavasse, *Sancti Leonis Magni romani
   pontificis tractatus septem et nonaginta*, CCSL 138 (Turnhout, 1973),
   pp. 85–89.

4. Fols. 7v–10v. SERMO CUIUS SUPRA. Inc.: Exultemus in domino
   dilectissimi et spirituali iocunditate laetemur ... Des.: In sua maies-
   tate regnantem cum deo patre et spiritu sancto. Amen.

   Leo the Great, *Tractatus* 22, ed. Chavasse, *Sancti Leonis Magni romani
   pontificis tractatus*, pp. 90–101. (This version belongs to the manuscript
   tradition Chavasse identifies as "α").

5. Fol. 10v. LECTIO SANCTI EVANGELII SECUNDUM LUCAM.
   Inc.: In illo tempore exiit edictum a cesare augusto

   Luke 2:1.

   Fols. 10v–12r. OMELIA BEATI GREGORII PAPAE. Inc.: QUIA
   LARGIENTE DOMINO

   Des.: Defende ergo tibi homo contra vitia honore dei quia propter te
   factus es deus homo.

   Gregory the Great, *Homilia* 8, ed. R. Étaix. *Homiliae in Evangelia*,
   CCSL 141 (Turnhout, 1999), pp. 54–56.

6. Fol. 12r. LECTIO SANCTI EVANGELII SECUNDUM LUCAM.
   Inc.: IN ILLO TEMPORE pastores loquebantur

   Luke 2.15.

   Fols. 12r–15r. OMELIA BEATI BEDAE PRESBITERI. Inc.: Nato in
   Bethleem DOMINO salvatore sicut sacra ... Des.: insidias servare
   contendit. TU AUTEM DOMINE MI.

   Bede, *Homilia* I.7 (excerpt), ed. D. Hurst and J. Fraipont, *Bedae Venerabilis
   Opera, Opera homiletica, Opera rhythimca*, CCSL 122 (Turnhout, 1955),
   pp. 46–49.

7. Fol. 15v. INITIUM SANCTI EVANGELI SECUNDUM
   IOHANNEM. Inc.: IN PRINCIPIO ERAT

   John 1:1.

Fols. 15v–18v. OMELIA AURELII AUGUSTINI. Inc.: Intuentes quod modo audivimus . . . Des.: a patre plenum gratia et veritate.

Augustine, *In Evangelium Iohannis*, excerpts from *Tractatus* I, II, and III, ed. R. Willems, *In Iohannis evangelium tractatus CXXIV*, CCSL 36 (Turnhout, 1954), pp. 1–31.

8. Fol. 20r. Lectio sancti evangelii secundum marcum. Inc. In illo tempore Maria magdalene et maria iacobi et salome

Mark 16:1.

Fols. 20r–24v. OMELIA BEATI GREGORII PAPAE. Inc: multis vobis lectionibus fratres karissimi per dictatum loqui . . . Des [mut.]: in galilea videre mereamur Aduiuet omnipotens.

Gregory the Great, *Homilia* 21, ed. Étaix, *Homiliae in Evangelia*, pp. 173–179. (The manuscript lacks the last thirty-six words.)

9. Fols. 25r–27v: Inc.: Post beatam gloriosam et resurrectione . . . Des.: inunitur spiritus sancti in saecula saeculorum.

Leo I the Great, *Sermon* 72, ed. A. Chavasse, *Sancti Leonis Magni romani pontificis tractatus septem et nonaginta*, CCSL 138a (Turnhout, 1973), pp. 450–454.

10. Fol. 27v. LECTIO SANCTI EVANGELII SECUNDUM MARCUM. Inc.: In illo tempore dixit Iesus discipulis suis

Mark 16:15–16.

Fols. 27v–28v. *OMELIA BEATI GREGORII*. Inc.: Quod Resurrectionem dominicam discipuli . . . Des.: simultudine aliena non sunt.

Gregory the Great, *Homilia* 29 (excerpt), ed. Étaix, *Homiliae in Evangelia*, pp. 244–246.

11. Fols. 28v–29r. Lectio sancti evangelii secundum iohannem. Inc.: In illo tempore dixit . . . Siquis diligit me

John. 14:23.

Fols. 29r–30v. *OMELIA BEATI GREGORII*. Inc.: Libet fratres karissimi evangelicae lectionis verba. Des. [mut.]: vocis intelligentia nisi qui per hoc quod

Gregory the Great, *Homilia* 30 (excerpt from c. 1–3), ed. Étaix, *Homiliae in Evangelia*, pp. 256–258.

12. Fols. 31v–42v. [no title] Inc.: prologus: Cum primum animum ad scribendum appuli ... Inc. *vita* (fol. 33v): Francorum regnum a primordio ... Des.: nunc et in secula seculorum permanentis. AMEN EXPLICIT VITA SANCTAE ESEBIAE [*sic*] VIRGINIS.

Anon., *Vita Eusebiae* (prose) (BHL 2736). AASS March, vol. 2, cols. 452B–55A.

13. Fols. 43r–60v. [No title] Inc. prol.: Ordinibus variis, quorum compagine ... Inc. liber I (fol. 44r): TEXTUS PRINCIPIO FRANCORUM quae sit origo ... Des.: te prece iudice flexo.

Vita Eusebiae (metric) (BHL 2737). Excerpts in AASS February, vol. 1, cols. 300A–302A, and March, vol. 2, cols. 455B–57C.

14. Fols. 61r–65r. APOLOGIA TEMERITATIS. Inc. prol.: MATERIA NON apparente ... Inc. apologia (fol. 61v): Venerabilem huius diei celebritatem ... Des.: Sepultus autem est Marcianis ... omnipotens et mirabilis Deus.

Anon, *Homily of Jonat* (BHL 4447) for the saint's feast, August 1.[3]

15. Fols. 65v–68r. Qualiter elevatum est corpus sancti Ionati ... Inc.: MARCIANIS EST monasterii locus a beato Amando. Des.: ... per omnia secula seculorum. Amen.

Ps-Hucbald, *Inventio corporis Ionati* (BHL 4448). AASS August, vol. 1, cols. 74B–75A, and Migne, PL 132, cols. 901D–903D.

16. Fols. 68v–93v. INCIPIT PRAEFATIO IN VITA SANCTAE RICTRUDIS. Inc. prol.: IN CHRISTI MEMBRORUM COMPAGE sicut excellentiori ... Inc. *vita* (fol. 72r): Cum Francorum gentem ... Des.: gloria per infinita secula seculorum. Amen.

---

[3] Tenth-century writers from Saint-Bavo, Ghent, inserted Landoald into their saint's family tree. Landoald's appearance (fol. 63r) in the *Homily* of Jonat (BHL 4447) suggests it was composed in or after the 980s when Landoald first appears or rises to prominence. (Numerous texts commemorate Landoald's translation of 980.) Van der Essen attributes the *Homily* of Jonat to Hucbald on stylistic grounds and therefore sees it as evidence for Landoald's cult around the beginning of the tenth century (Van der Essen, *Étude critique*, pp. 354, 363).

Hucbald,*Vita Rictrudis* (BHL 7247). Migne, PL 132, cols. 830D-848C, and AASS May, vol. 3, cols. 81D–89A.

17. Fol. 93v. VERSUS IOHANNIS AD EPISCOPUM ERLUINUM Inc.: Praesulis eximii laudes ornare . . . Des.: Omnes insidias spernet moderamine tanto.

Johannes of Saint Amand, Acrostic verse (BHL 7248a). Poncelet, "Catalogus," 405.

Fols. 94v-95r. EPISTULA IOHANNIS AD STEPHANUM MONACUM GANDENSEM. Inc.: PERFECTAE ERUDITIONIS doctrina undique adornato . . . Des.: utilitatem omnium bonorum perpetualiter.

Johannes of Saint Amand, *Epistula ad Stephanum*. MGH Poetae 5/3, p. 566.

Fols. 95r–95v. Rescriptio Stephani ad Eundem Iohannem. Inc.: Iohanni caro capiti et dilecto . . . Des.: Vale in Christo memor mei.

Stephen, *Rescriptio ad Johannem*. MGH Poetae 5/3, pp. 566–567.

Fols. 96r–124r. INCIPIT VITA SANCTAE RICTRUDIS METRICA ORATIONE DESCRIPTA PRAEFATIO SEQUENTIS OPERIS. (A later hand has added "Iohanne monacho marcianensi.") Inc. pref.: Haebraicus populus liber pharaone . . . Inc. liber 1 (fol. 98v): INCIPIT LIBER PRIMUS. Postquam summe bonus pastor grege . . . Des.: qui secla per omnia regnat.

Johannes, *Vita Rictrudis*. MGH Poetae 5/3, pp. 567–595.

Fols. 124r–124v. EPISTOLA IOHANNIS AD RAINERUM. Inc.: Divini splendoris fulgore . . . Des.: securius valeat stare.

Johannes of Saint-Amand, *Epistula ad Rainerum*. MGH Poetae 5/3, p. 595.

Fols. 124v–125v. EPISTULA RAINERI IN CONFIRMATIONE HUIUS OPERIS. Inc.: Domno Iohanni donato gratia . . . Des.: Inter sacra tui sis memor oro mei.

Rainer, *Epistula ad Iohannem*. MGH Poetae 5/3, pp. 595–596.

18. Fol. 125v. LECTIO SANCTI EVANGELIUM SECUNDEM MATTHEUM. Inc.: IN ILLO TEMPORE Loquente Iesus ad turbas

Matt. 12:46–50.

Fols. 126v–129v. OMELIA BEATI GREGORII PAPAE URBIS
ROMAE. Inc.: SANCTI EVANGELI fratres karissimi brevis est
lectio . . . Des.: regnat deus per omnia saecula saeculorum. AMEN.

Homily for Saint Rictrude based on Gregory, *Homilia* 3 (on the feast day
of Saint Felicity, following the reading of Matt. 12:46–50), adapted to
apply to Rictrude. Gregory, *Homilia* 3, ed. Étaix, *Homiliae in Evangelia*,
pp. 20–25.

19. Fol. 129v [no title] Inc.: Ade peccatum . . . Des.: homo gaudet
tartara merent. Eighteen lines (in a small, much later hand).

Anselm, *Versus Cur Deus Homo*, ed. Antoine Charma, *Saint Anselme:
notice biographique, littéraire et philosophique* (Paris, 1853), p. 234.

Description

230 mm × 190 mm. 129 folios. 21 lines per page, single column. The text
block, excluding initials, measures 170 mm × 140 mm with some variation
(the text occupies approximately three-quarters of the leaf; pages may have
been trimmed). The parchment is of "mediocre quality and of modest size"
as is typical of the region's eleventh-century sheepskin.[4] Pages are ruled in
dry point, and prickings are visible in the outer margins only, showing that
the bifolia were ruled, as was usual continental practice, before they were
assembled into quires.[5] The codex contains seventeen quaternios. Modern
restoration may obscure the original collation of the first four quires. A
note on the guard page dates the restoration to 1839. Modern vellum
binding. There are postmedieval cursive notes from Raphael de
Beauchamps, a monk of Marchiennes, and Charles Godin, its eighteenth-
century librarian.

The book comprises two sections, which may have originally been
separate. The first, folios 1–30 (quires I–IV) comprising the *lectiones*, is
incomplete. The second section (folios 31–129, quires V–XVII), on the
saints, begins with a blank page (fol. 31r), which would provide protection
for a booklet if it was intended to circulate independently.[6] The ruling

---

[4] Steven Vanderputten, "Hagiography and the Literalization Process. In Search of Significant
Changes in the Transmission of Texts in Manuscripts from the Southern Low Countries
(Tenth to Early Thirteenth Centuries)," *Quaerendo* 35 (2005): 46, n. 33.

[5] Clemens and Graham, *Manuscript Studies*, p. 16.

[6] The notes on fol. 31r are postmedieval.

differs between the two sections. Quires V–VIII (fols. 31–60) feature prose and verse lives of Eusebia. Quires IX–XVII (fols. 61–129) contain works on Jonat and Rictrude. The similarity of format, script, initials, and size all attest to the sections' contemporaneous production, but variations in rulings between the *lectiones* (quires I–IV) and the remainder of the codex suggest they could once have been separate.

Collation: i + I–III,^{8} IV,^{6} V–VII,^{8} VIII,^{6} IX,^{7} X–XII,^{8}
XIII,^{7} XIV–XVI,^{8} XVII^7 + i

The folios are arranged hair to hair and flesh to flesh, with the hair on the outside of each gathering.

Rulings

The top line of writing is generally above the first ruled line. In the first gathering of the manuscript (fols. 1–8), the lines of text are bounded by three vertical lines on each side of the page. In the rest of the manuscript, the text block is bounded on the left and right by a pair of vertical lines.

Script

Caroline minuscule with insular features. The script lacks the roundness of earlier Carolingian minuscule, but it is not as cramped and square as script from the late eleventh century (e.g., that of Valenciennes, BM, MS 39). It features a distinctive ct ligature, with an exaggerated bow, found in English manuscripts and eleventh-century manuscripts from the region.[7] It also features forked ascenders, e-caudata, e with serif, minims with feet, and both tall and short s. Uncial capitals are used to begin sentences. NS ligature occasionally occurs at the end of a word. The eleventh-century dating of Douai, BM, MS 849 is supported by the similarity of the script to

---

[7] For example, Harley Psalter, London BL Harley 603 (ca. 1010–1130), fol. 18r, reproduced in *The Utrecht Psalter in Medieval Art: Picturing the Psalms of David*, ed. Koert van der Horst, William Noel, and Wilhelmina C.M. Wüstefeld (Utrecht, 1996), p. 137. From Saint-Amand, Valenciennes, BM MSS 9 (Alard Bible, post-1075); 10 (xi); and 61 (x or xi). From Saint-Vaast, Boulogne-sur-Mer, BM, MS 9 (xi); from Marchiennes, Douai, BM, MS 494 (xi), *Lectiones Evangelii* written by the monk Amand of Marchiennes. Dehaisnes, *Catalogue*, p. 291; Anne-Marie Turcan-Verkerk, "Le Scriptorium de Saint-Vanne de Verdun sous l'abbatiat de Richard (1004–1046)," *Scriptorium* 46 (1992): 218.

that of the monk Amand of Marchiennes, who identifies himself as the scribe in several manuscripts.[8]

Rubrication

Half uncials and rustic capital rubrics serve as titles, with green and blue ink sometimes used. The epic lives feature alternating red and green capitals for the first letter of each line. The prose texts are marked with *lectio* numbers, suggesting they were read on feast days.

Decorative Initials

Acanthus-leaf initials typical of the Franco-Saxon style appear on 22 folios, usually at the incipit of a text.[9] Initials incorporate beast heads (2v, 33v, 96r) and in one instance a bird (94v). The initials, uncolored except for small red accents, are usually set off by areas of green and blue infill (occasionally red and yellow are also used).[10] Several appear unfinished.[11] Folios 2v and 33v feature entire pages of decorative text based on foliate motifs, and the upper half of folio 72r is similarly ornamented.

Other eleventh-century manuscripts from the area, particularly from Saint-Amand, feature similar foliate and beast-head initials.[12] The acanthus initials and the figures of the historiated initials attributed to

---

[8] Amand identifies himself as scribe in Douai, BM, MSS 300, 303, and 306 (where he is one of three). The eighteenth-century librarian of Marchiennes, Charles Godin and the cataloguer Dehaisnes have also identified this Amand as the probable copyist of numerous other manuscripts now held at Douai (MSS 47, 200, 255, 328, 342, 345) and as the creator of decorative initials (MSS 255, 344, 494). See Dehaisnes, *Catalogue*, pp. 28, 98, 133, 174, 180, 291.

[9] P. Černý, "Les manuscrits à peintures de l'abbaye de Marchiennes jusqu'à la fin du XIIe siècle," *Bulletin de la Commission départementale d'histoire et d'archéologie du Pas-de-Calais* 11 (1981): 52; fols. 2v, 7v, 10v, 12v, 15v, 20r, 25v, 31v, 33v, 51v, 52v, 61v, 65v, 68v, 72r, 94v, 96r, 98v, 110r, 126v. Fol. 44r features a plainer initial.

[10] The seven-line *M* on fol. 65v and the full-page *F* on fol. 33v also have a section of red infill. The nine-line *F* on fol. 51v, the half-page *C* on fol.72r, and the full page *I* on fol. 68v each have sections of pale yellow infill.

[11] On fol. 25r, the letter *O* is entirely infilled with green, whereas only a small portion of the letter *P* has been infilled.

[12] Valenciennes, BM, MS 9 (Alard Bible from Saint-Amand, post-1075), includes foliate initials very similar to those in 849, with a different color scheme (red, green, and light blue infill), fol. 4r, 29v and with beast heads incorporated into the design, fols. 48v and 61r. Numerous other eleventh-century manuscripts from Saint-Amand feature similar foliate initials, including Augustine's *Commentaries on the Psalms*, Valenciennes, BM, MS 39 (late xi) and MS 10, a Bible. (Molinier dates Valenciennes, BM, MSS 9 and 39 to early xii.) Molinier, *Catalogue*, pp. 195–196 and 206.

Amand of Marchiennes, mentioned above, are reminiscent of those in this codex. There are pronounced similarities between manuscripts produced at Marchiennes and Saint-Vaast in Arras, both houses ruled by abbot Leduin. Schulten identifies the foliate initials of a mid-eleventh-century Pontificale produced at Saint-Vaast (Cologne, Dombibliothek, Hs. 141), as the work of the same hand as those in Douai, BM, MS 849.[13]

Fol. 2v. **Decorative text page.** Full page acanthus beast-head *P* initial. White, partially infilled with green, against a blue ground. The rest of the text is in rustic capitals, a pair in red, a pair in green, another pair in red, and the final four letters in green.

Fol. 33v. **Decorative text page.** Full page acanthus initial F with beast head, white, accented with red and green, with red, blue, and green infill against a yellow ground. To the right, intertwined RA, and, below, CORU(M), all acanthus letters accented with red and green. A cursive hand has added "Francorum."

Miniatures

There are nine full- or half-page miniatures and two historiated initials. A miniature prefaces each main text or groups of texts.

Fols. **1v–2r: Nativity.** Facing page miniatures are each divided into two registers. In the upper register of fol. 1v, three yellow-haloed angels gesture toward the facing page. In the lower register, three shepherds herd three sheep. The ground of these registers is divided into four quadrants, with the upper left and lower right painted green and the others blue. In the upper register of 2r, Mary reclines in the foreground. Behind her, two cows watch over Christ in the manger. In the lower register, three figures and an angel converse to the left of a large, haloed enthroned figure. Celtic interlace frames the scenes on 2r, with a portrait roundel, probably an evangelist, in each corner. The sheep are similar to those of Boulogne-sur-Mer, BM, MS 107 (from Saint-Bertin ca. 1000). The angels' wings and beasts resemble those from the Saint-Vaast Pontificale.[14]

Fol. **19v. The women at the tomb.** Three women proceeding from the left encounter a wingless angel. The tomb has a distinctive rounded dome,

---

[13] A Pontificale of Cambrai. Černý, "Manuscrits," pp. 51–52; Sigrid Schulten, "Die Buchmalerei des 11. Jahrhunderts im Kloster S. Vaast in Arras," in *Münchner Jahrbuch der bildenden Kunst*, III series, vol. 7 (1956), p. 77; Andreas Odenthal and Joachim M. Plotzek, "Erweitertes Kurzkatalogisat: Köln, Dombibliothek, Codex 141," *Codices Electronice Ecclesiae Coloniensis*, http://www.ceec.uni-koeln.de (accessed May 15, 2011).

[14] Cologne, Dombibliothek, Hs. 141 fols. 33r and 77v for wings.

topped by an orb and flanked by thin towers, each with an orb. Unlike many depictions of this scene, there are no soldiers. A miniature from the English Sacramentary, Rouen, BM, MS 274, fol. 72v (ca. 1020), has a similar composition.[15] Although clearly not a copy, the Douai miniature closely approximates many of features of the Rouen Sacramentary, particularly the grouping of the women and the lines conveying the contours of their drapery, suggesting a common artistic heritage. The ninth- or tenth-century Cambrai Apocalypse (Cambrai, BM, MS 386) features similar architecture.[16]

Fol. 33r. Eusebia (Figure 8). The haloed, elongated figure stands against a blue ground in the center of a triple arch. In the shorter arch on each side, a censer hangs against a green ground. Her left hand holds a book, and her right is raised in benediction. Above her, the stylized roof is flanked by small towers.

Fol. 43r. Portrait initial prefacing the epic *VE*. Inside the half-page O, a kneeling tonsured figure holds a booklet or page, while a hand reaches down from heaven, suggesting divine inspiration.

Fol. 61v. Portrait initial (Figure 9) at the beginning of Jonat's homily. A nine-line historiated acanthus V shows Jonat, with tonsure and monastic habit, holding a crook and a book, against a vertically divided ground of blue and green.

Fols. 71v–72r: Saints of Marchiennes (Figures 10–11). The miniatures on the lower halves of the facing leaves feature the saints, labeled and framed in triplex arches. Folio 71v shows Jonat, Rictrude, and Mauront. Folio 72r features Adalsend, Eusebia, and Clotsend.

Fol. 126r: Christ and Rictrude preaching (Figure 12). In the upper register, framed on each side by towers, Christ, with cruciform halo, is surrounded by onlookers. In the lower part of the page, a haloed, long-haired figure, presumably Rictrude, addresses four people.[17]

Style of the Miniatures

The miniatures are outline drawings accented with a restricted palette of blue, green, red, and pale yellow, often against green or blue grounds. The figures, with their large hands, expressive gestures, and wildly fluttering

---

[15] Three women approach from the left, and a winged angel gestures in benediction. The tomb's tiled dome is surmounted by an orb and flanked by a tower. The historiated initial of the same scene in the Drogo sacramentary from Metz, Paris, BN, MS lat. 9428, fol. 58r (ca. 850–855), features a domed tomb, but an entirely different composition (reproduced in van der Horst et al., *Utrecht Psalter*, p. 197).

[16] Cambrai BM MS 386, fols. 34r, 35r. Cain, *Manuscrits*, p. 4, dates it to the ninth century.

[17] Johannes, *VR*, 2.191–192; Hucbald, *VR* c. 21.

hems are reminiscent of the English Winchester style.[18] The Pontificale from Saint-Vaast (Cologne Dombibliothek Hs. 141) features similar figures. The miniatures (like the decorative text pages and initials) show a synthesis of older Franco-Saxon features and newer Anglo-Saxon styles, but, as is typical of art from the region in the first half of the eleventh century, little Ottonian influence.[19] The line drawings, color washes, and minimal color reflect Anglo-Saxon technique.[20] This influence is the result of the close contact between Flanders and England in the later tenth and eleventh centuries,[21] when letters, manuscripts, scholars, and artists all traveled between England and the Continent.[22]

Although they exhibit general stylistic consistency, the figures in different parts of the codex have different proportions. The women at the tomb (fol. 19v) and Eusebia (fol. 33r) are both elongated, reminiscent of the Winchester style. Eusebia resembles figures from the Odbert Psalter, produced at Saint-Bertin in 999,[23] and from the later eleventh-century English Psalter, London BL Arundel 60.[24] The miniatures from later

---

[18] For example, the hem of the Mary's garment in Arras, BM, MS 732, fol. 2v (from Saint-Vaast), printed in Reilly, *Art of Reform*, fig. 36; from Saint-Bertin, in 1000, Boulogne-sur-Mer, BM, MS 107, fol. 6v.

[19] Reilly, *Art of Reform*, pp. 27–31; André Boutemy, "Le style franco-saxon, style de Saint-Amand," *Scriptorium* 3 (1949): 26–64.

[20] Cf. Reilly, *Art of Reform*, p. 25.

[21] Ph. Grierson, "The Relations between England and Flanders before the Norman Conquest," *Transactions of the Royal Historical Society* (1941): 71–112; Steven Vanderputten, "Canterbury and Flanders in the Late Tenth Century," *ASE* 35 (2006): 219–244; G. Dunning, "Trade Relations between England and the Continent in the Late Anglo-Saxon Period," *Dark Age Britain*, ed. D.B. Harden (London, 1956), pp. 218–233.

[22] One of the Gospelbooks of Judith of Flanders, Fulda, Hessische Landesbibliothek, Aa. 21, was written in English Caroline minuscule but completed by a scribe and artist from the Low Countries who contributed continental script, display capitals, and illuminations. McGurk and Rosenthal, "Anglo-Saxon Gospelbooks of Judith," p. 281. The Boulogne Gospels (Boulogne-sur-Mer, BM, MS 11) were illuminated by an Anglo-Saxon artist working at Saint-Bertin on the Continent around 1000. See van der Horst et al., eds., *The Utrecht Psalter in Medieval Art*, p. 244. For the miniatures in Boulogne-sur-Mer, BM, MS 11, see Thomas H. Ohlgren, *Anglo-Saxon Textual Illustration* (Kalamazoo, 1992), pp. 303–330.

[23] Odbert Psalter, Boulogne-sur-Mer, BM, MS 20, fol. 15, reproduced in van der Horst et al., *Utrecht Psalter in Medieval Art*, p. 131. The large expressive hands and faces in rondels are similar to Odbert Psalter, at Saint-Bertin in 999 (although the psalter is a much more assured and expensive production).

[24] London, BL, Arundel 60, fol. 5v. See also, Mary on fol. 12v. The British Library Catalogue dates this codex to the "3rd quarter of the 11th century, probably after 1073." *Catalogue of Illuminated Manuscripts*, http://www.bl.uk/catalogues/illuminatedmanuscripts/record.asp?MSID=8761&CollID=20&NStart=60 (accessed August 20, 2012).

folios (fols. 61v–end) are squatter and more crudely executed.[25] With their squarish faces, and large heads jutting forward on their necks, they resemble the figures of Valenciennes, BM, MSS 39 and 502, as well as earlier Carolingian depictions.[26]

Decoration and miniatures also strongly resemble examples from Saint-Vaast. In 1024, Leduin became reform abbot of Marchiennes and he was succeeded by five more abbots from Saint-Vaast.[27] Leduin probably promoted manuscript production at Marchiennes, as he did at Saint-Vaast.[28] The pronounced similarities between this codex and Saint-Vaast manuscripts from the first half of the eleventh century can be attributed to his influence and perhaps the exchange of artists between the houses.[29] Several scholars date Douai, BM, MS 849 specifically to his reign (1024–1033).[30] Schulten argues that the same hand created the foliate initials of Douai, BM, MS 849 and the Saint-Vaast Pontificale.[31] The latter, like other manuscripts of its house, is a far more luxurious object, using a greater range of colors and solid blocks of color. The quality of Douai, BM, MS 849 reflects the less prosperous abbey's resources, showing that it was made at Marchiennes.

---

[25] The figures on fols. 71v–72r and 126r are similar to the Christ in the historiated B on London, BL, Harley, MS 603, fol. 2r (reproduced in van der Horst et al., *Utrecht Psalter*, p. 123) and the "additional images," on fols. 29v–31v of the same manuscript. (For example, the central figure in the Harley Psalter, fol. 29v resembles Christ on fol. 126r.) *A Catalogue of the Harleian Manuscripts in the British Museum*, vol. 1 (London, 1808), no. 603.

[26] Christ on fols. 9 and 27r of Valenciennes, BM, MS 39 (a manuscript of Augustine's *Ennarrationes in Psalmos*) are particularly reminiscent of the Christ on fol. 126r. Molinier, *Catalogue*, p. 206. The images on Valenciennes, BM, MS 502, fols. 123v–124r and Douai, BM, MS 849, fols. 71v–72r exhibit particularly similar features. The Stuttgart Psalter (820–830) provides a Carolingian parallel. See examples reproduced in van der Horst et al., *Utrecht Psalter*, pp. 69, 96.

[27] Ugé, *Monastic Past*, p. 113; *Annales Marchianenses*, pp. 614–615. Monks from Saint-Vaast ruled Marchiennes until 1091.

[28] Černý, "Manuscrits," p. 51.

[29] Ibid., p. 52.

[30] Dion-Turkovics, *Representation de l'Invisible*, p. 64; Černý, "Manuscrits," p. 52.

[31] Schulten identifies the foliate initials of a mid-eleventh-century Pontificale produced at Saint-Vaast as the work of the same hand as those in Douai, BM, MS 849. Cologne, Dombibliothek, Hs. 141, a Pontificale of Cambrai, discussed by Schulten, "Die Buchmalerei des 11. Jahrhunderts," p. 77; Černý, "Manuscrits," pp. 51–52; Andreas Odenthal and Joachim M. Plotzek, "Erweitertes Kurzkatalogisat: Köln, Dombibliothek, Codex 141," *Codices Electronice Ecclesiae Coloniensis*, http://www.ceec.uni-koeln.de (accessed May 15, 2011). Hs. 141 has many similarities to this manuscript in script, initials, and miniatures, but it was much more carefully rendered, with fully colored miniatures and gold and silver illumination.

Date

Second quarter, eleventh century.[32] Marchiennes's stylistic conservatism (typical of a smaller house) makes dating difficult, but the script, miniatures, and initials find their closest *comparanda* in the region's early- to mid-eleventh-century manuscripts.[33] The *Elevatio* of Jonat was copied after the abbey was reformed as a house of monks, providing a *terminus post quem* of 1024.[34]

Catalogue

C. Dehaisnes, *Catalogue général des manuscrits des bibliothèques publiques des départements*, vol. 6 (Paris, 1878), pp. 594–596.

---

[32] Schulten and Boeckler date the manuscript to the turn of the millennium, Dehaisnes to the end of the tenth or the beginning of the eleventh century (pp. 594–596), and Porcher to the first half of the eleventh century. Černý and Dion-Turkovics date it to Leduin's abbacy (1024–1033). Ugé suggests it may have been produced pre-1024, based on its execution. Sigrid Schulten, "Die Buchmalerei des 11. Jahrhunderts im Kloster St. Vaast in Arras," *Münchner Jahrbuch der bildenden Kunst*, Ser 3, 7 (1956): 89, n. 51; Albert Boeckler, *Abendländische Miniaturen bis zum Ausgang der romanischen Zeit* (Berlin, 1930), p. 95; Dehaisnes, *Catalogue*, pp. 594–596; Porcher, *Catalogue Paris* 1954, no. 146, p. 62; Ugé, *Monastic Past*, p. 130. Černý, "Manuscrits," p. 52; M.P. Dion-Turkovics, *La répresentation de l'invisible: Trésors de l'enluminure romane en Nord-Pas-de-Calais* (Valenciennes, 2007), p. 64.

[33] Černý, "Manuscrits," p. 54.

[34] The *Elevatio* explains the presence of an abbess (Judith, who is named in a diploma of 976) "because the place was ruled by nuns" (per enim locus per sanctimoniales regebatur; PL 132, 902C). The explanation would be unnecessary before 1024. The *Elevatio*'s address to "fratres dilectissimi" (903B) does not itself provide evidence for a post-1024 date, because a writer might address only male members of a mixed congregation. The work was composed before Eusebia's translation to Marchiennes (before 1090), because it names the saints whose relics rested at Marchiennes as Jonat, Rictrude, and Mauront.

Index

Note: Saints are only given separate entries if they are discussed at length, otherwise only their *vitae* or *passiones* are listed below. Locators followed by 'n' indicates notes.

311